The Practice of Pluralism

Mark Häberlein

The Practice of Pluralism

Congregational Life and Religious Diversity in Lancaster, Pennsylvania, 1730—1820

The Pennsylvania State University Press
University Park, Pennsylvania

Max Kade German-American Research Institute Series
EDITED BY A. GREGG ROEBER

This series provides an outlet for books that reflect the mission of the Penn State Max Kade Institute: to integrate the history and culture of German speakers in the Americas with the major themes of early modern scholarship from the sixteenth century to the early nineteenth century.

The Max Kade German-American Research Institute, located on Penn State's University Park campus (http://www.maxkade.psu.edu/), was founded in 1993 thanks to a grant from the Max Kade Foundation, New York. The directors of the Penn State Max Kade German-American Research Institute are Daniel Purdy and A. Gregg Roeber.

Library of Congress Cataloging-in-Publication Data

Häberlein, Mark.
The practice of pluralism : congregational life and religious diversity in Lancaster, Pennsylvania, 1730–1820 / Mark Häberlein.
p.   cm.
Summary: "Studies the development of religious congregations in Lancaster, Pennsylvania, from 1730 to 1820. Focuses on German Reformed, Lutherans, Moravians, Anglicans, and Presbyterians. Also examines how Roman Catholics, Jews, and African Americans were absorbed into this predominantly white Protestant society"—Provided by publisher.
Includes bibliographical references (p.   ) and index.
ISBN 978-0-271-07483-2 (pbk : alk. paper)
1. Lancaster (Pa.)—Church history—18th century.
2. Religious pluralism—Pennsylvania—Lancaster—History—18th century.
3. Lancaster (Pa.)—Church history—19th century.
4. Religious pluralism—Pennsylvania—Lancaster—History—19th century.
I. Title.

BR560.L34H23 2009
277.48'1507—dc22
2008050362

For Maximilian and Teresa

Contents

Preface and Acknowledgments

Over the past three centuries religious pluralism has become a central feature of American life. While religion began to take on a more diverse character in Britain's North American colonies in the eighteenth century, this diversity was still of a limited nature. Many communities, especially in New England and the South, largely adhered to a single faith, and religious minorities only gradually made inroads into prevailing patterns of uniformity. Moreover, the vast majority of European colonists were British or central European Protestants; there were very few Catholics and even fewer Jews. It was mainly in the "middle colonies" of New York, New Jersey, and Pennsylvania that communities comprised a larger variety of creeds well before the American Revolution. One of these communities is the subject of this book. I intend to demonstrate how religious diversity emerged and how adherents of various faiths interacted with one another in a single town. Given the role of Lancaster as a major inland center of settlement in the eighteenth century and the remarkable diversity of its people, the town has not received the scholarly attention it deserves. This neglect is perhaps due to the fact that the relevant sources are scattered over a number of archives, and many documents are in an intricate Germanic handwriting.

Almost two decades ago I first walked into the Lancaster County Historical Society as a doctoral student in search of material on southwest German migration to eighteenth-century Pennsylvania. Debbie Smith, who was then the administrator of the society, and her husband, Bill, not only showed me extraordinary hospitality and generosity by hosting me for more than two months but also introduced me to the religious life of Trinity Lutheran Church and shared much of their deep knowledge of the city's and county's history. Over the past twenty years, Debbie Smith and the Reverend Frederick S. Weiser, a tireless student of Pennsylvania German culture, have also edited the early records of Trinity Church, thereby providing researchers with a most valuable source of information. If it weren't for Debbie, this book may have never been written.

After several years of working on other projects, I had a chance to return to the topic of Lancaster when the Alexander von Humboldt foundation granted me a Feodor Lynen fellowship for a year of postdoctoral research at The Pennsylvania State University in 1999–2000. A. G. Roeber, whose own work has set new standards for the study of German-American religious history, served as my mentor there. At Penn State's Max Kade Institute for German-American Research, I also benefited from the generosity and good cheer of its co-director, Frank Gentry. It was very good to have Barbara and Joe Strasser as neighbors and friends in State College. At nearby Juniata College, the late Donald F. Durnbaugh shared some of his immense knowledge of Pennsylvania German pietism and its sources with me. A shorter research trip to central Pennsylvania in 2002 was made much easier by the hospitality of Pauline and Scott Fogelsanger.

A number of archives in Pennsylvania and Germany gave me access to their collections, for which I would like to thank the Lancaster County Historical Society, St. James Episcopal Church, Trinity Lutheran Church, and the Evangelical and Reformed Historical Society, all in Lancaster, Pennsylvania; the Moravian Archives, Bethlehem, Pennsylvania; the Pennsylvania State Archives, Harrisburg; the Lutheran Archives Center, Mount Airy, Pennsylvania; the Presbyterian Historical Society, Philadelphia; the Historical Society of Pennsylvania; the Archives of the Francke Foundations, Halle/Saale; and the Württembergisches Landeskirchliches Archiv, Stuttgart.

A Heisenberg fellowship from the Deutsche Forschungsgemeinschaft (DFG) from 2001 to 2004 made the uncertainties of an academic career in Germany more bearable and provided further funding for research on this project. Moreover, by awarding me a Gerhard Hess prize in 1999, the DFG gave me the opportunity to direct a research group on the comparative history of foreigners and religious minorities in southwest Germany and Pennsylvania. Discussions with the members of this group, Irmgard Schwanke, Eva Wiebel, and Martin Zürn, as well as their own inspiring work have greatly advanced my understanding of the problems and practices of religious coexistence in the early modern period. In addition, at meetings and conferences on both sides of the Atlantic I had the opportunity to discuss my findings with numerous colleagues. For conference invitations and valuable comments I am especially indebted to Rosalind J. Beiler, Hans-Jürgen Grabbe, Walter G. Rödel, Helmut Schmahl, Claudia Schnurmann, and Marianne S. Wokeck.

Michael D. Driedger, Hermann Wellenreuther, and Ned C. Landsman have read the entire manuscript and made numerous valuable suggestions. Matthias Schönhofer, my student and research assistant at the University of

Bamberg, helped prepare the final manuscript. At Penn State Press, editors Peter J. Potter and Patrick H. Alexander and copyeditor Amanda E. Kirsten turned the manuscript into a book. Any remaining errors and omissions are entirely my own responsibility.

During the years in which this book was researched and written, my wife, Michaela, has been a constant source of inspiration and strength. In a sense, our children, Maximilian and Teresa, grew up with this book, venturing out to Penn's Woods with us as little kids and seeing it finally come to an end as almost grown-up teenagers. If they may have sometimes wondered what this was all about, my dedicating this book to them serves as a small way of acknowledging how much they mean to me.

Introduction

As the European population of British North America expanded in the eighteenth century and settlements spread from the Atlantic seaboard to the interior of the continent, hundreds of new towns were founded in the colonial backcountry. Some of these new settlements developed into sizable population and market centers that linked the major seaport cities to the expanding colonial frontier and performed a variety of commercial and administrative functions for the inhabitants of the backcountry. In Pennsylvania, several new counties were created after 1729 in response to demographic and territorial growth, and county seats such as Lancaster, Reading, York, and Carlisle thrived as market and supply centers for the surrounding countryside. "Political, commercial, craft, and social functions," historical geographer James T. Lemon wrote, "brought early rapid growth and later sustained growth to these county towns in the backcountry." The county courthouse became the focus of legal and political activity; wholesalers, retailers, and artisans provided an increasing variety of goods and services; and churches, fire companies, libraries, and eventually newspapers and secondary schools contributed to a thriving social life.[1]

The oldest of these towns in the Pennsylvania backcountry, Lancaster (founded in 1730), became the administrative center of the surrounding county and an important commercial hub connecting the colonial metropolis of Philadelphia to a rapidly expanding hinterland. The town had about twenty-eight hundred inhabitants in 1770, and its population grew to about four thousand by the end of the eighteenth century. While these figures seem rather modest from today's perspective, they made Lancaster one of largest inland towns in eighteenth-century North America, and Lancaster's commercial functions foreshadowed, on a smaller scale, the role that Midwestern cities such as

---

1. James T. Lemon, "Urbanization and the Development of Eighteenth-Century Southeastern Pennsylvania and Adjacent Delaware," *William and Mary Quarterly* 24 (1967): 501–42 (quote on 516); Jack P. Greene, *Pursuits of Happiness: The Social Development of Early Modern British Colonies and the Formation of American Culture* (Chapel Hill: University of North Carolina Press, 1988), 66–67, 90, 135–36.

Cincinnati, Chicago, and St. Louis would assume in the nineteenth century. Eighteenth-century Lancaster also resembled later Midwestern cities in one other crucial aspect: its ethnic and religious diversity. From its earliest days, German speakers formed a majority of Lancaster's inhabitants, and up to the 1750s the town absorbed growing numbers of German immigrants. While some of them prospered as shopkeepers, innkeepers, or artisans, many more moved on after a brief stay. English speakers accounted for only one-third to two-fifths of Lancaster's prerevolutionary population, but due to their command of the language and the legal system and their business connections and political ties to the Philadelphia elite, they were disproportionately influential. While Lancaster's population was highly mobile—population turnover in the years 1772–82 has been estimated at 5 percent annually—the town also had a stable core of long-time residents who became active in community affairs.[2]

Neither English nor German speakers were confessionally homogeneous groups. Describing the community to officers of the London-based Society of the Propagation of the Gospel in Foreign Parts, the Anglican minister Thomas Barton wrote in 1760 that "Lancaster is a large Town having near 600 Houses, inhabited chiefly by Germans of almost every Religious Denomination. It contains one Church of England, which is but small, a large German Calvinist Church, a Lutheran Church, a Moravian Church, a large Quaker Meeting House, a Popish Chapel; and a Presbyterian Church is now erecting." Thirty years after its founding, Lancaster housed seven Christian congregations, and all of them had built or were in the process of building their own places of worship. Only the small group of Jewish families, "who read and observe their Talmud with great exactness," did not have a synagogue.[3]

Apart from the small clusters of Catholics and Jews, both German and English speakers were thus divided into three major Protestant groups. Many German settlers were Lutherans, adherents of the creed dating back to Martin Luther's Reformation of the early sixteenth century. Spreading out from Saxony, Lutheranism had become the public religion in a number of German territories

<hr/>

2. Jerome H. Wood Jr., *Conestoga Crossroads: Lancaster, Pennsylvania, 1730–1790* (Harrisburg: Pennsylvania Historical and Museum Commission, 1979), 7–8, 17, 19, 47–49, 159. On geographic mobility, see James T. Lemon, *The Best Poor Man's Country: A Geographic Study of Early Southeastern Pennsylvania* (Baltimore: Johns Hopkins University Press, 1972), 74. For similar patterns of ethnic composition and mobility in another eighteenth-century Pennsylvania town, see Laura L. Becker, "The American Revolution as a Community Experience: A Case Study of Reading, Pennsylvania" (Ph.D. diss., University of Pennsylvania, 1978).

3. William Stevens Perry, ed., *Historical Collections Relating to the American Colonial Church*, 5 vols. (Hartford, 1870; repr., New York, 1969), 2:315.

and free imperial cities and received official recognition in the Holy Roman Empire with the religious peace of Augsburg in 1555. The German Reformed church originated in the teachings of the Swiss theologians Ulrich Zwingli and Jean Calvin, who shared Luther's emphasis on God's saving grace and the sole authority of the Bible but differed in their views on the sacraments and church discipline. Moreover, they sought to purify the liturgy from "popish" elements to a greater extent than the Lutherans. Reformed German princes fused Calvinist doctrine with a hierarchical church organization that resembled the Lutheran one. With the Peace of Westphalia that ended the Thirty Years' War in 1648, the Reformed religion also received official sanction in the Holy Roman Empire. In contrast to both Lutheran and Reformed churches, Moravianism remained outside the imperial constitution and was considered a "sect" by central European secular and ecclesiastical authorities. Originating in Jan Hus's Reformation in Bohemia and Moravia in the early fifteenth century, the Moravian Brethren had survived lengthy periods of persecution until their remnants found shelter on the estate of a Lutheran nobleman in Saxony, Count Nikolaus von Zinzendorf, in the early eighteenth century. The charismatic Zinzendorf first became a convert and then a leader of the Moravian brethren. Under his influence Moravianism developed into a highly personal "religion of the heart," and Zinzendorf's followers spread the message of the renewed Moravian church with considerable missionary zeal.[4]

Among the English speakers, Anglicans were adherents of the Church of England, established as the national church by the Tudor rulers Henry VIII, Edward VI, and Elizabeth I in the sixteenth century. While Anglicanism had absorbed elements of Calvinist doctrine, it retained a hierarchical, Episcopal form of ecclesiastical government. In the eighteenth century, the Church of England generally adopted a latitudinarian position, emphasizing reason and morality over fine points of doctrine, but the renewal movements of the revivalists George Whitefield and John Wesley also promoted a new emphasis on piety and spiritual rebirth. Presbyterians, heirs to Scottish Calvinism and English Puritanism who preferred congregational autonomy over hierarchical

---

4. The historical literature on the Lutheran and Reformed churches in early modern Europe is vast, but valuable surveys include Ronnie Po-Chia Hsia, *Social Discipline and the Reformation: Central Europe, 1550–1750* (London: Routledge, 1989); James D. Tracy, *Europe's Reformations, 1450–1650* (Lanham, Md.: Rowman and Littlefield, 1999); and Johannes Burkhardt, *Das Reformationsjahrhundert. Deutsche Geschichte zwischen Medienrevolution und Institutionenbildung, 1517–1617* (Stuttgart: Kohlhammer, 2002). On eighteenth-century developments in the Lutheran, Reformed, and Moravian churches, see Martin Brecht and Klaus Deppermann, eds., *Geschichte des Pietismus,* vol. 2, *Der Pietismus im 18. Jahrhundert* (Göttingen: Vandenhoeck and Ruprecht, 1995).

church organization, were restricted to the status of "dissenters" in eighteenth-century England but constituted the official church in Scotland. Finally, the Society of Friends, or Quakers—religious nonconformists who made their first appearance during the English Civil War of the mid-seventeenth century—emphasized the "inner light" within each individual over ecclesiastical and scriptural authority and suffered heavy persecution during the first decades of their existence on account of their antiauthoritarianism. Quakers were a relatively marginal and shrinking minority in eighteenth-century England but all the more prominent in Pennsylvania, a colony that their member William Penn had founded, in part, as an asylum for persecuted Christian minorities.[5]

As Thomas Barton's 1760 report indicates, church building in Lancaster had started almost as soon as town proprietor Andrew Hamilton had succeeded in making his town the new county seat: the German Reformed had completed their first wooden church by 1736, the Lutherans finished their first building two years later, the Roman Catholic chapel is referred to as early as 1741, and the Anglicans worshipped in their own church by 1744. Soon after their split from the Lutherans in 1746, the Moravians also built their own church.[6] In later years, the congregations would enlarge and sometimes completely rebuild these early edifices, add towering steeples, import church bells from England, and adorn church interiors with elaborate pulpits, organs, pews, and galleries. Contemporary views of the town confirm that Lancaster was thoroughly "sacralized" by the later eighteenth century.[7]

As these building activities demonstrate, congregations were of central importance to Lancaster's early residents. Laypeople in the new town began to build churches before the arrival of regular ministers, and the organization of several congregations predates the incorporation of Lancaster as a borough in 1742. In Lancaster, as elsewhere in early America, "congregations provided the

5. On the sixteenth-century origins of Protestantism in the British Isles, see Susan Brigden, *New Worlds, Lost Worlds: The Rule of the Tudors, 1485–1603* (London: Penguin, 2000), esp. chapters 3–4, 6–8; and Felicity Heal, *Reformation in Britain and Ireland* (New York: Oxford University Press, 2003). On religious persecution and dissent, see John Coffey, *Persecution and Toleration in Tudor and Stuart England, 1558–1689* (Harlow, England: Longman, 2000). On the eighteenth century, see Paul Langford, *A Polite and Commercial People: England, 1727–1783* (Oxford: Clarendon Press, 1989), chapter 6; and Frank O'Gorman, *The Long Eighteenth Century: British Political and Social History, 1688–1832* (London: Arnold, 1997), 6–8, 163–170, 294–309.

6. Caroline S. Coldren and M. Luther Heisey, "Religious Life in Lancaster Borough," *Papers Read Before the Lancaster County Historical Society* (hereafter *PLCHS*) 45 (1941): 125–44; Wood, *Conestoga Crossroads*, 13–14, 182, 187.

7. Jon Butler speaks of the "sacralization" of the North American landscape in Jon Butler, *Becoming America: The Revolution Before 1776* (Cambridge: Harvard University Press, 2000), 191–92.

only regular small-group activities that included every colonist—men, women, and children." Congregational administration also involved far greater numbers of people than town government or voluntary societies such as the fire companies or the library company. Whereas only thirty-six men served as burgesses of Lancaster from 1742 to 1789, several times that many officiated as trustees, wardens, elders, and deacons of the town's congregations. It was in the running of congregational affairs—the drafting of charters and bylaws, the acquisition of real estate for churches, schoolhouses, and graveyards, the management of funds—that many European immigrants acquired their first experiences in self-government on American soil. In their concern for public morality, the relief of poor members, and the schooling of the young, religious congregations fostered a "sense of communal responsibility."[8] Moreover, it was their congregations that dozens of eighteenth-century Lancasterians thought of when they made charitable bequests in their last wills, and it was in the congregations that pastors and laypeople fought and argued over questions of power, authority, obedience, and order. Even the religious enthusiasm of the "First Great Awakening" was a distinctly congregational affair: the town as a whole never experienced a religious revival in the eighteenth century, but "awakenings" repeatedly occurred within individual churches.[9] In the 1740s the inspired preaching and Moravian sympathies of the Lutheran pastor Laurence Thorstensson Nyberg split the local Lutheran congregation and resulted in the establishment of a Moravian congregation. In the 1750s the young pastor Philipp Wilhelm Otterbein's preaching invigorated piety and spirituality among Lancaster's German Reformed, and in the early 1770s a newcomer from Halle, Justus Heinrich Christian Helmuth, led the Lutherans through another period of awakening.[10] While Nyberg, Otterbein,

8. Quotes from E. Brooks Holifield, "Toward a History of American Congregations," in *American Congregations*, vol. 2, *New Perspectives in the Study of Congregations*, ed. James P. Wind and James W. Lewis (Chicago: University of Chicago Press, 1994), 23–53, 29, 31–32. On town government, see Wood, *Conestoga Crossroads*, 28–29. Charles H. Glatfelter has stressed the importance of congregations in introducing German immigrants to self-government in colonial Pennsylvania (Charles H. Glatfelter, *Pastors and People: German Lutheran and Reformed Churches in the Pennsylvania Field, 1717–1793*, 2 vols. [Breinigsville, Pa.: Publications of the Pennsylvania German Society, 1979–81], 2:162).

9. The Anglican minister Richard Locke reported in April 1747 that "Mr. Whitefield hath been here twice, invited by the Moravians; but he did not seem to answer their expectations" (William F. Worner, "The Church of England in Lancaster County [Part II]," *PLCHS* 40 [1936]: 89; see also *Pennsylvania Gazette*, August 29, 1746, and September 11, 1746; and Coldren and Heisey, "Religious Life," 135). When the revivalist returned to Lancaster and preached in the Lutheran church in 1770, the Anglican minister Thomas Barton considered him "a rambling Divine" whose "Popularity is almost expired. There is nothing new in him, and without change we are soon surfeited" (quoted in Wood, *Conestoga Crossroads*, 199).

10. Wood, *Conestoga Crossroads*, 197–200.

and Helmuth drew inspiration from continental European traditions of Reformed, Lutheran, and Moravian pietism, they were only loosely connected to the Anglo-American revivalist networks that created—or "invented," as some scholars have argued—the Great Awakening.[11] These observations suggest that congregations were pivotal social and cultural institutions in eighteenth-century Lancaster.

While scholars of colonial New England have long recognized the central significance of the church in the region's communities, churches in the middle colonies have often been described as weak, fledgling, strife-ridden institutions.[12] In the case of Pennsylvania and her neighbors, the Great Awakening of the 1740s has been interpreted as a response to crisis and decline, while the later eighteenth century has sometimes been described as a period of secularization. In her study of Germantown, for example, Stephanie Grauman Wolf has argued that individualism, geographic mobility, and the heterogeneity of the population led to a "growing lack of interest in the church as a vital center of life." Congregations were organized slowly, and close to half the population remained unchurched in the late eighteenth century. According to Wolf, Germantown's churches "seem to have played a very small role in the overall life of the community." Ministers exerted little influence in a place where the courts and taverns allegedly were much more important public forums than houses of worship. The slight impact of Germantown's congregations on education, charity, and public morality also indicated a "failure of institutional religion to carve out a meaningful niche for itself in the new secular world."[13]

11. On the influence of central European pietism on eighteenth-century American religion, see F. Ernest Stoeffler, ed., *Continental Pietism and Early American Christianity* (Grand Rapids, Mich.: Eerdmans, 1976); Jon Butler, "The Spiritual Importance of the Eighteenth Century," in *In Search of Peace and Prosperity: New German Settlements in Eighteenth-Century Europe and America,* ed. Hartmut Lehmann et al. (University Park: Pennsylvania State University Press, 2000), 101–14, esp. 102–3; A. G. Roeber, "The Problem of the Eighteenth Century in Transatlantic Religious History," in Lehmann, *In Search of Peace and Prosperity,* 115–38, esp. 125–26; and A. G. Roeber, "Der Pietismus in Nordamerika im 18. Jahrhundert," in *Geschichte des Pietismus,* vol. 2, *Der Pietismus im 18. Jahrhundert,* ed. Martin Brecht and Klaus Deppermann (Göttingen: Vandenhoeck and Ruprecht, 1995), 666–99. On revivalist networks, see Frank Lambert, *Inventing the "Great Awakening"* (Princeton: Princeton University Press, 2000).

12. On the central significance of the church in the region's communities, see Catherine Brekus and Harry S. Stout, "A New England Congregation: Center Church, New Haven, 1638–1989," in *American Congregations,* vol. 1, *Portraits of Twelve Religious Communities,* ed. James P. Wind and James W. Lewis, 14–102 (Chicago: University of Chicago Press, 1994).

13. Stephanie Grauman Wolf, *Urban Village: Population, Community, and Family Structure in Germantown, Pennsylvania, 1683–1800* (Princeton: Princeton University Press, 1976), 203–42 (quotes on 217, 229, 235). See also Dietmar Rothermund, *The Layman's Progress: Religious and Political Experience in Pennsylvania, 1740–1770* (Philadelphia: University of Pennsylvania Press, 1961), esp. 57–68; Martin Lodge, "The Crisis of the Churches in the Middle Colonies," *Pennsylvania Magazine of History and Biography* (hereafter *PMHB*) 95 (1971): 196–221; and John B. Frantz, "The Awakening of Religion Among the German Settlers in the Middle Colonies," *William and Mary Quarterly* 33 (1976): 266–88.

In the case of Lancaster nothing would be more misleading than to portray congregational development in terms of decline or secularization. Lancaster's congregations grew throughout the eighteenth century, and they continued to absorb a majority of the town's and many of the surrounding countryside's inhabitants. While the population of Lancaster has been estimated at roughly three thousand on the eve of the Revolution, pastor Helmuth wrote in 1772 that almost thirteen hundred people had registered themselves as members of the Lutheran congregation; this figure probably excluded children under fifteen. The following year the Reformed pastor Carl Ludwig Boehme reported 218 families in his congregation to the annual Coetus of Reformed ministers, and one historical demographer has put the size of the congregation at 850 to 900 people. In 1775 the Moravian congregation counted 320 members (including children). Anglican minister Thomas Barton had only twenty-five communicants in Lancaster in 1770, but the number of people who regularly attended his church was certainly not below 150. While the numbers of Presbyterians, Quakers, and Catholics can only be guessed, it is still clear that at least twenty-seven hundred people were affiliated with one of Lancaster's congregations in the early 1770s. Even if we estimate that one-fifth to one-quarter of these lived in surrounding townships, a significant majority of eighteenth-century Lancasterians adhered to a church. And these churches were experiencing steady growth. In the Lutheran church the number of Easter communicants increased by 78.5 percent, from 107 to 191, between 1749 and 1785, while the number of newly confirmed rose from fourteen to seventy over the same period. The 284 Lutherans who went to communion on Pentecost in 1785 represented a 67 percent increase over the 170 Pentecost communicants in 1749. The Reformed pastor Heinrich Wilhelm Stoy counted "about 100 families belonging to the congregation" upon his arrival in Lancaster in 1758. In 1790 his successor, Wilhelm Hendel, reported 183 families.[14]

14. See Wood, *Conestoga Crossroads*, 47–49, for population figures; W. J. Mann, B. M. Schmucker, and W. Germann, eds., *Nachrichten von den vereinigten Deutschen Evangelisch-Lutherischen Gemeinen in Nord-America, absonderlich in Pensylvanien*, 2 vols. (Allentown, Pa.: Brobst, Diehl and Co.; Halle: Buchhandlung des Waisenhauses, 1886–95), 2:690 (hereafter *Hallesche Nachrichten*); Lancaster Diaries, 1775, Moravian Archives, Bethlehem, Pennsylvania; William J. Hinke, ed., *Minutes and Letters of the German Reformed Coetus in Pennsylvania, 1747–1792: Together with Three Preliminary Reports of Rev. John Philip Boehm, 1734–1744* (Philadelphia: Reformed Church Publication Board, 1903), 184, 339, 386; Roger C. Henderson, "Matters of Life and Death: A Demographic Analysis of Eighteenth-Century Lancaster Reformed Church Records," *Journal of the Lancaster County Historical Society* (hereafter *JLCHS*) 91 (1987/88): 63–64; Perry, *Historical Collections*, 2:449; and Debra D. Smith and Frederick S. Weiser, eds. and trans., *Trinity Lutheran Church Records, Lancaster, Pennsylvania*, 4 vols. (Apollo, Pa.: Closson Press, 1988–2006), 1:336–44, 276–83. On the difficulties of defining membership in the German churches of eighteenth-century Pennsylvania, see Glatfelter, *Pastors and People*, 1:176–77.

When Lancaster's tax assessment lists are correlated with local church records, it becomes clear that church adherence was high even during a period for which many historians have claimed rising religious indifference.[15] Lancaster's earliest tax assessment dates from 1751 and includes 293 taxpaying householders. Sixty-three individuals (21.5 percent of the total) can be identified as Lutherans since they took communion in the Lutheran church at midcentury or were repeatedly present at pastoral acts there. A further fifty taxpayers (17.1 percent) appear in the Reformed church records at least twice or are identified as Reformed in the Lutheran church book, and thirty-four people (11.6 percent) are on a list of adherents compiled by the local Moravian pastor. Twenty-nine individuals (9.9 percent) on the tax list also appear on membership lists of the Anglican congregation, and fifteen (5.1 percent) can be identified as members of smaller religious groups in town—Catholics, Jews, Quakers, and Presbyterians. Altogether, 191 taxpayers or 65.2 percent of the people on the list were clearly affiliated with a religious group. At a time when Lancaster society was still in flux—the town was just twenty years old, German immigration to Pennsylvania was at its peak, geographical mobility rates were high, some religious groups were not yet formally organized, and others were experiencing interior conflict—a significant majority of the town's household heads were "churched."[16]

The 1773 tax list names 432 individuals and four estates of deceased persons. Of the 432 taxables, 93 (21.5 percent) could not be located in contemporary church records, but since there are no Presbyterian and Catholic records for the colonial period and the Anglican church books are patchy, we may assume that at least one-third of these taxables were not really "unchurched." A further twenty-six individuals (6.0 percent) could be found in only one church record; they may have been loosely affiliated with a local congregation or may have stayed in town only briefly. The remaining 313 individuals (72.5 percent), however, repeatedly appear in church records. At the very least, this means that they deemed religion important enough to have their children baptized or seek

15. For the middle colonies, the method of linking membership lists of congregations to tax and census data has been successfully employed by Joyce D. Goodfriend, "The Social Dimensions of Congregational Life in Colonial New York City," *William and Mary Quarterly* 42 (1985): 252–78. Record linkage enables Goodfriend to assert that "[m]ost residents belonged to a church during the seventeenth and eighteenth centuries, and their churches played a critical role in ordering community life" (252).

16. Information in this paragraph is based on Lancaster Borough Tax Assessment List, 1751, Lancaster County Historical Society; Smith and Weiser, *Trinity Lutheran Church Records*, vol. 1; F. Edward Wright, *Lancaster County, Pennsylvania Church Records of the Eighteenth Century*, vol. 2 (Westminster, Md.: Family Line Publications, 1994); *Transactions of the Moravian Historical Society* 1 (1858–76): 384–87; Vestry Minutes of St. James from October 3, 1744, to November 13, 1846, pp. 4–9, St. James Episcopal Church, Lancaster (hereafter St. James Vestry Minutes, St. James Episcopal Church).

a Christian burial for family members. But many were involved to a much larger degree. One-hundred-twenty-six individuals on the 1773 tax list—almost 30 percent of all taxables—had rented pews in the Lutheran church. Fifty-eight Lutheran, Reformed, and Anglican men were elected to church offices (trustee, elder, deacon, warden, vestryman) during the late 1760s and early 1770s. Since the Moravians, Presbyterians, Quakers, and Catholics also had their lay leaders, at least seventy individuals, or one out of six taxables, must have been active in congregational self-government. On the basis of the 1773 tax assessment it is also possible to give a rough estimate of the religious composition of prerevolutionary Lancaster. About 40 percent of household heads were Lutheran, 20 percent Reformed, and almost 10 percent Moravian; the three largest congregations were all German speaking and together comprised more than two-thirds of the town's inhabitants. Anglicans and Presbyterians together may have accounted for another 10 percent of household heads and the smaller religious groups (Quakers, Catholics, and Jews) about 5 percent. This would leave only 15 percent of the taxables who were not affiliated with any congregation. Comparing these percentages with the 1751 data, it appears that the Lutherans had gained most from the heavy German immigration of the early 1750s while the share of the Reformed, Moravians, Anglicans and smaller groups remained relatively stable.[17]

These figures suggest that Lancaster fits a pattern of continuing religious vitality, congregational growth, high levels of church adherence, and a proliferation of ecclesiastical institutions that some scholars have detected in eighteenth-century America. Jon Butler has noted an "expansion of diversity within colonial American Protestantism between 1680 and the 1770s," and Charles Cohen asserts that the work of Butler, Patricia Bonomi, and others amounts to a "post-Puritan paradigm"—a perspective on early American history that emphasizes "the varieties of colonial religious experience." According to Cohen, "the earnest if stolid fabrication of ecclesiastical institutions throughout Anglo-America during the so-called long eighteenth century" may have had a more lasting impact on religious patterns in the United States than either seventeenth-century New England Puritanism or nineteenth-century revivalism. Moreover, the construction of these institutions "engaged the laity; gathering churches, challenging ministerial prerogatives, and nurturing their own hermeneutics, they played a significant—at

17. The 1773 tax assessment list is printed in William H. Egle, ed., *Pennsylvania Archives*, 3rd series (Harrisburg: William Stanley Ray, 1897), 17:454–63; for the pew rent list of the Lutheran congregation, see Smith and Weiser, *Trinity Lutheran Church Records*, 2:302–465. For patterns of lay leadership, see chapters 1–4 below.

times paramount—role in defining their faiths."[18] The history of church-building in Lancaster allows us to test some of the major tenets of this "post-Puritan paradigm." More particularly, Lancaster provides ample evidence for the pivotal role of laypeople in shaping local congregations. As the subsequent chapters will show, the laity actively participated in church affairs throughout the colonial and early national periods, and even conflicts with pastors testify to its intense concern for the ordering of congregational life and the distribution of authority.

Since Lancaster, unlike colonial New England towns, never knew a religious establishment but housed a plurality of congregations from its beginning, a study of congregational development also illuminates the diverse, pluralist character of eighteenth-century Pennsylvania. To be sure, the microcosm of Lancaster does not fully represent the "crazy quilt" of religious groups that had formed in the colony on account of religious toleration and the diversity of immigration. German-speaking Anabaptist and radical pietistic groups such as the Mennonites, the Amish, the Dunkers, and Conrad Beissel's sabbatarian Ephrata commune were prominent in rural Lancaster County, for example, but few of their members resided in the borough and they did not build meeting-houses or form congregations there.[19] Nor did English-speaking residents establish Methodist or Baptist congregations in Lancaster before 1800. Still, a study of congregations in the borough and their relationships with one another can shed considerable light on the interactions of people from various national and religious backgrounds at the local level. With the exception of the small Catholic community, Lancaster's congregations also mirrored the town's ethnic divisions: the membership of the Reformed, Lutheran, and Moravian congregations was

18. Patricia U. Bonomi and Peter R. Eisenstadt, "Church Adherence in the Eighteenth-Century British American Colonies," *William and Mary Quarterly* 39 (1982): 245–87; Patricia U. Bonomi, *Under the Cope of Heaven: Religion, Society, and Politics in Colonial America* (New York: Oxford University Press, 1986); Richard W. Pointer, *Protestant Pluralism and the New York Experience: A Study of Eighteenth-Century Religious Diversity* (Bloomington: Indiana University Press, 1988), 4, 14, 21–22, 30–34; Goodfriend, "Social Dimensions of Congregational Life"; Jon Butler, *Awash in a Sea of Faith: Christianizing the American People* (Cambridge: Harvard University Press, 1990), 123–28, 174–80; Jon Butler, "Protestant Pluralism," in *Encyclopedia of the North American Colonies*, vol. 3, ed. Jacob E. Cooke et al. (New York: Scribner, 1993), 609–31 (quote on 615); Jon Butler, "The Future of American Religious History: Prospectus, Agenda, Transatlantic *Problématique*," *William and Mary Quarterly* 42 (1985): 167–83; and Charles L. Cohen, "The Post-Puritan Paradigm of Early American Religious History," *William and Mary Quarterly* 54 (1997): 695–722 (quotes on 697, 699–700).

19. On these groups, see Richard K. MacMaster, *Land, Piety, Peoplehood: The Establishment of Mennonite Communities in America, 1683–1790* (Scottdale, Pa.: Herald Press, 1985); Donald F. Durnbaugh, "Pennsylvania's Crazy Quilt of German Religious Groups," *Pennsylvania History* 68 (2001): 8–30; and Jeff Bach, *Voices of the Turtledoves: The Sacred World of Ephrata* (University Park: Pennsylvania State University Press, 2002).

overwhelmingly German speaking throughout the period covered here, while the vast majority of English speakers attended the Anglican and Presbyterian churches.[20] As historian E. Brooks Holifield has noted, however, "even the ethnic coloration of congregations exemplified their comprehensive character—their embrace of a larger community, their function in preserving larger communal values."[21] Steven M. Nolt has asserted that "religion and religious institutions were often the chief means of mediating and propagating culture" for minority groups in a pluralistic setting."[22] Significantly, no single religious group comprised the majority of Lancaster's inhabitants, and no group even came close to holding a monopoly on wealth or political influence. Among the thirty-four men with the highest assessment on the first borough tax list of 1751, we find eight Anglicans, eight Lutherans, seven Moravians, seven German Reformed, two Quakers, one Catholic, and one Jew. Members of all these groups except Catholics and Jews were elected to the borough council between 1742 and 1775.[23]

In order to assess the nature of religious pluralism in Lancaster, two approaches are combined here: comparison and the study of interactions. Much scholarship on religious development in the middle colonies has focused on particular denominations—Dutch Calvinists, German Lutherans and Moravians, or Scots-Irish Presbyterians—and traced the transfer of their religious institutions from the Old World to the new as well as their encounters with a dominant English culture. While these works have placed colonial religious history in a transatlantic context and outlined the "Americanization" of European churches, a comparative perspective allows us to identify what was actually unique about the development of specific religious groups within a particular environment.[24]

20. In New York City, by contrast, the "ethnically centered configuration of congregational life began to fracture in the early decades of the eighteenth century." See Goodfriend, "Social Dimensions of Congregational Life," 262.

21. Holifield, "Toward a History," 33.

22. Steven M. Nolt, *Foreigners in Their Own Land: Pennsylvania Germans in the Early Republic* (University Park: Pennsylvania State University Press, 2002), 4.

23. Lancaster Borough Tax Assessment List, 1751, Lancaster County Historical Society; Franklin Ellis and Samuel Evans, *History of Lancaster County, Pennsylvania, with Biographical Sketches of Many of Its Pioneers and Prominent Men* (Philadelphia: Everts and Peck, 1883), 373–74; Wood, *Conestoga Crossroads*, 28–31.

24. On the Dutch Calvinists, see Randall Balmer, *A Perfect Babel of Confusion: Dutch Religion and English Culture in the Middle Colonies* (New York: Oxford University Press, 1989); David G. Hackett, *The Rude Hand of Innovation: Religion and Social Order in Albany, New York, 1652–1836* (New York: Oxford University Press, 1991). Lutherans and Moravians are treated in A. G. Roeber, *Palatines, Liberty, and Property: German Lutherans in Colonial British America* (Baltimore: Johns Hopkins University Press, 1993); Thomas J. Müller, *Kirche zwischen zwei Welten: Die Obrigkeitsproblematik bei Heinrich Melchior Mühlenberg und die Kirchengründung der deutschen Lutheraner in Pennsylvania* (Stuttgart: Steiner, 1994); Wolfgang Splitter, *Pastors, People, Politics: German Lutherans in Pennsylvania, 1740–1790*

Thus the first three chapters of this study analyze the development of the major Protestant churches in colonial Lancaster—German Reformed, Lutheran, Moravian, Anglican, Presbyterian—in a comparative perspective. While each congregational history has its distinct features, there are also remarkable parallels. The argument pursued here is that a quest for order and stability was the dominant theme in each of these congregations. During the colonial period all major religious communities experienced similar problems: the adjustment of an immigrant population to a new environment, struggles between ministers and laymen for the control of congregational affairs, and conflicting concepts of church order. By later in the eighteenth century, however, congregations had achieved a large measure of stability and cohesion. They had built ornate churches, secured charters of incorporation, and attracted qualified ministers who usually served long, successful pastorates (chapter 5). Moreover, the Protestant congregations had developed traditions of charity and stewardship that had a significant impact on the establishment of local benevolent associations such as the Lancaster Bible Society, the German Society, and the Female Benevolent Society after 1815 (chapter 6).

In addition, this book examines the interactions between the various religious groups in the town. While pastors offered general comments on relations between Lancaster's inhabitants, a detailed analysis of church records, wills, letters, and a variety of other sources reveals how frequently eighteenth-century Lancasterians switched allegiance from one congregation to another, how commonly townspeople married across denominational lines, and how often they made bequests to more than one congregation. A close study of the relationships between Englishmen and Germans, "church" and "sect" people, Catholics and Protestants, Jews and Christians, as well as blacks and whites enables us to assess the character of ethnic and religious boundaries and the meanings of pluralism in a major population center of the Pennsylvania backcountry (chapter 4). While there are several fine studies on the growth of toleration and religious

---

(Trier: Wissenschaftlicher Verlag, 1998); John Fea, "Ethnicity and Congregational Life in the Eighteenth-Century Delaware Valley: The Swedish Lutherans of New Jersey," in *Explorations in Early American Culture* 5 (2001): 45–78; Beverly P. Smaby, *The Transformation of Moravian Bethlehem: From Communal Mission to Family Economy* (Philadelphia: University of Pennsylvania Press, 1988); and Craig D. Atwood, *Community of the Cross: Moravian Piety in Colonial Bethlehem* (University Park: Pennsylvania State University Press, 2004). For Presbyterians, see Leonard J. Trinterud, *The Forming of an American Tradition: A Re-examination of Colonial Presbyterianism* (Philadelphia: Westminster, 1949); Ned C. Landsman, *Scotland and Its First American Colony, 1683–1765* (Princeton: Princeton University Press, 1985); Marilyn J. Westerkamp, *Triumph of the Laity: Scots-Irish Piety and the Great Awakening, 1625–1760* (New York: Oxford University Press, 1988); and Leigh Eric Schmidt, *Holy Fairs: Scottish Communions and American Revivals in the Early Modern Period* (Princeton: Princeton University Press, 1989).

liberty in the middle colonies, these tend to look at general developments at the provincial level, and they rely heavily on sources authored by political and clerical leaders.[25] The adoption of a microhistorical perspective on actual inter-confessional relations in a specific community broadens our understanding of the nature and evolution of religious pluralism.

The sources for a study of congregational development and religious pluralism in Lancaster are remarkably rich. Apart from the Presbyterians, for which few eighteenth-century records exist, church books, vestry minutes, pastors' letters and diaries, and the protocols of ecclesiastical bodies such as the Lutheran Ministerium and the German Reformed Coetus of Pennsylvania provide a wealth of information on the major religious congregations. Indeed the Moravian diaries, with their day-to-day accounts of congregational affairs, tend to overwhelm the reader with their abundance of detail. While the pastors' voluminous writings privilege their perspective over that of laypeople, a careful reading of the sources sheds light on the laity's goals and aspirations as well. In addition, tax lists, deed books, wills, estate inventories, and newspaper advertisements reveal much about the social standing of laypersons who were involved in congregational leadership. While a local perspective is necessary to understand the importance of the congregation in the lives of eighteenth-century Lancasterians, the study of congregational life has implications far beyond the confines of one Pennsylvania town. The size and diversity of the community, as well as the quantity and quality of existing archival and printed sources, make Lancaster an ideal setting for a study of major problems in eighteenth-century American religious history: the development of institutional pluralism, the nature of religious toleration, the impact of the Great Awakening, and the meanings of power and authority within the churches.

A NOTE ON SPELLING

I have generally rendered the German spelling of the names of German and Swiss immigrants—pastors as well as laypeople—in the text since German speakers usually retained that spelling in congregational records and in their own correspondence. Thus, I write of Heinrich Melchior Mühlenberg (not Henry Melchior

25. Sally Schwartz, *"A Mixed Multitude": The Struggle for Toleration in Colonial Pennsylvania* (New York: New York University Press, 1987); Jerry William Frost, *A Perfect Freedom: Religious Liberty in Pennsylvania* (New York: Cambridge University Press, 1990); Pointer, *Protestant Pluralism;* Douglas C. Jacobsen, *An Unprov'd Experiment: Religious Pluralism in Colonial New Jersey,* Chicago Studies in the History of American Religion 9 (Brooklyn, N.Y.: Carlson, 1991).

Muhlenberg), Johann Wilhelm Hendel (not William Hendel), and Matthäus Jung (not Matthew Young). In the case of some second-generation Germans, particularly those who became well-known public figures in Pennsylvania, on the other hand, I use the anglicized spelling also found in other works. This applies, for example, to Matthias Slough (originally Schlauch) or Adam Hubley (originally Hubele).

1

A QUEST FOR ORDER:

THE GERMAN REFORMED CONGREGATION, 1733–1775

Reformed settlers from the Electoral Palatinate, smaller German principalities, and Swiss cantons were the first to erect their own church in the new county town on the Conestoga, and their congregation remained the second largest in Lancaster throughout the eighteenth century. To open this study with a close look at the German Reformed congregation is rewarding in several respects. First, the German Reformed church in the middle colonies has received much less attention from modern historians than the Lutherans, Dutch Reformed, Presbyterians, or Moravians, but it contributed to the colonies' religious diversity in significant respects. Second, the Lancaster congregation went through distinct stages, whose analysis provides a model for the study of the other German and English congregations. During the initial period from the 1730s to midcentury, the few resident German Reformed pastors in Pennsylvania viewed the nascent Lancaster congregation as chaotic and disorderly, while laypeople actively participated in church affairs and laid the foundations for future development. The subsequent period from the early 1750s to the eve of the American Revolution was marked by the presence of committed pietistic ministers, repeated struggles between these pastors and the congregation, and further organizational efforts culminating in the charter that the colony's proprietor granted to the Lancaster German Reformed church in 1771. Third, the evolution of this congregation highlights several of the issues that lie at the heart of this study, particularly the problems and achievements of congregation building in a pluralistic setting and the clashes between ministerial and lay conceptions of order and authority. In short, this chapter on the German Reformed congregation develops a theme whose variations will be explored in subsequent chapters on the other German and English churches.

ORIGINS

On February 13, 1733, Johann Conrad Tempelmann, a tailor from the Palatinate, wrote a letter to the Reformed Synods of North and South Holland that constitutes the most important source on the beginnings of the German Reformed church in Lancaster County. According to Tempelmann, "[t]he church at Chanastocka had its origin in the year 1725, with a small gathering in houses here, and there, with the reading of a sermon and with song and prayer, according to their High German Church Order upon all Sundays and holidays, but, on account of the lack of a minister, without the administration of baptism and the Lord's Supper." At the laypeople's request, the pious schoolmaster Johann Philipp Boehm started to preach in the Conestoga area, and after his ordination by the Dutch Reformed ministers of New York in 1729 Boehm also administered the sacraments and introduced a church order. The growth of the Conestoga settlement eventually led to the separation of the original community into six meeting places, which Boehm could not visit any longer on a regular basis because he lived too far away from them. While three congregations were supplied by the Reformed minister Johann Peter Müller, Tempelmann, one of the elders of the original Conestoga church, ministered to the other three. One of Tempelmann's congregations can be identified as the church in Lancaster because one of the elders, Johann Jacob Hock, later became its acting minister. Tempelmann reported that the Reformed congregation at the newly established county seat had thirty members.[1]

Three years later, on June 20, 1736, Johann Jacob Hock, now described as the "teacher, preacher, or pastor" of the congregation, entered the first six baptisms

---

1. William J. Hinke, ed., *Life and Letters of John Philip Boehm, Founder of the Reformed Church in Pennsylvania, 1683–1749* (Philadelphia: Publication and Sunday School Board of the Reformed Church in the United States, 1916), 62–64; Glatfelter, *Pastors and People,* 2:153. For accounts of Boehm and Tempelmann's careers, see James I. Good, *History of the Reformed Church in the United States, 1725–1792* (Reading, Pa.: Daniel Miller, 1899), 100–12, 120–33, 265–78; William J. Hinke, *Ministers of the German Reformed Congregations in Pennsylvania and Other Colonies in the Eighteenth Century* (Lancaster, Pa.: Historical Commission of the Evangelical and Reformed Church, 1951), 1–18; Glatfelter, *Pastors and People,* 1:21–22, 149–51 and 2:35–42.

into the church book "of the newly built Reformed church here in the island of Pennsylvania, in Cannastocken, in the new town named Langester." According to the protocol's preface, the wooden church building had been so far completed that the first worship service could be held on the festival of Pentecost. In the same year Johann Heinrich Basler, Felix Müller, Johann Gorner, and Peter Doerr were elected as the first elders of the congregation, and Carl Keller and Stephan Rammersberger as the first deacons. In a rotating election system, two elders were to be replaced annually. Until August 8, 1737, Hock recorded thirty-four baptisms. He then disappears from the records.[2]

As in many other early German-speaking congregations in Pennsylvania, pious laymen played a decisive role in the establishment of a German Reformed church in the new town of Lancaster. Men like Tempelmann and Hock lacked formal theological training and their pastoral acts were of dubious validity in the eyes of ordained ministers, but their efforts responded to the genuine desire of early German and Swiss settlers for spiritual guidance and a community of believers amid the bewildering variety of religious groups in the Pennsylvania backcountry. Thus Johann Philipp Boehm, who was generally critical of "irregular" ministers, wrote approvingly of Tempelmann "that he is very watchful against the sects, and that his congregations are very much united." Some pious laymen progressed almost inadvertently from the reading of Bible texts and sermons to regular preaching and the performance of pastoral acts, whereas others raised funds to build churches and support the poor. When regularly ordained ministers began to arrive in larger numbers in the 1740s and 1750s, they found well-established congregations in many places.[3]

In the Reformed congregation of Lancaster, the process of establishing a regular ministry was particularly long and arduous. Ministers changed frequently in the early years, there were long vacancies between pastorates, and the congregation had more than its share of inept pastors and outright scoundrels. After Hock had left (or died), the congregation was apparently without a settled minister until the arrival of Johann Bartholomäus Rieger in April 1739. Rieger, a native of Oberingelheim in the Palatinate who had begun his American career with a brief, controversial ministry in Philadelphia and then spent several years in New Jersey, antagonized his congregation when he extended a warm welcome to the leader of

2. W. Stuart Cramer, *History of the First Reformed Church Lancaster, Pennsylvania, 1736–1904* (Lancaster, Pa.: n.p., 1904), 8–9, 11; Ellis and Evans, *History of Lancaster County,* 450; Coldren and Heisey, "Religious Life," 131; Hinke, *Ministers,* 311–13; Glatfelter, *Pastors and People,* 1:65; Wood, *Conestoga Crossroads,* 13.

3. Hinke, *Ministers,* 15. Cf. Bonomi, *Under the Cope of Heaven,* 72–79.

the Moravian church, Count Nikolaus von Zinzendorf, during his tour through Pennsylvania in 1742. According to Johann Philipp Boehm, one of Rieger's sermons was "nothing but a glorifying and praising of the piety and doctrines of the Moravian brethren." His congregation refused to renew his contract when it expired in early 1743, and Rieger returned to Europe to study medicine at the University of Leiden in Holland. By the time he returned to Lancaster in the spring of 1745, the congregation had called another man, Caspar Ludwig Schnorr, as its preacher.[4]

Schnorr, a native of Westphalia who may have been a converted Catholic, had come to America with passage money and moral support from the Reformed Classis of Amsterdam, which found out too late that the man had an ill reputation. He accepted a call from Lancaster and began his ministry in November 1744; in addition, he agreed to preach at the Tulpehocken Reformed church in present-day Berks County once a month. In two letters to the Classis of Amsterdam, Schnorr reported that his congregation consisted of 106 members but could not provide him with a sufficient salary on account of its poverty. Therefore he asked the Classis to augment his salary and send him several hundred Bibles, hymn books, and catechisms for distribution. Schnorr also commented on Bartholomäus Rieger's efforts to regain the favor of his former congregation after his return. According to Schnorr, Rieger had offered to build a parsonage and obtain a church bell, causing rumors that he had secured funds from the church authorities in Holland. The conflict with Rieger and his feud with Moravian pastor Jacob Lischy, whom he once called a "sorcerer," may have been less damaging to Schnorr than the enmity of the influential Germantown printer Christoph Saur. After Schnorr had attacked Saur's printing of the Bible for its promotion of sectarian views, Saur published newspaper articles accusing Schnorr of drunkenness and immoral conduct and reporting that the pastor had been tried and sentenced for his misdeeds. The Lutheran minister Heinrich Melchior Mühlenberg likewise wrote that "the wanton sinner" Schnorr had been "lately punished by the provincial and city court for rape." Faced with these charges, Schnorr had to end his pastorate in Lancaster in disgrace in the spring of 1746.[5]

4. Good, *History (1725–1792)*, 166–70; Joseph Henry Dubbs, "The Reformed Church in Pennsylvania . . . Prepared at the Request of the Pennsylvania-German Society," in Proceedings and Addresses of the Pennsylvania German Society 11 (Lancaster, Pa.: n.p. 1902), 100–102; Hinke, *Boehm*, 417–18; Hinke, *Ministers*, 27–29; Wood, *Conestoga Crossroads*, 185, 190; Glatfelter, *Pastors and People*, 1:108–9 and 2:95; Schwartz, "*A Mixed Multitude*," 141–42.
5. Good, *History (1725–1792)*, 250–52; Dubbs, "Reformed Church," 103–4; Hinke, *Boehm*, 70; Hinke, *Ministers*, 339–42; *Pensylvanische Berichte*, May 16, 1746; Theodore G. Tappert and John W.

After vacancies of almost two years in 1737–39 and more than one and a half years in 1743–44, the congregation remained without a resident minister for almost four years. Michael Schlatter, the Swiss pastor who vigorously organized the Reformed church in the middle colonies after his arrival in America in 1746, visited Lancaster on a number of occasions. During his first stay in September 1746, Schlatter conferred with both Rieger and lay members of the congregation. The latter "were unanimous in desiring a stated minister" but would not accept Rieger again. Their opposition to Rieger, the Swiss pastor noted, "arises only from the claim that his Rev. is said not to have very agreeable delivery of his sermons and to be rather severe and exact, in his service." Schlatter "ordained and installed regular officers" and promised that he would try to recruit a minister, to whose salary the congregation pledged to contribute £40. When he held a communion service in June 1747 in Lancaster, 225 people participated. "The crowd of people," Schlatter wrote, "which had assembled on the occasion was so great that the church could scarcely contain the one-half, so great was the desire to hear the word of God, and the greatest portion returned to their homes with joy and thanksgiving." The pastor felt he had ample reason to thank God "for the goodness which he has shown toward this poor destitute people." In May 1748 when Schlatter returned, 265 people partook in the Lord's Supper, and the pastor reported that he did not leave "without much blessing and deep emotions."[6]

Schlatter's efforts to secure an ordained minister, however, repeatedly ended in frustration. In September 1748, he accompanied his newly arrived colleague Dominicus Bartholomäus to Lancaster, who preached there "to the satisfaction of all" but eventually accepted a call to Tulpehocken. A month later, Schlatter arranged for his Swiss countryman Johann Jacob Hochreutiner, who had sailed to America with Bartholomäus, to deliver two sermons in Lancaster. According

Doberstein, eds., *The Journals of Henry Melchior Muhlenberg*, 3 vols. (Philadelphia: Evangelical Lutheran Ministerium of Pennsylvania and Adjacent States, 1942–57), 1:154; Glatfelter, *Pastors and People*, 1:121–22 and 2:128; Schwartz, *"A Mixed Multitude,"* 142; William Reed Steckel, "Pietist in Colonial Pennsylvania: Christopher Sauer, Printer, 1738–1758" (Ph.D. diss., Stanford University, 1949), 46–47, 72, 74–75.

6. William J. Hinke, ed., "Diary of the Rev. Michael Schlatter, June 1—December 15, 1746," *Journal of the Presbyterian Historical Society* 3 (1905/6): 113–14, 118–19; Henry W. Harbaugh, *The Life of Michael Schlatter: With a Full Account of His Travels and Labors Among the Germans of Pennsylvania, New Jersey, Maryland and Virginia* (Philadelphia: Lindsay, 1857), 135, 158, 178. Cf. also ibid., 152, 155, 160, 170–71; Good, *History (1725–1792)*, 316, 327, 346, 349, 462; Ellis and Evans, *History of Lancaster County*, 451; Cramer, *History*, 18–19. For biographical accounts of Schlatter's career, see also Hinke, *Ministers*, 37–47; Glatfelter, *Pastors and People*, 2:112–22, 217–21; and Marthi Pritzker-Ehrlich, "Michael Schlatter von St. Gallen. Eine biographische Untersuchung zur schweizerischen Amerika-Auswanderung im 18. Jahrhundert" (Ph.D. diss., Zurich, 1981).

to Schlatter, Hochreutiner preached a preparatory sermon "to the satisfaction and edification of the people," and after the two Swiss had administered communion to 150 people, he delivered a thanksgiving sermon "to the great delight of the congregation." Hochreutiner accepted the call to Lancaster, but before he could take up his duties, he accidentally shot and killed himself in Schlatter's Philadelphia home in November 1748. "The amazement and sorrow . . . occasioned by this accident," Schlatter wrote, "was so much the greater on account of the great love which all bore him, and the expectations which his own congregation and others entertained of the services of such an excellent servant of Jesus Christ." Deeply impressed by this sudden tragedy, Schlatter published the introductory sermon that Hochreutiner had prepared for Lancaster under the title *Swan Song*, and Christoph Saur's newspaper *Pensylvanische Berichte* reported that the unfortunate pastor had been eagerly looking forward to his labors among the "rough and insolent people" of Lancaster. After Hochreutiner's death, Dominicus Bartholomäus agreed to supply Lancaster once a month from his Tulpehocken parish; Johannes Hoffman, the congregation's schoolmaster since May 1747, was also preaching and catechizing when neither Schlatter nor Bartholomäus were available.[7]

When another Swiss pastor, Johann Conrad Steiner, arrived in Pennsylvania in late 1749, the Lancaster congregation "earnestly entreated" the recently formed German Reformed Coetus of Pennsylvania "if it were possible, that this newly-arrived minister might be sent to them, and to this end they gave [Schlatter] authority to call him to be their regular pastor and teacher." Steiner agreed to go to Lancaster but then accepted a call from a faction of the Reformed congregation in Philadelphia that opposed Schlatter's ministry there.[8] A call to the Swiss minister Johann Joachim Zubly in South Carolina that the Reformed pastor Jacob Lischy prepared for Lancaster in September 1749 may have never been sent.[9]

7. Harbaugh, *Life of Michael Schlatter*, 181–86; Good, *History (1725–1792)*, 360–61, 492–93; Dubbs, "Reformed Church," 158–59; Hinke, *Boehm*, 439–40; *Pensylvanische Berichte*, November 16, 1748; Hinke, *Ministers*, 47–52; Glatfelter, *Pastors and People*, 1:65 and 2:172. According to P. M. Harbold, "Schools and Education in the Borough of Lancaster," *PLCHS* 46 (1942): 1, Hoffman remained the Reformed schoolmaster until 1776.

8. Harbaugh, *Life of Michael Schlatter*, 191; Good, *History (1725–1792)*, 372–73; Hinke, *Minutes of the Coetus*, 57–58; Cramer, *History*, 23; Pritzker-Ehrlich, "Michael Schlatter von St. Gallen," 114, 116. In a letter to Steiner dated November 14, 1749, the Presbyterian pastor Gilbert Tennent and his Lutheran colleagues Heinrich Melchior Mühlenberg and Peter Brunnholtz entreated Steiner not to abandon Lancaster and become involved in the dispute within the Philadelphia congregation (Kurt Aland, ed., *Die Korrespondenz Heinrich Melchior Mühlenbergs aus der Anfangszeit des deutschen Luthertums in Nordamerika*, 4 vols [Berlin and New York: de Gruyter, 1986–1997], 1:333–37).

9. Good, *History (1725–1792)*, 361.

At the suggestion of Schlatter, the congregation then extended a one-year call to Ludwig Ferdinand Vock, a fifty-nine-year-old man from Heidelberg in the Palatinate who had recently come to America. The agreement between pastor and congregation stipulated that Vock should receive a salary of £40, free lodging, and a cord of firewood. He was also allowed to charge a fee of seven shillings and six pence for each marriage and five shillings for each funeral sermon. Vock was free to preach at other places on four Sundays of the year and on weekdays. When Vock assumed his pastoral duties in January 1750, his Lutheran colleague Johann Friedrich Handschuh was "not a little delighted that the Reformed people have now also secured a pastor of their own." After a few months, however, dissatisfaction with his ministry had already become widespread. More than thirty men, including most leading church members, signed a declaration that they did not wish to retain Vock after the expiration of his contract. Before the year was over, the Coetus of Reformed ministers also demanded that the congregation oblige itself "to dismiss your present pastor, Mr. Fock, as soon as the term of his engagement . . . comes to an end, he having been admitted to the services of the ministry only for the time being, and being everywhere in evil repute because of his conduct." Johann Bartholomäus Rieger, who had himself been dismissed by the congregation several years earlier, seized the occasion to publish "a warning letter from Lancaster" in Christoph Saur's newspaper in September 1750. Rieger heaped scorn on the "sullied, discharged windbags" among the immigrant clergy, who believed "that the people are dumb, preachers are rare, the church without a fence and supervisors," but through their misbehavior soon became "the laughing stock of the prudent worldly people, a disgust to the wise Christians, and a burden and plague to those who saddle themselves with them." The writer explicitly referred to the Lancaster congregation, which had "disgraced itself" by accepting the services of unworthy ministers. From January 1751 until Philipp Wilhelm Otterbein's arrival in late 1752, the Reformed were once again without a settled pastor.[10] Writing a century ago, church historian James I. Good concluded that the Lancaster congregation "had been singularly

---

10. Cramer, *History*, 24–27; Hinke, *Minutes of the Coetus*, 60–61; Hinke, *Ministers*, 366–68; Wood, *Conestoga Crossroads*, 190–91; Glatfelter, *Pastors and People*, 1:151–52. Rieger's "warning letter" in *Pensylvanische Berichte*, September 16, 1750, is quoted in Splitter, *Pastors, People, Politics*, 27–28. While Hinke and Glatfelter assert that Vock "simply disappeared from view" after January 1751, there is evidence that he remained in Lancaster for some time. In June 1753 Vock and his wife mortgaged a lot on the east side of Church Street to Sebastian Graff for £30. The deed refers to Vock as a minister (R. Thomas Mayhill, comp., *Lancaster County, Pennsylvania, Deed Abstracts . . . Deed Books A through M [1729 through c1770] with Adjoining Landowners and Witnesses* [Knighttown, Ind.: The Bookmark, 1994], 40 [D48]).

unfortunate. Schnorr had disgraced them, Hochreutiner had accidentally killed himself, Steiner refused to come and Vock proved unworthy."[11]

The frequent change of ministers, the dubious qualifications and controversial behavior of several pastors, and numerous vacancies seemingly suggest a chronic instability of the congregation that was anything but unique in the early history of the German churches in Pennsylvania. Some historians have interpreted the 1720s to 1740s as a time of crisis in the churches of the middle colonies, which was then followed by a general "awakening" of religion. In the case of Lancaster, the beginnings of a religious awakening among the Reformed might be identified with Schlatter's visits in the late 1740s, and from the arrival of Otterbein to the War of Independence, several highly qualified pietist pastors successfully ministered there.[12] Upon closer inspection, however, it is doubtful whether a framework of crisis and renewal is appropriate for interpreting the experience of the Lancaster Reformed. During the alleged crisis period, the Reformed built their first church and introduced regular worship services. In October 1741, town proprietor James Hamilton granted to the "trustees" of the German Reformed church in Lancaster a lot on Orange Street "on which . . . a Meeting House Erected by the Said Congregation now Stands." Five years later, the trustees obtained a second lot adjacent to the first. In 1746, at a time when it lacked a resident pastor, the congregation built a steeple and spent £60 for the purchase of a church bell and clock.[13] This process of church-building continued throughout the colonial period.

Moreover, the Reformed laypeople repeatedly demonstrated that they had their own conceptions of how their church should work. As early as 1740, Johann Philipp Boehm wrote about "the congregation in Cannastocka, which has been gathered in the new town of Lancaster" that "up to this time they have acted according to their own pleasure. They have never cared for church order, but thus far have allowed themselves to be served by irregular men." Over the next decade, this "pretty strong congregation" fired three pastors even though they did not have an immediate prospect of replacement in either case. During the long vacancy from 1746 to 1749, the congregation might have called on the services of Johann Bartholomäus Rieger, who was practicing medicine in the town, ministering to two country congregations, and participating in the Reformed Coetus, but they refused to do so. According to a letter that Boehm wrote in 1748, the laity had told

---

11. Good, *History (1725–1792)*, 375.

12. Lodge, "Crisis of the Churches," 196–221; Frantz, "Awakening of Religion," 266–88. Cf. also Schwartz, *"A Mixed Multitude,"* 112–13, 143–44, 146.

13. Mayhill, *Deed Abstracts*, 96 (H89, H90); Cramer, *History,* 9–10, 18–19; Ellis and Evans, *History of Lancaster County,* 450–51; Coldren and Heisey, "Religious Life," 131.

Michael Schlatter "that they would have nothing to do with Mr. Rieger, and, because he had intercourse with all kinds of sects, they could not regard him as a true Reformed man, much less a Reformed minister, and would not tolerate such a minister in their congregation. They would rather help themselves as well as they could, hoping that through the grace of God they would not be left helpless." When the Reformed Coetus proposed in 1749 that Johann Conrad Steiner (who later declined the call) should not only serve several country congregations along with Lancaster but take up residence in the countryside as well, two elders from the borough who were present at the meeting "did not accept the above resolution of the Rev. Coetus, but most strenuously protested against it."[14] After midcentury, even popular pastors like Otterbein would complain about the obstinacy and assertiveness of the town's Reformed laity.

From the perspective of the laity, the growth of the Reformed congregation was a long process that included the building and rebuilding of the church edifice, its embellishment with a bell, clock, and organ, the maturing and growing prosperity of an immigrant population, and the development of social ties among its members, some of whom would rise to prominence in the community and leave significant bequests to the church. The history of Lancaster's German Reformed congregation can thus be seen as a successful case of institution-building and a prolonged quest for order and stability involving pastors, lay leaders, and ordinary parishioners. The ministers' concepts of order and authority repeatedly clashed with those of laymen who were well aware of their own pivotal role in the congregation's development. The significance of the congregational history of the German Reformed in colonial Lancaster lies neither in the presumed awakening of religious fervor nor in a gradual emancipation of the laity from clerical control, but in a persistent search for order amid numerical and institutional growth—a search that involved pastors and laymen and -women as equal, although often uneasy, partners. A profile of the early lay leaders, who have received much less scholarly attention than their counterparts in the ministry, is therefore essential for understanding the dynamics of the congregation.

LAY LEADERSHIP IN THE EARLY CONGREGATION

While there are no continuous lists of church officers for the first decades of the Reformed congregation, church books, deeds, and Coetus minutes allow us to

14. Hinke, *Boehm,* 275–76, 462; Hinke, *Ministers,* 29–30; Hinke, *Minutes of the Coetus,* 58.

identify nineteen elders and deacons during the period from 1736 to 1752.[15] In some respects, these men had much in common. First, they usually were recent immigrants who helped build a congregation at the same time that they established themselves in the New World. Second, almost all of them acquired property in the city or the surrounding countryside, and some of them demonstrated a remarkable entrepreneurial spirit. Third, the ties that developed among these men mark the formative stage of a social network among Reformed lay leaders.

With the notable exception of John DeHuff, who apparently came to Pennsylvania from Maryland's eastern shore, early Reformed leaders had arrived in America only shortly before they took up residence in Lancaster. Heinrich Basler, a linenweaver from Elsenz, a village in the Kraichgau region near Heilbronn, and his wife, Anna Barbara, landed in Philadelphia on the ship *Dragon* in September 1732 and had moved to Lancaster by 1735. The following year Basler became one of the first elders of the Reformed church there. The potter Peter Balsbach, who probably came from Fahrenbach in the Neckar-Odenwald region west of Heidelberg, reached the port of Philadelphia on the *Samuel* in August 1732; according to the ship list he was twenty-three years old. A year later, in October 1733, he first appears as a sponsor at a baptism in a Lancaster church book, and by 1735 he owned two lots in the new town. Friedrich Strubel, who like Balsbach became a Reformed elder in 1737, had immigrated to Pennsylvania on the *Pensilvania Merchant* in September 1731 and appears in Lancaster records by 1735. Johann Henneberger, a young ropemaker, was on the same ship with Peter Balsbach in 1732, but it may have taken him longer to reach Lancaster, for his presence there is first recorded in 1739. His name appears among the trustees of the Reformed church in 1746. The locksmith Johann Gorner was born in

15. In 1736 Johann Heinrich (Henry) Basler, Felix Müller, Johann Gorner, and Peter Doerr were elected as the congregation's first elders; in 1737 Peter Balsbach and Friedrich Strubel replaced Basler and Doerr (Cramer, *History*, 11–12). When the Lancaster congregation subscribed £15 annually toward the support of a Reformed minister in 1740, the pledge was signed by Jost Freuler, Nicolas Treber (Drewer), and John DeHuff (Hinke, *Boehm*, 291). The trustees to whom James Hamilton granted a lot in October 1741 were Basler, DeHuff, Balsbach, Gorner, Müller, and Nicolaus Kendel (Mayhill, *Deed Abstracts*, 96 [H89]). When James Hamilton granted the church a second lot in November 1746, the trustees were Heinrich Basler, Johann Henneberger, Heinrich Walter, and Nicolas Treber (ibid., 96 [H90]). In 1747 Caspar Schaffner and Friedrich Partemer acted as elders, Nicolas Treber and Heinrich Walter as deacons (cf. Records of the First Reformed Church, vol. 1, microfilm no. 88/1, p. 256, Evangelical and Reformed Historical Society, Lancaster [hereafter Records of the First Reformed Church, Evangelical and Reformed Historical Society]). Paul Weitzel and Caspar Schaffner were elders in 1749 (Hinke, *Minutes of the Coetus*, 57–58; Cramer, *History*, 23). Weitzel and Philipp Leonhard occupied the same position in 1750 (Wright, *Lancaster County Church Records*, 14). The elders elected for 1751 were Bernhard Becker, Peter Spicker, Johann Henneberger, and Peter Wolf (Cramer, *History*, 27). Spicker is misspelled here as Peter Sticker.

Grindelwald in the Swiss canton of Berne and had migrated to the German duchy of Zweibrücken on the Rhine River before crossing the Atlantic in 1733. Caspar Schaffner, who came to Philadelphia as a twenty-one-year-old man on the *Samuel* in the same year, was married to Anna Maria Knobel by the Lutheran pastor Johann Caspar Stoever in late December 1735.[16]

Nicolas Treber crossed the Atlantic as a middle-aged man of forty-four years on the ship *Harle* in 1736. The thirty-four-year-old Maria Anna Treberin and the seventeen-year-old Christoph on the same ship most likely were his wife and son. By 1740 Treber had become a property owner in Lancaster as well as an elder of the Reformed congregation. Two years after Treber, the thirty-three-year-old Heinrich Walter, a clothmaker from Kusel in the western Palatinate, set out on his journey to the New World with his young family. He had married Christina Margaretha Finck, a tailor's daughter, in October 1735, and two daughters were born in September 1736 and January 1738. The Walters' arrival in Philadelphia on the ship *Glasgow* is recorded in the fall of 1738, and their first American-born daughter was baptized in Lancaster in October 1739. The child's godfather, Johann Heinrich Klein, came from the same Palatine village as the Walters. Jost Freuler, a gunmaker of Swiss origin, married Anna Catharina Hirshy, another Swiss migrant, in the Palatine town of Zweibrücken in 1721, and seven children were born to the couple over the next fourteen years. In 1738 the family migrated to Pennsylvania, and Freuler appears among the officers of the Lancaster Reformed church as early as 1740. Another Palatine, the twenty-six-year-old baker Paul Weitzel from Oberingelheim on the Rhine River, disembarked from the *Loyal Judith* in the port of Philadelphia in September 1742. He married Jost Freuler's

16. DeHuff: Martha B. Clark, "Some Early Lancaster Notables," *PLCHS* 8 (1903/4): 3–13, 9–10; M. Luther Heisey, "The Borough Fathers," *PLCHS* 46 (1942): 49–50. Basler: Ralph B. Strassburger and William J. Hinke, *Pennsylvania German Pioneers: A Publication of the Original Lists of Arrivals in the Port of Philadelphia from 1727 to 1808*, 3 vols. (Philadelphia, 1934; repr., Baltimore: Genealogical Publishing Company, 1966), 1:96, 98; Annette K. Burgert, *Eighteenth-Century Emigrants from German-Speaking Lands to North America*, vol. 1, *The Northern Kraichgau* (Breinigsville, Pa.: Publications of the Pennsylvania German Society, 1983), 42; Heisey, "Borough Fathers," 69; Balsbach: Lancaster County Historical Society genealogical notes in family file folder; Strassburger and Hinke, *Pennsylvania German Pioneers*, 1:59, 64–65; Smith and Weiser, *Trinity Lutheran Church Records*, 1:10; Heisey, "Borough Fathers," 57, 61, 69; Strubel: Strassburger and Hinke, *Pennsylvania German Pioneers*, 1:43, 45–46; Heisey, "Borough Fathers," 57, 61; Henneberger: Lancaster County Historical Society genealogical notes in family file folder; Strassburger and Hinke, *Pennsylvania German Pioneers*, 1:59, 63–64; Wright, *Lancaster County Church Records*, 2:3; Gorner's European origins can be determined from his *Lebenslauf* in the diary of the Moravian congregation, which he joined a few years before his death. See Lancaster Diaries, 1752, entry for October 12, Moravian Archives. For Schaffner, see Strassburger and Hinke, *Pennsylvania German Pioneers*, 1:107, 111–12; Smith and Weiser, *Trinity Lutheran Church Records* 1:20, 44; Elizabeth Clarke Kieffer, "Three Caspar Shaffners," *PLCHS* 42 (1938): 181.

eldest daughter, Charlotte Elisabeth, and in October 1746 Michael Schlatter baptized their son John Peter during one of his brief sojourns in Lancaster.[17]

These immigrants' adaptation to their new environment coincided with a period when Lancaster was a new town made up of rough-hewn wooden buildings and most lots were still vacant. Since the town's proprietors Andrew and James Hamilton were interested in reaping quick financial rewards from their property, the acquisition of town lots was relatively easy, and most early Reformed leaders did not miss the opportunity. Heinrich Basler acquired two lots on Queen Street in November 1736 and a third in 1745. He quickly resold one of these to his fellow congregation member Friedrich Strubel, a second to the shopkeeper Conrad Schwartz in 1742, and the third for £550 to Jacob Schlauch in 1747. Basler also owned some land in the town's vicinity and obtained a patent for a large tract in Manheim Township in 1743. In November 1744 the enterprising Reformed leader was charged in court for illegally "selling Rum, Wine, Beer, Cyder & Liquor."[18]

Felix Müller, who like Basler became one of the congregation's first elders, was a farmer in Hempfield Township west of Lancaster, where he had obtained a warrant for two hundred acres on Little Conestoga Creek. In the German will he wrote in 1748, Müller declared that he had advanced £30 to his daughter Elizabeth and £45 to each of his two sons. When his personal estate was inventoried in the same year, it consisted mainly of animals, farm implements, and a bond of £50, but also included £12 for an indentured servant's remaining time. Peter Balsbach owned two town lots in 1735 and acquired a third in 1740 but resold it four years later. In the will he made in 1748, he stipulated that his wife was to retain occupation of his house during her widowhood while his two youngest children were to receive £50 in advance for their upbringing. His personal property consisted mainly of bond notes and was valued at close to £330 after the discharge of his debts. Balsbach's inventory also included £10 for an

17. Treber: Strassburger and Hinke, *Pennsylvania German Pioneers*, 1:155, 158–59; Heisey, "Borough Fathers," 69; Walter: Annette K. Burgert, *Eighteenth-Century Emigrants from German-Speaking Lands to North America*, vol. 2, *The Western Palatinate* (Birdsboro, Pa.: Publications of the Pennsylvania German Society, 1985), 204, 326; Strassburger and Hinke, *Pennsylvania German Pioneers*, 1:204, 206, 208; Wright, *Lancaster County Church Records*, 2:3; Freuler: Burgert, *Western Palatinate*, 125–26; Weitzel: Strassburger and Hinke, *Pennsylvania German Pioneers*, 1:323–24, 326; Wright, *Lancaster County Church Records*, 2:11.

18. On the early development of the town, see Wood, *Conestoga Crossroads*, chap. 1. For Basler's property holdings, see Warrant Register, vol. 16, p. 14, no. 277, Pennsylvania State Archives (hereafter Warrant Register, Pennsylvania State Archives); Mayhill, *Deed Abstracts*, 21 (B460), 36 (C455), 77 (G8), 116–18 (I51, I94, I119); Lancaster County Deed Books R551, U186, QQ247–249, Pennsylvania State Archives Harrisburg; cf. Ellis and Evans, *History of Lancaster County*, 396; Heisey, "Borough Fathers," 69. For Basler's court indictment, see Lancaster County Manuscripts, vol. 1, 1724–72, p. 49, Historical Society of Pennsylvania, Philadelphia.

indentured laborer's remaining term of servitude.[19] Friedrich Strubel and Johann Gorner also owned several town properties. When he made his will in 1752, Gorner left two lots to his widow and descendants.[20]

The most enterprising man among the early Reformed leaders, however, was certainly the saddler John DeHuff, who served as church elder in 1740 and 1741. In 1733 DeHuff obtained a warrant to 250 acres of land on Pequea Creek, 268 acres on Little Conestoga Creek in 1737, and several town lots between 1735 and midcentury. On the first borough tax list of 1751 his estate was assessed at £90— the fifth highest assessment among almost three hundred taxables. It may have been due to his economic success that DeHuff was appointed an assistant burgess when Lancaster was incorporated in 1742, and he became the town's chief burgess in 1744. When he died in 1752, he left his widow and five children a house on Queen Street, three further lots, the 268-acre tract in Lancaster Township, and additional land in Hempfield Township.[21]

After his arrival in Lancaster in the late 1730s, the clothmaker and dyer Heinrich Walter also accumulated property at a remarkable rate. When he died at age forty-nine in 1754, he left three houses and a five-acre outlot to his wife and two children and £20 to the Reformed congregation.[22] Caspar Schaffner acquired two lots in 1740 and remained active on Lancaster County's real estate market during the following decades. From 1744 to 1749 Schaffner was one of the town's assistant burgesses.[23] Like Schaffner, Nicolaus Kendel and the saddler Philipp Leonhard were active on the land market. In 1751 Walter, Schaffner, Leonhard, and the baker Paul Weitzel were all assessed among the top fifth of Lancaster's taxables.[24] Leonhard, who provided saddlery and other leatherware

19. For Müller, see Warrant Register, vol. 16, p. 132, no. 832, Pennsylvania State Archives; Felix Miller's German will (not entered in will book), March 18, 1748; Felix Miller Estate Inventory, 1748, Lancaster County Historical Society. For Balsbach, cf. Mayhill, *Deed Abstracts*, 119 (I162); Heisey, "Borough Fathers," 57, 61, 69; Lancaster County Will Book A-I-155, Pennsylvania State Archives; and Peter Balspach Estate Papers, 1748, Lancaster County Historical Society.

20. Strubel: Mayhill, *Deed Abstracts*, 36 (C455), 80 (G113), 118 (I131), 123 (K70); Heisey, "Borough Fathers," 57, 61; Gorner: Mayhill, *Deed Abstracts*, 14 (B160), 21 (B452), 119 (I152), 127 (K138); Heisey, "Borough Fathers," 76; Lancaster County Will Book I-I-78, Pennsylvania State Archives.

21. Warrant Register, vol. 16, p. 47, no. 11, Pennsylvania State Archives; Mayhill, *Deed Abstracts*, 21 (B443), 86 (G306, G311), 117 (I96), 140 (L165); Clark, "Early Lancaster Notables," 13; Heisey, "Borough Fathers," 49–50, 61, 76; Lancaster County Will Book A-I-201, Pennsylvania State Archives.

22. Mayhill, *Deed Abstracts*, 31–32 (C225, C228, C229), 119 (I163); Heisey, "Borough Fathers," 77; Lancaster County Will Book B-I-92, Pennsylvania State Archives; Lancaster County Orphans Court Records, vol. 1, pt. 3, pp. 76–77, Pennsylvania State Archives. Cf. also Wood, *Conestoga Crossroads*, 126.

23. Mayhill, *Deed Abstracts*, 17 (B306); Heisey, "Borough Fathers," 53, 68, 77; Ellis and Evans, *History of Lancaster County*, 363, 373; Kieffer, "Three Caspar Schaffners," 183–84.

24. Lancaster Borough Tax Assessment List, 1751, Lancaster County Historical Society. In 1744 Kendel and his wife acquired a town lot from Michael Shryack. They sold it in 1748, but Kendel

to colonial troops during the French and Indian War, was elected burgess in 1757 and 1758.[25] Peter Spicker, an elder of the Reformed congregation in 1751, seems to have moved to Lancaster only a short time before, for he offered two farms for sale in December 1748. By 1750 he had set up a shop where he sold ironware and other goods imported from London.[26]

Not all early Reformed leaders were quite as successful. When Bernhard Becker and Peter Wolf were elected as elders for 1751, each was assessed near the median of Lancaster's taxpayers.[27] Johann Henneberger, Reformed elder in 1746 and 1751, owned a town lot and five acres in Adamstown, a "suburb" founded by the German physician Adam Simon Kuhn. Even though he had sold the town lot a year before his death in 1752, his widow and administrator, Magdalena, found Henneberger's personal estate insufficient to discharge his debts. While his assets totaled £122, Henneberger owed almost £165 to Lancaster's former Reformed pastor Caspar Schnorr and twenty-one other people. Magdalena therefore had to sell the Adamstown property in order to meet her husband's liabilities.[28]

While these early Reformed leaders pursued their economic interests and social aspirations, they also began to form ties among one another. Baptismal, court, and property records reveal the outlines of a social network in the making.[29] Heinrich Basler's standing in the young congregation is underlined by the fact that he became the godfather of more than a dozen children baptized in the Reformed church between 1736 and 1747 as well as several children baptized in the Lutheran church. Among his godchildren were a son of John DeHuff in

bought it again the next year and finally disposed of it for £380 in 1751 (Mayhill, *Deed Abstracts*, 27 [C1]). In December 1744 the Kendels also bought a lot from John Musser, which they resold after only two months (Mayhill, *Deed Abstracts*, 94 [H42b]). Philipp Leonhard had obtained a first lot in 1745 (Mayhill, *Deed Abstracts*, 119 [I147]; Heisey, "Borough Fathers," 68. In 1748 he paid £125 for a second lot, half of which he sold to Jacob Friedrich Curteus for £230 only two and a half years later (Mayhill, *Deed Abstracts*, 42–43 [D104, D110]).

25. Wood, *Conestoga Crossroads*, 39, 123, 142.

26. *Pensylvanische Berichte*, December 16, 1748, and December 16, 1750.

27. Becker was assessed at £18, Wolf at £15. The median was £18 (Lancaster Borough Tax Assessment List, 1751, Lancaster County Historical Society). For their town properties, cf. Mayhill, *Deed Abstracts*, 69 (E346), 70 (E362), 72 (F95), 73 (F178).

28. Mayhill, *Deed Abstracts*, 31 (C189), 119 (I144); Heisey, "Borough Fathers," 62, 82; John Henneberger Estate Papers, 1752, Lancaster County Historical Society; Lancaster County Orphans Court Records, vol. 1, pt. 2, p. 58, Pennsylvania State Archives; cf. Sophie Selden Rogers, "Genealogical Gleanings from Orphans Court Records of Lancaster County," *Pennsylvania Genealogical Magazine* 24 (1965/66): 133, 202.

29. On the concept of social networks, see Andrejs Plakans, *Kinship in the Past: An Anthropology of European Family Life, 1500–1900* (Oxford: Blackwell, 1984), esp. chapter 10. For networks among German speakers in eighteenth-century America, cf. Roeber, *Palatines*, 120–31.

1735 and a daughter of Heinrich Walter in 1743.[30] Caspar Schaffner held Peter Balsbach's daughter Anna Maria at the baptismal font in 1735. John DeHuff was sponsor at the baptisms of children of his fellow Reformed leaders Johann Gorner and Felix Müller. In 1742 Peter Balsbach stood as sponsor for Gorner's daughter Maria Philippina, and Paul Weitzel, a son-in-law of Reformed leader Jost Freuler, became the godfather of Philipp Leonhard's daughter in 1750. Weitzel and Caspar Schaffner developed particularly close ties, sponsoring baptisms of each other's children and repeatedly acting as joint guardians of orphaned children.[31] When Heinrich Walter made his will in 1754, he named the current elders of the Reformed church, Caspar Schaffner, Jacob Kuntz, and Johannes Baer (John Barr), as executors of his estate.[32]

By midcentury, however, fissures began to appear in this network of Reformed leaders. Heinrich Basler, arguably the most active layman in the new congregation, announced his intention to travel to Germany in 1747, and after the completion of this journey he did not return to Lancaster but remained in Philadelphia.[33] Jost Freuler was dead by 1746, and Peter Balsbach, Felix Müller, Johann Gorner, John DeHuff, Johann Henneberger, and Heinrich Walter all died between 1748 and 1755. Nicolaus Kendel, Peter Doerr, Friedrich Strubel, and Friedrich Partemer

30. Wright, *Lancaster County Church Records*, 2:1–3, 5–6, 8–9, 12; Smith and Weiser, *Trinity Lutheran Church Records*, 1:18, 41, 415–16.

31. Wright, *Lancaster County Church Records*, 2:5–7, 12, 14–15; Smith and Weiser, *Trinity Lutheran Church Records*, 1:20. In 1749 the Lancaster County Orphans Court appointed Paul Weitzel and Caspar Schaffner as guardians over Christian Smink; in 1754 Weitzel and Schaffner became guardians of the children of Adam Schreiber (Lancaster County Orphans Court Records, vol. 1, pt. 1, p. 59, and pt. 3, p. 19, Pennsylvania State Archives; Rogers, "Genealogical Gleanings," 35). In 1758 Schaffner sold a town lot to Weitzel for £112 (Mayhill, *Deed Abstracts*, 158 [L119]). Cf. also Kieffu, "Three Caspar Schaffners," 182, 186.

32. Lancaster County Will Book B-1-92, Pennsylvania State Archives; Lancaster County Orphans Court Records, vol. 1, pt. 3, p. 76, April 25, 1757, Pennsylvania State Archives; cf. Rogers, "Genealogical Gleanings," 215.

33. The Orphans Court record of March 1747 states that because Basler planned to depart for Germany in a short time, he had to give security for the estate of Matthias Haines's children. In 1753 Andrew Hersey and his wife of Lancaster County and "Henry Bostler" and his wife of Philadelphia sold a house and half lot in Lancaster Borough to Christoph Graffort for £140 (Lancaster County Orphans Court Records, vol. 1, pt. 1, p. 21, Pennsylvania State Archives; Rogers, "Genealogical Gleanings," 24; Mayhill, *Deed Abstracts*, 87 [G351]). In November 1761 Basler dictated his will in Philadelphia, and it was probated on July 13, 1762. The childless Basler left his real and personal property, including a house in the city and a lot in the Northern Liberties, to his wife, Mary, during her lifetime. After her death, Basler stipulated £100 for the instruction of poor children in the German Reformed school in Philadelphia, while the remainder of his estate was to go to two stepchildren and several other relatives (Philadelphia Will Book M320. For the public sale of his property, see *Der Wöchentliche Philadelphische Staatsbote*, no. 89, September 26, 1763).

may have left Lancaster by the early 1750s since they disappear from the records. Peter Spicker, an elder in 1751, moved to Berks County and set up his shop in Tulpehocken Township. He was appointed a justice of the peace for Berks County in 1777 and sat on the bench of the County Courts of Common Pleas and Quarter Sessions.[34] Early Lancaster was a mobile society, and several families who appear in the Reformed records of the 1730s and 1740s are known to have migrated to outlying townships, westward across the Susquehanna River, or Virginia's Shenandoah Valley by midcentury.[35]

Perhaps most ominously for the plight of the congregation in the late 1740s, three of its elders—Peter Balsbach, Johann Gorner, and John DeHuff—joined the Moravians. Pastor Bartholomäus Rieger's early endorsement of Zinzendorf and his movement probably had less influence on their decisions to leave the Reformed fold than the prolonged vacancies of the pulpit and the poor performance of some its occupants. Lutheran minister Heinrich Melchior Mühlenberg claimed that "some of the respectable people of the congregation are adhering to the Moravian church because they will have nothing to do with [Caspar] Schnorr." Since the earliest days of Lancaster, moreover, Reformed laypeople had never hesitated to call on the services of Lutheran clergymen when there was no Reformed minister at hand. Thus the Lutheran pastor Johann Caspar Stoever sponsored the baptisms of two of Johann Gorner's children, and two of Peter Balsbach's and John DeHuff's children were each baptized by Stoever and Laurentius Thorstensson Nyberg in 1735 and 1744. Caspar Schaffner was married by the Lutheran pastor in 1735 and brought a child to baptism in the Lutheran church in 1743. Nicolaus Kendel was married to a Lutheran wife. During a troubled period of their own congregation's history, therefore, Balsbach, Gorner, and DeHuff seem to have been more attracted by Laurentius Nyberg's preaching

34. Peter Spicker is identified as a resident of Tulpehocken Township in Lancaster County Deed Books (Mayhill, *Deed Abstracts*, 66–67 [E229, E252]) and in *Pensylvanische Berichte*, June 15, 1759. For his public career, see Kurt Aland and Hermann Wellenreuther, eds., *Die Korrespondenz Heinrich Melchior Mühlenbergs aus der Anfangszeit des deutschen Luthertums in Nordamerika*, vol. 5, *1777–1787* (Berlin and New York: de Gruyter, 2002), 421n1, and Splitter, *Pastors, People, Politics*, 275, 357.

35. Rudolph Brack and his family, who had left the duchy of Pfalz-Zweibrücken and journeyed to Philadelphia in 1733, appear in the baptismal records of the Lancaster Reformed church in 1736. In 1749, however, Brack made his will in Augusta County, Virginia (Burgert, *Western Palatinate*, 62–63). Johann Jacob Klund and his wife from Kusel in the Palatinate arrived in Philadelphia in 1738 and had a son baptized in Lancaster in October 1739. From 1741 onward, however, the Klunds appear in the church records of Conewago in present-day Adams County, Pennsylvania (ibid., 208–9). David Fortinet (Fortney), another Palatine immigrant, came to America in 1739, and three of his children were baptized in the Lancaster Reformed church between 1745 and 1749. After midcentury, though, Fortinet became a resident of Warwick Township in northern Lancaster County (ibid., 121–22).

than by the likes of Caspar Schnorr. All three "defectors" had died by 1752, but the descendants of John DeHuff remained faithful Moravians throughout the remainder of the eighteenth century, and the loss of such an influential family probably gave the Reformed ample cause for regret.[36] Only a handful of early lay leaders—notably Caspar Schaffner and his family—continued to play a role in congregational affairs after midcentury. The pastors of the late colonial period—Otterbein, Stoy, and Hendel—would therefore face a new generation of Reformed lay leaders.

PIETISM AND THE SEARCH FOR ORDER: THE PASTORATES OF OTTERBEIN, STOY, AND HENDEL

After several futile attempts, Michael Schlatter finally succeeded in recruiting a new pastor for Lancaster when Philipp Wilhelm Otterbein, one of six young ministers Schlatter had recruited on a journey to Europe, accepted the congregation's call in 1752. Born in Dillenburg in 1726 and educated at the University of Herborn, a stronghold of Reformed pietism, Otterbein was an exceptionally qualified candidate for a ministry in the colonies. His teacher Valentin Arnoldi, professor of systematic theology at Herborn, stated on his behalf that he "has always lived an honest, pious, and Christian life; and not only by much preaching . . . but also by his godly life has built up the church. Wherefore we do not doubt that he will faithfully and fruitfully serve the Church in Pennsylvania, to which he has been called." Otterbein remained in Lancaster for six years. He received an annual salary of £45 plus £15 donated from Holland and assigned to him by the Reformed Coetus of Pennsylvania. He also served two country congregations and in 1755 was appointed to supply the Reformed churches in Reading and Conewago (York County).[37]

While Michael Schlatter had come under the influence of pietism in his Swiss hometown of St. Gall and encouraged "expressions of religious emotion that resembled revivalism" in Pennsylvania, Philipp Wilhelm Otterbein became the preeminent representative of a distinctive strand of German Reformed pietism in

36. Tappert and Doberstein, *Journals of Henry Melchior Muhlenberg*, 1:154; *Transactions of the Moravian Historical Society* 1 (1858–76): 384–87; Clark, "Early Lancaster Notables," 10–13; *Burial Book of the Lancaster Moravian Church, 1744–1821* (Lancaster: n.p., 1928), 4; Smith and Weiser, *Trinity Lutheran Church Records*, 1:17–18, 20, 40, 44, 277, 325, 343, 419, 421.

37. Hinke, *Ministers*, 71–72 (quote on 72); cf. Hinke, *Minutes of the Coetus*, 64, 86, 117, 149; Dubbs, "Reformed Church," 234–35; Glatfelter, *Pastors and People*, 1:101–2 and 2:482.

the American colonies.[38] Otterbein was the son of a pastor, and several of his
brothers, who remained in Germany but stayed in touch with their American
brother, became renowned theologians in their own right. Steven O'Malley, who
has studied their writings, argues that the Otterbeins' pietism was characterized
by a strong emphasis on the Heidelberg catechism. They sought to transform
this central document of the Reformed faith into a "'heavenly guide' whereby an
individual might attain salvation by progressive stages." Salvation, according to
Philipp Wilhelm Otterbein, could only be attained by searching for "inner holiness" and experiencing Christ within oneself. A person who "builds his salvation
upon Christ solely outside himself," he declared in a sermon delivered in Germantown in 1760, "remains in his sin and builds upon a foundation of sand.
Whatever such a person may believe and hope about deliverance and blessedness,
is only a dream and an empty imagination." It was not enough to believe "that
Christ has completed all things on the cross and He has made us holy just as we
are." On the contrary, Christ had "only laid the groundwork of our salvation" and
provided man with a model of how Satan could be overcome. According to
Otterbein, "a person can easily know whether the Holy Spirit has His work in a
person . . . when he knows and feels with agony the inner corruption of his
heart." The "work of redemption, Christ in us" manifests itself "where lusts and a
tendency to sin are lost, where sin ceases. . . . The fruit of this is holiness . . . the
new man . . . and a step-by-step progression toward perfection." By emphasizing
the importance of inner religious experience, the Otterbein brothers came to
embrace the idea of an "invisible church" of true believers within the larger visible
church. Attempting to put this concept into practice, Philipp Wilhelm Otterbein
had begun to hold special prayer meetings during a supply pastorate in Germany,
and he continued the practice in Pennsylvania.[39]

The Reformed congregation in Lancaster was thus confronting a very
demanding—but at least to some of its members, highly inspiring—pastor,
whose rhetoric of sin and redemption, conversion, and the "new birth" may have
reminded them of Anglo-American revivalists like George Whitefield and Gilbert

38. Stephen L. Longenecker, *Piety and Tolerance: Pennsylvania German Religion, 1700–1850*, Pietist
and Wesleyan Studies 6 (Metuchen, N.J.: Scarecrow, 1994), 86–88 (quote on 86); cf. James Tanis,
"Reformed Pietism in Colonial America," in *Continental Pietism and Early American Christianity*, ed.
F. Ernest Stoeffler (Grand Rapids, Mich.: Eerdmans, 1976), 34–73, esp. 64–68, 70.

39. J. Steven O'Malley, *Pilgrimage of Faith: The Legacy of the Otterbeins* (Metuchen, N.J.: Scarecrow, 1973), 94, 104, 132–34, 175. Otterbein's Germantown sermon is printed in an annotated English
translation in J. Steven O'Malley, ed., *Early German-American Evangelicalism: Pietist Sources on Discipleship and Sanctification*, Pietist and Wesleyan Studies 7 (Lanham, Md.: Scarecrow, 1995), 19–41 (quotes
on 25–28).

Tennent. Although the sources on Otterbein's pastoral work during his first years in Lancaster are few, the available evidence indicates that his ministry had a profoundly invigorating effect on the congregation. Several men who were affiliated with the Moravians in 1749—Jacob Kuntz, Martin Bamberger, Georg Reitzel, Jacob Hoening, Jacob Gallatin—returned to the Reformed fold, and Kuntz and Bamberger even became church elders.[40] In 1753 the congregation began building a new stone church, financed by a subscription, which was largely completed two years later. A final account of the building expenses drawn up in 1758 revealed that the new church had cost more than £1,018 and the congregation remained indebted to the amount of £215. Thus the congregation, which numbered about one hundred families in the late 1750s, had raised more than £800, or an average of £8per family.[41]

Despite his popularity, Otterbein had become displeased with his congregation by 1757. During the Coetus held in Lancaster in the summer of that year, "the question arose about Do. Otterbein and his ministry in the congregation in Lancaster. The elders of his church asked us [the members of the Coetus], his five years being ended for which he had pledged himself to the congregation . . . whether they might, in accordance with the wish and the hope of the congregation, expect his ministry in the future." Otterbein answered that "he would not in the future bind himself to any congregation for a fixed time" and "complained of many grievances by which his mind during the time of his ministry had been vexed in various ways." The pastor desired "that all disorderly customs be done away with as much as possible or changed in the future through the just and legitimate use and exercise of church discipline. . . . Finally he promised that if he be allowed to act in this matter according to the conviction of his conscience, and his hearers would obey him, he would then further remain with them and discharge his pastoral office." According to the Coetus minutes Otterbein was successful: "The congregation in Lancaster has not only promised to their pastor, whom they most earnestly longed to keep, the obedience they owed, but also the desired correction. Do. Otterbein has again taken upon himself the care of that congregation."[42]

40. Jacob Kuntz served as elder in 1754, Martin Bamberger in 1755 and 1758 (Records of the First Reformed Church, vol. 3, microfilm no. 88/1, pp. 13, 18, 28, Evangelical and Reformed Historical Society). For the association of these men with the Moravian congregation, see *Transactions of the Moravian Historical Society* 1 (1858–76), 384–87.

41. Cramer, *History*, 36–38; Ellis and Evans, *History of Lancaster County*, 452–53; Good, *History (1725–1792)*, 498–99; O'Malley, *Pilgrimage*, 169–70; Hinke, *Minutes of the Coetus*, 126, 184.

42. Hinke, *Minutes of the Coetus*, 157–58.

While the minutes remain vague about the pastor's "many grievances" and the congregation's "disorderly customs," an agreement drawn up in Otterbein's handwriting and signed by eighty members throws more light on his concerns. The document stated that, since "for some time matters in our congregation have proceeded somewhat irregularly," the pastor and the lay officers of the church had agreed

> to request that every one who calls himself a member of our Church, and who is concerned to lead a Christian life, should come forward and subscribe his name to the following rules of order:
>
> First of all, it is proper that those who profess themselves members should subject themselves to a becoming Christian Church discipline, according to the order of Christ and his Apostles, and thus to show respectful obedience to minister and officers in things that are proper.
>
> Secondly, To the end that all disorder may be prevented, and that each member may become more fully known, every one, without exception, who desires to receive the Lord's Supper shall, previous to the preparation service, upon a day appointed for that purpose, personally appear before the minister for the purpose of an interview. No one by this arrangement will be deprived of his liberty or be in any way bound. This we deem necessary for the preservation of order, and it is our desire that God may bless it to this end. Whoever is truly concerned to grow in grace will not hesitate to subscribe his name.[43]

The document reveals two distinct concerns. One was that the members of the congregation "grow in grace"—a central tenet of pietists and evangelicals during the Great Awakening. It is known that Otterbein, who would decades later emerge as one of the founders of a new denomination, "passed through a profound spiritual experience" during his pastorate in Lancaster, and by closely monitoring his parishioners' development he obviously hoped to combat religious indifference and promote piety and spiritual growth. Moreover, since the Otterbein brothers claimed that true religion was experienced in the heart and the true church was invisible, it became a central concern to distinguish

---

43. Cramer, *History*, 31–32; reprinted in Arthur C. Core, ed., *Philip William Otterbein: Pastor, Ecumenist* (Dayton, Ohio: Board of Publication, Evangelical United Brethren Church, 1968), 107. Cf. also O'Malley, *Pilgrimage*, 170; Wood, *Conestoga Crossroads*, 193–94; Glatfelter, *Pastors and People*, 2:482–84.

worthy from unworthy communicants. As communion was reserved for the truly regenerate, it was important to screen parishioners before admitting them to the Eucharist.[44]

Otterbein's second concern, and the one that receives more emphasis in the document, was with church discipline, order, and obedience. By making mandatory interviews with the pastor a prerequisite for communion and full membership, the pastor attempted to control his parishioners' moral behavior and impose stricter standards of personal conduct. Had Otterbein's program of imposing church discipline succeeded, it would have invested the pastor with considerable authority over the laity.[45] But his concern with discipline and good order should also be seen in its European context. Since the middle of the sixteenth century, the imposition of church discipline had been a central element of Reformed confessionalism in many areas of central Europe, including Otterbein's native principality of Nassau-Dillenburg. Presbyteries and consistories of pastors and lay elders censured parishioners for immorality, laziness, drunkenness, breaches of the Sabbath, and nonattendance at church; monitored their spiritual development; and defined the boundaries of the community of believers.[46] Otterbein apparently deemed the introduction of similar disciplinary standards necessary to preserve the integrity of Reformed pietism and ensure the success of church building in the New World.

Although his congregation agreed to his demand for "obedience" in 1757, Otterbein remained in Lancaster for only one more year. His place was taken by Heinrich Wilhelm Stoy, who had also studied at Herborn and come to the New World with Otterbein. As pastor in Philadelphia, Stoy had alienated his congregation by marrying "a stocking weaver's daughter"— a curious parallel to the experience of the Lutheran pastor Johann Friedrich Handschuh, who had also married a poor woman while serving Lancaster in 1750. Stoy took up his duties in Lancaster in October 1758, and at the Coetus meeting in 1760 he reported that he had found a congregation of about one hundred families.

---

44. Hinke, *Ministers*, 72–73; Good, *History (1725–1792)*, 500–501; O'Malley, *Pilgrimage*, 139–40, 170–72.

45. The example of Otterbein supports Jon Butler's argument that the pietist and evangelical wings of the colonial American clergy were no less concerned with power over and control of their parishioners than their orthodox counterparts. Jon Butler, *Power, Authority, and the Origins of the American Denominational Order: The English Churches of the Delaware Valley, 1680–1730* (Philadelphia: American Philosophical Society, 1978); Butler, *Awash in a Sea of Faith*, 180–84.

46. Cf. Heinz Schilling, ed., *Die reformierte Konfessionalisierung in Deutschland: Das Problem der "Zweiten Reformation." Wissenschaftliches Symposion des Vereins für Reformationsgeschichte 1985* (Gütersloh, Germany: Mohn, 1986); Hsia, *Social Discipline*, 26–38, 124–29.

Sixty children were attending the parochial school. A year later, Stoy informed the Coetus that the number of students had risen to seventy and "[t]wo families formerly connected with the congregation have returned, being received from the Moravians with whom they had united." After serving Lancaster for slightly over four years, during which he also became a founding director of the local library company, Stoy returned to Europe in early 1763 to study medicine. After his departure, the Coetus "arranged with Do. Waldschmidt, and occasionally with one of the remaining brethren, to conduct services for them."[47] Financial records of the congregation document several payments to Johann Waldschmidt, whose field of activity encompassed northern Lancaster County along with neighboring Berks and present-day Lebanon counties, for pastoral services, food, and lodging expenses between February 1763 and December 1764. They also list payments to pastors Alsentz and Weyberg, probably for occasional visits, in the summer of 1764.[48]

After Stoy's departure the congregation was without a resident minister for more than a year, and in May 1764 the Coetus reported to Holland that Lancaster and several other Reformed congregations were "in a deplorable condition." These "important places for preachers, request, beg, and pray through us for help." When a new minister from the Palatinate, the twenty-four-year-old Johann Wilhelm Hendel, arrived in Pennsylvania in late 1764, Lancaster was eager to secure his services. The president and secretary of the Coetus, Johann Georg Alsentz and Caspar Dietrich Weyberg, wrote to the congregation in December 1764 that they consented to send Hendel there and hoped "that you will receive him with all the love and respect which he deserves." "We do not doubt," the Coetus officers continued, "that his ministry will be agreeable to you all, and will tend to the salvation of your immortal souls. We only regret that you have sent your delegated brother so early, without our knowledge, which has only increased the expenses, and shows too much zeal." In a sarcastic rebuke of Lancaster's impatience, which can also be read as an ironic comment on the congregation's earlier history, the Coetus leaders wrote they wished "that your fervor may not too soon become cold." Alsentz and Weyberg added that

47. Hinke, *Minutes of the Coetus*, 167, 184, 198–99, 215; Charles I. Landis, "The Juliana Library Company in Lancaster," *PLCHS* 33 (1929): 195–96, 239. On Stoy, see Good, *History (1725–1792)*, 506–7; Hinke, *Ministers*, 84–89; Glatfelter, *Pastors and People*, 1:144–45.

48. Records of the First Reformed Church, vol. 3, microfilm no. 88/1, pp. 38–39, 43–48, Evangelical and Reformed Historical Society. In November 1764 there was a payment of £2, 2s. 4p. to pastor Kern and Mr. Weill from New York (ibid., 47). On Waldschmidt, see Hinke, *Ministers*, 89–94; and Glatfelter, *Pastors and People*, 1:157.

they expected Lancaster to reimburse them for a part of Hendel's travel expenses and provide him with a yearly salary of £75 "besides his free residence."[49]

Four years later, the congregation's enthusiasm for Hendel seems indeed to have cooled. During the annual Coetus meeting held at Easton in September 1768, a lay delegate from Lancaster, Wilhelm Bausman, speaking "in behalf of a part of the . . . congregation," brought forward several complaints. Bausman criticized the minister for not visiting the school regularly, neglecting the examination of the children, and not catechizing every Sunday. Hendel defended himself by pointing out his many preaching duties outside Lancaster and offered to visit the school each week if his other duties allowed it. Indeed, the Coetus minutes show that Hendel was preaching to the congregation at Pequea once a month and conducted services at "York, Donegal, Maytown, White Oaks, Lebanon, Kreutz Creek, Seltenreich and Muddy Creek." In 1766 he had traveled as far as Virginia to visit congregations there. Two decades after Schlatter had organized the Reformed Coetus, ministers were still in short supply in the Pennsylvania countryside, and the Coetus tried to make amends for this by asking its members to visit outlying country congregations as often as possible. From the perspective of the Lancaster congregation, however, these supply duties were clearly unwelcome. Bausman challenged the Coetus to prohibit Hendel's visits to Pequea, claiming that this rural congregation could thereby be "compelled to unite with Lancaster, and thus united, give them their assistance." Hendel, on the other hand, deemed it "very unreasonable" that people living twelve miles away should be asked to come to Lancaster each Sunday and offered to share the salary he received from Pequea with Lancaster. Bausman's final charge against Hendel was that the minister "kept many children from the Lord's Supper," to which Hendel replied that "this has never happened except for the weightiest reasons." While the Coetus attempted to mediate between pastor and congregation on the other issues, it clearly supported the minister in this instance and resolved "that Do. Hendel, like every minister, act in this matter after the conviction of his own conscience," and "the officers of the church shall sustain him in this."[50]

The conflict between Bausman's party and the minister touched on some key themes of Reformed pietism that concerned the congregation since Otterbein's time—the necessity of catechizing and instructing the children and the

---

49. Hinke, *Minutes of the Coetus,* 224–25, 230. On Hendel, see Good, *History (1725–1792),* 546–47; Hinke, *Ministers,* 111–16; Glatfelter, *Pastors and People,* 1:58–59.

50. Tappert and Doberstein, *Journals of Henry Melchior Muhlenberg,* 2:465; Hinke, *Minutes of the Coetus,* 250, 270–71; cf. Glatfelter, *Pastors and People,* 2:209; Wood, *Conestoga Crossroads,* 191.

prerequisites for communion—but it was also a power struggle. This is particularly evident in the pastor's complaint that "the things which were invented by certain persons were presented as grievances of the whole congregation." Hendel pointed out that a faction of the laity had "arbitrarily" drawn up "certain regulations" subscribed to by twenty-seven members. These regulations "specified, that the minister shall supply no other congregation, that the congregation in certain cases has even the right to dismiss the minister, and other things besides. . . ." A worried Coetus concluded that "this action of the congregation was contrary to the Netherland Church-order" and admonished the Lancaster Reformed to apply to the Coetus instead of acting on their own.[51]

As in the case of Otterbein a decade before, the compromise struck between Hendel and the congregation in 1768 did not last. When the Reformed ministers and elders convened in Germantown the next year, Hendel returned to the issue and "complained that there were seven or eight men, some of them officers of the congregation and all of them self-willed and obstinate men, who in a very rude manner found fault with the best and most sincere performance of his duties, and thereby constantly caused him vexation." The lay delegate from Lancaster, who was more sympathetic to the pastor than Wilhelm Bausman the year before, affirmed that Hendel spoke for "the majority of the congregation" and "conducted himself in his office without giving offense, as becomes a true minister of God's word." The Coetus, clearly displeased that the conflict was dragging on, offered Hendel a call to Tulpehocken that the minister reluctantly accepted. From September 1769 to December 1770, Lancaster was temporarily supplied by the young preacher and catechist Caspar Wack—the congregation's first American-born minister—until another Palatine clergyman, Carl Ludwig Boehme, filled the vacant position. During its 1771 meeting, the Coetus remarked that "Mr. Boehm[e] has conducted himself so well that not the least improper action can be charged against him in his life or in doctrine, and has won the undivided love and esteem of his congregation," which he served until 1775.[52]

The conflict over Hendel's ministry demonstrates that the presence of pietist pastors had finally resulted in a confrontation over control of congregational

---

51. Hinke, *Minutes of the Coetus*, 271–72.

52. Ibid., 281–82, 298, 308–9; cf. Records of the First Reformed Church, vol. 10, microfilm no. 88/3, pp. 26–28, Evangelical and Reformed Historical Society; Glatfelter, *Pastors and People*, 2:206. On Wack and Boehme, see Good, *History (1725–1792)*, 554–55, 570–72; Hinke, *Ministers*, 155–58, 181–86; Glatfelter, *Pastors and People*, 1:22, 153.

affairs. While pietist ministers sought to monitor access to the communion table, impose discipline, and spread the gospel in rural communities, a part of the laity felt that the pastor should limit his activities to the town proper and submit to the ultimate authority of the laity. Although the Coetus minutes indicate that lay officers were divided over this issue and opponents of ministerial control may have constituted a minority, the available sources do not allow us to identify the size of the two parties. What is certain, however, is that a new generation of lay leaders had emerged during the 1750s and '60s. These men often prospered in worldly affairs, and they played a decisive role in congregational development during a time of demographic and institutional growth.

Demographic growth manifested itself in a steep rise in the number of recorded baptisms during the 1750s, caused by the surge of German and Swiss immigration at midcentury, and a steady increase afterward. According to Rodger C. Henderson, the size of the congregation swelled from between 530 and 630 in the early 1750s to about 850 to 900 in the early 1770s.[53] Institutional development is reflected in the purchase of real estate and in building activities. In 1760 the congregation bought a lot on Duke Street and built a parsonage on it by 1766. Lotteries held in 1761 and, jointly with the Anglican congregation, in 1765 yielded funds for a schoolhouse. In 1769 the Reformed spent £250 on the purchase of an organ from the renowned Moravian organ-builder David Tannenberg for which a member of the congregation, the joiner and cabinetmaker Georg Burkhard, made the organ case. When the new instrument was completed in December 1770, a contributor to the *Pennsylvania Gazette* wrote that it "was never equalled in any place of worship in the province or perhaps on the continent." And while they attempted to keep the services of their minister confined to the town, the lay officers did not hesitate to contribute money for the relief of Pennsylvania's frontier inhabitants during Pontiac's War in 1764.[54] Just as the first generation of lay leaders had established the congregation and kept it alive in difficult times, the second generation continued the process of church-building and remained reluctant to yield power to the ministry. It is therefore important to find out who these men were.

53. Henderson, "Matters of Life and Death," 43–77, esp. 44–46, 63–64.

54. Records of the First Reformed Church, vol. 3, microfilm no. 88/1, pp. 26–30, 42, Evangelical and Reformed Historical Society; Mayhill, *Deed Abstracts*, 89 (G413); Cramer, *History*, 41–43, 46; Ellis and Evans, *History of Lancaster County*, 453; *Pennsylvania Gazette*, July 23 and August 20, 1761, and January 10, 1771; Raymond J. Brunner, *"That Ingenious Business": Pennsylvania German Organ Builders* (Birdsboro: Publications of the Pennsylvania German Society, 1990), 76–78.

THE REFORMED LAITY AFTER MIDCENTURY

There are no complete lists of Reformed elders and trustees for the 1750s and 1760s, but an early account book of the congregation allows us to identify twenty-four men who held either office between 1755 and 1769.[55] Apart from veteran elder Caspar Schaffner, these men were newcomers to the ranks of the Reformed leadership. They had arrived later than the first generation of leaders, but in the relatively mobile colonial society many of them succeeded in establishing themselves, and some became quite wealthy. Moreover, the still fragile network of the early leaders was now replaced by a denser and more durable web of social relations.

Jacob Kuntz and Johannes Baer (John Barr), who were both elected as elders in 1755, prospered as traders and shopkeepers. In 1759 both men were in the top decile of the town's taxpayers. Kuntz probably came to Pennsylvania in the late 1730s and acquired farmland on Conestoga Manor in 1741. He originally was a carpenter by trade and was paid £80 for work on the new Reformed church building in 1753, but he mortgaged his land to Philadelphia merchant Caspar Wistar in order to raise capital for the shop he opened in Lancaster. When Kuntz's estate was inventoried in 1763, the goods in his store were valued at about £285. He sold an assortment of dry goods but also had a stock of ironware, looking glasses, buttons, sugar, spices, rum, and wine from the Canary Islands. He also left his children four houses in the town and a farm in Manor Township. His daughter Elizabeth had married Caspar Schaffner Jr., the son of an early Reformed leader, and when Kuntz wrote his will he named Schaffner and Wilhelm Bausman, one of the new leaders of the congregation, as executors.[56]

Johannes Baer arrived in Philadelphia as a twenty-three-year-old man in 1743. He held the office of clerk in Lancaster Borough from 1752 to 1756 and was treasurer of the Reformed church in 1758. During the French and Indian War, Baer acted as a forage contractor for troops on the frontier, and for a while he was a co-owner of Elizabeth Furnace, an ironworks in northern Lancaster County, in partnership with Heinrich Wilhelm Stiegel and the Stedman brothers

55. Records of the First Reformed Church, vol. 3, microfilm no. 88/1, pp. 13, 18, 23, 28, 33, 41, 59, 65, 72, Evangelical and Reformed Historical Society. For the names of the church elders in 1760, see Mayhill, *Deed Abstracts*, 89 (G413).

56. Lancaster Borough Tax Assessment List, 1759, Lancaster County Historical Society. Two persons named Jacob Kuntz appear on the ship lists in 1737 and 1739 (Strassburger and Hinke, *Pennsylvania German Pioneers*, 1:169–70, 172, 252–53, 255). See also Cramer, *History*, 36–37; Mayhill, *Deed Abstracts*, 33 (C275), 106 (H271); Lancaster County Will Book B-I-597, Pennsylvania State Archives; and Jacob Kuntz Estate Papers, 1763, Lancaster County Historical Society.

of Philadelphia. In 1761 he made a first unsuccessful bid for the office of county sheriff. The Anglican pastor Thomas Barton, who considered him "a worthy honest Man, well regarded by all his Acquaintance," wrote to Provincial Secretary Richard Peters that Baer was "unwilling to continue any longer in the disagreeable Business of a Tavern-keeper, having a Number of Female Children growing up" and therefore ran for public office. Since another candidate had been promoted through "Schemes & low Artifice," however, Baer lost by three votes, "tho' every Body expected he would have been as many hundreds above him." Baer eventually won the office in 1765 and served as sheriff until 1767. He was well connected among the Reformed leadership: Caspar Schaffner, Christoph Graffort, and Wilhelm Bausman were godfathers of his children, and Baer himself sponsored the baptisms of children of Schaffner, Bausman, and Michael Fortinet. He also acquired substantial real estate: 476 acres on Conestoga Manor, three houses in Lancaster, two lots in the town of Manheim, and a brick house with some land in Millersburg, Manor Township. These purchases apparently overstretched his means, for Baer was indebted to Philadelphia merchant Henry Keppele for the considerable sum of £1,576 in 1769 even though he had already sold him several properties. His remaining Lancaster and Millersburg properties were seized in 1770 and sold to Keppele and Adam Reigart.[57]

Like Kuntz and Baer, Jacob Friedrich Rieger and Christoph Graffort, elders in 1756 and 1757, were assessed among the wealthiest 10 percent of Lancaster's taxpayers in 1759. Graffort, whose name was anglicized to Crawford, arrived in Philadelphia in 1743 on the same ship that carried Bernhard Becker, Daniel May, and Jacob Wilhelm—all to become elders of the Reformed congregation. In the early 1750s he purchased two houses and obtained a warrant for one hundred acres in Rapho Township. He served as an assistant burgess from 1750 to 1754 and again in 1763 and was elected as elder once more in 1764. Seven years later Graffort advertised a large assortment of recently imported dry goods. He also sold books and English tinware and offered a house and some land at the Donegal

57. Strassburger and Hinke, *Pennsylvania German Pioneers*, 1:332–34; Ellis and Evans, *History of Lancaster County*, 373; Cramer, *History*, 37; *Pennsylvania Gazette*, October 10, 1765, and October 9, 1766; Sylvester K. Stevens and Donald H. Kent, eds., *The Papers of Col. Henry Bouquet* (Harrisburg: Pennsylvania Historical and Museum Commission, 1940), 2:286–88, 473, 494, 629; George L. Heiges, *Henry William Stiegel and His Associates: A Story of Early American Industry*, 2nd ed. (Manheim, Pa.: The Arbee Foundation, 1976), 30, 33; Mayhill, *Deed Abstracts*, 29 (C79), 50 (D319), 52 (E65), 113 (H368), 138 (L109), 141 (L190), 147 (L319), 178 (M55, M60), 182 (M151); Wright, *Lancaster County Church Records*, vol. 2, pp. 27, 31, 37, 41, 44, 48, 49, 60; Lancaster County Deed Books N11, N18, O385, O554, O570, Q671, Pennsylvania State Archives. Cf. the not completely reliable data in Splitter, *Pastors, People, Politics*, 330–31.

road, reportedly well suited for a country tavern, for lease.[58] Jacob Friedrich Rieger, a surgeon and brother of the Reformed minister Johann Bartholomäus Rieger, advertised that he was selling Bibles in 1744. By the time of his death in 1761 he owned two houses in town and land on Swatara Creek in western Lancaster County.[59] The blacksmith Daniel May, who served as elder with Rieger and Graffort in 1756–57, had arrived in Pennsylvania in 1743 and was listed among the top fifth of Lancaster's taxables by 1759.[60]

The tavernkeeper Wilhelm Bausman, a Reformed elder in the early 1760s and the spokesman for pastor Hendel's opponents in 1768, was both a successful businessman and an important figure in local civic affairs. In some respects he occupied a similar position within the congregation in the third quarter of the century as John DeHuff had before he joined the Moravians. Born in Freilaubersheim in the northern Palatinate in 1724, Bausman came to America in 1746 and can be located in Lancaster shortly after midcentury. He was elected as assistant burgess in 1760–61, burgess in 1763, chief burgess in 1764, was returned to the same office in 1774–75 and 1777, and served as county commissioner during the War for Independence. He also became treasurer of the Lancaster Library Company in 1760 and was among the charter members when it was incorporated as the Juliana Library Company three years later. From the 1750s to the Revolution, he accumulated an impressive amount of real estate and employed several indentured laborers. After the iron and glass manufacturer Heinrich Wilhelm Stiegel had defaulted, Bausman, his fellow Reformed leader Michael Diffendorfer, and three Lutheran residents of Lancaster formed a partnership that took over the glassworks in 1775. In the early years of the War for Independence he sat on the Lancaster Committee of Observation (1775) and was appointed barracks master (1777). When Bausman dictated his will in 1784, he enumerated three houses in Lancaster and several other town properties, thirty-one acres in Manheim Township, thirteen acres on Conestoga Creek, the Manheim glassworks, one-half of a 262-acre tract in Northumberland County, two tracts comprising almost six hundred acres in Westmoreland

58. Strassburger and Hinke, *Pennsylvania German Pioneers,* 1:266, 269, 272; Ellis and Evans, *History of Lancaster County,* 373; Warrant Register, vol. 16, p. 40, no. 381, Pennsylvania State Archives; Mayhill, *Deed Abstracts,* 87 (G351), 176 (M25); *Der Wöchentliche Pennsylvanische Staatsbote,* no. 498, August 6, 1771.

59. Good, *History (1725–1792),* 167–68; *Pensylvanische Berichte,* April 16, 1744; Mayhill, *Deed Abstracts,* 119 (I172), 122 (K38, K40); Lancaster County Will Book B-I-364 (Jacob Rieger), Pennsylvania State Archives.

60. Lancaster Borough Tax Assessment List, 1759, Lancaster County Historical Society; Mayhill, *Deed Abstracts,* 72 (F124).

County, loan office certificates, and several slaves. The mention of a spinnet, a clock, mahogany chairs, and a "family wagon" in his will indicate that he had attained a genteel lifestyle. Bausman frequently appears as a sponsor in the Reformed and Lutheran baptismal records and was repeatedly called on to execute wills and administer estates.[61]

The stocking weaver Lorenz Marquedant, a Reformed elder in 1765–66, immigrated to Pennsylvania in 1750 and appears among the top fifth of borough taxpayers nine years later. In 1762 he offered his services as a dyer in the *Wöchentliche Pennsylvanische Staatsbote*. Marquedant was a close associate of Wilhelm Bausman, who was the godfather of his son William. Their names appear together in mortgages, Bausman purchased real estate from Marquedant, and they jointly obtained land in Northumberland County in the 1770s.[62] Jacob Wilhelm, an elder of the congregation in 1768, had come to America as a thirty-seven-year-old man in 1743. He was able to pay more than £500 for three hundred acres of land in Manheim Township as early as 1748 and disposed of extensive property holdings when he made his will in 1771. He left his wife and five children a house in Lancaster he had acquired ten years before, a three-hundred-acre tract including two stone houses in Manheim Township, and 160 acres in Tulpehocken Township, Berks County.[63]

The butcher Michael Fortinet (also spelled Fortney or Fordney), a trustee in 1769, was probably the only member of the congregation to match Wilhelm

---

61. Strassburger and Hinke, *Pennsylvania German Pioneers*, 1:363; Mayhill, *Deed Abstracts*, 48 (D215), 56 (D463), 99 (H146), 109 (H316); Lancaster County Deed Books Q247, Q578, R103, R452, R454–457, S295, S301, X295–298, EE271, FF508–9, Pennsylvania State Archives; Henry Frank Eshleman, "Early Lancaster Taxables—1754," *JLCHS* 13 (1909): 266; Landis, "Juliana Library Company," 196, 213, 242–43; *Record of Indentures of Individuals Bound Out as Apprentices, Servants, Etc. and of German and Other Redemptioners in the Office of the Mayor of the City of Philadelphia, October 3, 1771, to October 5, 1773* (repr., Baltimore: Genealogical Publishing Company, 1973), 34–35, 134–35, 316–17; *Heinrich Millers Pennsylvanischer Staatsbote*, no. 741, October 27, 1775; "Local Items from an Old *Gazette*," *PLCHS* 16 (1912): 116–17; Lancaster County Will Book E-I-16, Pennsylvania State Archives; Ellis and Evans, *History of Lancaster County*, 366, 373–74, 395; Egle, *Pennsylvania Archives*, 67; Wright, *Lancaster County Church Records*, 2:34, 37, 40, 51, 52, 55; Smith and Weiser, *Trinity Lutheran Church Records*, 1:117, 120, 130, 134; Heiges, *Henry William Stiegel*, 139, 148; Splitter, *Pastors, People, Politics*, 331. Bausman was executor of Leonhard Notz's will in 1758, Jacob Fortney's will in 1761, and Jacob Kuntz's will in 1763 (Lancaster County Will Books B-I-201, B-I-355, and B-I-597, Pennsylvania State Archives).

62. Strassburger and Hinke, *Pennsylvania German Pioneers*, 1:445; Lancaster Borough Tax Assessment List, 1759, Lancaster County Historical Society; *Der Wöchentliche Philadelphische Staatsbote*, no. 44, November 15, 1762; no. 45, November 22, 1762; no. 47, December 6, 1762; Wright, *Lancaster County Church Records*, 2:40; Mayhill, *Deed Abstracts*, 66 (E206); Lancaster County Deed Book EE271, Pennsylvania State Archives; Wood, *Conestoga Crossroads*, 110, 126.

63. Strassburger and Hinke, *Pennsylvania German Pioneers*, 1:336–39; Mayhill, *Deed Abstracts*, 51 (D360), 83 (G190); Lancaster County Will Book J-I-350, Pennsylvania State Archives.

Bausman's economic success in the years before the Revolution. Born in Land-stuhl in the Palatinate in 1714, Fortinet came to America earlier than most other Reformed leaders of the second generation; he arrived with his brothers Franz and Melchior in 1737, and their parents and several siblings had followed them by 1742. He married a sister of Paul Weitzel's wife, bought and sold a number of properties in and near the town, and developed ties of godparentship with Reformed leaders Caspar Schaffner, Christoph Graffort, and Johannes Baer. When Michael Fortinet made his will in 1778, he specified how his two town houses, three five-acre plots near Lancaster, and his brick house and land in Manheim were to be divided among his wife and four surviving children.[64] The skinner Wilhelm Busch, a lay leader in the 1760s, established close ties to the Fortinet family when he married Melchior Fortinet's widow, Anna Barbara, in 1756 and helped raise the deceased butcher's children. These ties were further strengthened when Michael Fortinet's son Caspar married Busch's daughter Elizabeth in 1778. In the same year Michael Fortinet appointed Busch as one of the executors of his will.[65]

While men like Christoph Graffort, Wilhelm Bausman, Johannes Baer, and Michael Fortinet represent the wealthy mercantile element among the Reformed leadership, other church officers were artisans of middling rank and modest means.[66] In 1759 the shoemakers Peter Bier and Georg Reitzel, the turner Valentin Weber, and the saddler Jacob Backenstos, who were elected to the position of elder at some point between 1758 and 1766, were taxed at nine to ten shillings each, the median being eight shillings. Martin Bamberger, repeatedly mentioned as an elder between 1755 and 1760 and assessed at ten shillings in 1759, was listed as a laborer in 1773. The saddler Jacob Hildebrand, who served as elder in 1764–65, was taxed below the median five years before.[67]

64. Burgert, *Western Palatinate*, 121–24; Evajean Fortney McKnight, *The Fortineux—Fortinet Family (Fortney, Fortna, Fordney, Furtney) in America* (Salem, W.Va.: Walsworth, 1989), 90–97; May-hill, *Deed Abstracts*, 7 (A132), 21 (B460), 63 (E117), 77 (G11), 100 (H154); Lancaster County Will Book C-I-504, Pennsylvania State Archives; Wright, *Lancaster County Church Records*, 2:13, 21, 25, 40, 49.

65. Wright, *Lancaster County Church Records*, 2:158, 170; Lancaster County Will Book C-I-504, Pennsylvania State Archives; Lancaster County Orphans Court Records, 1760–63, p. 143; 1763–67, p. 21, Pennsylvania State Archives; McKnight, *Fortineux—Fortinet Family*, 94–95.

66. Like the Dutch Reformed congregation in colonial New York City studied by Joyce D. Good-friend, the German Reformed church of Lancaster was "socially inclusive." According to Goodfriend, the Dutch Reformed elders and deacons in New York City "were men of stature in the community but by no means were drawn exclusively from the mercantile elite" (Goodfriend, "Social Dimensions of Congregational Life," 252–78 [quotes on 257]).

67. Lancaster Borough Tax Assessment List, 1759, Lancaster County Historical Society; Egle, *Pennsylvania Archives*, 17:454–63.

Eberhard Michael, finally, earned the gratitude of his fellow parishioners by playing the new Tannenberg organ free of charge. In January 1773, the church consistory voted to acknowledge Michael's service through an annual gift of £10. Before coming to Lancaster, where he became a trustee of the congregation in 1771, Michael was listed as a "clerk at Mr. Stiegel's furnace" in Elizabeth Township. The eccentric ironmaster Heinrich Wilhelm Stiegel was renowned as a music enthusiast and directed the choir at Trinity Lutheran Church, and it is quite likely that Stiegel stimulated and encouraged Michael's musical activities.[68] Michael's 1789 estate inventory also reveals a remarkable breadth of literary and intellectual interests. At a time when the bookshelf of most of his fellow parishioners consisted mainly of a Bible, a copy of Johann Arndt's *True Christianity*, and a couple of sermon and hymn books, Michael's inventory listed "Musical Notes" and more than seventy books, mostly works on religion, history, and education. Besides a large Bible, two sermon books, Arndt's work, and several dictionaries, he owned an *Ecclesiastical History* in two volumes, Calvin's *Institutiones*, Robertson's *History of Charles the 5th*, a *History of England*, and a four-volume edition of *Don Quixote*.[69]

The identification of prosperous laypeople with the Reformed church is also reflected in an increasing number of bequests for the benefit of the congregation and its poor.[70] These charitable bequests, however, also highlighted the problem that the German Reformed congregation had not yet attained the status of a chartered corporation and therefore had no legal right to receive and administer money or real estate. If the heirs of a testator refused to comply with his will, the congregation also lacked the power to take the case to court. This issue came up when the heirs of Abraham Im Obersteg refused to release a tract of land in Hempfield Township, which Im Obersteg had acquired for £400 in 1763 and willed to the Reformed church four years later.[71] When the congregation finally applied for a proprietary charter, it specifically pointed out that it had lost valuable bequests because it lacked corporate status.

The charter that the Penn family granted the German Reformed congregation on February 16, 1771, represents a milestone in the latter's history in several

68. Records of the First Reformed Church, vol. 10, microfilm no. 88/3, pp. 39–41, Evangelical and Reformed Historical Society; Lancaster County Tax Lists, Elizabeth Township, 1758, Lancaster County Historical Society; Mayhill, *Deed Abstracts*, 125 (K93); Heiges, *Henry William Stiegel*, 70–71, 78, 81.

69. Eberhart Michael Estate Inventory, 1789, Lancaster County Historical Society.

70. These are treated in detail in chapter 6.

71. Mayhill, *Deed Abstracts*, 120 (K16); Lancaster County Will Book B-I-597, Pennsylvania State Archives; Cramer, *History*, 79. As the consistory minutes of 1811/12 show, the congregation never regained the land (Records of the First Reformed Church, vol. 10, microfilm no. 88/3, pp. 150–51, 153–54, Evangelical and Reformed Historical Society).

respects. First, the document stipulated that the pastor, three trustees, six elders, and six deacons constituted a permanent corporation with full rights to acquire, receive, and administer real estate, annual rents, interest payments, or other funds and privileges in Pennsylvania and Delaware. The income of the congregation, which was not to exceed £300 annually (or £500 in the event of the construction of a second church), was to be used for the support of the pastor and other employees or for the maintenance of church, parsonage, and schoolhouse. The charter explicitly provided for the building of a second Reformed church in the town. Secondly, church officers were authorized to make laws, regulations, and ordinances for the administration of the congregation in accordance with the laws of Pennsylvania. They were entitled to make their own seal and go to court. Finally, the charter provided for annual elections of one-third of the church officers; trustees, elders, and deacons were to serve three-year-terms.[72] After almost four decades, the congregation's search for order had thus culminated in a charter—the first for a Lancaster church—which considerably enhanced its economic and legal autonomy, provided for orderly church government, and made sure that extensive lay participation would continue to play a vital role in the future.

THE REFORMED CONGREGATION ON THE EVE OF THE REVOLUTION

The 1771 charter ensured a fairly broad representation of active laymen by setting up a corporation of fifteen lay officers along with the pastor and providing for the annual replacement of one-third of the officers. Under the terms of the new charter, twenty-eight laymen filled church offices during the years from 1771 to 1775. At least one-third of these men had already served as officers before 1770, and one-quarter were elected more than once during the early 1770s. At the expiration of his term as elder in 1772, for example, Wilhelm Bausman was immediately reelected. Trustee Michael Diffendorfer and elder Georg Reitzel served from 1771 to 1773 and were elected to the same offices in 1775, while Lorenz Marquedant was chosen as trustee in 1774 after having served three years as elder. Deacons Caspar Brunner, Jacob Weber, and Bernhard Wolf were reelected as elders.[73]

72. The charter was entered in German into the Records of the First Reformed Church, vol. 10, microfilm no. 88/3, pp. 1–7, Evangelical and Reformed Historical Society. Cf. Ellis and Evans, *History of Lancaster County*, 453–54.

73. The names of officers were compiled from the Records of the First Reformed Church, vol. 10, microfilm no. 88/3, pp. 1–7, 30, 31, 36, 39, 45, 47, 51, Evangelical and Reformed Historical Society.

An analysis of the social profile of these men reveals that most of them (twenty-four of twenty-eight) resided in the town itself, while the remaining four lived in neighboring townships. Of the twenty-four townsmen, one-third were assessed in the top two deciles of the 1773 taxpayers. The prestigious office of trustee was largely reserved for wealthy members of the congregation: five of the six trustees came from the top fifth of the town's taxpayers. The only exception, Caspar Schaffner the younger, was the son of a long-time lay leader and occupied the position of town clerk for a number of years. In contrast to the trustees, many elders and deacons were artisans of middling rank. Reformed church officers in the years before the War of Independence were in fact chosen from all ranks of Lancaster society except the poorest (see Table 1). The occupational backgrounds of Reformed lay leaders were as varied as their assessed wealth. While some earned their living as merchants, retailers, and innkeepers, others came from the town's textile, metal-, leather-, and woodworking trades. The social composition of the Reformed leadership suggests that the congregation sought to maintain a balance between the aspirations of the few genuinely wealthy laymen and the larger number of artisans of more modest means who were also active in the affairs of the congregation.

The Reformed leaders' concern for maintaining the order achieved in the 1771 charter by striking a balance between pastor, lay leaders, and the congregation-at-large formed a central theme of the consistory meetings held in the following years. Before the 1774 consistory elections, several members reportedly complained that the elections were not free since the church council preselected the candidates. In response to these rumors, the consistory left the first proposal to the congregation; "since nobody wished to submit a proposal, the matter once again fell to the consistory, which accordingly proposed 13 men besides the six whose term had expired."[74] Repeated complaints about the assignment of pews that members brought before the consistory demonstrate that laymen and -women jealously guarded their rank and status. While the church council generally tried to accommodate dissatisfied members, it became exasperated when the quarrelling did not cease and finally refused to hear further complaints.[75]

---

74. Records of the First Reformed Church, vol. 10, microfilm no. 88/3, p. 47, Evangelical and Reformed Historical Society; translation mine.

75. Records of the First Reformed Church, vol. 10, microfilm no. 88/3, pp. 29–30, 33–34, 41, 44, Evangelical and Reformed Historical Society. Quarrels over church seats were a common phenomenon in Catholic as well as Protestant central Europe, and historians have repeatedly interpreted them as struggles for prestige and status (see Jan Peters, "Der Platz in der Kirche. Über soziales Rangdenken im Spätfeudalismus," *Jahrbuch für Volkskunde und Kulturgeschichte* 28 [1985]: 77–196; Rainer Beck, "Der Pfarrer und das Dorf. Konformismus und Eigensinn im katholischen Bayern des 17./18. Jahrhunderts,"

Table 1   Officers of the Reformed church, 1771–1775

Residents of Lancaster Borough

Name	Office and year of election	Profession	Decile on 1773 tax list
Bausman, Wilhelm	E 1771, 1772	"Yeoman"[a]	1
Brunner, Caspar	D 1772, E 1775	Locksmith	4
Burkhard, Georg	E 1771	Joiner	2
Busch, Wilhelm	E 1771	Skinner	2
Diffendorfer, Michael	T 1771, 1775	Tavernkeeper	1
Franciscus, Christoph	E 1774	Skinner	3[b]
Frey, Jacob	D 1771	Taylor	6/7
Graffort, Christoph	T 1772	Shopkeeper	1
Hatz, Johannes	D 1771	Weaver	7
Isch, Peter	D 1771	Blacksmith	3
Job, Nicolaus	E 1771	Shoemaker	3
König, Conrad	D 1774	Cooper	7/8
Lambert, Franz	D 1774	Cooper	7/8
Marquedant, Lorenz	E 1771, T 1774	Stockingweaver	2
Martin, Stephan	T 1773	Tavernkeeper	2
Michael, Eberhard	T 1771	—	1
Miller, Johannes	E 1772	Gunsmith	6/7
Peter, Ludwig	D 1772	Brickmaker	5/6
Reitzel, Georg	E 1771, 1775	Shoemaker	4
Rublet, Abraham	D 1773	Tobacconist	5/6
Schaffner, Caspar Jr.	T 1771	Dyer	4
Schaffner, Peter	D 1775	Bluedyer	7/8
Weber, Jacob	D 1772, E 1773	Turner	4/5
Wolf, Bernhard	D 1771, E 1773	Saddler	4

Residents of other townships

Name	Office and year of election	Place of residence	Landholdings on 1773 township tax list
Buschong, Philip	D 1771	Lampeter Twp.	200
Manderbach, Johann	D 1773	Lancaster Twp.	130
Schweitzer, Heinrich	E 1774	Hempfield Twp.	60
Wilhelm, Jacob	D 1775	Donegal Twp.	140

ABBREVIATIONS: T = trustee, E = elder, D = deacon.

NOTE: The occupational information is taken from the 1773 borough tax list printed in Egle, *Pennsylvania Archives*, 17:454–63. The position of the Reformed church officers on the town's wealth scale has been calculated from the same source. For the landholdings of the four men who lived outside Lancaster, see ibid., 325, 346, 394, 427.

[a] Bausman was a shopkeeper in the 1750s and 1760s, but he may have given up this occupation before 1773. In his 1784 will, he called himself a yeoman (Lancaster County Will Book E-I-16).

[b] Two persons of that name were listed on the 1773 borough tax list. The other was listed as a carpenter in decile 6.

The consistory's difficulties in charting a middle course between its own conception of order and church government and the demands of a self-conscious congregation-at-large are even more obvious in the discussions about the prerequisites for membership. Throughout the colonial period, the criteria for membership—participation in communion, regular financial contributions, or simple attendance—and the corresponding question of the congregation's boundaries had never been settled.[76] As we have seen, earlier attempts to impose uniform standards had failed. In April 1771 a majority of the consistory voted that members should be charged pew rents in the future, but on second thought the officers deemed it advisable to obtain the congregation's consent. Although a bare majority of the members voted in favor of pew rents, the consistory still hesitated to implement its decision and decided to defer the introduction of pew rents until after the next election. In March 1772, however, it postponed the issue for another year. Less than a year later the matter came up again because almost half the congregation had fallen behind on their contributions to the minister's salary. The consistory discussed a proposal for raising the pastor's salary by subscription and limiting pastoral services to those who had submitted written pledges. Those who did not contribute anything were to have no right to call on the pastor for baptisms and funerals or share in the congregation's privileges. Although a majority of twenty-nine members present at a meeting in January 1773 voted in favor of pew rents, the twenty-four negative votes were sufficient cause for the consistory to defer their introduction another year. Eventually the congregation did not begin to charge its members for their seats until the 1790s. That the Reformed leaders were still hesitant to impose this means of

---

in *Armut, Liebe, Ehre: Studien zur historischen Kulturforschung,* ed. Richard van Dulmen, 107–143 [Frankfurt am Main: Fischer Verlag, 1988]; and David Gugerli, *Zwischen Pfrund und Predigt. Die protestantische Pfarrfamilie auf der Zürcher Landschaft im ausgehenden 18. Jahrhundert* [Zurich: Chronos-Verlag, 1988], 86–87. On the importance of seating and social rank in colonial American churches, see Robert J. Dinkin, "Seating the Meetinghouse in Early Massachusetts," *New England Quarterly* 43 (1970): 450–64; Hackett, *Rude Hand of Innovation,* 18–20; and Holifield, "Toward a History," 32. Heinrich Melchior Mühlenberg recorded several quarrels over seating among the married women of the Lutheran congregations in Philadelphia during the 1760s and 1770s. In early 1764 Mühlenberg claimed that he attended a meeting of St. Michael's church council "with fear and trembling" as it "had been called to regulate the seatings in the church, which is a critical matter because there is too little room and there is a great deal of strife over the seats." The meeting lasted several hours and was "constantly interrupted by members of the congregation, some of them desiring seats closer to the front and others applying for seats for the first time etc." (Tappert and Doberstein, *Journals of Henry Melchior Muhlenberg,* 1:498, 581, 637–38, 649; 2:14 [quote]; Aland, *Die Korrespondenz,* 4:666; Christine Hucho, *Weiblich und fremd: Deutschsprachige Einwandererinnen im Pennsylvania des 18. Jahrhunderts* [Frankfurt am Main: Lang, 2005], 384–85).

76. This also holds true for other German Reformed congregations (see Wolf, *Urban Village,* 219–20).

raising revenue after several majority votes had sanctioned its decision testifies to the potential divisiveness of the measure, which might have offended many poorer members.[77]

While the consistory remained reluctant to stir up trouble within the congregation, their conflict with Pequea demonstrated that the Lancaster Reformed continued to live up to their reputation as an independent-minded and difficult congregation. In March 1771, two delegates from Pequea, a rural Reformed church that had been served every four weeks by Otterbein, Stoy, and Hendel, appeared before the Lancaster consistory and demanded that the new pastor Boehme visit them every third Sunday. They claimed to have a right to regular visits since they had given pastor Stoy a substantial sum for the Lancaster congregation and Stoy in turn had promised them that Pequea should "always" be supplied from Lancaster. The latter turned down the request, however, because it feared that frequent pastoral visits to Pequea would interfere with the catechizing of the youth. On Easter Sunday 1771, the male members voted that Boehme should visit Pequea only two Sundays a year and never go there on holidays. Unwilling to accept this setback, Pequea brought the case before the next Coetus meeting in October 1771. In a letter to Lancaster, the Coetus deemed it fair that Boehme should either visit Pequea every fourth Sunday or Lancaster should return the contribution received from Pequea. When the letter was read to a meeting of male church members, a majority found that Pequea had no right to demand the money back, but in order to show the Coetus due respect, Lancaster offered to make a contribution to Pequea if the latter congregation made a serious effort to build a church in the future. Although it is doubtful whether this resolution satisfied Pequea, there is no evidence that the conflict was pursued any further.[78]

CONCLUSION

Although its members failed to live in complete harmony with their neighbors and one another, the German Reformed congregation in Lancaster had undeniably achieved a considerable degree of order and stability by the early 1770s. It worshipped in a spacious stone church and listened to an organ that was thought to be among the finest in North America. Its pastor and elected church officers

77. Records of the First Reformed Church, vol. 10, microfilm no. 88/3, pp. 25, 32, 37–41, Evangelical and Reformed Historical Society; cf. Cramer, *History,* 50–51.

78. Records of the First Reformed Church, vol. 10, microfilm no. 88/3, pp. 23–24, 26–29, Evangelical and Reformed Historical Society; Hinke, *Minutes of the Coetus,* 308–9; Cramer, *History,* 48–49.

effectively practiced congregational self-government and deliberated on a variety of administrative, financial, and disciplinary questions. Since the 1750s, it had been served by a string of dedicated pietist ministers who may have been frustrated by their parishioners' independence and assertiveness, but who undoubtedly left their mark on the congregation. Wealthy laypeople as well as some of more modest means continued to bequeath substantial amounts to what had become their church. During the first four decades of its history, the German Reformed congregation repeatedly experienced times of crisis and once, during the 1750s, a period of "awakening." But most important, the colonial history of their church was one of impressive growth and a successful quest for order. This stability would not have been possible without the organizational efforts and material contributions of immigrant laypeople, who would not miss the community of fellow believers while they were striving to establish themselves in the colonial backcountry.

2

GROWTH AND DISRUPTION:

LUTHERANS AND MORAVIANS

In 1745 the Swedish-born pastor Laurentius Thorstensson Nyberg alienated the majority of the Lutheran congregation by openly embracing the ecumenical movement initiated by the Moravian leader Count Nikolaus von Zinzendorf and attending Moravian-sponsored meetings. When about seventy members tried to prevent Nyberg from entering the Lutheran church, fistfights broke out and Nyberg's supporters took the case to court. After public officials and German Lutheran ministers had failed to resolve the conflict, the schism became permanent when the Moravians formed their own congregation. The Lutheran-Moravian schism—probably the best-known episode in the religious history of Lancaster in the eighteenth century—has usually been placed in the context of the Great Awakening of the 1740s. Historians have interpreted the events as evidence that the religious fervor of the Great Awakening affected German speakers as much as their English counterparts.[1]

When the history of the Lutheran and Moravian congregations is viewed from a long-term perspective, however, their institutional growth and search for stability emerge as the dominant themes. The Lutheran and Moravian experiences, in other words, in many ways resemble the experience of Lancaster's German Reformed congregation. Both the Reformed and the Lutherans went

---

1. Glatfelter, *Pastors and People,* 2:87, 105–6, 109–10, 128; Schwartz, *"A Mixed Multitude,"* 140–41.

through initial periods of instability that were also marked, however, by the leading laymen's commitment to establishing a lasting congregational order. Both achieved a remarkable degree of stability after midcentury and built elaborate new churches in the 1750s and 1760s. The pastors of both congregations, finally, continued to complain about their parishioners' obstinacy and independence. Not even the Moravian schism sets the history of the Lutheran congregation completely apart, for the Moravian church attracted a number of Reformed families as well. The history of Lutheranism and Moravianism in early Lancaster should therefore be approached on similar terms as the Reformed congregation in the preceding chapter. The role of laypeople and the changing relationship between clergy and laity merit particular attention.

JOHANN CASPAR STOEVER AND THE EARLY LUTHERAN CHURCH

Like Conrad Tempelmann and Johann Jacob Hock, the pious laymen who ministered to the Reformed people of Lancaster in their early years, Johann Caspar Stoever Jr. was not an ordained clergyman when he began to preach and administer the sacraments in the Conestoga settlement, which had been organized as Lancaster County in 1729. Stoever, who had arrived in Pennsylvania in 1728, was the first person to minister to the Lutherans in the new town of Lancaster, and although his name does not appear on a request for an ordained pastor that sixteen members of the Conestoga congregation sent to the University of Tübingen in the duchy of Württemberg in 1731 or 1732, he possibly helped draft it. The signers of the petition mostly came from the Kraichgau in southwest Germany, and their appeal to Tübingen was forwarded through two Kraichgau pastors. The document was written by a "poor farmer" named Johann Georg Dieter, a native of Schwaigern near Heilbronn, and set forth that the "abandoned and shepherdless sheep, scattered in the wilderness" of the Pennsylvania backcountry "must lead [their] life among so many mobs and false spirits in this wilderness" and "must daily live with God-mocking words which press through a true Christian's body and soul." Whereas many Lutherans were "led astray from the true Evangelical doctrine," others sought to "resist all hordes and sectarian spirits that creep around in the world, to withstand them with a joyous spirit." Therefore they entreated the university faculty to "send us a pious, true servant of God who may enlighten us and bring us scattered sheep together in this wilderness to edify our souls in Christian love and the truth of God."

They promised that the pastor, who was to serve the Tulpehocken settlement along with Conestoga, would be well supported and that his parishioners would "suffer him obediently."[2]

Although the rhetoric of watchfulness against sectarian groups, so common among early Lutherans in Pennsylvania, was certainly calculated to convey the urgency of the request to the Tübingen professors, the petition did not produce any results. Still, the Lutherans of Conestoga unexpectedly received an ordained minister when Johann Christian Schultz, who briefly served the congregations in and near Philadelphia, ordained Stoever and his father of the same name before his return to Germany in the spring of 1733. Until the arrival of Johann Valentin Kraft and Heinrich Melchior Mühlenberg in 1742, Stoever was the only ordained Lutheran clergyman in Pennsylvania. He acquired a large tract of land in Lancaster County in 1735, organized a number of congregations in present-day Lancaster and Lebanon Counties, and performed hundreds of baptisms and marriages. In 1733 he administered the Lord's Supper to 159 communicants in the new town of Lancaster. Five years later, in October 1738, Stoever dedicated the newly erected Evangelical Lutheran church there "by prayer and the preaching of God's Word and the administration of the Holy Sacraments." Although the building was completed two years after the German Reformed church in the town, an early traveler's account points out that it was a stone church far superior to the crude log building that initially housed the Reformed. While he continued to visit a number of country congregations, Stoever demonstrated his attachment to Lancaster by presenting the congregation with a pewter host box and a host plate left behind by Johann Christian Schultz in 1735 and donating a black altar cloth four years later.[3]

Although Stoever played a larger role in organizing religious life than any of the early Reformed pastors in Lancaster, laymen were just as important in the founding of the Lutheran congregation. At least seven of the sixteen members of the original Conestoga congregation who had signed the request for a pastor

2. Glatfelter, *Pastors and People*, 1:139; Annette K. Burgert and Frederick S. Weiser, "Seeking a Pastor for Conestoga, ca. 1732," *Der Reggeboge* 24, no. 2 (1990): 62–65; Frederick S. Weiser, "The Origin of Organized Lutheranism in Lancaster County, Pennsylvania," *JLCHS* 107 (Winter 2005): 110–33.

3. Smith and Weiser, *Trinity Lutheran Church Records*, 1:3; Ellis and Evans, *History of Lancaster County*, 438; Theodore Emanuel Schmauk, "The Lutheran Church in Pennsylvania, 1638–1800 . . . Prepared at the Request of the Pennsylvania-German Society," in Proceedings and Addresses of the Pennsylvania German Society 11 (Lancaster, Pa.: n.p. 1902), 293–96; Coldren and Heisey, "Religious Life," 128; George L. Heiges, "The Evangelical Lutheran Church of the Holy Trinity, Lancaster, Pennsylvania. Part One, 1730–1861," *JLCHS* 83 (1979): 3–5; Wood, *Conestoga Crossroads*, 13–14; Glatfelter, *Pastors and People*, 1:140, 316, and 2:24–29.

in the early 1730s can be identified as later residents of the town and members of the congregation.[4] In 1742 Martin Lantz, Georg Graff, Caspar Lochmann, and Michael Beyerle acted as trustees when the Lutheran church obtained two lots on Duke Street from town proprietor James Hamilton.[5] Moreover, a number of donations to the church between 1733 and 1743 recorded in the earliest church book provide a unique glimpse of the contributions of laymen toward the establishment of a Lutheran congregation in the Pennsylvania backcountry. In September 1733, Johann Martin Weybrecht donated a pewter flagon "with a cover and spout," and the following year he bought a pewter chalice. In 1737 several women, including the wives of Hans Georg Barth and Michael Kurr, made a white altar cloth. Zacharias Barth presented an hourglass in 1738, while Caspar Lochmann and Jacob and Michael Beyerle had a stone altar made. The following year, Christoph Trenckel donated velvet for a collection bag and Captain John Stedman a small church bell. Wilhelm Ziegler gave a white damask altar cloth in 1741 and Adam Simon Kuhn a cloth "to cover the bread and wine when holding Holy Communion" in 1742. Peter Grung, an English officer, and the unmarried baker Michael Beyerle donated books—a Hamburg hymnal and the Lutheran liturgy of the southwest German principality of Baden-Durlach. In May 1743 Christoph Trenckel, Adam Löffler, and Georg Honig had church pews made, and the joiner Ludwig Detteborn donated the wooden boards for them. Detteborn also gave the church a baptismal table, and the wife of the saddler Philipp Schütz contributed a napkin to cover it. A second napkin came from Adam Löffler and his wife, while Christoph Trenckel donated £2 for funeral cloths. Georg Honig, finally, "had the rail made at his own expense of walnut wood around the altar" in the summer of 1743, and Jacob Lochmann "donated the iron rod on the pulpit for the hour glass."[6] Several of these benefactors also contributed money toward the building of a Lutheran church in Germantown in 1738.[7]

Taking into consideration that two of the donors, Captain Stedman—a ship captain active in the transporting of German immigrants from Rotterdam to

4. Hans Philipp Fernsler (or Firnsler), Friedrich Stein (an elder of the Conestoga congregation), Friedrich Eichelberger, Johann Michael Beyerle, Philipp Schaufelberger, Johann Georg Barth, and Philipp Heinrich Rudesill (Burgert and Weiser, "Seeking a Pastor," 63–65).

5. Mayhill, *Deed Abstracts*, 96 (H50); Heisey, "Borough Fathers," 63; Heiges, "Evangelical Lutheran Church," 6–7.

6. Smith and Weiser, *Trinity Lutheran Church Records*, 1:3–4. The list also appears in Coldren and Heisey, "Religious Life," 127–28, but several names are not accurately transcribed in this older publication. See also Heiges, "Evangelical Lutheran Church," 5, 9.

7. Frederick S. Weiser, ed., "Donors to the Lutheran Church in Germantown in 1738," *Der Reggeboge* 19, no. 1 (1985): 8–10.

Pennsylvania—and the officer Peter Grung, were not residents of Lancaster, it is possible to identify twenty-three people as leaders in the Lutheran congregation between 1732 and 1743—that is, as people who either served as church officers or made donations to the new church.[8] A social profile of this group therefore illuminates the composition of the core of the Lutheran laity in the new town. By identifying these lay leaders in ship lists, property records, church books, and genealogical works, some conclusions can be reached about their social status and group cohesion.

A majority of these early leaders came from a cluster of small towns and villages in the northern Kraichgau, a politically and confessionally fragmented region near the city of Heilbronn in the southwestern part of the Holy Roman Empire. No less than fourteen of the twenty-three elders and donors can be traced back to the Kraichgau, which most of them left between the mid-1720s and the late 1730s. If emigration and vital records were more complete, the number that can be traced back to the region might even be higher. In the early eighteenth century, Kraichgau villagers suffered from economic hardship and the demands of petty princes for feudal rents and labor. After a first wave of emigrants had successfully established themselves in the New World, a chain migration took off that made the Kraichgau one of the major emigration centers from central Europe to colonial America.[9] Given their common regional background, it is not surprising to find that social ties existed among the Lutheran leaders even before their emigration to Pennsylvania.

One of the most active of the early Lutheran leaders was Hans Georg Barth: he signed the petition to Tübingen in the early 1730s, his wife helped make an altar cloth in 1737, and he served as a church elder in 1748. Zacharias Barth, who gave the hourglass to the congregation in 1738, was his son. A native of Franconia, Hans Georg Barth had married Anna Barbara Klein in the Kraichgau village of Kirchardt in 1715, and three children were born to the couple between 1717 and 1721. The family apparently came to Pennsylvania in the mid-1720s, and three more baptisms of Barth children were recorded in Lancaster between 1730 and 1736. Barth took up 250 acres of land on Conestoga Creek in Lampeter

---

8. Marianne S. Wokeck, *Trade in Strangers: The Beginnings of Mass Migration to North America* (University Park: Pennsylvania State University Press, 1999), 74–75.

9. Burgert, *Kraichgau.* For patterns of emigration from the Kraichgau, see Roeber, *Palatines*, 41–43, 101–108; and Aaron S. Fogleman, *Hopeful Journeys: German Immigration, Settlement, and Political Culture, 1700–1775* (Philadelphia: University of Pennsylvania Press, 1996), chapters 1–2. Fogleman also observes the clustering of emigrants from particular villages of the Kraichgau in Lancaster (*Hopeful Journeys*, 74–75, 79).

Township, a few miles from the county seat, in 1733 and was naturalized in March 1735. He repeatedly stood as godfather of children of fellow Kraichgau immigrants and Lutheran leaders. Thus Barth sponsored the baptisms of four children of Sebastian Finck, who had emigrated from the same village as the Barth family. He also was the sponsor of a son of the fellow Kraichgau immigrant and Lutheran leader Friedrich Eichelberger in 1730 and became the godfather of Michael Kurr's daughter in 1744. Barth's and Kurr's wives had collaborated in making the altar cloth for the church. At midcentury, three of Barth's servants—probably recently arrived redemptioners—are mentioned in communion lists. Barth lived to a great age: he was eighty-nine years old when he died on his farm in 1769.[10]

Even more conspicuous in the affairs of the young congregation than the Barths was the Beyerle family from Sinsheim in the Kraichgau. Hans Michael Beyerle, born in 1698, arrived in Pennsylvania in 1730 and moved to the new town of Lancaster, where he had acquired two lots by 1735. He signed the request for a pastor from Tübingen and, together with his younger brother Jacob, oversaw the making of a stone altar for the new church in 1738. He acted as a trustee in 1742 and served as an assistant burgess from 1742 to 1744. Beyerle helped transfer inheritances of German immigrants from Kraichgau villages to Pennsylvania, and in the 1730s and 1740s he was frequently asked to sponsor the baptisms of Lutheran children, including several children of his fellow Kraichgau immigrants Philipp Firnsler, Philipp Rudesill, and Jacob Spanseiler. In the 1740s, the Lancaster Orphans Court repeatedly appointed him as a guardian of orphaned children. In 1749, for example, he became the guardian of Christian Kurr, a surviving child of the deceased Lutheran leader Michael Kurr. In addition to his real estate in town, Beyerle acquired eighty acres on Conestoga Creek in 1741.[11]

The baker Jacob Beyerle, who was five years younger than his brother Hans Michael, had married in Neckarbischofsheim in 1725, and four children had been born before the family migrated to the New World in 1732, where three more children were baptized in Lancaster from 1736 to 1740. Like his brother, Jacob was a frequent sponsor at baptisms and acquired several town lots as well

10. Burgert, *Kraichgau*, 41, 111; Smith and Weiser, *Trinity Lutheran Church Records*, 1:5–6, 347, 361, 364, 423, and 2:145; Warrant Register, vol. 16, p. 8, no. 86, Pennsylvania State Archives; Lancaster County Will Book B-I-562, Pennsylvania State Archives.

11. Burgert, *Kraichgau*, 58; Mayhill, *Deed Abstracts*, 12 (B75), 41 (D59), 46 (D177), 117 (I105); Ellis and Evans, *History of Lancaster County*, 362, 373; Heisey, "Borough Fathers," 49, 71; Smith and Weiser, *Trinity Lutheran Church Records*, 1:4, 6, 8, 14, 15, 19, 22, 24, 26, 34, 38, 39, 416, 418–20; Burgert and Weiser, *Seeking a Pastor*, 65; Roeber, *Palatines*, 126–27; Lancaster County Orphans Court Book, vol. 1, pt. 1, pp. 25, 56, and pt. 2, p. 21; Rogers, "Genealogical Gleanings," 25.

as land on Conestoga Creek.[12] In 1738 the brothers Andreas and Michael Beyerle, younger cousins of Hans Michael and Jacob, crossed the Atlantic and also found their way to Lancaster. The second Michael Beyerle, a baker who was sometimes referred to as "the younger" in county records in order to distinguish him from his cousin, donated the Baden-Durlach liturgy to the church in 1743, the year in which he married Anna Maria Schmiedin.[13]

The careers of Philipp Rudesill, Philipp Schaufelberger, Philipp Schütz, Christoph Trenckel, and Adam Löffler provide further insight into the role of Lutherans from the Kraichgau in early Lancaster. Rudesill, who signed the request for a pastor in the early 1730s and made a donation to the Germantown church in 1738, was born in Michelfeld in 1697 and married Anna Maria Schopff, daughter of the *Schultheiss* (bailiff) of Weiler, in 1722. Five years later the Rudesills crossed the Atlantic with their young son Georg Philipp and settled in Lancaster, where Philipp remarried twice and fathered seven more children. The Lutheran leaders Caspar Lochmann and Hans Michael Beyerle were among the children's godfathers. Rudesill's third wife, Susanna Beyer, was Reformed, which may account for the fact that he sponsored several baptisms in the Reformed church between 1736 and 1742. In November 1748, Rudesill informed the Lutheran pastor of his intention to go to communion but did not come "on account of the excuse of an argument with his Ref[ormed] wife." Rudesill obtained land on Conestoga Creek next to Caspar Lochmann and was living in Manheim Township in 1751. At that time he had at least one indentured servant.[14]

The saddler Philipp Schütz was born in Neckarbischofsheim in the Kraichgau in 1708 and arrived in Philadelphia in 1732. He obtained several properties in Lancaster from 1735 to 1744 and some land in nearby Lampeter Township. Schütz donated money for the Germantown church, and his wife gave a napkin for the baptismal table in 1743, but their marriage ran into difficulties shortly thereafter, for in September 1744 Schütz advertised in two Pennsylvania newspapers that his wife had run away with one Jacob Frederick Kurtz. When he died in 1761, the Lutheran pastor referred to him as a "separatist," but it is not

---

12. Burgert, *Kraichgau*, 58–59; Smith and Weiser, *Trinity Lutheran Church Records*, 1:18, 23, 28, 38, 412–14, 425; Wright, *Lancaster County Church Records*, 3; Warrant Register, vol. 16, p. 8, no. 95, and p. 14, no. 298, Pennsylvania State Archives; Mayhill, *Deed Abstracts*, 6 (A108), 56 (D463), 118 (I135), 119 (I167), 122 (K39), 178–79. (M78); Heisey, "Borough Fathers," 65; Roeber, *Palatines*, 127.

13. Burgert, *Kraichgau*, 57; Smith and Weiser, *Trinity Lutheran Church Records*, 1:4, 49.

14. Burgert and Weiser, *Seeking a Pastor*, 65; Burgert, *Kraichgau*, 304–6; Smith and Weiser, *Trinity Lutheran Church Records*, 1:6, 44, 335, 354, 379, 423; Wright, *Lancaster County Church Records*, 2:1, 5, 8; Mayhill, *Deed Abstracts*, 25 (B589); Lancaster County Tax Lists, Manheim Township, 1751, Lancaster County Historical Society; Lancaster County Will Book B-I-112, Pennsylvania State Archives.

clear whether Schütz had joined another denomination or had simply stopped
attending services. He had remarried in the late 1740s but died childless; therefore he willed £150 to each of his three siblings in Neckarbischofsheim, half of
the property on King Street where he had been living to Friedrich, Engelhard,
and Philipp Yeiser, prominent members of the Lutheran congregation, and the
remainder of his estate to his wife.[15]

Philipp Schaufelberger, a signer of the petition to Tübingen and an elder in
1748, had been born in the Kraichgau village of Michelfeld in 1682 and was
forty-five years old when he journeyed to America with wife and three children
in 1727. His presence in Lancaster is recorded as early as 1730. Like his fellow
congregational leaders Philipp Rudesill and Caspar Lochmann, Schaufelberger
farmed land on Conestoga Creek, where he acquired 150 acres in 1736. In the
will he made in 1755, he left the bulk of his estate to his only surviving daughter,
Anna Margaretha, and his son-in-law, Martin Schreiner, while his two sisters
or their children were to receive £4 each "when ever they shall come from Germany." According to the Lutheran burial book, the seventy-six-year-old widower
died "at his own place" in 1759.[16]

Christoph Trenckel and his son-in-law Adam Löffler were very active in congregational affairs around 1740. They donated money and various objects and
had pews made for the church. A native of Allmersbach, Trenckel had married
the daughter of a master potter in the town of Sinsheim in 1715. Three children
were born to the couple between 1716 and 1723, and after Trenckel had remarried
he fathered another child in 1737. The year before Trenckel's twenty-year-old
daughter, Anna Margaretha, had been impregnated by the apprentice potter
Johann Adam Löffler, a baker' son from Hohenhaslach in Württemberg. The
young woman married the apprentice in June 1736 and gave birth to a son three
months later. The Löfflers migrated to America in 1737, and Trenckel followed
them a year later. Christoph Trenckel obtained a lot and five acres in Lancaster
in 1740 and married a third time; his wife was the widow of another Kraichgau
immigrant. He employed a servant in 1750 and was naturalized in the same year.
When he died in 1752, the sixty-one-year-old Trenckel declared on his deathbed
that his wife should receive £30 before the division of his estate. In January 1754

15. Burgert, *Kraichgau*, 334–35; Mayhill, *Deed Abstracts*, 38 (C516), 43 (D120), 91 (G463), 118 (I121);
Heisey, "Borough Fathers," 62, 74; Smith and Weiser, *Trinity Lutheran Church Records*, 1:4, 308; *Pensylvanische Berichte,* September 16, 1744; Lancaster County Will Book B-I-360, Pennsylvania State Archives.

16. Burgert, *Kraichgau*, 314; Smith and Weiser, *Trinity Lutheran Church Records*, 1:9, 60, 304, 331,
347, 365, 375; Warrant Register, vol. 16, p. 191, no. 118, Pennsylvania State Archives; Lancaster County
Will Book B-I-283, Pennsylvania State Archives.

his widow, Anna Maria, testified before the Orphans Court that the deceased's estate was worth about £195 after the deduction of debts. This left £165 to be divided among the widow and Michael Ott, the husband of Trenckel's only surviving daughter.[17] Adam Löffler had acquired real estate in Lancaster and served as an assistant burgess between 1745 and 1749, but he appears to have died or moved away shortly thereafter.[18]

While most early Reformed leaders resided in the town itself, the leadership of the Lutheran congregation was somewhat more rural. In addition to Barth, Lochmann, Rudesill, and Schaufelberger, Martin Weybrecht became a substantial landholder when he acquired 284 acres on Conestoga Creek in 1733.[19] As the example of the Beyerle family illustrates, moreover, outmigration was as common for early Lutheran leaders as for their Reformed counterparts. The elder Hans Michael Beyerle moved to Virginia in the 1750s. Andreas Beyerle joined General Braddock's ill-fated expedition to Fort Duquesne in 1755 and remained in western Pennsylvania after the French and Indian War. Jacob Beyerle removed to Philadelphia, where he joined an important network linking the major emigration areas of southwest Germany to the Delaware Valley. This left only the younger Michael Beyerle in Lancaster, where he died childless in 1766.[20] Other Lutheran leaders also left Lancaster around midcentury. Friedrich Eichelberger, a native of Ittlingen in the Kraichgau who had come to America in 1728, frequently appears in early church records and signed the appeal for an ordained minister in the early 1730s. By 1750, however, he had moved to Warwick Township in northern Lancaster County. Another signer of the petition to Tübingen was Philip Firnsler, probably from Berwangen in the Kraichgau, who immigrated to Pennsylvania in 1727 and was married by Johann Caspar Stoever in 1731. Firnsler took up a town lot and five acres in 1735 but later moved to Lebanon County, where he became a member of Hill Lutheran Church.[21] Georg Honig, whose place of origin is not known,

17. Burgert, *Kraichgau*, 241, 349, 368–69; Smith and Weiser, *Trinity Lutheran Church Records*, 1:3–4, 287, 349; Heisey, "Borough Fathers," 58, 60, 63–64; Mayhill, *Deed Abstracts*, 54 (D429), 117 (I75); Lancaster Borough Tax Assessment List, 1751, Lancaster County Historical Society; Lancaster County Will Book J-I-326, Pennsylvania State Archives.

18. Mayhill, *Deed Abstracts*, 117 (I80); Heisey, "Borough Fathers," 60, 63; Ellis and Evans, *History of Lancaster County*, 373.

19. In 1738 Weybrecht obtained a further warrant for 200 acres on Little Conestoga Creek. This second tract was later patented to another person Warrant Register, vol. 16, p. 224, no. 10, and p. 226, no. 135, Pennsylvania State Archives.

20. Mayhill, *Deed Abstracts*, 57 (D473A); Burgert, *Kraichgau*, 57–59; C. H. Martin, "Life of Andrew Byerly," *PLCHS* 33 (1929): 3–8; Roeber, *Palatines*, 127.

21. Burgert and Weiser, "Seeking a Pastor," 62–65; Burgert, *Kraichgau*, 97–99; Smith and Weiser, *Trinity Lutheran Church Records*, 1:5, 45, 49, 238, 435 (Eichelberger); ibid., 14, 43 (Firnsler); Mayhill, *Deed Abstracts*, 118 (I130); Heisey, "Borough Fathers," 61.

married in Lancaster in 1739, acquired town property, and had an indentured servant at midcentury but in a 1755 newspaper announced his intention to move from Lancaster.[22] Even before these men left, the controversy over pastor Nyberg's Moravian leanings had caused a permanent rift in the congregation.

THE MORAVIAN SCHISM

The first signs that the Lutherans were heading for trouble appeared in 1740 when the number of baptisms performed by Stoever declined precipitously and the congregation invited the Swedish pastor Johann Dylander to visit them on occasion. Then, in late 1742, Johann Valentin Kraft appeared in town. A native of Hesse-Darmstadt, Kraft had come to America as a sixty-two-year-old man in the summer of 1742 and begun a pastorate among Lutherans in and near Philadelphia. Since he lacked formal credentials from European church authorities and since Heinrich Melchior Mühlenberg, who arrived in Pennsylvania shortly afterward, challenged the validity of his ministry, Kraft was forced to move to the Conestoga area, where he could count on the support of his former student Johann Caspar Stoever. As early as February 1743, however, Mühlenberg reported that Kraft was dividing the Lancaster congregation. One part wanted to call him as their pastor, but another faction strenuously opposed him. Mühlenberg added that the old pastor "had promised to marry a seventeen-year-old girl in Philadelphia, and up in Lancaster he wanted to become engaged to a widow, and his wife is said to be still living in Germany. This has again given occasion among the sects for renewed slander and ridicule of the Lutheran pastors. Mr. Sauer, the Germantown newspaper publisher, is also having a great deal of fun over it."[23]

While Kraft moved on to several rural congregations in Lancaster and York Counties, Lancaster's Lutherans followed the suggestion of Johann Dylander and the Philadelphia merchant Peter Kock and sent a call for a new pastor to Uppsala in Sweden. Laurentius Thorstensson Nyberg accepted the call, was ordained in Sweden, and arrived in Lancaster in late 1743 or early 1744. In November 1744, he purchased a lot in the suburb of Adamstown. It soon became apparent, however, that Nyberg was sympathetic to the ecumenical movement of Count Nikolaus von Zinzendorf's Moravian brethren. He started to correspond with Moravian

22. Smith and Weiser, *Trinity Lutheran Church Records,* 1:47, 363; Mayhill, *Deed Abstracts,* 117 (I109); Heisey, "Borough Fathers," 60, 64; *Pensylvanische Berichte,* March 16, 1755.

23. Glatfelter, *Pastors and People,* 1:71–73 and 2:30, 87; Tappert and Doberstein, *Journals of Henry Melchior Muhlenberg,* 1:90; Aland, *Die Korrespondenz,* 1:77, 95, 98n8, 109.

leaders in Bethlehem, and in January 1745 he invited the Moravian minister Abraham Reinke to Lancaster to "preach there in German and English." In March Nyberg began attending the quarterly synods organized by the Moravians, and in May he married a Moravian woman. Around that time Nyberg reported to Bethlehem "how hostile the people at Lancaster were toward him because of his association with the Brethren."[24] Heinrich Melchior Mühlenberg now began to comment on Nyberg's Moravian leanings and the resulting divisions within his congregation. Mühlenberg and Nyberg had both participated in a meeting organized by the Swedish pastor Bryzelius and the merchant Peter Kock at Wicaco in the spring of 1745 and had immediately taken a deep dislike of each other. As the meeting had been called to consider a formal union of the Swedish and German Lutheran churches in Pennsylvania, Nyberg made it clear that neither himself nor his congregation "should be subject to any unnecessary subordination." When Nyberg insinuated that Zinzendorf's writings agreed more with the Augsburg confession than the "suspect" doctrines and "nice morals" of the Halle pietists, Mühlenberg could barely keep his composure; according to Nyberg he "twisted his eyes in Halle fashion and began to feel rather badly."[25] In any case, a furious Mühlenberg wrote that Nyberg "broke his sworn obligation concerning the symbolical books. He rejected and ridiculed the chief doctrines concerning the Law, repentance, faith, and sanctification. He mutilated the doctrine of Christ."[26] When the Moravians held a conference in Lancaster in late 1745, the attendance of Nyberg and some of his parishioners, according to a report which Mühlenberg penned in December 1745, openly split the congregation:

> The *Moravians* arranged a great conference in Lancaster and this prompted Mr. Neuberg and the brethren he had won over from his congregation to show themselves in their true colors. They attended the meetings of the conference. When, after this, Mr. Neuberg undertook to preach in the Lutheran church, about eighty persons opposed it and refused to allow him inside the church any more. The other party stood up for him and took him inside the church. The two parties came very near to blows and violence. Some of

24. Kenneth G. Hamilton and Lothar Madeheim, trans. and eds., *The Bethlehem Diary*, vol. 2, *January 1, 1744–May 31, 1745* (Bethlehem, Pa.: Archives of the Moravian Church, 2001), 103, 123, 203, 243–44, 274, 280, 295, 300, 309, 327, 348.

25. Nyberg's report on the Wicaco conference is printed in Rothermund, *Layman's Progress*, 154–58; cf. Glatfelter, *Pastors and People*, 1:100–101 and 2:124–25; Heiges, "Evangelical Lutheran Church," 6–8; Müller, *Kirche zwischen zwei Welten*, 119–20; Mayhill, *Deed Abstracts*, 9 (A205); Aland, *Die Korrespondenz*, 1:157.

26. Tappert and Doberstein, *Journals of Henry Melchior Muhlenberg*, 1:164.

them went to the church with guns and swords, and even the women took a hand in the fray and began to lay about them boldly. The affair will doubtless end in a bitter lawsuit before the *court*.[27]

Mühlenberg went on to report that Nyberg presented himself as a faithful Lutheran pastor while brandishing his opponents as pietists, "against whom many royal mandates have been promulgated." Nyberg allegedly claimed that it was possible to be an orthodox Lutheran and a Moravian at the same time—a claim that Mühlenberg found dubious but nevertheless forwarded to Halle and London for comment.[28]

Meanwhile both sides in this "wretched, bitter dispute" sent petitions to the governor, who had ordered chief burgess Thomas Cookson to lock the church. When the governor suggested that the Lutheran clergy should arbitrate the dispute, Nyberg denied the authority of the German and Swedish pastors in Pennsylvania and declared that he "would let the affair be decided by the archbishop in Sweden." The governor thereupon told Nyberg's opponents—whom Mühlenberg referred to as the "united seventy"—that they should pursue their case in court and permitted Nyberg to reenter the church and preach in the morning, while the opposing faction was permitted to hold services in the afternoon. A dispute over the use of the church on the festival of Epiphany caused the opposition to lock the church again, and Nyberg's party forcibly entered it once more. Upon repeated requests of Nyberg's opponents, pastors Mühlenberg, Brunnholtz, and Wagner traveled to Lancaster in January 1746 and offered to mediate between the two parties. The Lutheran pastors suggested that a committee of English ministers or two justices of the peace should act as arbitrators and admonished the Nyberg party that "it will be a blame for us and our Neighbours and friends abroad, if we devour one another and destroy one another and make Expences and give more offences by further acting like unchristians." Nyberg and three of his adherents—Sebastian Graff, Matthäus Jung, and Jacob Schlauch—rejected the pastors' initiative since they were not impartial and had not been invited by the congregation.

At about the same time, the case was heard in the county court where the Nyberg party had indicted nine of their opponents for disturbing the peace and

27. Tappert and Doberstein, *Journals of Henry Melchior Muhlenberg*, 1:109; Aland, *Die Korrespondenz*, 1:209. Cf. also Schmauk, "Lutheran Church," 296–304; Wood, *Conestoga Crossroads*, 185; Müller, *Kirche zwischen zwei Welten*, 120–29. The active participation of women in this violent confrontation indicates that they saw their rights and interests at stake (see Hucho, *Weiblich und fremd*, 387–89).

28. Tappert and Doberstein, *Journals of Henry Melchior Muhlenberg*, 1:109–10.

obstructing religious services. The court, however, returned a verdict of not guilty. On February 7, Mühlenberg's father-in-law, the respected justice of the peace and Indian agent Conrad Weiser, entered the scene and attempted to negotiate a settlement. He suggested that both parties should use the church property alternately on equal terms. Twenty-six men of the anti-Nyberg party then drafted an agreement that spelled out their terms for a settlement; Nyberg's faction answered with a counterproposal. After Weiser had failed to harmonize the two agreements, apparently because Nyberg vetoed the final draft, he and Mühlenberg left. When Mühlenberg returned to deliver a sermon at the beginning of May, the atmosphere was still tense.[29]

After the courts, the political authorities, and the Lutheran ministers had all failed to reach a settlement, the two parties took their case to the public forum of Christoph Saur's newspaper, *Pensylvanische Berichte*. In March 1746, Saur had published an "impartial" report on the dispute written by a man who allegedly preferred to stay away from the "many-headed Pennsylvanian religious monster" (in fact, Saur may well have written the piece himself). The report was critical of Nyberg, who was portrayed as a gifted man who had alienated his congregation with his Moravian sympathies and devious behavior. The article mirrored Saur's disdain for professional clergymen and lawyers and heaped sarcasm on the attorneys of both sides who, it claimed, suddenly became theologians and talked religion in court. The writer also poked fun at a layman, Christophel Franciscus, who got beaten up in front of the church despite the fact that he was rarely seen near it. The article also predicted that Nyberg's appeal to the Swedish archbishop would not work. In "our free Pennsylvania," it declared, "the people do not allow the clerics to lead them by the nose, and much less will the authorities be led in such a way—unless they do not know their powers, like wild horses are unaware of their strength."[30]

This article provoked a letter to the publisher from four of Nyberg's supporters—Sebastian Graff, Michael Immel, Jacob Schlauch, and Matthäus Jung—that was printed two months later. Nyberg's party defended the minister and claimed that the Swedish pastor in Philadelphia had kindled the flames of contention. This was a rather oblique reference to the Wicaco conference. But

29. The preceding two paragraphs are based on Tappert and Doberstein, *Journals of Henry Melchior Muhlenberg*, 1:111–14, 164–66; Aland, *Die Korrespondenz*, 1:215–20, 253 (quote on 218); *Hallesche Nachrichten*, 1:146–49; cf. Splitter, *Pastors, People, Politics*, 72.

30. *Pensylvanische Berichte*, March 16, 1746. On Saur's social and political views, see Roeber, *Palatines*, 175–96.

Graff, Immel, Schlauch, and Jung reserved most of their criticism for Heinrich Melchior Mühlenberg. The "black robe," they claimed, had broken his promise to stay out of the Lutheran church and had cheated the Nyberg party when he delivered a sermon there on short notice.[31] The opposing faction, represented by six elders and deacons, replied with a letter defending Mühlenberg and laying the blame on Nyberg, who became caught in the fire "on account of the Moravian fantasies and plans with which he went pregnant." They chastised their opponents for their violent behavior—even insinuating that the Nyberg party planned to start a "Munsterian peasants' war"—and accused the Moravian leader Count Nikolaus von Zinzendorf of plotting to rule over the souls, bodies, and goods of the Pennsylvania Germans.[32] Nyberg finally had to yield when the Lutheran consistory of Uppsala, Sweden, condemned his Moravian views, and he and his supporters withdrew from the Lutheran church and started their own congregation.[33]

Historians of Pennsylvania German religion have noted the importance of the Lancaster schism in the context of the colony-wide struggle between Lutherans and Moravians for power and influence in the 1740s. They have also interpreted the conflict as a learning process in the course of which Pennsylvania Germans adapted to concepts of civil and religious authority very different from the ones they knew in the Old World. Lutherans and Moravians in Lancaster found that neither the provincial government and the courts nor European ecclesiastical authorities and colonial clergymen were able to offer them much help. As self-governing bodies, the churches essentially had to find their own ways of resolving such disputes. Since the laity was deeply involved in the conflict and a reconciliation of the opposing viewpoints proved impossible, the permanent split of the congregation became inevitable.[34] What remains to be explored, however, is the composition of the two factions. It has been demonstrated above that successful immigrants from the Kraichgau who had come to Pennsylvania in the 1720s and 1730s and maintained a close web of social ties among each other had dominated the affairs of the congregation during the first dozen years

31. *Pensylvanische Berichte*, May 16, 1746. On the Wicaco meetings, see Glatfelter, *Pastors and People*, 1:100–101.

32. *Pensylvanische Berichte*, June 16, 1746. Mühlenberg commented on this exchange: "So then, since the Zinzendorfers could not belabor me with their flails, they put me in the German newspaper and reviled and abused me to the best of their ability in signed articles, which the others moderately and discreetly answered in the next issue of the newspaper, making public the whole course of the affair" (Tappert and Doberstein, *Journals of Henry Melchior Muhlenberg*, 1:166).

33. Tappert and Doberstein, *Journals of Henry Melchior Muhlenberg*, 1:115; Glatfelter, *Pastors and People*, 1:100–101, and 2:106.

34. Glatfelter, *Pastors and People*, 2:105–6, 109–10; Müller, *Kirche zwischen zwei Welten*, 118–29.

of its existence. How did the Moravian schism affect this early group of leaders and who were the people who sided with Nyberg?

Of the twenty-three men who have been identified as early Lutheran leaders, only two, Georg Graff and Wilhelm Ziegler, and the son of another, Martin Weybrecht Jr., clearly supported the Nyberg party.[35] According to the burial book of the Moravian congregation, Graff, a Lutheran elder in 1742, "was among our first brethren in Lancaster who were awakened by Br. Nyberg's preaching and united with the Communion of the Brethren." Since his brother Sebastian was a leader of the Nyberg party, family ties may have played a major role in bringing Georg Graff into the Moravian fold.[36] By contrast, eight of the twenty-six men whom Heinrich Melchior Mühlenberg identified as Nyberg's opponents were early Lutheran leaders. It thus appears that Nyberg was mainly supported by people who had not yet played leading roles in congregational affairs, while the "old" leadership group mostly opposed him.[37]

In most other respects, however, a close look at the leaders of the pro- and anti-Nyberg camps reveals that they had very similar regional backgrounds and social profiles. Mühlenberg identifies five men—Sebastian Graff, Matthäus Jung, Michael Immel, Jacob Schlauch, and Leonhard Bender—as leading supporters of Nyberg, and all of them except Bender also signed the letter in defense of the Swedish pastor that appeared in the *Pensylvanische Berichte*. By contrast, the six Lutheran elders and deacons who rebuked Nyberg in the same newspaper—Philipp Schaufelberger, Ludwig Stein, Adam Simon Kuhn, Bernhard Hubele (Hubley), Jacob Yeiser, and Michael Gross—may be identified as his leading opponents.[38] Virtually all of these eleven men came from the wealthiest segment of the town's population or were prosperous farmers in the vicinity, and immigrants from the Kraichgau and neighboring regions ended up on both sides of the divide.

35. Long after the Moravian controversy in Lancaster had subsided, Mühlenberg claimed in 1753 that Jacob Beyerle, an early Lutheran leader who had relocated from Lancaster to Germantown, had been an "intimate friend" of Nyberg's, but there is no corroborating evidence of his involvement in the controversy. His cousin Andreas Beyerle, by contrast, was a vehement opponent of the Swedish pastor (see Aland, *Die Korrespondenz*, 2:41; and Tappert and Doberstein, *Journals of Henry Melchior Muhlenberg*, 1:114).

36. Clyde L. Groff, Walter B. Groff, and Jane Evans Best, *The Groff Book*, vol. 1, *A Good Life in a New Land* (Ronks, Pa.: Groff History Associates, 1985), 25; *Moravian Burial Book*, 12; *Transactions of the Moravian Historical Society* 1 (1858–76), 384–87.

37. Christoph Trenckel, Ludwig Detteborn, Philipp Rudesill, Philipp Schütz, Georg Honig, Philipp Schaufelberger, Jacob Lochmann, and Hans Georg Barth (Tappert and Doberstein, *Journals of Henry Melchior Muhlenberg*, 1:114).

38. Tappert and Doberstein, *Journals of Henry Melchior Muhlenberg*, 1:112–13; Aland, *Die Korrespondenz*, 1:216; *Pensylvanische Berichte*, May 16, 1746, and June 16, 1746.

Three of the five leading Nyberg supporters came from regions of the Palatinate. The butcher Leonhard Bender was born in Kirchardt in the Kraichgau in 1703 and immigrated to Pennsylvania before 1727. Two of his children were christened in Lancaster in 1730 and 1734, and his wife, a former Mennonite, was baptized as a Lutheran by Johann Caspar Stoever in October 1737.[39] Matthäus Jung's brother, Marcus, was born in a village near Kreuznach in the Palatinate, so Matthäus probably also came from there. His age was given as twenty-one when the two Jung brothers came to Pennsylvania in 1732; he married three years later.[40] Jacob Schlauch, born in the village of Adelshofen near Eppingen in the Kraichgau in 1708, arrived in Philadelphia in 1728 and married Ursula Elisabeth Stein in Lancaster five years later. The couple had seven children, four of whom were still living at the time of Schlauch's death in 1750.[41] Sebastian Graff, the son of a farmer, was born in Offenheim in the margravate of Ansbach, a Franconian principality, in 1711 and came to Pennsylvania in 1730. After surveying the opportunities in Penn's colony, Graff returned to his native land where he handled business transactions for Philadelphia merchant Caspar Wistar and married. In 1736 he returned to Pennsylvania with his wife and his brother Georg. The Graffs had seven children baptized in Lancaster between 1737 and 1747.[42] Like Graff, Michael Immel may have been a native of Franconia. When Leonhard Immel, probably his brother, married in 1733, he was described as a farmer's son from the territory of the imperial city of Rothenburg. Michael Immel had arrived in Pennsylvania on the same ship with Leonhard and was the godfather of one of Leonhard's children. Michael had four children baptized in Lancaster between 1738 and 1745, with Sebastian Graff acting as sponsor for three of them.[43]

39. Burgert, *Kraichgau*, 50; Smith and Weiser, *Trinity Lutheran Church Records*, 1:8, 407.

40. *Moravian Burial Book*, 24; Strassburger and Hinke, *Pennsylvania German Pioneers*, 1:89, 91–92; Heisey, "Borough Fathers," 49.

41. Burgert, *Kraichgau*, 320.

42. Lancaster Diaries, 1763, entry for October 8, Moravian Archives; Heisey, "Borough Fathers," 48–49; Groff, *Groff Book*, 1:26–27; Jane Evans Best, *The Groff Book*, vol. 2, *A Continuing Saga* (Ronks, Pa.: Groff History Associates, 1997), 66–67; Smith and Weiser, *Trinity Lutheran Church Records*, 1:24, 407–8, 415. On Graff's career as a "newlander," see Rosalind J. Beiler, "'Smuggling Goods or Moving Households?'" The Legal Status of German-Speaking Immigrants in the First British Empire," in *Menschen zwischen zwei Welten: Auswanderung, Ansiedlung, Akkulturation*, ed. Walter G. Rödel and Helmut Schmahl (Trier: Wissenschaftlicher Verlag, 2002), 9–23, esp. 19–20; and Mark Häberlein, "Transatlantische Beziehungen im 18. Jahrhundert. Die Kontakte südwestdeutscher und Schweizer Einwanderer in Pennsylvania zu ihren Heimatregionen," in ibid., 45–60, esp. 45–46.

43. Strassburger and Hinke, *Pennsylvania German Pioneers*, 1:66, 69–70; Smith and Weiser, *Trinity Lutheran Church Records*, 1:16, 24, 28, 43, 432.

Of these five men, Sebastian Graff and Matthäus Jung were particularly active in the economic and political life of the town. When Lancaster was incorporated as a borough in 1742, Sebastian Graff was appointed as burgess and Matthäus Jung as assistant burgess.[44] Sebastian Graff and his brother Georg were among Lancaster's early shopkeepers and "stocked a variety of wares in the establishments they opened before 1740." In January 1746, Sebastian Graff placed an announcement in the *Pensylvanische Berichte*, summoning his debtors to settle their accounts and declaring that he had given up his shop but was still selling sugar, wine, rum, and brandy. From the late 1730s, he accumulated sizable real estate and engaged in land speculation. By midcentury he was living as a "gentleman farmer" on a large estate in Manheim Township, where he ran a gristmill. When Graff made his will in 1763, he left to his wife and children four houses in Lancaster, his 140-acre farm in Manheim Township, and more than £5,000—certainly one of the largest estates in Lancaster County at that time.[45] Numerous mortgages entered in the Lancaster County Deed Books reveal Graff's importance in local credit networks.[46] The shopkeeper Matthäus Jung took up two lots in Lancaster in 1735 and had a female servant in 1745. According to historian Jerome Wood, he "appears to have traded extensively." After his death in 1749, his estate inventory, which "included large supplies of hardware and other items generally stocked by shopkeepers," was valued at £1,000 in goods and £1,200 in outstanding debts. Like Graff, Jung engaged in land speculation.[47]

Like Matthäus Jung, Michael Immel—owner of a 260-acre farm in Manheim Township—obtained a female indentured servant in 1746. Five years later he recovered an inheritance that his parents-in-law in Franconia had left to his four children.[48] Jacob Schlauch (named Slaugh or Slough in English-language records)

44. Ellis and Evans, *History of Lancaster County*, 373; Heisey, "Borough Fathers," 48; Mayhill, *Deed Abstracts*, 12 (B75); Wood, *Conestoga Crossroads*, 29, 32.

45. Wood, *Conestoga Crossroads*, 12, 29, 50, 174; *Pensylvanische Berichte*, January 16, 1746; Warrant Register, vol. 16, p. 75–76, nos. 118, 126, 181, Pennsylvania State Archives; Mayhill, *Deed Abstracts*, 4 (A35), 9 (A200), 10 (A242), 16 (B275–277), 17 (B301), 77 (F409), 107 (H 290), 119 (I169); Lancaster County Tax Lists, Manheim Township, 1751, Lancaster County Historical Society; Lancaster County Will Book A-I-230, Pennsylvania State Archives.

46. Mayhill, *Deed Abstracts*, 4 (A34), 17 (B307), 21 (B450, B461), 25 (B588), 27 (B641), 31 (C217), 40 (D48–50), 60 (D546), 66 (E213), 67 (E246, 248), 69 (E323), 86 (G318), 93 (H25, H30).

47. Heisey, "Borough Fathers," 61; Wood, *Conestoga Crossroads*, 100; George W. Neible, "Account of Servants Bound and Assigned Before James Hamilton, Mayor of Philadelphia," *PMHB* 31 (1907): 100; Mayhill, *Deed Abstracts*, 13 (B120), 67–68 (E274), 71 (F88); Warrant Register, vol. 16, p. 241, no. 5, Pennsylvania State Archives; Lancaster County Will Book A-I-177, Pennsylvania State Archives.

48. Neible, "Account of Servants (1907)," 31, 355; Lancaster County Tax Lists, Manheim Township, 1751, 1756–59, Lancaster County Historical Society; Lancaster County Orphans Court Book, vol. 1, pt. 2, p. 28; Lancaster County Will Book B-I-221, Pennsylvania State Archives.

was an innkeeper who also took advantage of opportunities for land speculation. Three hundred acres in Manheim Township were patented to him in 1747, and when Schlauch sold the property a year later, he took in more than £500.[49] According to the burial book of the Moravian congregation, Leonhard Bender was "one with the first here in Lancaster who became acquainted with the Brethren. In 1748 he was received in the Congregation in Bethlehem, as the first in Lancaster." Bender owned a 215-acre farm on Conestoga Creek, which he mortgaged to Philadelphia merchant Caspar Wistar in 1752. The preaching schedule of two Moravian itinerants, Christian Rauch and Leonhard Schnell, for the summer of 1747 shows that the traveling preachers regularly held services "at Leonhardt Bender's, 4 miles from Lancaster via Conestocke."[50]

In the late 1730s and 1740s these men frequently stood as sponsors of one another's children. Sebastian Graff and his wife were godparents of Matthäus Jung's son in 1745, while the Jungs were sponsors at the baptisms of three of Sebastian and Eva Graff's children. Michael Immel and Sebastian Graff repeatedly picked each other as sponsors, and Jacob Schlauch and his wife became the godparents of Leonhard Bender's daughter in 1745.[51] But despite these ties, two of the five leading supporters of Nyberg had returned to the Lutheran fold by 1748. When Michael Immel and his wife brought a daughter to be baptized in the Lutheran church in November of that year, the new Lutheran pastor, Johann Friedrich Handschuh, personally acted as sponsor. From that time on, Immel regularly appears in the records of the Lutheran congregation until his death in 1758. Pastor Handschuh noted that Immel had reluctantly joined the congregation again and many people were against him because of his former support for the Moravian cause. Immel had realized, however, that the Moravians had "cheated" him and became a regular church-goer again.[52] Jacob Schlauch was buried in the Lutheran churchyard in May 1750 "with an extraordinarily large funeral attendance of all sorts of persons."[53] Even more ominously for the Moravians, their leader Matthäus Jung committed suicide in 1749. For his fellow parishioners, this was "a Blow to our Happiness, particularly as such a thing is quite unheard of among Brethren," and the

49. Mayhill, *Deed Abstracts*, 51 (D360), 109 (H319b); Lancaster County Will Book A-I-204, Pennsylvania State Archives.

50. *Moravian Burial Book*, 13; Mayhill, *Deed Abstracts*, 36 (C443); Rothermund, *Layman's Progress*, 158–59.

51. Smith and Weiser, *Trinity Lutheran Church Records*, 1:24, 28, 415, 428, 431.

52. Smith and Weiser, *Trinity Lutheran Church Records*, 1:64, 85, 97, 120, 122–23, 135, 137, 140, 245, 282, 299, 360, 378, 394; *Hallesche Nachrichten*, 1:532–33.

53. Smith and Weiser, *Trinity Lutheran Church Records*, 1:280.

Moravians' critics would certainly not miss "the opportunity to slander and to annoy the Brethren."[54]

If the leading supporters of Nyberg were established men of means, the same was true of the leaders of the anti-Nyberg faction. Philipp Schaufelberger, a prosperous farmer from the Kraichgau who was in his sixties when the conflict broke out, has already been portrayed above as one of the congregation's early leaders. The butcher Jacob Yeiser, who was registered in Philadelphia as a twenty-three-year-old immigrant in 1736, acquired real estate in Lancaster but died shortly after the Moravian controversy in 1747, leaving all his real and personal estate to his wife.[55] The other four leading opponents of the Swedish pastor were all among the twenty borough residents with the highest tax assessments in 1751.[56] The shopkeeper Ludwig Stein, possibly the son of early Lutheran leader Friedrich Stein, not only signed the article defending Mühlenberg in the *Pensylvanische Berichte* but became involved more directly in the Moravian controversy when, in a tense confrontation of the two factions in front of the locked church in late 1745, he "grabbed Nyperg and pushed him into the [sacristy]."[57] Since the late 1730s, Stein bought and sold a number of town properties, investing no less than £1,900 in real estate transactions from 1747 to 1753. Stein seems to have made business trips to Germany as well, for on the occasion of his return from one of his European journeys he "gave the congregation and church a beautiful silver chalice, a similar little bowl and a fine cloth with the heartfelt wish that all who would be served by them might be true Christians or thereafter would at least become them." In 1750–51 he served as town burgess.[58]

Adam Simon Kuhn has been identified by genealogist Annette K. Burgert as the son of a swineherder who emigrated from the Duchy of Pfalz-Zweibrücken with his parents and siblings as a nineteen-year-old lad in 1733. If this identification is correct, Kuhn's rise in colonial society was remarkable indeed. He seems to have come to Lancaster shortly after his marriage to Anna Maria Schrack in the Trappe Lutheran Church near Philadelphia in 1740. Kuhn engaged in large-scale

---

54. Quoted in Wood, *Conestoga Crossroads*, 187. See also *Hallesche Nachrichten*, 1:540.

55. Mayhill, *Deed Abstracts*, 50 (D319), 89 (G413), 97 (H100), 116 (I36); Lancaster County Will Book A-I-130, Pennsylvania State Archives.

56. Lancaster Borough Tax Assessment List, 1751, Lancaster County Historical Society.

57. Tappert and Doberstein, *Journals of Henry Melchior Muhlenberg*, 1:111. Wood, *Conestoga Crossroads*, 64, mentions that Stein was later convicted for "breaking down the door of the Lutheran Church, the property of Michael Byerly and George Groff" but fails to make the connection to the Moravian controversy.

58. Mayhill, *Deed Abstracts*, 36 (C438, C455), 43 (D107), 44 (D127, D131–32) 123 (K70); Smith and Weiser, *Trinity Lutheran Church Records*, 1:51; Ellis and Evans, *History of Lancaster County*, 373.

real estate speculation when he laid out a whole section at the southeastern edge of Lancaster, which became known as Adamstown, into forty-six lots in 1744. He sold most of these lots within a year and in 1749 disposed of all his Adamstown ground-rent holdings to Lancaster proprietor James Hamilton. Kuhn, who practiced medicine and pharmacy and opened a second pharmacy in Reading in the 1750s, paid the second highest tax assessment in the borough in 1751 and served as the town's chief burgess from 1750 to 1756. He also became a justice of the peace and a director of the Lancaster Library Company. In 1775 he was a delegate to the Second Provincial Convention. One historian has asserted that he was "without a doubt the most prestigious 'Dutchman' in the borough in the eighteenth century."[59]

The merchants and shopkeepers Bernhard Hubele and Michael Gross were almost as prominent in the affairs of the Lutheran congregation and the borough as Adam Simon Kuhn. A native of Maulbronn in Württemberg, the thirteen-year-old Bernhard Hubele came to Pennsylvania with his father and brother in 1732 and was trained as a tanner in Valentin Krug's business in Lancaster before opening his own shop. In the 1740s, Hubele established close relations with Adam Simon Kuhn; the two men repeatedly chose each other as godfathers of their children. He was already among Lancaster's wealthiest taxpayers in 1751 and served a term as assistant burgess. His business and political careers peaked in the two decades before the Revolution. Hubele was elected burgess in 1759 and 1760, and Lancaster County deeds show that he was a frequent creditor of farmers and townsmen and a purchaser of town property as well as land on Conestoga Creek.[60] The merchant Michael Gross bought two lots from the early Lutheran leader Jacob Beyerle in 1743 and had at least two indentured servants in the late 1740s. In 1752 he obtained patents to three hundred acres in the northwest section of the county. Gross purchased dry goods, wine, and tea from Philadelphia merchants and supplied goods and credit to iron furnaces and forges in the Lancaster area. A large number of artisans and farmers were indebted to this prosperous Lutheran merchant. When the Lancaster Library Company was founded in 1759

59. Annette K. Burgert, *Eighteenth-Century Emigrants from the Northern Alsace to America* (Camden, Me.: Picton, 1992), 316–18; Lancaster Borough Tax Assessment List, 1751, Lancaster County Historical Society; *Pensylvanische Berichte,* December 16, 1759; Heisey, "Borough Fathers," 53, 80–82; Ellis and Evans, *History of Lancaster County,* 364, 373; Landis, "Juliana Library Company," 195–96, 213, 241; Wood, *Conestoga Crossroads,* 28–29, 49, 177–78; Splitter, *Pastors, People, Politics,* 225n10, 236, 346.

60. John W. Lippold, "The Distinguished Hubley Family of Lancaster," *PLCHS* 40 (1936): 55–58; Mayhill, *Deed Abstracts,* 42 (D88), 67 (E264), 133 (K232b), 138 (L96), 140 (L151–157), 185 (M204), 192 (M320), 196 (M405); Smith and Weiser, *Trinity Lutheran Church Records,* 1:42, 422; Wood, *Conestoga Crossroads,* 29, 32, 99, 148; Ellis and Evans, *History of Lancaster County,* 363, 373.

Gross was its first treasurer. A year later he became a co-owner of Tulpehocken Forge but sold his share to his partner Heinrich Wilhelm Stiegel after eighteen months. At the time of his death in 1771, he owned a house in Lancaster, several houses in Philadelphia, where his daughter Catherine was married to merchant Henry Keppele Jr., and a farm in Paxton Township.[61]

In comparing the profiles of the leaders of the two factions in the Lutheran congregation during Nyberg's pastorate, it needs to be emphasized how much alike they were. Both groups were dominated by traders, innkeepers, and substantial landholders of roughly similar age and regional origins. While ties of kinship and godparentship may have been a factor in determining an individual's loyalties, the bitter dispute cut across social and regional cleavages and solidarities. And the rift remained permanent.

THE TRIALS OF JOHANN FRIEDRICH HANDSCHUH

After a visit to the Lancaster congregation in mid-1747, Heinrich Melchior Mühlenberg gave a gloomy assessment of its situation. "Unfortunately," he wrote after discussions with the elders and deacons, "the outlook is very disappointing as a whole and in detail. The Evangelical Lutheran congregation is now completely split. The largest group has kept the church and with our consent has been served by necessity up to this time by the assistant, Mr. [Nicolaus] Kurtz, from Tulpehocken," since a Swedish pastor who had briefly supplied Lancaster from Philadelphia did not want to continue his services. Mühlenberg went on to describe the organizational efforts of the Moravians:

> About eight or ten families, including the most well-to-do, separated and in a short time built themselves an entirely new stone church, in which Mr. Nyberg and other impartial preachers, that is, Moravian preachers, but none of ours, are to have the liberty to preach. So Mr. Nyberg preached the Zinzendorf principles more boldly than ever in this church and still

61. Smith and Weiser, *Trinity Lutheran Church Records*, 1:231, 324; Landis, "Juliana Library Company," 196, 242; Heiges, *Henry William Stiegel*, 39; Wood, *Conestoga Crossroads*, 101, 104–5, 140–41, 174; Warrant Register, vol. 16, p. 79, nos. 306–7, Pennsylvania State Archives; Mayhill, *Deed Abstracts*, 40 (D37, D39, D40), 49 (D268b, D279), 56 (D463), 60 (D539), 66 (E231), 73 (F217), 92 (H15), 97 (H106), 101 (H167), 107 (H285, H288), 112 (H351b), 113 (H368), 124 (K83, K84), 127 (K125), 130 (K178), 131 (K202b), 132 (K213), 136 (L41), 179 (M93–96), 184 (M192), 186 (M220b), 189 (M273), 194 (M359b); Lancaster County Will Book C-1-1, Pennsylvania State Archives.

claimed to be a pure Lutheran preacher. Alternating with him, there was another preacher from the Synod of Bern. He is a Swiss named Jacob Lischy who came to this country with Count Zinzendorf and has been preaching here in Lancaster. Finally Bishop Kammerhof and several more came and preached there.

Since Nicolaus Kurtz could visit Lancaster only two Sundays a month, many Lutherans went to the Moravian church on the other two Sundays "[b]ecause they want a sermon every Sunday, and also because they are urged and enticed to go." The Lutheran schoolmaster was of little help since he was "a careless, lazy fellow and he has few pupils," whereas the Moravians sent schoolmasters from Bethlehem who attracted many students. While ill feeling persisted between Moravians and Lutherans, the Lutheran elders and deacons were also divided among themselves, and the "common people" were "becoming completely unruly and stubborn because there is no real preacher who remains there constantly and there is no discipline or order. In short, it looks as though the whole thing is going to pieces." To make matters worse, Lancaster's pioneer Lutheran pastor, Johann Caspar Stoever, "recently had a lawsuit in the city and in anger drank himself drunk in an inn and vomited in the presence of all sorts of sectarian people, which is charged up to our account because he is called a Lutheran preacher, even though we have no fellowship with him."[62] In later reports, Mühlenberg indicated that Nicolaus Kurtz also became embroiled in factional struggles.[63]

Mühlenberg and his colleague Peter Brunnholtz made a new attempt to impose order on the congregation in April 1748. At the pastors' suggestion, the Lutherans elected a new church council of twelve members "since the congregation had been ruled heretofore by a number of deacons and elders, almost every one of whom had his own following and party." The new council, which was to promote congregational unity, consisted of the six men who had led the opposition to Nyberg—Schaufelberger, Stein, Kuhn, Hubele, Gross, and Yeiser— and six new officers. The council members signed thirteen "articles" declaring their intention to seek "the true best" of the congregation and agreeing on general rules for council meetings. The clergymen then presented their newly arrived colleague, Johann Friedrich Handschuh (1714–1764), like Mühlenberg and Brunnholtz a

62. Tappert and Doberstein, *Journals of Henry Melchior Muhlenberg*, 1:153–54; cf. also *Hallesche Nachrichten*, 1:350; Aland, *Die Korrespondenz*, 1:287; Schmauk, "Lutheran Church," 305; Heiges, "Evangelical Lutheran Church," 10. For Nicolaus Kurtz, see Glatfelter, *Pastors and People*, 1:76–77.

63. Tappert and Doberstein, *Journals of Henry Melchior Muhlenberg*, 1:169–70, 173, 184–85.

pietist from Halle, as Lancaster's new minister. When three members of the church council objected and declared their preference for Nicolaus Kurtz, the pastors resorted to outright threats: "We told them . . . that if even one of them were troublesome and dissatisfied with our counsel and arrangement, they would get neither one of the men with our consent and we would turn to the other vacant congregations and withdraw our aid entirely; they must consider it a special favor we came to their aid at all." Faced with this prospect, the council relented and agreed to Handschuh. For the time being, ministerial authority prevailed.[64]

Once settled in Lancaster, Handschuh engaged in an ambitious program of church discipline, catechizing, and spreading the gospel. One hundred eighty-three people—ninety-four men and eighty-nine women—participated in his first communion service in July 1748. Before the year ended, Handschuh had held two more communion services and confirmed thirty-four young people. A peak was reached on Easter Sunday 1750, when more than 240 people attended communion.[65] Handschuh's communion records show that men and women participated in roughly equal proportions. Before the Pentecost service in May 1749, eighty men and eighty-nine women announced their intention to come, and before Pentecost 1750, seventy-four men and sixty-seven women had themselves registered as communicants. The "feminization" of eighteenth-century churches that historians have noted for Protestant denominations in New England and New York had not yet affected Lancaster's Lutherans.[66] Handschuh preached regularly in country congregations such as Earltown and performed baptisms and marriages there. In the borough he visited the members of his congregation in their homes, initiated extensive repairs of the church building, and recruited Johann

64. Tappert and Doberstein, *Journals of Henry Melchior Muhlenberg*, 1:192; cf. Splitter, *Pastors, People, Politics*, 31–32. The "articles" that the council members signed are printed in Smith and Weiser, *Trinity Lutheran Church Records*, 1:51–54. On Handschuh, see Glatfelter, *Pastors and People*, 1:50–51.

65. Smith and Weiser, *Trinity Lutheran Church Records*, 1:327–36, 351–57; *Hallesche Nachrichten*, 1:532–33, 547; Glatfelter, *Pastors and People*, 1:316–17.

66. Smith and Weiser, *Trinity Lutheran Church Records*, 1:340–44, 357–60; cf. *Hallesche Nachrichten*, 1:535, 537. On the feminization of eighteenth-century churches, see Richard D. Shiels, "The Feminization of American Congregationalism, 1730–1835," *American Quarterly* 33 (1981): 46–62; Mary Beth Norton, "The Evolution of White Women's Experience in Early America," *American Historical Review* 89 (1984): 593–619, esp. 608–9; Bonomi, *Under the Cope of Heaven*, 113–15; Balmer, *Perfect Babel of Confusion*, 100; Hackett, *Rude Hand of Innovation*, 85–86; Marilyn J. Westerkamp, *Women and Religion in Early America, 1600–1850: The Puritan and Evangelical Traditions* (London: Routledge, 1999), 78–80. In some New England churches, this process started as early as the 1660s (see Brekus and Stout, "Center Church," 40–43). Jon Butler has noted, however, that the German Lutheran and Reformed congregations were a "possible exception" from this general trend (Butler, *Becoming America*, 205). Christine Hucho finds a slight female majority in Lutheran congregations in Pennsylvania (Hucho, *Weiblich und fremd*, 373, 376).

Jacob Loeser, a loyal aide of Mühlenberg, as the new Lutheran schoolmaster. He mediated disputes and counseled individuals who experienced personal awakenings. In August 1749, Handschuh had the male members sign eight articles of agreement, in which they promised to obey the elders and deacons, submit themselves to church discipline, pay more attention to the catechizing of the youth, and maintain order and sobriety during funerals. Moreover, the congregation should annually audit the church's financial records and the council should collect the pastor's salary. By November the pastor was convinced that the circumstances of his congregation had improved considerably.[67]

As a close associate of Mühlenberg and the Halle pietists, Handschuh also led the Lancaster congregation into the Lutheran Ministerium of Pennsylvania, which was formed in 1748 as an association of the "regular," orthodox pastors of the province. Six leading laymen accompanied Handschuh to the first meeting of the ministerium in Philadelphia. At the meeting, the Lutherans of Lancaster and nearby Earl Township declared that they were "well satisfied with Mr. Handschuh" and reported that the parochial school "has been flourishing now for a year" and was attended by seventy children. The Lancaster delegates also raised the question under what conditions people who had left the congregation should be accepted again. While the delegates, who were obviously thinking of returning Moravians, wished to require written acknowledgements of membership, "[t]he meeting admonished the Lancaster people to act wisely in the matter, and to entrust it to their preacher." When a few laymen remained unconvinced, one of the ministers rather imperiously "exhorted all elders who were not yet entirely converted, to be converted from the heart, because otherwise they could not fill their office as they ought."[68]

While Handschuh sought to impose his conception of order on a congregation that had recently gone through a period of turmoil and division, the influx of new immigrants made his task even more demanding. German immigration

67. *Hallesche Nachrichten,* 1:531–548, and 2:58–68 (an abridged and heavily edited version of Handschuh's 1748–53 diary, the original of which is located in the Archiv der Francke'schen Stiftungen, Missionsarchiv, Abt. Nordamerika). Cf. also J. F. Handschuh to G. A. Francke, November 16, 1749, Johann Friedrich Handschuh Correspondence, 4 C 3: 33, Missionsarchiv, Abteilung Nordamerika, Archiv der Franckeschen Stiftungen, Halle/Saale, Germany; Schmauk, "Lutheran Church," 306–7; Heiges, "Evangelical Lutheran Church," 11–13; Wood, *Conestoga Crossroads,* 193; Splitter, *Pastors, People, Politics,* 57.

68. *Documentary History of the Evangelical Lutheran Ministerium of Pennsylvania and Adjacent States: Proceedings of the Annual Conventions from 1748 to 1821* (Philadelphia: Board of Publication of the General Council of the Evangelical Lutheran Church in North America, 1898), 5, 7, 9–12; Heiges, "Evangelical Lutheran Church," 11; Splitter, *Pastors, People, Politics,* 32. On the early history of the Lutheran Ministerium, see Glatfelter, *Pastors and People,* 2:124–26, 221–37.

to Pennsylvania peaked during his pastorate in Lancaster, and the presence of many poor immigrants is reflected in the marriage, burial, and communion records.[69] Of the eighty-one people who announced their intention to participate in communion at Christmas 1749, Handschuh identified more than twenty as recent arrivals. More than one hundred people in the church records are characterized as servants—probably redemptioners—between 1746 and 1756.[70] Meanwhile, Handschuh's effectiveness was diminished almost from the beginning of his pastorate by bouts of illness, and his insistence on church discipline seems to have provoked resentment. The baptism of Philipp and Eva Dannbach's son, for example, was canceled by the child's father because, Handschuh claimed, "they absolutely could not take certain people to be the sponsors." The pastor also invited "sinners" to make public confession in front of the congregation and designated several women who wished to come to communion as "prostitutes." Particular ostracism was reserved for Anna Gertraut Flimmer, "a prostitute, who let her first born child fall from a wagon into the Conestoga, and who was acquitted by the Appellate Court of the crime of child murder." Although Flimmer "showed public penitence for her former sinful life," she "was notified from the pulpit" that she was not admitted to the communion table. Heinrich Melchior Mühlenberg later claimed that Handschuh attempted to "convert" his congregation all at once, and when he compared Lancaster to "Sodom and Gomorrha" in one of his sermons and exclaimed that he wished there were just one righteous man among the elders and deacons, some of his parishioners believed he was losing his senses.[71]

Handschuh's severeness, his insistence on strict church discipline, and perhaps a lingering feeling that he had been forced upon the congregation by Mühlenberg and his colleagues in the first place help explain why the elders and deacons objected so strenuously when the pastor married his maidservant Susanna Barbara

69. Wokeck, *Trade in Strangers*, 40–46.

70. Smith and Weiser, *Trinity Lutheran Church Records*, 1:230, 232, 234, 276, 279, 332, 345–49, 351, 353 passim. Handschuh himself commented on the large number of Lutheran immigrants arriving at midcentury (*Hallesche Nachrichten*, 1:544). For a close analysis of these servants' experiences, see Mark Häberlein, "Unfreie Dienstknechte und -mägde im Nordamerika des 18. Jahrhunderts: Migrationserfahrungen, kolonialer Arbeitsmarkt und soziale Mobilität," in *Über die trockene Grenze und über das offene Meer: Binneneuropäische und transatlantische Migrationen im 18. und 19. Jahrhundert*, ed. Mathias Beer and Dittmar Dahlmann (Essen: Klartext Verlag, 2004), 191–219, esp. 202–19. On Lutheran pastors' concern about the spiritual neglect of redemptioners, see Splitter, *Pastors, People, Politics*, 45.

71. Smith and Weiser, *Trinity Lutheran Church Records*, 1:69, 90, 345, 362–63, 369–70. Cf. *Hallesche Nachrichten*, 1:531–48, and 2:58–68; Aland, *Die Korrespondenz*, 1:345, 362, 394, 408–9; Schmauk, "Lutheran Church," 309, 314–15; Splitter, *Pastors, People, Politics*, 57–58; Hucho, *Weiblich und fremd*, 381.

Belzner, the daughter of a poor tailor and Lutheran deacon, on May 1, 1750.[72] Mühlenberg and his colleagues Brunnholtz and Kurtz traveled to Lancaster for the occasion because Handschuh "had extended to us a pressing invitation to be present at his wedding and perform the ceremony." Upon their arrival, they found Handschuh "in great distress. He was in a constantly changing state of mind, now too depressed and then too elated, as is usually the case with those who are subject to *malum hypochondriacum*." No elders or deacons were present at the wedding, and Mühlenberg learned soon thereafter that Handschuh's troubles were just beginning. "Wherever I went I was asked whether it was true that Pastor Handshue had gravidated his maid servant and been forced to marry her. . . . From Lancaster I have learned to my pain that most of the older and most prominent people are staying away from divine services, that the young people have lost their respect for Pastor Handshue, and that they are singing all kinds of songs about his marriage." For the women in the congregation a poor girl who had peddled goods at local markets and enjoyed herself at country dances was simply unacceptable as the pastor's wife. The elders and deacons reportedly withheld Handschuh's salary and "had torn him to pieces with derogatory expressions in the taverns."[73]

In February 1751, Mühlenberg received a report from Nicolaus Kurtz that revealed how far Handschuh's position had deteriorated:

> He said that Mr. Handshue must really be living by faith, for many a time there was nothing to eat in the house. Several of the most prominent people in the congregation had arranged a sleigh ride, had become drunk, and had danced and made fun of their preacher. He was also made the subject of songs in the taverns and was called by his wife's nickname. Besides, a church councilman, who was the mayor of the city, had evicted him from his residence in the coldest time of winter so that he was obliged to move into a small new house which still smelled of fresh lime and whitewash. He was not receiving his salary and had to go into debt.

72. For Simon Belzner, who had emigrated from the village of Adelshofen in the Kraichgau to Pennsylvania in 1732, see Burgert, *Kraichgau*, 46. On the 1751 Lancaster Borough Tax List, Belzner's estate is assessed at a mere £9, considerably below the median of £15 for that year (Lancaster Borough Tax Assessment List, 1751, Lancaster County Historical Society).

73. Smith and Weiser, *Trinity Lutheran Church Records*, 1:234; Tappert and Doberstein, *Journals of Henry Melchior Muhlenberg*, 1:240–42, 261, and 2:128; Aland, *Die Korrespondenz*, 1:409; J. F. Handschuh to J. H. Schaum, March 19, 1750, and April 24, 1750, Schaum Correspondence, PS 313 C, Lutheran Archives Center, Mount Airy, Pennsylvania. Cf. Schmauk, "Lutheran Church," 315–20; Heiges, "Evangelical Lutheran Church," 13–14; Splitter, *Pastors, People, Politics*, 58–59.

According to the schoolmaster Johann Jacob Loeser, the church council was "completely disorganized and split" and the "young people were becoming unbridled and were telling tales about their pastor." Faced with this unbearable situation, Handschuh had no choice but to leave Lancaster in March 1751, after a pastorate of slightly less than three years. Mühlenberg reported that his colleague "was sick and tired of the place," while the "wild and raw rabble" was losing all order and discipline. Handschuh went on to a pastorate in Germantown that turned out to be just as troubled as his time in Lancaster.[74]

Even if Handschuh was a strict disciplinarian, it is not easy to understand why his marriage to a poor young woman caused such an outrage and the lay leaders boycotted him so adamantly. The prominent physician and church elder Adam Simon Kuhn, for example, had asked Handschuh to stand as godfather at the baptism of his son Johann Friedrich in September 1748. The following year, Handschuh repeatedly expressed his delight over Kuhn's spiritual awakening, and he was pleased when the Lutheran leader was elected as Lancaster's chief burgess.[75] Yet it was Kuhn's wife who met the new Mrs. Handschuh with unmitigated hostility and Kuhn himself who, according to Mühlenberg, evicted his pastor from the parsonage in the middle of winter! Another lay leader, the shopkeeper Bernhard Hubele, did not come to the pastor's support even though he was married to a sister of Handschuh's wife.[76] These observations suggest that the marriage was less the cause than the catalyst for Handschuh's estrangement from the congregation. The lay leaders' objections to the pastor's wife may have revealed some genuine concern about the reputation of the minister and the Lutheran church, but it may also have been a mere pretext for their rejection of the pastor's claim to authority, his attempts to implement a particular conception of order, and, ultimately, of Halle pietism.

At least two underlying causes of the estrangement can be identified. First, the rumors that the pastor had impregnated his maid suggest that the minister was perceived as a phony—a disciplinarian who failed to meet his own high

74. Tappert and Doberstein, *Journals of Henry Melchior Muhlenberg*, 1:268–69, 271; Aland, *Die Korrespondenz*, 1:408–9, 448–49, 455, 457; Glatfelter, *Pastors and People*, 1:50–51. On Handschuh's conflicts with the Germantown congregation, see Müller, *Kirche zwischen zwei Welten*, 129–77; and Splitter, *Pastors, People, Politics*, 68–72.

75. Smith and Weiser, *Trinity Lutheran Church Records*, 1:63; *Hallesche Nachrichten*, 1:542.

76. Johann Friedrich Handschuh Diarium, 4 H 10, entries for March 19, 21, and 26, 1749, and December 10, 1750, Missionsarchiv, Abteilung Nordamerika, Archiv der Franckeschen Stiftungen, Halle/Saale, Germany (hereafter Handschuh Diarium, Archiv der Franckeschen Stiftungen); Lippold, "Hubley Family," 58. Mühlenberg was well aware of this connection (cf. Tappert and Doberstein, *Journals of Henry Melchior Muhlenberg*, 2:324, 341).

standards. Second, Lancaster's Lutherans came mainly from southwest Germany, particularly from the Duchy of Württemberg, but also from the Palatinate, the margravate of Baden-Durlach, and a number of smaller Hessian, Franconian, and Palatine territories.[77] The Hallensian Handschuh was unfamiliar with the cultural and social background of most of his parishioners. As A. G. Roeber has pointed out, Halle pietism was actively concerned with the well-ordering and moral reform of society and with the accumulation of property for charitable purposes. Halle's missionary activism was alien to southwest Germans for whom piety was an inward, private, and domestic concern and who conceived liberty as freedom from state interference.[78] That regional background may have played a role in the laity's rejection of Handschuh is supported by the fact that the congregation bypassed the Halle-dominated Lutheran Ministerium and sent their call for a new pastor to Stuttgart, the capital of the duchy of Württemberg. In its—temporary—rejection of Halle pietism, the Lancaster congregation affirmed its desire for local autonomy and the limitation of clerical power.

JOHANN SIEGFRIED GEROCK AND THE
MATURING OF THE LUTHERAN CONGREGATION

After Handschuh had left, the congregation was temporarily supplied by Tobias Wagner, a native of Württemberg who had ministered to German settlers in Waldoboro (Maine) and the Tulpehocken Valley and had become a bitter opponent of Heinrich Melchior Mühlenberg. After preaching to a large crowd in November 1751, Wagner produced a pastoral call to Stuttgart that he had prepared at a congregational meeting in Friedrich Yeiser's house and convinced a number of members to sign it. Mühlenberg later claimed that Wagner had attempted to secure a call to Lancaster for himself, but "the congregation found no pleasure

---

77. This regional background becomes especially evident in Lancaster's Lutheran marriage records, in which Handschuh's successor, Johann Siegfried Gerock, entered the places of origin of many people he married between 1753 and 1762. Gerock registered about seventy spouses as natives of Württemberg; more than twenty came from the Electoral Palatinate and the Kraichgau region, while more than a dozen were from the margravate of Baden-Durlach. On emigration of Lutherans from southwest German territories to colonial Pennsylvania, see Roeber, *Palatines;* Mark Häberlein, *Vom Oberrhein zum Susquehanna: Studien zur badischen Auswanderung nach Pennsylvania im 18. Jahrhundert* (Stuttgart: Kohlhammer, 1993); Mark Häberlein, "German Migrants to Colonial Pennsylvania: Resources, Opportunities, and Experience," *William and Mary Quarterly* 50 (1993): 555–74; Fogleman, *Hopeful Journeys,* chapters 1–2; Wokeck, *Trade in Strangers,* 1–35.

78. Roeber, *Palatines,* 68–72, 75–77; cf. Splitter, *Pastors, People, Politics,* 29–30; Nolt, *Foreigners in Their Own Land,* 31–32.

in him."[79] In early 1753, two more pastors made brief appearances: Johann Theophilus Engelland, an unordained Württemberger who pursued an independent ministry in Pennsylvania, and Heinrich Burkhard Gabriel Wortmann, a North German who resided in the colony for only a few years. Mühlenberg stated that Wortmann "was a powerful speaker in the pulpit, but in his social relations he was a hot-tempered bully and battler." He reportedly beat his wife exceedingly hard and struck church member Michael Hubele in a quarrel.[80] When Lancaster's new pastor, Johann Siegfried Gerock, arrived from Württemberg, he entered a memorandum in the baptismal book that was obviously designed to underscore the legitimacy of his ministry: "At the end of May 1752 the call sent by the Evangelical Lutheran congregation in the city of Lancaster in Pennsylvania was given to me Johann Siegfried Gerock, M.A. by the unanimous vote of the honorable Consistory in Stuttgart, as a result of which I as their regularly called and ordained pastor and teacher travelled to America and after a hard trip of a duration of eight months finally arrived here healthy and well at the beginning of March 1753 and baptized the following children thereafter."[81]

Gerock, a graduate of the University of Tübingen who was in his late twenties when he came to America, received an annual salary of £60 of Pennsylvania currency in "local goods and sound money" for his pastoral services.[82] He evidently took a very different approach to his pastorate from Handschuh. According to Mühlenberg, "Pastor Gerock was so shy that he did not like to visit the members of the congregation—not even the sick—unless he was strongly urged to do so, nor did he have the gift for conducting edifying *Kinderlehre*, although this is certainly an important part of the office." Gerock's sermons were reported to be

79. Johann Jacob Loeser to Tobias Schaum, November 21, 1751, Schaum Correspondence, PS 313 C, Lutheran Archives Center. As Mühlenberg told the story, Wagner "maneuvred some of the influential elders so cleverly that, in defiance of the preachers who had been sent from Halle, they petitioned the Reverend Consistory in the Duchy of Württemberg, as it seems, for an orthodox pastor in the congregation of Lancaster" (Tappert and Doberstein, *Journals of Henry Melchior Muhlenberg*, 2:318–19; cf. Schmauk, "Lutheran Church," 320–22; Glatfelter, *Pastors and People*, 1:154–56; Splitter, *Pastors, People, Politics*, 21–24).

80. Tappert and Doberstein, *Journals of Henry Melchior Muhlenberg*, 2:319; Glatfelter, *Pastors and People*, 1:35, 167–68; Aland, *Die Korrespondenz*, 2:55–56, 65, 76–77; Heiges, "Evangelical Lutheran Church," 14. Two receipts that Trinity Lutheran Church in Lancaster acquired for its archives in 1989 show that Wortmann received £10 for his pastoral services on February 21, 1753, and £24 on March 23, 1753 (Trinity Lutheran Church Documents Acquired at John W. Aungst sale, no. 1459, Trinity Lutheran Church Archives, Lancaster).

81. Smith and Weiser, *Trinity Lutheran Church Records*, 1:107. Cf. Aland, *Die Korrespondenz*, 2:15–16, 44.

82. Trinity Lutheran Church Documents Acquired at John W. Aungst sale (no. 1453), Trinity Lutheran Church Archives. For Gerock's call and his ordination, see Best. A 26, Bü 373, 1d, nos. 8–10, Landeskirchliches Archiv Stuttgart.

long and rather tedious, and his parishioners later complained that "in public worship he used neither the Württemberg Order nor the liturgy customarily employed in the United Congregations here." The new pastor also discontinued the practice of regularly recording communicants; when Mühlenberg visited Lancaster after Gerock had left in 1767, he complained about the Swabian's poor record-keeping. Moreover, he declined the invitation to attend the Lutheran Ministerium's meetings in 1753 and 1754. While everyone agreed that Gerock led an "honest and orderly life," Mühlenberg later saw the "principal achievements" of his fourteen-year pastorate in "the construction of the new church, which was brought about in the meantime by the elders, and a fair measure of harmony and external peace in the congregation."[83]

Initially Gerock had some difficulties with Gabriel Wortmann, who kept preaching to a faction of the congregation in the courthouse and continued to occupy the parsonage but finally eloped in 1754, leaving his wife and children behind. Mühlenberg reported in the same year that Gerock was still struggling with some elders who believed that they were ruling the congregation. Mühlenberg thought that Gerock declined the first invitations to the Lutheran Ministerium because his "patrons," as he called the Lancaster elders, would not have permitted him to go.[84] Gerock initially kept up a correspondence with Mühlenberg, but then kept his distance from the Halle ministers, and there are few references to him in Mühlenberg's diaries and correspondence between 1754 and 1760.[85] As Mühlenberg later saw it, the lay leaders "gradually grew weary of him," while the congregation "was disturbed again and again by secret grumbling" about Gerock's limited pastoral gifts and the fact that Lancaster "was never visited by the United Preachers, and that the congregation as a consequence was never refreshed by an exchange with other regular preachers." These concerns seem to have paved the way for a rapprochement between Lancaster and the Lutheran Ministerium; in Mühlenberg's view Lancaster's powerful lay leaders hoped this association would lead to Gerock's transfer to another congregation.[86] In September 1760, Mühlenberg

83. Tappert and Doberstein, *Journals of Henry Melchior Muhlenberg*, 1:319, 342–43, 353. Cf. Aland, *Die Korrespondenz*, 3:631; Glatfelter, *Pastors and People*, 1:43; Schmauk, "Lutheran Church," 322; *Documentary History of the Lutheran Ministerium*, 41.

84. Aland, *Die Korrespondenz*, 1:55–56, 131–32, 144 (quote), 182; Tappert and Doberstein, *Journals of Henry Melchior Muhlenberg*, 2:319. In July 1754 Mühlenberg claimed that Jacob Beyerle—a former inhabitant of Lancaster who now led the opposition to Mühlenberg and Handschuh in the Germantown congregation—had enticed Wortmann to go to Lancaster (ibid., 208).

85. Aland, *Die Korrespondenz*, 1:213. In 1759 Mühlenberg reported on a visit with Gerock in Lancaster, who was unhappy about "certain occurrences" in his congregation (ibid., 2:357).

86. Tappert and Doberstein, *Journals of Henry Melchior Muhlenberg*, 1:319.

invited his colleague to attend a pastoral conference in New Providence and preach a sermon there. Gerock attended the conference together with two elders, Adam Simon Kuhn and Johannes Schwab, and he participated in further meetings of the Lutheran Ministerium until 1763. In 1761 Mühlenberg reported to Europe that Gerock and the Lancaster congregation were once more in harmony with the Lutheran Ministerium, and three years later he counted Gerock among the "impartial" pastors who were not Hallensians but maintained friendly relations with them.[87]

During the period of Gerock's rapprochement with the Ministerium, the Lancaster congregation was completely rebuilding its church. The decision to construct a new brick church to replace the dilapidated and cramped old stone building was taken in January 1761, at a time when interior strife had largely subsided. Moreover, the congregation had received a number of testamentary bequests during the 1750s, providing it with an initial capital stock.[88] The major part of the funds for the new church was raised by subscription. The surviving subscription list is difficult to use since later subscribers were inserted amid the original ones.[89] It appears, however, that some 260 subscribers originally pledged more than £1,700. More than 20 percent of this sum—£350—were subscribed by just six men: Michael Gross, who gave £100, and Adam Simon Kuhn, Bernhard Hubele, Friedrich Yeiser, Gerhard Brenner, and Ludwig Laumann, who pledged £50 each. Eight more people promised to contribute £20 or more, while forty-one planned to give between £10 and £19. The vast majority—205 of the 260 subscribers—pledged less than ten pounds. Not all pledges were actually honored; Dietrich Schopf, for example, never paid the £15 he had promised, and Johannes Dörr failed to pay the ten pounds he had pledged. On the other hand, a number of people increased their original pledges, and more than 130 people contributed money for the church during the later 1760s and 1770s, so total revenue between 1761 and 1779 exceeded £2,400. While most paid their share in cash, some contributed labor or materials to the building project.

The building of the new church, which lasted from 1761 to 1766, was overseen by a committee made up of pastor Gerock and elders Adam Simon Kuhn,

87. Aland, *Die Korrespondenz*, 2:387–89, 480, 528–30; 3:101, 230; Tappert and Doberstein, *Journals of Henry Melchior Muhlenberg*, 1:442, 529, 531, 685; *Documentary History of the Lutheran Ministerium*, 44–45, 48–49, 58–61, 63, 70–71; Glatfelter, *Pastors and People*, 1:43; Splitter, *Pastors, People, Politics*, 24.
88. See chapter 6.
89. Trinity Lutheran Church Documents, vol. 103, pp. 1–67, Trinity Lutheran Church Archives. On the building of Trinity Lutheran Church, see also Schmauk, "Lutheran Church," 324–27; Heiges, "Evangelical Lutheran Church," 15–20.

Bernhard Hubele, and Friedrich Yeiser. After Yeiser's untimely death in February 1762, his place was taken by Ludwig Laumann, who also served as treasurer. In January 1761 Kuhn, Hubele, and Yeiser acquired two half lots on Duke Street from the blacksmith Johannes Epple and Stophel Franciscus. The cornerstone was laid in May in the presence of several ministers from Pennsylvania, New Jersey, and Delaware. Heinrich Melchior Mühlenberg, the pastor of New Germantown in New Jersey, Bryzelius, and the Swedish provost of Philadelphia, Carolus Magnus Wrangel, delivered sermons on the occasion. After the ceremony, the pastors were invited to the courthouse, where Justice of the Peace Adam Simon Kuhn addressed them and his sons demonstrated their skills as orators. In the evening elder Michael Gross invited the pastors and several lay leaders to a musical entertainment at his house. In sum, the roles of pastors and lay leaders were carefully balanced on the occasion.[90]

Throughout the year, large amounts of red brick, stone, lime, sand, and wood were delivered to the building site. Wooden boards and planks were hauled from Cumberland County on the west side of the Susquehanna River, while other materials such as cedar shingles had to be bought in Philadelphia. Bricklayers Thomas Milnor and George Moore were constantly at work on the building, and the outside work as well as the roof framework were completed by November 1761. The following year smiths Nicolaus Reitenauer and Nicolas Knight and joiner Peter Dennig, who made six wooden pyramids, were paid for their work. Carpenter Johannes Grosch was remunerated in 1763. Three years later, stone cutter Jonas Metzger, joiner Peter Dennig, glazier Michael Frank, and Adam Hardt, who worked on the pulpit and altar, were among those who finished the building and its interior decoration. In addition, numerous people were employed hauling materials, laying shingles, painting, and performing a variety of other tasks, while local merchants and storekeepers supplied many needed items.[91] Since the funds raised by subscription proved insufficient to cover all expenses, the elders Kuhn, Gross, Hubele, and Laumann were authorized on New Year's Day 1765 to borrow up to £1,000.[92]

90. Mayhill, *Deed Abstracts*, 94 (H52, H54); Trinity Lutheran Church Documents, vol. 103, loose leaves 9–12 and pp. 68–71, and Bills and Receipts, 1761–69, Trinity Lutheran Church Archives, Lancaster.

91. A number of additional receipts from the building period are among the Trinity Lutheran Church Documents Acquired at John W. Aungst sale in 1989, Trinity Lutheran Church Archives, and in Society Misc. Collection, Lutheran Church, Lancaster, Pa., box 10a, Historical Society of Pennsylvania, Philadelphia.

92. Trinity Lutheran Church Documents, vol. 103, pp. 112–15, Trinity Lutheran Church Archives.

The red brick exterior of the finished church was "devoid of any decoration except six finials (urns) at the two peaks and at the four corners of the roof and two stone tablets placed high on the west wall of the building" rendering the name of the church and the date of the laying of the cornerstone in Latin and German. The churchyard was also enclosed by a brick wall. The interior was entirely taken up by the sanctuary, measuring eighty by sixty feet and dominated by the altar and a raised pulpit. A baptismal font, box pews, and a gallery for the organ completed the furnishings. Two pewter communion flagons made for the dedication of the new building by Johann Christoph Heyne, a member of the Moravian congregation who produced numerous altar candlesticks, flagons, and chalices for Pennsylvania German churches, are still in existence.[93]

The consecration of the new church building on May 4, 1766, was a festive occasion that was marked by a careful balancing of roles between pastors, lay leaders, and the congregation at large. On the day before the event, pastor Gerock, the elders and deacons, and Heinrich Melchior Mühlenberg, who had been invited by the church council, agreed on a schedule, according to which the Lutheran ministers and their congregations' delegates were to assemble in the schoolhouse at nine o'clock in the morning. An hour later, a carefully arranged procession was to move from the schoolhouse to the new church. The schoolmaster, Johann Jacob Loeser, and his students were to lead the procession, followed by the deacons carrying the sacred vessels, the pastors, and finally the elders and trustees from Lancaster and the deputies from other Lutheran congregations. In the new church building the pastors were to stand inside the altar railing, while the lay officers were to form a half circle around the altar outside the railing. Mühlenberg was to open the ceremony with a reading of the hundredth psalm, followed by choir and instrumental music conducted by Heinrich Wilhelm Stiegel, ironmaster at Elizabeth Furnace. Next, Gerock was to deliver an address on the occasion and, after another musical interlude, each of the pastors present was to recite a verse from the Bible that "is suitable for the consecration of the whole or its parts." The inclusion of Johann Caspar Stoever in this ceremony acknowledged his pioneering role in the history of the congregation as well as his recent reconciliation with the Lutheran Ministerium of Pennsylvania. Mühlenberg was to deliver the morning sermon and Gerock to preach in the afternoon, each sermon again framed by music. Sermons by the

93. Heiges, "Evangelical Lutheran Church," 19–20. On Heyne, see Eric de Jonge, "Johann Christoph Heyne: Pewterer, Minister, Teacher," *Winterthur Portfolio* 4 (1968): 168–84; and Donald L. Fennimore, "Metalwork," in *Arts of the Pennsylvania Germans,* ed. Scott T. Swank et al. (New York: Norton, 1983), 213, 215–16.

Anglican minister Thomas Barton, Johann Caspar Stoever, and Johann Andreas Krug as well as further musical recitals rounded out the ceremonies. Mühlenberg later commented that the whole event proceeded in a peaceful and harmonious spirit. The festivities thus struck a balance between ministerial authority and lay participation; between the Lutheran Ministerium and Lancaster's independent-minded pastor Gerock; and between confessional self-consciousness and accommodation with the Lutherans' English-speaking neighbors. The church protocol did not forget to mention that £137 were raised on the occasion.[94]

Altogether, the building of Trinity Lutheran Church—the only eighteenth-century church building in Lancaster still in existence—was a major accomplishment that highlights the importance of lay leadership among German Protestants in colonial Pennsylvania. Heinrich Melchior Mühlenberg, who was often critical of the Lancaster Lutherans, wrote to Germany in 1769 that the congregation had one of the most impressive brick churches in the country, which had cost several thousand pounds without burdening it with heavy debts. This was possible because, he noted, "most members of the numerous congregation are prosperous and zealous in religious matters."[95]

Scattered sources allow us to identify nineteen Lutheran elders during Gerock's tenure from 1753 to 1767.[96] Some of them, such as Georg Honig (elder in 1755) and Philipp Schaufelberger (elder in 1758), had already been among the congregation's leaders before midcentury. The innkeeper Jacob Eichholtz, a Kraichgau immigrant and temporary supporter of Nyberg who had returned into the Lutheran fold, served as church elder in 1755. Like Eichholtz, the cooper Friedrich Dannbach, an elder in 1759, was a native of the Kraichgau. He had been born in Ittlingen in 1723 and come to Pennsylvania with his family as a child. In 1746 he had married Elisabeth Spanseiler, a woman of Reformed origin, and the couple had six children between 1748 and 1764. Dannbach owned some real estate in the town and was among the wealthiest fifth of Lancaster's taxables in 1759.[97] Yet

94. Trinity Lutheran Church Documents, vol. 103, pp. 124, 138–41, Trinity Lutheran Church Archives; Tappert and Doberstein, *Journals of Henry Melchior Muhlenberg*, 1:298–99. Cf. also Schmauk, "Lutheran Church," 327–28; Heiges, "Evangelical Lutheran Church," 17–19; and Wood, *Conestoga Crossroads*, 196.
95. Aland, *Die Korrespondenz*, 4:65.
96. From receipts in the archives of Trinity Lutheran Church in Lancaster, it is possible to identify several elders for the years 1753 to 1755, while a ledger of the congregation in the same archives names a number of elders for the period from 1756 to 1766 (Trinity Lutheran Church Documents, vol. 101, ledger 1754–82, and Trinity Lutheran Church Documents Acquired at John W. Aungst sale, nos. 1459, 1461, 1462, Trinity Lutheran Church Archives).
97. Burgert, *Kraichgau*, 86–87; Mayhill, *Deed Abstracts*, 76 (F356), 104 (H227), 201 (M490, M493b); Lancaster Borough Tax Assessment List, 1759, Lancaster County Historical Society.

another Kraichgau immigrant was the hatter Martin Offner, who was born in the village of Schwaigern in 1718 and married there in 1747. The Offners emigrated to Pennsylvania in 1749, and Martin lost his wife and remarried shortly thereafter. He was a church elder by 1756. Like Dannbach, Offner was assessed among the top fifth of Lancaster's taxpayers in 1759. When he made his will a year later, Offner stipulated that his wife, Barbara, should have "free use" of one of his houses during her widowhood and one-third of his personal estate. While his eldest son, John, should receive his hatter's tools, the remainder was to be equally divided among his three surviving children.[98]

Elders Philipp Schreiner (1759), Johannes Schwab (1756–60), and Gerhard Brenner (1761, 1765–67) were farmers in nearby townships. The Schreiner family immigrated to Pennsylvania in 1738, and Philipp inherited land in Manheim Township from his father in the mid-1740s. He was taxed for a two-hundred-acre farm in 1759. When he made his will in 1790, he also owned a house in Lancaster, a large tract of land on the west side of the Susquehanna River, and an island in the river.[99] Johannes Schwab was a potter and yeoman in Leacock Township, where he occupied a 445-acre farm in 1758. In the will he made in 1780, Schwab provided four of his sons with sizable farms and bequeathed money to his daughters and their children. Gerhard Brenner, who had arrived in Pennsylvania in 1737, obtained a patent to almost three hundred acres of land in Manor and Hempfield Townships in 1745. He also owned a lot in the town and acquired a second farm in Manor Township as well as land in York County. In 1773 he was taxed for three hundred acres of land and one servant.[100]

Although they shared the office of elder with other men, Adam Simon Kuhn, Bernhard Hubele, Michael Gross, Friedrich Yeiser, and Ludwig Laumann clearly were the most powerful Lutheran leaders after midcentury. Kuhn, Gross, and Hubele had emerged as leaders during the tumultuous 1740s, while Friedrich Yeiser, a prosperous butcher, was a brother of the deceased Lutheran leader Jacob Yeiser.[101] Ludwig Laumann had worked as an indentured servant for Michael

---

98. Lancaster County Will Book C-I-13, Pennsylvania State Archives; Lancaster Borough Tax Assessment List, 1759, Lancaster County Historical Society.

99. Strassburger and Hinke, *Pennsylvania German Pioneers*, 1:198, 200, 202; Mayhill, *Deed Abstracts*, 35 (C384); Lancaster County Tax Lists, Manheim Township, 1759, Lancaster County Historical Society; Lancaster County Will Books A-I-94 and F-I-279, Pennsylvania State Archives.

100. Strassburger and Hinke, *Pennsylvania German Pioneers*, 1:195–97; Warrant Register, vol. 16, p. 16, no. 362, Pennsylvania State Archives; Mayhill, *Deed Abstracts*, 62 (E75), 181 (M124); Lancaster County Tax Lists, Manor Township, 1759, and Leacock Township, 1758, Lancaster County Historical Society; Egle, *Pennsylvania Archives*, 17:193 (Schwab/Swope), 111, 400 (Brenner); Lancaster County Will Books C-I-127 (Brenner) and D-I-195 (Schwab), Pennsylvania State Archives.

101. On Friedrich Yeiser, see Wood, *Conestoga Crossroads*, 141–42.

Gross after his arrival in Pennsylvania in 1746, but he had apparently married a relative of his master and become an enterprising shopkeeper and church leader by the mid-1750s.[102] These men paid the highest taxes of all German Lutherans, subscribed the largest sums to the new church building, and served the longest terms of all Lutheran officers.[103] Kuhn seems to have been in office continuously from 1757 to 1767, while Bernhard Hubele occupied the position of elder in 1758, 1760–64, and 1766. Adam Simon Kuhn also gave a substantial loan to the congregation—between 1757 and 1760 it paid him back more than £55.[104] The importance of this group of leaders is further underscored by the fact that Friedrich Yeiser's brother Engelhard and Bernhard Hubele's brother Michael also served as elders during this period.

While construction of the new church building was under way, growing dissatisfaction of the lay leadership with its pastor manifested itself in complaints before the Lutheran Ministerium. At the 1763 meeting a delegate from Lancaster, deacon Caspar Singer, claimed that "[t]he majority of the elders and members of the congregation would be happy to see Pastor G[erock] exchange with somebody for a time, first, because the congregation was involved in the heavy expenses of building a church, and second, because many did not want to give the amount they had promised, alleging that everything was too cold in the congregation, that

102. Laumann is identified as Michael Gross's servant in a 1747 Lutheran communicant list. In 1749 he married Elisabeth Gross, who is also referred to as Gross's servant maid in the marriage record, but the common last name indicates that she may have been related to her master. When he made his will in 1771, Gross called Laumann his "kinsman" (Strassburger and Hinke, *Pennsylvania German Pioneers*, 1:360–61; Smith and Weiser, *Trinity Lutheran Church Records* 1:231, 324; Lancaster County Will Book C-I-1, Pennsylvania State Archives). In the February 1, 1755, issue of the newspaper *Pensylvanische Berichte*, Laumann advertised that he was selling books, dry goods, wine, rum, and molasses in his shop in Lancaster near the courthouse. In the 1770s he regularly advertised handkerchiefs and a variety of European and East Indian goods for sale. By that time he was one of Lancaster's wealthiest citizens (cf. *Der Wöchentliche Pennsylvanische Staatsbote*, no. 506, October 1, 1771; no. 509, October 22, 1771; no. 520, January 7, 1772; and Wood, *Conestoga Crossroads*, 99–100, 103, 105, 148). Laumann also played an important role in local credit networks, extending credit to numerous artisans and farmers (sometimes in collaboration with his former master Michael Gross) (Mayhill, *Deed Abstracts*, 51 [D327], 60 [D539], 69 [E340], 85 [G291], 87 [G341, G344], 107 [H286], 126 [K109], 184 [M191], 186 [M230], 197 [M416]; Wood, *Conestoga Crossroads*, 140).

103. In 1759 Michael Gross was assessed at £7, Bernhard Hubele at £3 10s., Adam Simon Kuhn at £3 5s., Laumann and Yeiser at £3. These assessments put all of them among the town's twenty wealthiest taxpayers (Lancaster Borough Tax Assessment List, 1759, Lancaster County Historical Society). In 1770 Friedrich Yeiser's personal estate was valued at £575 total and £421 after deduction of expenses. His real estate, which consisted of three houses in Lancaster, fifteen acres on Conestoga Creek, and several other properties on the outskirts of town, was valued at £1,625 in 1773 (Lancaster County Orphans Court Records, 1768–72, pp. 33, 58, 203–4, Pennsylvania State Archives; Orphans Court Records, 1772–76, pp. 122, 147–50, Pennsylvania State Archives).

104. Trinity Lutheran Church Documents, vol. 101, Ledger 1754–82, entries for November 28, 1757; July 22, 1760; and October 7, 1760, Trinity Lutheran Church Archives.

the pastor made no pastoral visits, etc." Gerock answered that a change could only be made if both the congregation and the Württemberg consistory approved it and denied that he had neglected his duties. But he also hinted that if the congregation actually wanted a change, "he knew a place to which he could go."[105]

After having been criticized before the assembled pastors, Gerock did not attend further meetings of the ministerium, and his correspondence indicates that his relations with the Hallensian pastors cooled again.[106] In 1764 Gerock wrote a letter to Mühlenberg in which he referred to a gift of books that had been sent to the Pennsylvania congregations by a wealthy person in Leipzig. "Since," he wrote sarcastically, "to my understanding, it was the intent and will of the testator in Leipzig that these books were to be divided among the eight faithful laborers who had been sent or acknowledged by Halle, a Swabian who shared in goods that belonged to others would surely be charged with vanity and presumption and with considering himself to be equal with others." Gerock's claim that the Halle pastors regarded ministers like him as inferior reappears in a letter in which he declined Mühlenberg's request to preach a sermon in Philadelphia's St. Michael's church in his stead. He would not dare, Gerock declared, "to mount a pulpit that appears to be dedicated only to and reserved for Swedish doctors of theology, ecclesiastical councilors, royal court preachers, and a few others who are considered select, fit, and worthy enough." The letter, which was especially resentful of the Swedish provost Carolus Magnus Wrangel, a close friend of Mühlenberg's, closed on a defiant note: "I respect, honor, and love all colaborers, though I recognize none as superiors in this country."[107] Mühlenberg claimed that Gerock had only reluctantly agreed to invite the members of the ministerium to the dedication of the new church in 1766 and that the pastor and his elders haggled over a closer association between Lancaster and the ministerium.[108]

In early 1767, Gerock informed Mühlenberg that he had received a call to the Lutheran congregation in New York City, which he had temporarily supplied a few years earlier. He emphasized that he did not leave Lancaster with any ill

---

105. *Documentary History of the Lutheran Ministerium,* 79–80; Tappert and Doberstein, *Journals of Henry Melchior Muhlenberg,* 1:693; Heiges, "Evangelical Lutheran Church," 16–17; Wood, *Conestoga Crossroads,* 191–92.

106. Aland, *Die Korrespondenz,* 3:389; Glatfelter, *Pastors and People,* 1:50–51.

107. Tappert and Doberstein, *Journals of Henry Melchior Muhlenberg,* 2:38, 220–21; Aland, *Die Korrespondenz,* 3:283–84. In a letter written on April 8, 1767, Mühlenberg noted that Gerock held certain prejudices against the Hallensians, the precise reasons for which he claimed he could never find out (ibid., 3:504).

108. Tappert and Doberstein, *Journals of Henry Melchior Muhlenberg,* 2:320.

feeling but considered himself to be well understood and loved by his parishioners. After Gerock had already preached his farewell sermon, the church council and congregation extended a new call to him and offered to raise his annual salary from £60 to £100. This sudden turn of events started intense negotiations between Gerock, the Lutheran Ministerium, and delegates from Lancaster and New York City into which Mühlenberg was drawn as a reluctant and rather uneasy middleman. Mühlenberg claimed that Lancaster's elders had initially "rejoiced secretly" at Gerock's intention to leave, but the congregation now pressured them to keep their pastor. Gerock's final pastoral acts reportedly "evoked more feeling, love, confidence, benefactions, and awakening than had been manifest in the previous fourteen years of his ministry." According to Mühlenberg, moreover, the Anglican minister Thomas Barton had told the lay leaders that Lancaster had "the first and best claim to Mr. Gerock's." Characteristically, the men who led the negotiations with Gerock, Mühlenberg, and the New York delegates were the same who had dominated the congregation's affairs for two decades: Adam Simon Kuhn, Bernhard Hubele, and Michael Gross. They were unable to keep Gerock, however, who eventually turned down the new call and went to New York in May 1767.[109]

In retrospect, relations between Lancaster and the Lutheran Ministerium went through two distinct phases during Gerock's pastorate. A first phase from 1753 to 1759, during which the Swabian pastor and his congregation had kept their distance from the Halle pietists, had been followed by a second phase from 1760 to 1767, during which leading laymen gradually edged the congregation and its reluctant minister toward a closer association with Mühlenberg and his colleagues. After Gerock had left, therefore, the way was clear for a more formal union between Lancaster and the ministerium, and Adam Simon Kuhn, Bernhard Hubele, Ludwig Laumann, and their associates once again took the lead in bringing this union about. They invited the members of the ministerium to supply the vacant congregation, and the Swedish provost Carolus Magnus Wrangel, Heinrich Melchior Mühlenberg, and other pastors took turns visiting Lancaster and performing pastoral acts there during the latter half of 1767 and throughout 1768. Mühlenberg believed that these visits "opened the eyes of the people to the differences in teaching, catechization, visitation of the sick, etc.

109. Tappert and Doberstein, *Journals of Henry Melchior Muhlenberg*, 2:320–27 (quotes on 321, 323–24), 332; Aland, *Die Korrespondenz*, 3:491–93, 504–7; cf. Heiges, "Evangelical Lutheran Church," 21. For Gerock's testimony on behalf of his congregation, see Archiv der Francke'schen Stiftungen Halle/Saale, Missionsarchiv, Abt. Nordamerika, 4 D 1: 14, and Trinity Lutheran Church Documents, vol. 103, pp. 127–29, Trinity Lutheran Church Archives.

between Halle pastors on the one hand and pastors from Tübingen on the other." During his visit in the summer of 1767, the church council and congregation agreed to send a call for a new pastor to the Lutheran Ministerium. The latter would forward the call, which offered an annual salary of £100 besides free lodging and firewood, to Europe, and after the new clergyman's arrival, the ministerium and the Lancaster church council would determine whether the newly arrived man or a pastor with more experience in the Pennsylvania field was best suited for the congregation. For a while Lancaster hoped that Christian Emanuel Schultze, Mühlenberg's assistant in Philadelphia, would become their new pastor, but eventually a newcomer from Halle, Justus Heinrich Christian Helmuth, received the call and was presented to the congregation by Mühlenberg in the spring of 1769.[110]

A few months later, Mühlenberg returned to introduce a new constitution for the congregation, to which 118 heads of families subscribed on September 7 and over one hundred more during the following days. The first part of the constitution spelled out the rights and duties of the pastor in preaching, catechizing, administering the sacraments, visiting the sick, overseeing the school, and attending meetings of the church council and the Lutheran Ministerium. Several provisions were designed to strengthen the authority of the pastor and tie the congregation closer to the ministerium. Thus the pastor had the right to reject obvious sinners as communicants and sponsors at baptisms, and the congregation was obliged to call on the help of the ministerium in cases of the pastor's sickness or absence. The constitution also made it more difficult to dismiss a pastor who had become unpopular. If at least two thirds of the members of the church council had complaints against a pastor's life or doctrine that could not be resolved internally, they had to lay them before two neighboring pastors affiliated with the ministerium, and, if that did not solve the problem, to turn to a committee of the ministerium itself. Finally, the first section specified in what manner the congregation could call a pastor from the ministerium or from Europe.

The second section was concerned with the lay officers. The church council was to be composed of the pastor, three trustees, six elders, and four deacons. While the trustees were to remain in office during good behavior, elders served three-year-terms, after which they were eligible for reelection, and deacons two-year-terms.

---

110. Tappert and Doberstein, *Journals of Henry Melchior Muhlenberg*, 2:337–49, 353–56, 377, 384–87, 392–97, 424 (quote), 427–28; Aland, *Die Korrespondenz*, 3:527–30, 543, 559, 572, 590, 597–98, 602–3, 605–7, 642–43, 656; *Hallesche Nachrichten*, 2:681–84; Trinity Lutheran Church Documents, vol. 103, pp. 130–34, Trinity Lutheran Church Archives; Schmauk, "Lutheran Church," 329–31; Heiges, "Evangelical Lutheran Church," 21–24; Splitter, *Pastors, People, Politics*, 53–54.

The church council had the right to propose three candidates for each position to be filled, while the members of the congregation could make their choice from the preselected slate of candidates. While three long-time elders—Adam Simon Kuhn, Michael Gross, and Bernhard Hubele—were promoted to trustees and the other three elders—Gerhard Brenner, Michael Hubele, and Ludwig Laumann—remained in office, the constitution also contained an element of change by providing for the election of three new elders. Those who were elected had to accept the office or pay a fine. This section also set general rules for decision making, stipulating that important decisions required a two-thirds majority and had to be presented to the congregation for approval. The third part of the constitution, finally, detailed the requirements for membership—members had to be baptized and confirmed, must not lead an openly sinful life, had to subscribe to the constitution, respect the pastor and council, and pay their pew rents—and declared that the church council had the right to expel members for weighty reasons.[111]

In several respects, the church constitution—which Mühlenberg had obviously modeled on the church order introduced at St. Michael's church in Philadelphia several years before—resembled the Reformed congregation's charter of 1771. By spelling out the rights and duties of pastor, church council, and congregation, setting rules for the election of lay officers and deliberations of the council, and defining criteria for membership, the document sought to strike a balance between ministerial authority and lay participation and impose order and stability on the congregation. In this concern for an equilibrium between pastoral authority and lay expectations, the document mirrored Mühlenberg's views on discipline and church government after a quarter century of experience in the Pennsylvania field. Mühlenberg's influence is particularly evident in the importance attached to catechization, the attempt to forge a close alliance between Lancaster and the Lutheran Ministerium, and the limitation of the powers of the congregation at large, which could not nominate officers.[112] How successful Mühlenberg had been in adapting his views on church government to American circumstances and reconciling the needs and demands of pastors and parishioners became evident during the long pastorates of two other Halle pietists in Lancaster—Justus Heinrich Christian Helmuth (1769–79) and Mühlenberg's son Gotthilf Heinrich Ernst (1780–1815).

---

111. Tappert and Doberstein, *Journals of Henry Melchior Muhlenberg*, 2:415–16, 418–19, 427. For the text of the constitution, see Trinity Lutheran Church Documents, vol. 103, back pages 1–29, Trinity Lutheran Church Archives.

112. Cf. *Hallesche Nachrichten*, 2:435–41; Roeber, *Palatines*, 257–58; Müller, *Kirche zwischen zwei Welten*, 246–48; Splitter, *Pastors, People, Politics*, 80–86.

HALLE PIETISM RETURNS TO LANCASTER

Justus Heinrich Christian Helmuth (1745–1815), a native of Helmstedt who had studied at the University of Halle, was in his mid-twenties when he took up the ministry in Lancaster. The Halle-trained pastors in the Pennsylvania field naturally regarded him as an ally, and although relations with Heinrich Melchior Mühlenberg temporarily soured when Helmuth married a daughter of the prominent Philadelphia merchant and church elder Henry Keppele in 1770 without informing the senior pastor, Helmuth generally fulfilled his colleagues' expectations. In 1774 Mühlenberg approvingly noted that his younger colleague was "employing the powers bestowed on him by God's grace toward the best of the large congregation in Lancaster," was regularly visiting vacant congregations in the countryside, and was "eager to build up the kingdom of Christ in his parts." In contrast to Gerock, Helmuth placed a strong emphasis on catechizing, and soon after he began his pastorate he started to give private instruction to six young candidates for the ministry. As a gifted and popular preacher, Helmuth drew large crowds every Sunday. In an early report to Europe, the new pastor reported that harmony prevailed in his congregation and the debts remaining from the building of the new church were reduced from £1,000 in 1769 to £500 in 1771. The church council had introduced pew rents after the completion of Trinity Church in 1766, and although there were some complaints about members not paying, the rents put the congregation on a sounder financial basis and allowed for more speedy debt reduction.[113]

During Helmuth's pastorate, the church-building process continued with the decision to purchase a new organ in July 1771. While the congregation had acquired its first organ before midcentury, Lutheran pastor Peter Brunnholtz described it in 1752 as a "small and a noisy patchwork." The Moravian organ-builder David Tannenberg, who had already repaired and set up the old organ for the new Trinity Church in 1766 and constructed an instrument for the Reformed Church three years later, received the order for Trinity's new organ. The case was built by Peter Frick, a local cabinetmaker and member of the congregation. To finance the new instrument, which probably cost several hundred pounds, a subscription was started that drew 321 pledges. The largest came from

113. Aland, *Die Korrespondenz,* 4:91–92, 100, 171–74, 604 (quote; translation mine); *Hallesche Nachrichten,* 2:683, 689, 692; Tappert and Doberstein, *Journals of Henry Melchior Muhlenberg,* 2:396–97; Schmauk, "Lutheran Church," 331–34; Heiges, "Evangelical Lutheran Church," 24–27; Glatfelter, *Pastors and People,* 1:57–58. The first pew rent book of the congregation has been edited in Smith and Weiser, *Trinity Lutheran Church Records,* 2:303–465.

shopkeeper Paul Zantzinger, who gave £25, merchant Henry Keppele Jr., and innkeeper Matthias Slough, who promised £20 each (though only Slough actually paid). Pastor Helmuth, shopkeepers Christian Wertz and Ludwig Laumann, the tanner Jacob Krug, and Peter Frick, the maker of the ornamented organ cabinet, each contributed £10. All other subscribers donated six pounds or less, more than half of them less than £1. When the new organ was completed in December 1774, the Lutherans invited the Moravian trombone choir from Lititz to perform during the consecration ceremonies. In 1773 the congregation also purchased a new parsonage.[114]

The composition of the church council, which had been dominated by a small group for more than two decades, underwent some significant changes in the years around 1770. The wealthy shopkeeper Bernhard Hubele, who had emerged as "an outstanding leader" during the Nyberg controversy in the 1740s and served as deacon and elder for more than a quarter century, had to resign amidst a public scandal in 1769. While Hubele had been a member of the church council during Gerock's pastorate, Mühlenberg considered him to be the most loyal and persistent supporter of the Lutheran Ministerium among Lancaster's independent-minded lay leaders. According to Mühlenberg, it was Hubele who prevailed upon his colleagues to send the call for a new pastor to the minis-terium in 1767, and he accommodated visiting Lutheran preachers as well as the newly arrived pastor Helmuth in his house free of charge. Hubele's troubles started when he "unfortunately struck an insolent Mennonite with a stone" during the building of the new church, "and this resulted in the Mennonite's death about two weeks later. This was judged unpremeditated manslaughter," Mühlenberg reported, "but it was handled in such a way that the court acquitted him without penalty because the Mennonite was a drunkard and was, it is said, at the point of death anyhow." Several years after this incident, Hubele "suffered great anguish on account of his wife, who was afflicted more than a half-year with a *mania* or madness and died in this wretched condition." The aging elder employed a twenty-six-year-old woman "from his large circle of relatives" as his housekeeper. Hubele's grown-up children objected to their father's plan of marrying the young woman, but Mühlenberg secretly married the couple after the elder confided to him that he had impregnated his maid. This put both Hubele and Mühlenberg in an embarrassing situation when Hubele's relatives found out what had happened,

114. Trinity Lutheran Church Documents, vol. 103, pp. 74–82, 184, Trinity Lutheran Church Archives; Schmauk, "Lutheran Church," 331, 334; Heiges, "Evangelical Lutheran Church," 27–28; Brunner, *That Ingenious Business,"* 49–51, 71–72, 79–80.

and "it was spread far and wide . . . as the greatest *criminal* case in the city and province." According to Mühlenberg, Hubele's fellow parishioners were outraged over his alleged hypocrisy and fornication and threatened to keep him from the church by force. The anguished Mühlenberg had to urge his loyal ally to resign from office before the turmoil got out of hand, and Hubele followed the advice, although he defiantly noted: "It vexes me somewhat that such a harsh sentence should be passed upon me, as if I were guilty of a criminal act against the congregation, when I have always sought the best interests of the congregation and not my own."[115]

The second major change was the death of a long-time lay leader, the wealthy merchant Michael Gross, in 1771. Under the new church constitution, Gross had become a trustee in 1769. His only daughter had married Henry Keppele Jr., the son of the prominent Philadelphia trader and Lutheran leader, and pastor Helmuth had married into this family connection when he took Keppele's daughter Barbara as his wife in 1770. When he dictated his will in January 1771, Gross not only remembered a number of relatives in Pennsylvania and Germany but left significant bequests to the Lutheran congregations in Lancaster and Philadelphia and to the Pennsylvania Hospital.[116]

After Hubele's resignation and Gross's death, Ludwig Laumann emerged as a central figure among the "old" lay leaders. He was elected trustee in Gross's stead in 1772 and repeatedly used his connections to Mühlenberg and the ministerium to secure Bibles and religious books from Halle for sale in his shop in Lancaster.[117] Besides, several new men were elected to the office of elder in the final years before American independence. While some, such as the baker Christian App, the hatter Christian Liebe, and the tavernkeeper Veit Müller, had served as deacons before, many new church officers were artisans of middling wealth (see Table 2). The constitution of 1769 and the gradual demise of the "old guard" thus resulted in a socially more inclusive church council. It is notable that the group of congregational leaders, which had always included a number of farmers from surrounding townships in earlier decades, had now taken on a distinctly urban profile.

Throughout the eventful period from midcentury to the Revolution, Johann Jacob Loeser, who taught in the Lutheran parish school from 1749 until at least

---

115. Tappert and Doberstein, *Journals of Henry Melchior Muhlenberg*, 2:424–26; Aland, *Die Korrespondenz*, 4:103–4.

116. Lancaster County Will Book C-I-1, Pennsylvania State Archives. See also chapter 6.

117. Tappert and Doberstein, *Journals of Henry Melchior Muhlenberg*, 2:417, 491, 505, 702; Aland, *Die Korrespondenz*, 4:137.

Table 2   Elders and deacons of the Lutheran congregation, 1769–1775

Name	Office and first year of service*	Profession	Decile on 1773 borough tax list
App, Christian	E 1773	Baker	4
Benedict, Leonhard	D 1771	Weaver	5/6
Breitenhart, Christoph	E 1773	Tavernkeeper	2
Gross, Michael	T 1769	Merchant	1 (estate)
Hoff, Georg	D 1773	Clockmaker	3
Hubele, Bernhard	T 1769	Shopkeeper[a]	1
Hubele, Michael	E 1769	Not given	3
Keppele, Johann	D 1774	Baker	6/7
Kuhn, Adam Simon	T 1769	Doctor	1
Laumann, Ludwig	E 1769, T 1772	Shopkeeper	1
Liebe, Christian	E 1769	Hatter	3
Lindeberger, Georg	D 1772	Brickmaker	6/7
Moser, Georg	D 1770	Tanner	3
Moser, Michael	D 1772	Tanner	4
Müller, Veit	E 1769[b]	Tavernkeeper	4/5
Reitenauer, Nicolaus	D 1769	Smith	3
Roemele, Friedrich	D 1769	Wheelwright	4
Rudesill, Melchior	D 1769	Saddler	4
Schindel, Michael	D 1769	Tailor	4
Schlauch, Matthias	D 1773	Shopkeeper	1
Schmidt, Christian	D 1769	Butcher	5/6
Schneider, Mathias	D 1775	Mason	7
Schwartz, Conrad	D 1771	Saddler	6/7
Stahl, Jacob	D 1775	Tailor	6/7
Weidele, Christian	D 1770	Potter	5/6
Yentz, Jacob	D 1774	Butcher	5/6
Zehmer, Anton	D 1769	Stiller	2

*Under the new church constitution.

Residents of other townships

Name	Office and year of election	Township	Landholdings on 1773 tax list
Brenner, Gerhard	E 1769	Manor Twp.	300 acres
Rody, Daniel	E 1769	Manheim Twp.	150 acres

ABBREVIATIONS: T = trustee, E = elder, D = deacon.

SOURCES: Trinity Lutheran Church Documents, vol. 7, pp. 103:123, 130, 134, 136–37, 148, Trinity Lutheran Church Archives, Lancaster, Pa.; Tappert and Doberstein, *Journals of Henry Melchior Muhlenberg*, 2:428.

NOTE: The occupational information is taken from the 1773 borough tax list printed in Egle, *Pennsylvania Archives*, 17:454–63. The position of the church officers on the town's wealth scale has been calculated from the same source. For the landholdings of the two men who lived outside Lancaster, see ibid., 400, 430.

[a] The tax list gives his occupation as coppersmith.

[b] He was reelected in 1773.

1786, embodied continuity. In 1762 the school had "from fifty to sixty children in summer, but from eighty to ninety in winter. It is supported by the congregation itself, without outside assistance." Loeser was reputed to be "a ready and gifted man, who would be well capable of still more important service." After Mühlenberg had visited the school in 1767, he wrote: "Not all the school children were there because the harvest season happened to be at its height, but we found a fine group of children who were well instructed in spelling, reading, writing, and singing." In addition to teaching, Loeser played the organ and conducted the singing during services, opened and closed the church, and oversaw the graveyard. His popularity is highlighted by the fact that several German testators appointed their "trusted friend" Jacob Loeser as executors of their wills.[118]

While the congregation appeared to be outwardly flourishing, pastor Helmuth was concerned about the spiritual state of his parishioners. In a report to Europe written in 1771, Helmuth claimed that most members of his congregation were unfamiliar with "true conversion." By the end of the next year, however, he noticed "an enormously blessed awakening" among the Lancaster Lutherans. In a manner resembling Otterbein's work among the German Reformed two decades earlier, Helmuth now sought to monitor access to the communion table and reserve the Lord's Supper for the truly converted and awakened. Initially, he announced communion services two weeks in advance and held interviews with prospective communicants in the mornings on a voluntary basis. To Helmuth's dismay, however, a number of religiously indifferent or even "wicked" persons still participated in communion and disregarded the "very good church order" that Mühlenberg had introduced. Helmuth therefore went a step further and requested those who were willing to be members and participate in communion to register their names with him. Although members of the council warned Helmuth that the people of Pennsylvania did not like to have their names registered and might regard this as a bond, a "Stamp Act," or a Moravian practice, the pastor got almost thirteen hundred Lutherans to have their names registered. Helmuth then announced that new members would hitherto be registered on the first Wednesday in September of each year, while "obvious sinners" who did

118. *Documentary History of the Lutheran Ministerium*, 63; Tappert and Doberstein, *Journals of Henry Melchior Muhlenberg*, 2:344; Ellis and Evans, *History of Lancaster County,* 403, 440; Schmauk, "Lutheran Church," 327; Harbold, "Schools and Education," 1; Wood, *Conestoga Crossroads,* 218. See the wills of Christian Peterson (probated 1760), Johannes Utzmann (probated 1764), and Gerhard Brenner (probated 1774) in Lancaster County Will Books B-I-326, C-I-99, and C-I-127, Pennsylvania State Archives; Lancaster County Orphans Court Records, 1776–82, p. 233, December 8, 1779, Pennsylvania State Archives.

not heed admonitions to reform themselves would be publicly proclaimed and struck from the membership list on the first Wednesday in October.[119]

In his next reports to Europe, Helmuth observed that the awakening progressed under his vigorous leadership. He began to conduct mandatory interviews with his communicants on their spiritual state, some of which lasted up to an hour. This innovation met with opposition, and unrest in the congregation grew when some of his followers assembled for private prayer meetings and Bible readings, which were interpreted as pietist conventicles or even as the beginnings of a new sect. According to Helmuth, opponents started to throw rocks against the windows of houses where the "pietists" had assembled and shouted insults at them. The pastor had not initiated these meetings and did not participate in them but encouraged and defended them. Helmuth wrote that he found himself confronted with rumors and even challenges from council members that he was promoting separatist tendencies. While these attacks saddened him, Helmuth deemed them understandable in the light of the Moravian schism that had split the congregation in the 1740s and was still vivid in the minds of older members. Though Helmuth was able to restore unity, the young pastor regarded the crisis as a valuable lesson on the vicissitudes of a ministry in Pennsylvania. He considered the "main harvest" in Lancaster to be finished by 1773 but still expected to reap some souls in the countryside.[120]

Like the German Reformed, the Lutherans experienced significant growth during the colonial period. If Helmuth's observations that thirteen hundred members were registered in 1772 and the fifteen hundred seats in the church were filled on many Sundays are accurate, the Lutherans had by far the largest congregation in the town on the eve of American independence. Heavy immigration at midcentury had helped the congregation overcome the painful loss of members caused by the Moravian schism, which had resulted in a small but prosperous and viable Moravian congregation. Lancaster's Lutherans had built a formidable brick church and adorned it with a fine organ. In terms of wealth

119. *Hallesche Nachrichten*, 2:683–84, 689–91. Cf. Schmauk, "Lutheran Church," 334–35; and Splitter, *Pastors, People, Politics*, 60–61.

120. *Hallesche Nachrichten*, 2:691–701; see also J. H. C. Helmuth Diary, entries for August 7, 1772; November 29 and 30, 1772; and February 16, 1773, Lutheran Archives Center, Mount Airy, Pennsylvania. Around that time Helmuth also began to enter remarks on the state of his confirmands in the church records: Mathias Grünn and his sister, for example, seemed "both uninformed," while Michael Reinhardt "appears to have a little beginning of goodness," and Georg Boehler "promised to seek Jesus more seriously than happened" (Smith and Weiser, *Trinity Lutheran Church Records*, 2:255–56).

and prestige as well as in terms of size, they were second only to St. Michael's in Philadelphia among the German Lutheran congregations in Pennsylvania.

This impressive growth had been accompanied by a prolonged quest for stability that resembles the experience of the Lancaster Reformed. Assertive lay leaders had repeatedly opposed attempts to impose stronger ministerial control, and the relationship between the congregation, which was mainly composed of immigrants from southwest Germany, and the Halle-dominated Lutheran Ministerium remained ambivalent. The boundaries between pastoral authority and lay participation were as precarious as the balance between Halle pietism and Swabian Lutheranism. The main source of stability amid the many changes and challenges affecting the congregation, it seems, was the small group of lay leaders that emerged during the Moravian schism and remained extraordinarily influential throughout the remainder of the colonial period. Toward the end of this period, the constitution introduced by Mühlenberg and the energetic pastoral leadership of his younger colleague Helmuth tended to shift authority toward the pastor, but they also reinforced the concern for order and stability that occupied many German-speaking laypeople.

THE MORAVIAN CONGREGATION, 1746–1775

After Laurentius Thorstensson Nyberg and his supporters had left the Lutheran church, they formed their own congregation, which became known as St. Andrew's Moravian Church. Nyberg and Jacob Lischy dedicated St. Andrew's as a "free church" in November 1746, and when the Swedish pastor removed to Bethlehem in 1748, the trustees Georg and Sebastian Graff, Leonhard Bender, and Michael Kraemer wrote to the Moravian headquarters there, requesting a resident minister and the formal establishment of a Moravian congregation. Bethlehem sent another Swedish minister, Abraham Reinke, who arrived in Lancaster in the company of Richard Utley in early 1749 and celebrated the first Lord's Supper on April 15. Although Lutheran and Reformed pastors and some English speakers continued to regard their activities with suspicion, the Moravians embarked on a vigorous course of congregation building. A subscription raised more than £200 for the building of a schoolhouse and parsonage, which were completed in 1750 with the help of the Moravian congregation in Lititz. The congregation was able to discharge the remainder of its debt only four years later. The congregational diary for 1754 also notes the completion of the common hall (*Gemein Saal*), the covering of the pulpit, the purchase of a new clock, the introduction of a regular postal service between Lancaster and Bethlehem, the organization of a church council (*Gemein Rath*), and the distribution of new hymn books. In 1761 the Moravians obtained a lot for their churchyard as a gift from governor and town proprietor James Hamilton. Robert Hartaffel, a member of the congregation, was working on an organ for the church by 1756, but the work proceeded slowly and an impatient church council decided to contract with David Tannenberg for the completion of the instrument in 1762. In 1765 the congregation held a collection to pay for the finished instrument.[121]

After his arrival in 1749, Abraham Reinke drew up a list of twenty "members of the Brethren's congregation in Lancaster" that included eleven men and nine women. Between November 1749 and January 1751, Reinke added six more male and nine female members. A second list of fifty-five men and thirty-nine women compiled in 1749 contained the names of those "attached" to the Brethren—in other words, people who were attending worship services but were not considered full members. Many of these attached people were still single. Finally, twenty-seven boys and twenty-nine girls attended the Brethren's school.[122] The distinction between communicant members of the *Gemeine* and affiliated members of the *Societaet* was crucial in Moravian communities. Whereas Lutherans and German Reformed admitted all who were confirmed and led an orderly life to the Lord's Supper, Moravians limited access to the communion table to those who had been formally examined and admitted. In 1758 the Lancaster congregation had fifty-three communicant members while the total number, including members of the *Societaet* and children, came to 254. Of the three hundred members in 1767, seventy participated in the Eucharist. On the eve of the Revolution, eighty-four of the congregation's 320 members were communicants.[123] The Moravians emphasized that both the *Gemeine* and the *Societaet* were composed of individuals, not families. Each person had to apply for membership individually, and in 1754

121. Kurze Relation von den Anfängen der Brüder Gemeine in Lancaster und derselben gnädiger Entfaltung biß zum Jahre 1772, pp. 9–15, 19, Moravian Archives, Bethlehem, Pennsylvania (hereafter Kurze Relation, Moravian Archives); Lancaster Diaries, 1754, entries for January 26, March 17, July 13, August 23, September 22, and September 25, Moravian Archives; Protocoll vom Lancasterischen Gemein-Rath angefangen den 23. August 1754, entries for September 21, 1754; February 7, 1756; October 23, 1756; November 20. 1757; November 5, 1758; January 20, 1760; March 9, 1760; September 13, 1761; June 6, 1762; September 12, 1762; August 26, 1764; and July 7, 1765, Moravian Archives, Bethlehem, Pennsylvania (hereafter Protocoll, Moravian Archives); J. Max Hark, "The Beginnings of the Moravian Church in Lancaster, Pennsylvania," in *Transactions of the Moravian Historical Society* 11 (1931): 179–86; Coldren and Heisey, "Religious Life," 138; Wood, *Conestoga Crossroads*, 185–87.

122. *Transactions of the Moravian Historical Society* 1 (1858–76): 386–87.

123. Kurze Relation, 22, 24, Moravian Archives; Lancaster Diaries, 1775, "Memorabilien," Moravian Archives.

the church council decided that members and nonmembers were to be buried in separate sections of the graveyard.[124]

Who were the people attracted to the Moravian congregation? Considering that the Moravians had broken away from the Lutheran church, a surprising number of Reformed joined their ranks. Of the seventy men on Reinke's lists, at least a dozen can be identified as people of Reformed origin. They included the former elders John DeHuff and Johann Gorner with their grown sons, Martin Bamberger, and the brothers Jacob and Abraham Gallatin. As noted in the preceding chapter, the Reformed congregation was without a settled minister for several years in the late 1740s, and some defectors returned to the Reformed fold when the charismatic pastor Otterbein served Lancaster in the 1750s. The wealthy DeHuff family, however, remained faithful Moravians throughout the remainder of the eighteenth century.[125] Some of Reinke's parishioners also returned to the Lutheran congregation in the 1750s. The innholder Jacob Eichholtz was affiliated with the United Brethren in 1749, and the Lutheran pastor Handschuh referred to "Eichholtz the Zinzendoerffer." In 1756, however, one of his minor children was buried in the Lutheran graveyard, and Eichholtz himself had a Lutheran funeral in 1760. When he dictated his will shortly before his death he named two prominent Lutherans, the brothers Bernhard and Michael Hubele, as executors.[126] The glazier David Dressler, who was affiliated with the Moravians in 1749, was likewise buried in the Lutheran graveyard when he died five years later.[127]

But most Lutherans who had decided to follow Nyberg's lead and left the congregation in 1746 remained faithful Moravians. Members of the wealthy Graff family continued to play an important role in the affairs of the congregation. Tobias Riem, an immigrant from Theisbergstegen in the Palatinate who was reared in the Reformed faith but "was awakened in Br. Neuberg's time" and became a member of the Brethren, was buried in the Moravian congregation in 1775. Georg Schenk, a native of the margravate of Ansbach, was another early follower of Nyberg who remained a stalwart Moravian until his death in 1777. Leonhard Bender, who had sided with Nyberg in 1746, died as a Moravian in 1779, and Marcus Jung, brother of the suicide Matthäus Jung, was a leading

124. Protocoll, entries for October 21, 1754, and April 16, 1755, Moravian Archives.
125. See chapter 1.
126. Smith and Weiser, *Trinity Lutheran Church Records*, 1:293, 305, 334; Lancaster County Will Book B-I-407, Pennsylvania State Archives; cf. Janice Eichholtz-Rodriguez, "The Lancaster of Leonard Eichholtz, 1750–1817," *JLCHS* 79 (1975): 175–207, esp. 176.
127. Smith and Weiser, *Trinity Lutheran Church Records*, 1:290. For other examples of Lutherans returning from the Moravians, see ibid., 330, 338, 344; *Hallesche Nachrichten*, 1:535, 538, 541, and 2:60.

member of the congregation until his death in 1796. Jung's identification with the United Brethren is revealed in his estate inventory, which included, in addition to a large folio Bible and Bunyan's *Pilgrim's Progress*, David Cranz's *History of Greenland* (a two-volume work about the Moravian missions to the Inuit), a Zinzendorf text on Luther, and the *Bohemian Protestation against the Council of Constance*.[128] The saddler Johann Georg Schwartz, a native of Neckargemünd in the Palatinate who had come to America in 1743 and joined the Moravians when he was in his late twenties, remained a faithful member of the United Brethren until his death in 1800, more than half a century after the schism occurred in the Lutheran congregation.[129] Finally, the smith Johannes Eberman, who had migrated from Schwaigern in the Kraichgau to Pennsylvania with his family in 1732, found his way into the Moravian community by midcentury and was affiliated with it until his death in 1805.[130]

The Moravian congregation was sustained not only by the offspring of the original members but by migration as well. Jacob Vetter, a Reformed immigrant from the Palatinate who had come to Pennsylvania in 1729, was "awakened through the preaching of the blessed Disciple" Nikolaus von Zinzendorf in 1741 and lived in Bethlehem for seven years before moving to Lancaster in 1750. He died there in 1777. The clockmaker Rudy Stoner (1728–69) came to Lancaster in 1755 and established close relations with the DeHuff family, whose church he joined about 1760. Christopher Demuth, the son of an early Moravian immigrant from Herrnhut who had come to America in the 1730s, took up residence in Lancaster in 1767 and established a tobacco shop there.[131] Although the Moravian congregation was primarily made up of German speakers, a few prominent English-speaking residents joined their ranks.[132]

Since the Moravian church conceived itself as a missionary church and was expanding its field of activity to western Pennsylvania, Maryland, and North Carolina throughout the 1750s and 1760s, the pastors who served Lancaster were frequently transferred to other places. The congregation therefore experienced a frequent turnover of ministers. Abraham Reinke was succeeded by Georg Neisser

128. *Moravian Burial Book*, 11–13, 24; Marcus Young Estate Inventory, 1796, Lancaster County Historical Society.

129. Burgert, *Kraichgau*, 335–36; *Moravian Burial Book*, 26.

130. Burgert, *Kraichgau*, 96–97; Stacy B. C. Wood Jr., "A John Eberman Legacy: Eight Lancaster, Pennsylvania, Clockmakers," *JLCHS* 91 (1987/88): 90–128, esp. 90–94.

131. *Moravian Burial Book*, 12; Stacy B. C. Wood Jr., "Rudy Stoner, 1728–1769: Early Lancaster, Pennsylvania, Clockmaker," *JLCHS* 80 (1976): 112–27; Miloslav Rechcigl Jr., "The Demuth Genealogy Revisited: A Moravian Brethren Family from Czechoslovakia," *JLCHS* 92 (1989/90): 55–67, esp. 58–60.

132. See Chapters 4 and 6.

(1750–53), Anton Wagner (1753), Otto Krogstrup (1753–55), Christian Russmeyer (1755–57 and 1758), Karl G. Rundt (1757–58), Christian Bader (1758–62), Russmeyer again (1762–66), and Andrew Langgaard (1766–72). On the eve of the Revolution, Otto Krogstrup returned to Lancaster. Eight different men can thus be identified as regular pastors during the thirty-year period from the congregation's founding to the American Revolution.[133] Meanwhile the stability of the congregation and its integration into the network of Moravian communities and missions in North America were promoted by the visits of Moravian bishops and leading members of the communities at Lititz and Bethlehem. Matthäus Gottfried Hehl and Nathaniel Seidel were frequent visitors throughout the 1750s and 1760s, but the diaries also recorded visits from Johann Cammerhoff (1751), August Gottlieb Spangenberg (1761), and Johann Ettwein (1771).[134] The Lancaster congregation also contributed to projects in other communities. In 1757 its members subscribed £50 toward the building of two choir houses in Lititz, and in subsequent years they repeatedly collected money to help defray the debts of the Bethlehem *Societaet*, support the widows' choir in Bethlehem, and promote the Indian missions.[135]

Like other Moravian communities in the Old and New Worlds, the Lancaster congregation kept an extensive written record of its day-to-day activities, and the annual diaries and church council protocols reveal the features of their congregational life in considerable detail. Under Zinzendorf's leadership, the United Brethren had constructed an "intricate round of devotional services," in which daily and weekly devotions, monthly communion services, and annual festivals interlocked and built on each other.[136] The devotional life of the Lancaster Moravians adapted the ritual life of communities such as Bethlehem in somewhat attenuated form. Events of central importance were the six to eight annual communions and the "love feasts," which were held after the Lord's Supper or

---

133. Kurze Relation, 15–24, Moravian Archives. The list of Moravian pastors in Ellis and Evans, *History of Lancaster County,* 471, is inaccurate, especially since it does not distinguish regular pastors from pastoral helpers, traveling ministers, and temporary supplies.

134. Kurze Relation, 15–26, Moravian Archives.

135. Lancaster Diaries, 1761, entry for May 3, Moravian Archives; Protocoll, entries for September, 18, 1757; February 11, 1759; May 27, 1759; August 31, 1760; April 25, 1762; February 6, 1763; October 23, 1763; July 3, 1764; February 17, 1765; May 25, 1766; February 15, 1767; July 19, 1767; December 13, 1767; and April 10, 1768, Moravian Archives; Kurze Relation, 23, Moravian Archives. The Moravian church in Germany had accumulated heavy debts during the 1740s and 1750s, and as creditors called these after Nikolaus von Zinzendorf's death in 1760, all Moravian congregations in the Old and New Worlds were required to contribute toward their liquidation (see Smaby, *Transformation of Moravian Bethlehem,* 32, 36).

136. Smaby, *Transformation of Moravian Bethlehem,* 14–21. Cf. Atwood, *Community of the Cross,* 148–70.

on the occasion of visits from other communities. Since Lancaster never was a communal mission like Bethlehem, it did not formally organize its members into separate "choirs" by age, sex, and marital status. On a more modest scale, however, separate meetings of single men and women were held. In 1752 twenty single men came together for a separate meeting in February, and eighteen unmarried women had a "love feast" with two visiting sisters from Warwick in April. November 27, 1753, marked the first celebration of the "elders' feast" (*Ältestenfest*), and a year later the first "congregational day" (*Gemeintag*) was held. On these days, readings from the *Gemeinnachrichten*, reports and biographies from Moravian communities and missions all over the world, affirmed and strengthened the bonds of the local congregation to the larger Unitas Fratrum.[137] In a typical year, 1761, the congregation celebrated seven communions, eight *Gemeintage*, twenty-eight love feasts, the Mother Festival of the Holy Spirit (*Mutterfest*), the *Gemeinfest* celebrating the founding of the congregation, and the elders' feast, while the church council met eleven times.[138]

In accordance with their strong communal ethos, Moravian communities such as Herrnhut in Saxony and Bethlehem closely monitored the spiritual and temporal life of their members. During the first two decades of its existence, Bethlehem formed a general economy in which property was held in common and members contributed all their labor to the community. A congregation like Lancaster, which was made up of nuclear families living in separate households, could not exercise the same kind of oversight, but the protocols of the elders' conference and church council demonstrate that these governing bodies did use admonition, counsel, and threats of expulsion to influence members' conduct and economic behavior. At least in the early years of the congregation the elders' conference resorted to the Moravian practice of drawing lots to decide applications for membership, and members were required to submit economic decisions such as the sale of real estate or the borrowing of money to the church council for approval. When Johannes Eberman announced his intention to start "a little shop" in December 1754, the council agreed only hesitantly and urged him to stay out of debt. A few weeks later the council approved Jacob Gallatin's plan to sell his house in order to liquidate his debts, and in June 1755 it warned the indebted Tobias Riem against entering the "difficult and dangerous" business of

137. Lancaster Diaries, 1752, entries for February 16/27 and April 15/26, Moravian Archives; Lancaster Diaries, 1753, entry for November 17, Moravian Archives; Lancaster Diaries, 1754, entry for November 3, Moravian Archives. Cf. Smaby, *Transformation of Moravian Bethlehem*, 16–17.

138. Lancaster Diaries, 1761, Moravian Archives. On the *Mutterfest*, see Atwood, *Community of the Cross*, 155–56.

tavern keeping. In 1757 Gallatin and Riem were reproached for taking renters into their houses without informing the council.[139]

These interferences into the private lives and concerns of individuals were not only motivated by a desire to control the members of the congregation but also reflected a genuine concern for their welfare. Moravians felt obliged to help brothers and sisters in need, and the records show that Lancaster's brethren took these obligations seriously. In October 1754, for example, the council decided to support the poor member Michael Kraemer. In 1757 it granted financial aid to the "poor sister Koch." When the Quaker Isaac Whitelock got the Moravian Johann Georg Schwartz into debtor's prison, several council members pledged to help Schwartz get rid of his debts. In March 1756 all members who ran into economic difficulties were urged to turn to the council for advice, and brethren who had an argument were to request the arbitration of two or three council members. The dual concern for the discipline and welfare of congregation members became especially evident when Sebastian Graff proposed in 1758 that the council look after the affairs of widows and orphans "more precisely and carefully." Graff pointed to the example of the orphan boy Andreas Balsbach, whose stepfather and only guardian had just remarried after the mother's death. Since the boy would soon turn twelve years old, the brethren decided to take him under their care. Graff and Johannes Eberman, whom the Orphans Court appointed as guardians, promised to see to it that Andreas Balsbach started an apprenticeship with a local artisan.[140]

In the competitive religious environment of colonial Lancaster, Moravians selectively adapted the complex sets of rules governing religious, social, and economic life in closed Moravian communities such as Herrnhut and Bethlehem. The communal economy and the choir system characterizing these communities could be replicated only in rudimentary form. Still, Lancaster became an integral part of the far-flung Moravian network of travel and correspondence linking the communities in New York, Pennsylvania, Maryland, and North Carolina, and readings from missionary diaries during the *Gemeintage* continued to remind Lancaster Moravians that they belonged to a church with a worldwide

139. Lancaster Elders Conference, 1753–1804, entries for April 6–8, 1754; July 16–18, 1754; and May 19, 1764, Moravian Archives Bethlehem, Pennsylvania; Protocoll, entries for December 14, 1754, January 3, 1755, June 28, 1755, and November 20, 1757, Moravian Archives. See also entries for August 2, 1755; July 23, 1757; June 1, 1760; and June 22, 1760. On the exercise of discipline and control in the Bethlehem community, see Smaby, *Transformation of Moravian Bethlehem*, 22–24.

140. Protocoll, entries for October 23, 1754; April 10, 1756; March 3, 1756; May 8, 1756; March 6, 1757; March 31, 1757; April 29, 1757; May 21, 1758; and September 10, 1758, Moravian Archives.

mission.[141] In their emphasis on personal piety, congregational ritual, and communal responsibility, the Moravians added a distinct element to the pluralistic religious landscape of this colonial town.

CONCLUSION

Heeding historian Jon Butler's challenge to "pay more attention to the multiplicity of religious choices exercised by individuals within and outside churches," this chapter has shown that most German speakers in colonial Lancaster did have to make a choice after the split within the Lutheran church and the establishment of a Moravian church in the 1740s.[142] Their decisions eventually gave shape to two very different religious communities. For the Lutheran congregation, which absorbed large numbers of recent immigrants at midcentury, the main concerns were the accommodation of rapid growth and the relationship with the Lutheran Ministerium of Pennsylvania, which was dominated by pastors from Halle. While the Lancaster Lutherans remained largely independent of ministerial control until the 1770s, the smaller and more tightly organized Moravian congregation was firmly integrated into a hierarchical organization tying Lancaster to the transatlantic network of Moravian communities. The local autonomy and inclusiveness of Trinity Lutheran Church therefore contrasts sharply with the outside supervision and exclusiveness that characterized St. Andrew's Moravian Church. The development of these two different strands of German Protestant pietism within the same community is all the more remarkable in the light of the common origins of the immigrants who eventually joined the Lutheran and Moravian folds. The large, flourishing, increasingly prosperous but occasionally tumultuous congregation that worshipped in Trinity Lutheran Church and the smaller, close-knit, financially secure and highly disciplined Moravian church therefore constitute two variations on the themes of order, growth, and lay participation that lie at the heart of Lancaster's religious history in the eighteenth century. These variations illuminate the breadth of individual and congregational religious experience within a single Pennsylvania town.

141. Cf. Atwood, *Community of the Cross*, 3.
142. Butler, *Future of American Religious History*, 167–83 (quote on 178).

3

THE ENGLISH CHURCHES OF COLONIAL LANCASTER

English speakers were a minority among the town's inhabitants in the colonial period, they were as divided confessionally as the German-speaking population, and they organized congregations later than their German neighbors. In the Conestoga Valley as in the Penn family's province as a whole, the Church of England constituted "one denomination among many."[1] St. James' Anglican Church in Lancaster was formed in 1744, and the Presbyterians did not build their own church until the 1760s. In addition, the few Quaker families built a meeting-house that was associated with the Sadsbury Monthly Meeting. Compared to their Lutheran and Reformed colleagues, the Anglican pastors tended small flocks. While the Lutheran pastor Johann Friedrich Handschuh recorded the names of 242 people in preparation for Easter communion in April 1750 and noted that there were "many more who communed without announcing their intention," the Anglican minister George Craig reported merely twenty-four communicants on Christmas Day 1751. Eight years later his successor, Thomas Barton, counted about fifty communicants.[2]

Although their congregations were much smaller than those of their Lutheran and German Reformed neighbors, some English speakers were disproportionately

1. John Frederick Woolverton, *Colonial Anglicanism in North America* (Detroit: Wayne State University Press, 1984), 135.

2. Smith and Weiser, *Trinity Lutheran Church Records*, 1:351–57; Benjamin F. Owen, "Letters of the Rev. Richard Locke and Rev. George Craig, Missionaries in Pennsylvania of the 'Society for Propagating the Gospel in Foreign Parts,' London, 1746–1752," *PMHB* 24 (1900): 478; Perry, *Historical Collections*, 2:283.

influential on account of their wealth, political connections, and knowledge of the English legal system. While the vast majority of early German residents were immigrants, English speakers often came from established colonial families and used their superior social ties to their advantage. As the following account of the English-speaking congregations will demonstrate, moreover, their early histories show some remarkable similarities to the German congregations. The English as well as the German churches moved from fledgling beginnings in the middle decades of the eighteenth century to order and stability on the eve of the American Revolution, and both experienced similar conflicts between ministers and laymen along the way. The experience of the English-speaking congregations, therefore, helps put the case of the German churches in perspective and highlights the common problems and experiences of Protestant communities in a pluralistic colonial environment. The search for order, stability, and the proper distribution of power and authority between pastors and people characterized both of Lancaster's major ethnic groups during the colonial period.

ANGLICANS

Like the German Lutherans and Reformed, the Anglicans in Pennsylvania depended on ministers who were trained and ordained in Europe and received at least part of their salaries from there. For the first fourteen years of the town's existence, no such minister was available to its Anglican inhabitants, and they had to content themselves with occasional visits from itinerants who ministered to members of the Church of England in the Conestoga Valley since the late 1720s.[3] The Reverend Richard Locke, who became Lancaster's first Anglican pastor in 1744, seems to have ended up in the Pennsylvania backcountry by accident rather than design. According to a letter he sent to the secretary of the Society for the Propagation of the Gospel in Foreign Parts (SPG) in London, Locke originally sailed to "Barmudas" in 1743 but left the island after eight months because the salary did not meet his expectations and the inhabitants had "neither Bread nor Water only Rain Water." On the advice of the governor, Locke took a ship passage to Charleston, South Carolina, "but the Captain a villain carryed me to Philadelphia." As the war with France known as King George's War was just breaking out and Locke's wife, "being a weak woman," could not be persuaded to return to England, he decided to stay in Pennsylvania

3. Perry, *Historical Collections*, 2:161–62, 167; Ellis and Evans, *History of Lancaster County*, 464.

even though he did not like what he saw there. Like many of his Lutheran and German Reformed counterparts, Locke was bewildered by the multitude of ethnic and religious groups surrounding him.[4] After he had "accidentally" come "into this our Borough," the earliest vestry minutes note, the Anglican inhabitants "agreed to give him what Encouragement we could for his Residence amongst us." Though "destitute of any Sett Place of Worship for performing ye Divine Service of ye Church of England, & Its Members here but very few," Lancaster's Anglicans seized the opportunity to secure a resident minister. "In order to Keep up & maintain ye polity or Government of ye Church," a congregation was organized and church wardens and vestrymen were elected on October 3, 1744. Town proprietor James Hamilton gave three lots to St. James' Church and started a subscription for the construction of a church building. Meanwhile, the small congregation worshipped in the courthouse.[5]

Even after he received an appointment from the SPG as an itinerant minister for Pennsylvania and New Jersey in the summer of 1746, Richard Locke retained his home base in Lancaster, where he preached every other Sunday. "I have had nine Communicants at one time," he reported to London in October 1746, "and have baptised abundance brought from ye Country, several whole Families." In addition, he served Bangor Church, an Anglican congregation in eastern Lancaster County that was mostly made up of Welsh settlers, visited communities across the Susquehanna, and organized churches in present-day Huntington and Adams counties.[6] While Locke was gradually expanding his missionary activities in the Pennsylvania backcountry, the church building project launched in Lancaster in 1744 languished. One of the first wardens, chief burgess Thomas Cookson, had been chosen to receive subscriptions and pay the workmen and had raised additional funds amounting to more than £60 for the completion of the roof among his friends in Philadelphia, including Governor George Thomas, Richard Peters, Edward and Joseph Shippen, and Andrew and James Hamilton. Still, "ye Congregation being small & many of them in low Circumstances," resources were too limited and the building remained unfinished. Locke blamed the delay on "mismanagement" and on "ye leading men being too much

4. Owen, "Letters of the Rev. Richard Locke and Rev. George Craig," 467; see also Worner, "Church of England (Part II)," 79.

5. St. James Vestry Minutes, 1, St. James Episcopal Church; Ellis and Evans, *History of Lancaster County*, 464–65; Worner, "Church of England (Part II)," 80, 85–86; Coldren and Heisey, "Religious Life," 134; William F. Diller and Harry M. J. Klein, *The History of St. James' Church (Protestant Episcopal), 1744–1944* (Lancaster, Pa.: St. James Church Vestry, 1944), 12–13; Wood, *Conestoga Crossroads*, 182.

6. Owen, "Letters of the Rev. Richard Locke and Rev. George Craig," 467–71; Worner, "Church of England (Part II)," 83–85; Diller and Klein, *History of St. James' Church*, 14–16.

inclined to the new Lights, that they have run the Parish in Debt." The mounting cost of church building and Locke's frequent absences caused relations between the pastor and the congregation, which by now counted thirty-three communicants, to deteriorate. Looking back on a pastorate of three years, Locke stated that he had "not received £ 20. & have had neither surplis or Common Prayer Book, but what I carry in my pocket." In April 1747, he complained that he had "met wth very severe and hard usage" from public officials who were biased against the Church of England, and in September 1748 he reported to London that he was still living in the town, "as there is no clergyman near that place, tho' I meet with a great deal of opposition." He expressed his hope that "the Society will not be offended if I take the first opportunity of returning home" and left Lancaster shortly afterward.[7]

Locke's situation in 1748 strikingly resembles that of some early Lutheran and Reformed pastors. The financial burdens associated with church-building and salary payments, the laypeople's claims on the pastor's time, and dissatisfaction with his doctrinal views caused a rift in the congregation that the minister was unable to overcome. While it is difficult to ascertain whether the "leading men" were actually "inclined to the new Lights," as the minister claimed, there is evidence that several prominent Anglican laymen did not attend Locke's services and preferred the Swedish Lutheran pastor Laurence Thorstensson Nyberg, whose preaching gifts the Moravian leaders in Bethlehem compared to George Whitefield's. During Locke's tenure in Lancaster, Anglicans George Duke and Thomas Cookson let Nyberg baptize their children.[8]

A closer look at lay leadership during Locke's ministry shows that, like their Lutheran and Reformed counterparts, early Anglican leaders were actively striving for wealth and recognition and asserting their interests. Ten men are mentioned as leaders during the congregation's first years of existence. Thomas Cookson and John Postlethwait became wardens, while William Bristow, John Connolly, John Foulk, Morgan Morgan, Edward Smout, and Daniel Syng were elected vestrymen in 1744; Patrick Carrigan and Edward Taylor joined the vestry in 1745.[9] Several of these men held public office in the borough and county and

7. St. James Vestry Minutes, 3–4, St. James Episcopal Church; Owen, "Letters of the Rev. Richard Locke and Rev. George Craig," 467, 469, 472–74; Perry, *Historical Collections*, 2:252–53; Worner, "Church of England (Part II)," 81–83, 87–92; Diller and Klein, *History of St. James' Church*, 13–16; Wood, *Conestoga Crossroads*, 183, 197–98.

8. Worner, "Church of England (Part II)," 82; Smith and Weiser, *Trinity Lutheran Church Records*, 1:433.

9. St. James Vestry Minutes, 1, St. James Episcopal Church; Worner, "Church of England (Part II)," 80–81; Diller and Klein, *History of St. James' Church*, 13.

acquired substantial real estate. Thomas Cookson (1710–53), certainly the most prominent among the early Anglican leaders, became chief burgess in 1742 and held that office again from 1745 to 1749, while John Foulk served as assistant burgess from 1742 to 1744. Moreover, Cookson, who originally came from Sunderland in the county of Durham, England, had been appointed justice of the peace in 1738, became prothonotary and registrar of deeds for Lancaster County in 1744 and was a surveyor for the proprietors, while William Bristow, Edward Smout, and John Postlethwaite were appointed auditors of court in 1745. Smout was a justice of the peace for many years and served on several commissions.[10]

Several Anglican leaders frequently appear in property records. By the mid-1740s, Thomas Cookson, John Foulk, and Edward Smout had acquired town lots, while Smout, Cookson, John Connolly, and Patrick Carrigan obtained warrants to large tracts of land in the countryside.[11] Smout repeatedly advertised land for sale in English- and German-language newspapers.[12] John Postlethwaite is mentioned as an innkeeper as early as 1729. When his farm in Conestoga Township was advertised for sale after his death in 1750, it included a water gristmill, a sawmill, and £50 acres of good land."[13] In the will he dictated in 1747, John Connolly bequeathed £50 of Pennsylvania currency to each of his three siblings in Ireland if they should come to America and declared that the expenses of their passage should be paid from his estate.[14] The tanner John Foulk had an indentured servant from Ireland assigned to him in 1746; when

---

10. Ellis and Evans, *History of Lancaster County*, 362, 373; Heisey, "Borough Fathers," 47, 59; Mayhill, *Deed Abstracts*, 18 (B315); Wood, *Conestoga Crossroads*, 18, 30, 175.

11. Heisey, "Borough Fathers," 47, 50, 59. Smout: several hundred acres in Hempfield Manor and 200 acres near the Susquehanna, December 29, 1736; 250 acres on Bermudian Creek, September 16, 1742; 50 acres in Donegal Township, January 7, 1744; 150 acres on Bermudian Creek, July 20, 1747 (Warrant Register, vol. 16, p. 196, no. 320; p. 197, no. 214; p. 201, no. 525; p. 261, no. 27, Pennsylvania State Archives). Cookson: 200 acres in Heidelberg Township, January 10, 1744; 50 acres in Manheim Township, April 6, 1744 (ibid., p. 35, nos. 245, 254). In a letter to colonial proprietor Thomas Penn, Cookson stated in 1749 that he had purchased 1,400 acres on the Susquehanna River and wished to buy an additional 200 acres on a river island (Cookson to Penn, December 4, 1749, Lancaster County MSS, vol. 1, 1724–72, p. 65). Connolly: 150 acres on Conestoga Creek, January 12, 1744; 150 acres in Lebanon Township, April 6, 1744; three 150-acre tracts on Conestoga Creek, May 22, 1744; 150 acres west of the Susquehanna, December 12, 1745 (Warrant Register, vol. 16, p. 35, nos. 238, 246, 249–51, and p. 36, no. 272, Pennsylvania State Archives). Carrigan: 200 acres on Little Conestoga Creek, May 19, 1742; 200 acres in Earl Township, November 30, 1751 (ibid., p. 34, no. 204, and p. 40, no. 403). At the time of his death in 1756, Carrigan owned 700 acres in Leacock and Earl townships (Lancaster County Orphans Court Records, 1763–67, pp. 117–19, December 27, 1764, Pennsylvania State Archives; see also pp. 103–4, 130–31, 174, 203, 215, 237, 263–65).

12. *Pennsylvania Gazette*, January 15, 1745, and October 3, 1745; *Pensylvanische Berichte*, December 16, 1748; May 1, 1750.

13. Wood, *Conestoga Crossroads*, 9, 17; *Pennsylvania Gazette*, April 26, 1750.

14. Lancaster County Will Book A-I-141, Pennsylvania State Archives.

he made his will the next year in the presence of the Reverend Richard Locke and other witnesses, he mentioned four properties in and near Lancaster and a tract called "the point." Foulk also valued his books, for he ordered them to be divided equally among his two sons.[15]

When he made his will in 1751, Edward Smout, "Gentleman," conveyed three houses in Lancaster, a house in Trenton, New Jersey, two slaves, and various sums to his wife and a number of relatives. In addition, he ordered his four-hundred-acre tract in Manchester Township, York County, to be sold and half of the proceeds to be applied "towards the repairing and Glazeing the Church of England in the Borough" of Lancaster. The other half was to go to the Moravian congregation, with which Smout had established close relations during his final years. Smout's personal estate, consisting mostly of bonds, notes, and cash, came to £978.[16] The administration account of John Connolly revealed a balance of more than £980 in 1753, and Patrick Carrigan's personal belongings were valued at £1,172 three years later.[17] Their material success enabled these men to contribute substantial sums to the subscription for the Anglican church building. All the early lay leaders were among the thirty people who pledged a total of £114 and four shillings. Thomas Cookson alone contributed £35, nearly a third of the total, while seven vestrymen promised £5 to £6 each. Only William Bristow and Daniel Syng could merely afford £2. Syng, the son of a Philadelphia silversmith, seems to have come to Lancaster only recently and was merely thirty-two years old when he died in 1745.[18]

Although the Reverend Richard Locke may have shared some of the business drive of these lay leaders—he acquired a plot of land near the borough for £10 in 1745 and sold it for a handsome £120 in 1748—the leading parishioners did not respect his authority. According to Locke's colleague at Pequea, Richard Backhouse, several prominent laymen, "who are got into commissions in the government, and who have not religion much at heart," actually "despise[d] Mr. Locke . . . and never

15. Neible, "Account of Servants (1907)," 462; Lancaster County Will Book I-I-138, Pennsylvania State Archives; Wood, *Conestoga Crossroads*, 11. Wood erroneously identified Foulk as a Quaker (ibid., 123). Edward Smout advertised Foulk's properties for sale in the *Pennsylvania Gazette* on September 15, 1748, noting that "on one of them is a house, and a very good tan yard" (cf. also *Pennsylvania Gazette*, May 28, July 18, July 23, 1747).

16. Lancaster County Will Book A-I-196, Pennsylvania State Archives; Edward Smout Estate Inventory, 1751, Lancaster County Historical Society.

17. John Connolly Administration Account, 1753, Lancaster County Historical Society; Patrick Carrigan Estate Inventory, 1756, Lancaster County Historical Society.

18. St. James Vestry Minutes, 3–4, St. James Episcopal Church; Worner, "Church of England (Part II)," 86–87; Vivian S. Gerstell, *Silversmiths of Lancaster, Pennsylvania, 1730–1850* (Lancaster, Pa.: Publications of the Lancaster County Historical Society, 1972), 92–93.

go to public worship with him, or maintain a friendly, kind, Christian-like intercourse or correspondence with him." In sum, "these gentlemen of caprice at Lancaster town do not pay a just deference to Mr. Locke, as they ought."[19]

After Richard Locke left, the congregation was without a resident pastor for three years. The SPG had already appointed the Reverend George Craig to succeed Locke as missionary to Pennsylvania and New Jersey in January 1748, but Craig was licensed by the bishop of London only in September 1750 and did not arrive in America before May 1751.[20] Meanwhile the town's Anglicans depended on the services of occasional itinerants or the resident German pastors. While Edward Smout joined the Moravian fold, most Anglicans preferred the services of the Lutheran Johann Friedrich Handschuh, who baptized children of Samuel Price, George Gibson, George Sanderson, Patrick Carrigan, and other members of the Church of England. In July 1749 he buried Thomas Cookson's wife Margaret, who had died in childbirth, "with a large funeral attendance of all kinds of people." The sponsors that Anglican parents chose for the baptisms of their children in the Lutheran church demonstrate a clear preference for their own ethnic and religious group: Price and Gibson picked Thomas Cookson as their sons' godfather, while David Stout, his wife, and Martha Gibson stood as sponsors of George Sanderson's daughter in 1749.[21]

A new opportunity to secure a pastor arose when the congregation learned that George Craig had arrived as a missionary to Pennsylvania and New Jersey "with a Liberty to reside in any part of either Provinces." Craig accepted the invitation to settle in Lancaster after a visit to the town in June 1751, and the congregation opened a new subscription for the completion of the still unfinished church building. Twenty-seven people subscribed a total of slightly more than £100, the largest contributions coming from Governor James Hamilton, Thomas Cookson, and William Jevon. In August 1751, a meeting of church members elected Cookson and Jevon as wardens and chose a board of thirteen vestrymen, and the next year Cookson and Jevon pledged the largest sums for the support of Reverend Craig.[22] Jevon, who had resided in Philadelphia and imported ironmongery and textiles from England in the 1740s, moved to Lancaster around midcentury, where he worked as an attorney and shopkeeper and

19. Worner, "Church of England (Part II)," 80–81, 90–91. Cf. Wood, *Conestoga Crossroads*, 192.

20. Worner, "Church of England (Part III)," 25–26.

21. Smith and Weiser, *Trinity Lutheran Church Records*, 1:72, 73, 77–79, 85, 88, 90, 278.

22. St. James Vestry Minutes, 4–8, St. James Episcopal Church; Worner, "Church of England (Part III)," 26–30; Diller and Klein, *History of St. James' Church*, 19–20. The pledges for the rector's support amounted to £38 4s.

was among the twenty largest taxpayers in 1751. He remained an important figure in congregational and public affairs into the 1760s, receiving an appointment as justice of the peace in 1761. The fact that in 1762 he brought a lawsuit against Indian trader George Croghan for more than £200 shows that Jevon continued to look out for business opportunities. When he died in 1767, his estate was valued at £1,411. Jevon's household included such items as an "Eight Day clock," mahogany and walnut bookcases, tea tables, china bowls, and silver spoons. His library included the charter and laws of Pennsylvania, legal books, English and American magazines, two English dictionaries, a *History of the Czar of Muscovy*, and a number of theological works. The books in the latter category not only demonstrate a general interest in religious matters but reveal a definite concern with piety and the new birth. Along with a Bible, an *Epistol of the Apostolical Fathers*, a *Divine Dialogue*, and *The General Dilection of the Christians*, Jevon owned a three-volume edition of Johann Arndt's *True Christianity*, William Laid's *The Generation of the New Birth*, and "Tenant's Sermon," possibly Gilbert Tennent's famous 1741 sermon on *The Danger of an Unconverted Ministry*. Since Jevon died childless, the beneficiaries were his wife, his former bookkeeper, and three nieces in England.[23]

Several other men who joined the vestry in 1751 were important figures in the town. The tavernkeeper George Gibson, who became a warden in 1753, engaged in land speculation and paid the seventh-highest property tax in the borough at midcentury.[24] The physician Dr. Samuel Boudé, who was repeatedly chosen as church warden from 1753 to 1761, was elected burgess in 1755, served as chief burgess for three years, and became a county coroner in 1759. He owned substantial real estate and, together with the Jewish merchant Joseph Simon, engaged in the manufacture of potash. After 1763 he apparently moved to Cecil County, Maryland.[25] David Stout, town clerk from 1757 to 1760, was an attorney who

23. *Pennsylvania Gazette*, January 13, 1746/7; September 15, 1748; Lancaster Borough Tax Assessment List, 1751, Lancaster County Historical Society; Mayhill, *Deed Abstracts*, 74 (F239), 144 (L259b); Lancaster County Will Book B-I-531, Pennsylvania State Archives; William Jevon Estate Inventory, 1767, Lancaster County Historical Society; Wood, *Conestoga Crossroads*, 118.

24. St. James Vestry Minutes, 11, St. James Episcopal Church; Diller and Klein, *History of St. James' Church*, 22; Wood, *Conestoga Crossroads*, 117, 174, 206, 213; Mayhill, *Deed Abstracts*, 13 (B138), 22 (B487), 38 (C537); Lancaster County Will Book B-I-515, Pennsylvania State Archives. At midcentury Gibson advertised two houses and lots in Lancaster for sale (*Pensylvanische Berichte*, April 16, 1750; *Pennsylvania Gazette*, June 20 and October 31, 1751). For the assignment of an Irish indentured servant to him in 1746, see Neible, "Account of Servants (1907)," 93.

25. St. James Vestry Minutes, 11, St. James Episcopal Church; *Pennsylvania Gazette*, October 11, 1759; Ellis and Evans, *History of Lancaster County*, 373; Landis, "Juliana Library Company," 243; Diller and Klein, *History of St. James' Church*, 22–24, 31, 36, 38, 52, 326–27; Mayhill, *Deed Abstracts*, 31 (C225),

surveyed and laid out the new town of Manheim for the Stedman brothers of Philadelphia and their partner, the ironmaster Heinrich Wilhelm Stiegel, in 1762. The following year he left his whole estate "both here and in New York Province" to his wife and only son. Stout's personal estate included 120 books—works on law and history, a "French Bible," and sixty-eight French books. At the time of his death, however, Stout was heavily in debt and even the sale of several houses and tracts of land in Lancaster and environs did not suffice to defray his obligations estimated at £1,060 in 1765.[26]

The innkeepers George Sanderson (who was appointed as Lancaster's first town clerk in 1742), Edward Berwick, and John Hart also belonged to the top decile of Lancaster's taxpayers in 1751, while the tax assessments of vestrymen Thomas Butler and Denis Connolly indicate that they were men of more modest means.[27] Matthew Atkinson was a fuller and farm owner in nearby Lampeter Township, while John Murphy was variously referred to as a tanner and a farmer in deed records.[28] Finally, the attorney George Ross (1730–79), who would eventually become a signer of the Declaration of Independence, joined the circle of Anglican lay leaders shortly after midcentury. The son of a Church of England minister from New Castle, Delaware, Ross had studied law in Philadelphia and been admitted to the bar in 1750. His background and education enabled him to establish a flourishing law practice and brought him election to the vestry as early as 1753. He was chosen as church warden the following year.[29]

One of the major concerns of Craig and his congregation was the completion of the church. In June 1752, Craig reported to the SPG that Lancaster had "a very good Stone Church, which will be compleately finished this summer, I

38 (C551), 40 (D33), 43 (D122), 44 (D144), 63 (E118), 70 (F13), 71 (F44), 87 (G349), 117 (I112); Wood, *Conestoga Crossroads*, 32, 134.

26. Ellis and Evans, *History of Lancaster County*, 373; Heiges, *Henry William Stiegel*, 48–49; Lancaster County Will Book C-I-52, Pennsylvania State Archives; David Stout Estate Inventory, 1764, Lancaster County Historical Society; Lancaster County Orphans Court Records, 1763–67, pp. 90–92, 179–81, Pennsylvania State Archives; Wood, *Conestoga Crossroads*, 167, 225.

27. Lancaster Borough Tax Assessment List, 1751, Lancaster County Historical Society. For Sanderson, see Mayhill, *Deed Abstracts*, 12 (B75), 76 (F380); for Berwick's sale of substantial landholdings in Salisbury Township in 1751–53, see ibid., 32 (C244), 38 (C521). John Hart styled himself "merchant" when he sold a town lot in 1746 but was referred to as innholder when he mortgaged another town property to Philadelphia merchants Nathan Levy and David Franks (ibid., 19 [B362], 31 [C196], 117 [I78]).

28. Lancaster County Will Book B-I-148, Pennsylvania State Archives; Mayhill, *Deed Abstracts*, 28 (C44), 39 (D15).

29. St. James Vestry Minutes, 11–12, St. James Episcopal Church; Diller and Klein, *History of St. James' Church*, 22–24, 36, 38, 49, 51; *Dictionary of American Biography* 8, pt. 2, 177–78; Wood, *Conestoga Crossroads*, 118, 167, 176; Rodger C. Henderson, "Ross, George," in *American National Biography*, vol. 18, ed. John A. Garraty and Mark C. Carnes (New York: Oxford University Press, 1999), 911–12.

hope. It would have been so before now, but ye want of a Minister discouraged ye people, which is a common Case in this province."[30] Several weeks later the wardens Cookson and Jevon were asked to purchase materials and employ laborers for the plastering and glazing of the church, and in early January 1753 they reported completion of the work. The building measured forty-four by thirty-four feet and was made of "rough limestone." The vestry then discussed several plans for the construction of a platform for the communion table and the arrangement of the pews. While Thomas Cookson donated the wood for the ground sills of the platform, the members had to build the pews at their own expense. St. James' Anglican Church became the first in Lancaster in which the twenty-four pewholders, five of whom were widows, were assessed for pew rents. Although arrears on rent payments and transfers of pews without the vestry's knowledge soon became a problem, the pew rents were a permanent source of revenue.[31] The following year the vestry appointed the congregation's first sexton, who also officiated as undertaker, and in 1755 it arranged for the completion of the pulpit, communion table, font, and wooden "servant seats." A new subscription drew contributions from twenty-two people, the largest coming from the Philadelphian Richard Peters and minister George Craig.[32]

While Craig resided in Lancaster and took part in the community's affairs, he saw himself primarily as an "itinerant" with "several Congregations to attend."[33] These included St. John's Church at Pequea and Bangor Church in Caernarvon Township as well as congregations in Huntington and Carlisle.[34] By the summer of 1753, however, Craig found himself in ill health and longed for a "settled mission" where he would be relieved from the duties of an itinerant. In response to his request, the SPG transferred him to Lewes (Delaware) and rather insensitively reappointed his predecessor, Richard Locke, to Lancaster and the other backcountry congregations in Pennsylvania. If the society had hoped that the congregation would give Locke a second chance, they soon found out otherwise.

30. Owen, "Letters of the Rev. Richard Locke and Rev. George Craig," 476; cf. Perry, *Historical Collections*, 2:187.

31. St. James Vestry Minutes, 8–14, St. James Episcopal Church; Worner, "Church of England (Part III)," 31–34; Diller and Klein, *History of St. James' Church*, 20.

32. St. James Vestry Minutes, 13–14, St. James Episcopal Church; Worner, "Church of England (Part III)," 38–39; Diller and Klein, *History of St. James' Church*, 22.

33. The Reverend George Craig and James Wright were appointed guardians over Thomas Ewing's son John and John Connolly's son John in September 1753 (Lancaster County Orphans Court Records, vol. 1, pt. 2, p. 63, Pennsylvania State Archives. In the will she made in 1754, Margaret Young named Craig her sole executor (Lancaster County Will Book B-I-65, Pennsylvania State Archives).

34. Owen, "Letters of the Rev. Richard Locke and Rev. George Craig," 476–77; Worner, "Church of England (Part III)," 30–31.

The wardens and vestrymen sent a lengthy petition to the SPG stating that they thought Locke unfit for Lancaster on account of "some unhappy divisions that were, in the time of his late ministry here, between him and several of the principal men of the congregation, which, we have good reason to think, will not subside." The congregation's leaders painted a vivid picture of the church's decline and destitution before Craig's arrival and its revival under his ministry. Not only were they "unanimously joining together and exerting themselves to the utmost of their power in doing all they can for the welfare of the Church," but Craig was laboring so diligently and successfully among them that "several dissenters of different denominations have already become members of the Church of England, and we have an agreeable prospect of more following their example." They therefore asked "that the Rev. Mr. Craig may be continued among us, instead of Mr. Locke." Craig himself declared that he was willing to continue his itinerant mission, while Locke had consented to settle at Lewes instead. Moved by the "affections of the people of all denominations in his itinerant mission," Craig resumed his pastoral activities with renewed vigor in 1754. In letters to Richard Peters in Philadelphia, he requested support for a charter for St. James' Church and referred to the congregation's plans for finishing the altar, constructing a pulpit, and adding a steeple.[35]

Like his predecessor, Richard Locke, however, Craig eventually clashed with the lay leaders over questions of authority. The conflict began in April 1756, when the whole vestry except David Stout opposed Craig's choice of Charles Morse as church warden because "they did not look upon it to be regular as he was not one of the Vestry." While it was agreed that one warden was to be selected by the minister, the other by the vestrymen, "it had been the practice in this church to choose Wardens out of the vestry." Craig remained unconvinced by this line of reasoning—possibly because the vestry had chosen John Clark, who had just become a vestryman on the same day, as their warden—and insisted on his choice. The vestry then withdrew its own candidate and resolved that the two incumbents, George Sanderson and George Ross, should remain in office instead. While Craig consented to this arrangement, a new dispute arose when the vestry charged Craig with making an unauthorized entry into the vestry book. According to the laity, the claim that pew rents were levied "for the Maintainance and Support of the Minister" did not conform to the vestry's intentions. The quarrel over the selection of wardens thus broadened into a struggle

---

35. George Craig to Richard Peters, April 17, 1754, Lancaster County MSS, vol. 1, 1724–72, p. 95; Worner, "Church of England (Part III)," 36–38; Diller and Klein, *History of St. James' Church*, 21–22.

over control of the congregation's finances. In Craig's interpretation, the pew rents should have secured the minister a steady income independent from the whims of the laity, whereas the vestry sought to remain in charge of revenues and expenditures.[36]

The conflict soon extended to the only major legacy that the congregation had received so far, Edward Smout's testamentary bequest of 1751. The sale of Smout's land had yielded £21 and 14s. and this sum was now administered by church warden George Ross. However, the wardens and three vestrymen privately had to give the executors of Smout's will a bond of indemnity because Charles Morse endeavored to prevent the executors from paying the money to the leaders of the congregation "by saying the wardens and vestry had not a right to receive it." As Morse had been Reverend Craig's unsuccessful candidate for the warden's office, this may have been his and Craig's attempt to take revenge on the vestry. In Craig's absence, the congregation elected eight vestrymen on April 1757 and then notified the pastor that he might select one "for his warden." The fact that the former officers were reelected almost to a man—only the fuller Stephen Atkinson was chosen for the first time—signaled that the laity was not prepared to compromise with the minister. Predictably, Craig refused, "not thinking himself obliged to be confined to choose out of the Vestry." The vestry then resolved to abide by "their old and former rules" and chose George Ross and Samuel Boudé as wardens. Since these "old and former rules" were just thirteen years old at the time, the vestry's reference to the power of tradition barely masked the ongoing power struggle. The 1758 election was merely a reenactment of the preceding one: the congregation selected eight men, confirming seven former vestrymen in their positions. When Craig once again refused to make his choice, the vestry confirmed George Ross and Samuel Boudé as wardens. Ross and Boudé were then asked "to waite on Mr. Craige and inform him that the vestry desire to know whether he has any notice of or received orders for his removal to another mission & when." The rift between minister and vestry was now unbridgeable and Craig, who had repeatedly asked the SPG to be transferred to Chester, left Lancaster in 1758, to be replaced by Thomas Barton.[37]

Like similar disputes in the German Reformed and Lutheran churches, Craig's conflict with the vestry centered on issues of authority and control of the

---

36. St. James Vestry Minutes, 14–15, St. James Episcopal Church; Diller and Klein, *History of St. James' Church*, 22–24; Wood, *Conestoga Crossroads*, 192.

37. St. James Vestry Minutes, 15–17, St. James Episcopal Church; Worner, "Church of England (Part III)," 40–41; Diller and Klein, *History of St. James' Church*, 24.

congregation's finances. Like a number of German pastors, George Craig found that harmonious relations among pastor, lay leaders, and congregation could quickly disintegrate once the balance of power between clergy and laity seemed at risk. Craig's experience resembled that of several of his German colleagues in other respects as well: like Johann Friedrich Handschuh, he was a newcomer to America and found that the colonial climate and the pastoral labors in a large geographical area severely taxed his weak constitution. Both men entered the conflicts with their congregations in a physically weakened state. Moreover, like the German Reformed who refused to give Bartholomäus Rieger another try in 1748, Lancaster's Anglicans would not have Richard Locke back after their negative experiences with him. Given the small number of ordained ministers in the colonies, the congregations' intransigence thus limited the alternatives for replacement.

The new Anglican minister Thomas Barton, who held his first service on Easter Sunday 1759 and would remain pastor of the Lancaster, Bangor, and Pequea congregations until the end of the colonial period, was one of the most remarkable figures in the colonial Pennsylvania backcountry. Born in Ireland in 1730, he came from a family of the Anglo-Irish ascendancy in County Monaghan and was educated at Trinity College in Dublin. Barton first arrived in America in 1751 and, after keeping school in the Norristown area for one and a half years, began to teach at the Academy of Philadelphia. In 1753 he married Esther Rittenhouse, a sister of the scientist David Rittenhouse. After returning to England in the fall of 1754, Barton was ordained in January 1755 and appointed by the SPG as minister to the Anglican congregations in York, Cumberland, and Huntington west of the Susquehanna River. Originally interested in an Anglican mission to the American Indians, Barton soon lost his enthusiasm for Pennsylvania's native people when Indian attacks struck backcountry settlements in this early phase of the French and Indian War. He participated in efforts to organize the defense of the frontier and rallied distressed frontier settlers after Braddock's defeat with a sermon entitled *Unanimity and Public Spirit*, which was published in Philadelphia with a foreword by William Smith, provost of the College of Philadelphia and a leader of the Proprietary Party in Pennsylvania politics. Unfortunately for Smith and Barton, word reached Pennsylvania that Barton had plagiarized most of his exhortation to the frontier settlers from a sermon preached by an English clergyman during the Jacobite Rebellion of 1745. According to scholar James P. Myers, the rumors about his plagiarism "tarnished Barton's career and fed his uncommonly profound insecurity." Moreover, the "opprobrium under which he had to continue in his priestly offices must certainly have fueled Barton's determination to leave the Carlisle—Huntington—York circuit." In 1758 he participated as an army chaplain in General Forbes's expedition that captured Fort Duquesne from the French.[38]

In the early 1760s Barton's interest in the Indian missions revived, only to be shattered once again by the bloodshed on the frontier during Pontiac's War. In 1764 he penned an anonymously published pamphlet defending the actions of the Paxton Boys, Scots-Irish backcountry settlers who had murdered peaceful Conestoga Indians in Lancaster and marched on Philadelphia, and attacking Pennsylvania's Quaker-dominated assembly. The pamphleteer's "unmitigated hatred for all Indians" does not seem to fit an author who had repeatedly shown interest in missionary work among Native Americans, and it has been suggested that Barton wrote the pamphlet "under some kind of pressure, or even coercion." Three years later Barton made a final foray into the field of Native American education when he took the half-Mohawk son of the British Indian agent Sir William Johnson into his house for private instruction. The minister's hope that "many Indian Youths would follow the Example & chuse to come to Lancaster" soon proved illusory as the youth turned out to be "the most dissatisfied, sullen, careless Creature imaginable" and wished to return home after a few months in Barton's home. The Anglican pastor also took a lively interest in imperial politics, supporting the idea of a colonial bishop and critically observing the Stamp Act riots in the colonies.[39]

Barton shared at least some of his brother-in-law David Rittenhouse's enthusiasm for science: he purchased books for Rittenhouse in London, kept up a lively correspondence with him on a variety of topics, and acquired glass instruments for his brother-in-law at Heinrich Wilhelm Stiegel's glassworks in Manheim

38. For accounts of Barton's background and early career, see William Barton, *Memoirs of the Life of David Rittenhouse* (Philadelphia: Parker, 1813), 100–102, 111–12; Perry, *Historical Collections*, 2:275–81, 285–86; Diller and Klein, *History of St. James' Church*, 27–30; Theodore W. Jeffries, "Thomas Barton (1730–1780): Victim of the Revolution," *JLCHS* 81 (1977): 39–64, esp. 39–46; Marvin F. Russell, "Thomas Barton and Pennsylvania's Colonial Frontier," *Pennsylvania History* 46 (1979): 313–34, esp. 313–18; James P. Myers Jr., "The Rev. Thomas Barton's Conflict with Colonel John Armstrong, c. 1758," *Cumberland County History* 10 (1993): 3–14. The plagiarism case is reconstructed in James P. Myers Jr., "Thomas Barton's *Unanimity and Public Spirit* (1755): Controversy and Plagiarism on the Pennsylvania Frontier," *PMHB* 119 (1995): 225–48 (quotes on 244).

39. Thomas Barton to Richard Peters, October 2, 1761, July 5 and July 25, 1763, Peters Papers, vol. 5, p. 103, vol. 6, pp. 10, 14, Historical Society of Pennsylvania; Perry, *Historical Collections*, 2:348–49, 401–2, 408; Worner, "Church of England (Part IV)," 60–61, 73–74; Russell, "Thomas Barton," 325–30; Jeffries, "Thomas Barton," 49–52; Diller and Klein, *History of St. James' Church*, 39–41; Robert C. Batchelder, "A Lancaster Footnote in American History," *PLCHS* 64 (1960): 227–33 (quote on 230–31); James P. Myers Jr., "The Rev. Thomas Barton's Authorship of *The Conduct of the Paxton Men, Impartially Represented* (1764)," *Pennsylvania History* 61 (1994): 155–84 (quotes on 163, 176); Nancy L. Rhoden, *Revolutionary Anglicanism: The Colonial Church of England Clergy During the American Revolution* (New York: New York University Press, 1999), 20, 61, 91, 100–101.

near Lancaster. When Rittenhouse and "some other gentlemen of ingenuity and talents" gathered at Norristown to observe the transit of Venus in 1769, Barton joined them "and rendered such assistance as [he] could, to the committee." When the scientist constructed an orrery in the late 1760s, Barton's son William believed that "there was some correspondence and some understanding, respecting it," between the two men. In 1766 the clergyman asked provincial secretary Richard Peters to forward "a Box of Fossils etc." to proprietor Thomas Penn, adding that it "contains a Collection of Curiosities which cost me much pains" to obtain. In recognition of his scientific interests, Barton was elected to the American Philosophical Society in 1768 and received an honorary M.A. degree from King's College in New York two years later.[40] When the Lancaster Library Company was formed in 1759, Barton and his parishioners Edward Shippen, George Ross, and Joseph Rose were among its first directors while Samuel Magaw, teacher at the local charity school and later an Anglican clergyman, became its librarian. The Anglican leaders Samuel Boudé, William Atlee, James Burd, and Jasper Yeates joined the board of directors in subsequent years and Barton, Ross, and Atlee remained active in the library's affairs until at least 1775.[41]

In December 1759, Lancaster's new minister wrote to the SPG that upon his arrival he had "found the mission in great confusion occasioned by some unhappy disputes which long subsisted between the Gentleman I have the honour to succeed and the people." He hoped that he could be "instrumental in putting an end to them." At the beginning of his pastorate, Barton had in fact taken an important step toward ending these "unhappy disputes" when he deferred to the vestry's wishes and selected one of the vestrymen, Samuel Boudé, as his warden, thereby eliminating the source of conflict that had driven Craig out. By the end of his first year in Lancaster Barton was convinced that he had "a favorable prospect of doing service here" and reported that the congregation

40. Barton, *Memoirs*, 104, 118–22, 146–57, 162 (quote), 173–74, 192–98, 204–22, 230–35; Thomas Barton to Richard Peters, November 17, 1766; Peters Papers, vol. 6, p. 46, Historical Society of Pennsylvania; Jeffries, "Thomas Barton," 53–54. In 1760 Barton wrote to Governor Thomas Penn about "a scheme proposed here for making the Schuylkill navigable for small craft" (Worner, "Church of England [Part III]," 47). In 1773 he informed Penn that "[a] Subscription is now on Foot here for making the Susquehanna navigable for large Boats, which will undoubtedly succeed, will greatly promote the Prosperity of the Backcountry in particular, and the Reputation and Commerce of the Province in general." Barton's continuing interest in public improvements is also evident from the essay "Observations upon Public Roads, and Proposals for a Kind of Turnpike from Wright's Ferry to Philadelphia," which appeared in the *Pennsylvania Gazette* in 1772 and to which Barton referred in his letter to the proprietor (Thomas Barton to Thomas Penn, April 28, 1773, Penn Papers, Official Correspondence, vol. 11, p. 77, Historical Society of Pennsylvania); see also Wood, *Conestoga Crossroads*, 143, 242–43).
41. Landis, "Juliana Library Company," 195–96, 198, 213, 215–16, 238–44.

planned to enlarge its church, which was becoming too small for its growing membership. "In short," he concluded hopefully, "a real Spirit of Religion and learning seems to rise amongst us." Still, he realized that he had to beware of the lay leaders. The "misfortune" in Lancaster, he informed the SPG in December 1760, was "that some people puffed up with a notion of their superior knowledge, fortunes and families seem apprehensive of ranking with the meaner sort." Their sense of superiority, he thought, might be more justified "if they showed that respect to religion which is due to it."[42]

As for his predecessors, church-building became a major concern for Thomas Barton. In 1761 he wrote that although the "[n]umber of people belonging to the Church" in Lancaster was "very small" and most members were "people of contracted fortunes," they were "yet willing to give posterity some evidence of their attention to the great duty of promoting the credit of the Church." By means of a lottery they had raised "a considerable sum of money" for a steeple, the construction of galleries, the purchase of a church bell, and the completion of the stone wall around the graveyard. The leaders of the congregation published their "Scheme for a lottery, for raising $1,350 for the use of St. James's church, in the Borough of Lancaster," in the March 12, 1761, issue of the *Pennsylvania Gazette* and cooperated with the German Reformed church council in a further lottery to raise an additional $565 a few months later. The vestry had appointed the wardens George Ross and Samuel Boudé to receive the surplus from the managers of the lottery and contract with masons, carpenters, and laborers for the construction of a steeple. The building managers promised to "do all in their powers to make the house of God not only useful and convenient in its structure but also to add such decent ornaments to the same as becometh pious Christians." The next year Barton reported that the "people committed to my care" in Lancaster, Caernarvon, and Pequea "have shewn a remarkable spirit in finishing, enlarging and ornamenting their Churches," and in the summer of 1763 he wrote that "the Churches in this Mission make now as decent an appearance as any Churches in the province, those of Philadelphia excepted." Meanwhile the wardens and vestry had written to London in October 1762 that they had started a new subscription for the construction of a gallery and the acquisition of a church bell, which the Anglicans "alone of the many societies in this populous place are destitute of." To promote this project, they asked the SPG for whatever contribution it could afford. Since the subscription had already raised £100, the vestry made arrangements for the importation of a large and small bell from London, but the purchase through Philadelphia merchant Joseph Swift was only concluded after another subscription in 1770.[43] In the latter year Thomas Barton and William Atlee also bought a plot of land in Manheim Township north of Lancaster, probably on behalf of the congregation.[44] By 1771, moreover, Barton had secured a yearly allowance of £10 for a parochial school in which the children of poor members received free instruction. The schoolmaster Joseph Rathell reported in 1772 that twelve children had "been carefully instructed in reading, writing and arithmetic, in their catechism and the first principles of religion."[45]

Like many colonial Anglican pastors, Barton tried to steer a middle course between the extremes of religious enthusiasm and strict orthodoxy. No friend of revivalism, he was relieved in 1762 to find "the rage of enthusiasm and bitter zeal much abated, and religious dissension calmed." In a sermon that according to historian Jerome Wood may have been preached in Lancaster, Barton criticized the revivalist doctrine of "instantaneous" conversion and asserted that "Man cooperates with Grace, and by the Strength he receives from this Assistance, is able to will and to do according to God's good pleasure." On the other hand, Barton revealed pietist sentiments when he wrote in 1766 that "the young people in my congregations show a seriousness and warmth in matters of religion not common in persons of their years—several of them came to the Lord's Table at Christmas & presented their souls & Bodies with so much devotion and contrition of heart as not only pleased but affected the whole congregation." The same year he reported that he was preaching to "numerous, orderly & attentive" congregations, catechizing and lecturing the children during Sunday services and exhorting families during private visits. A social conservative and supporter of the proprietary interest in Pennsylvania politics, Barton noted with satisfaction that "[m]y people have continued to give proof of that submission and obedience to civil authority, which it is the glory of the Church of England to

43. St. James Vestry Minutes, 18–24, 29, St. James Episcopal Church; Jasper Yeates to Joseph Swift, April 9, 1770, Jasper Yeates Letterbook, 1769–71, AM 196, pp. 61–62, Historical Society of Pennsylvania, Philadelphia (hereafter Yeates Letterbook, Historical Society of Pennsylvania); Joseph Swift to Jasper Yeates, June 2, 1770, Jasper Yeates Papers, MG 207, box 1, folder 17, Lancaster County Historical Society; Perry, *Historical Collections*, 2:329, 343; Worner, "Church of England (Part III)," 49–54, "Church of England (Part IV)," 58, 69, 72; William F. Worner, "Old St. James's Church Bell," *PLCHS* 35 (1931): 239–46; Diller and Klein, *History of St. James' Church*, 35–39; Rhoden, *Revolutionary Anglicanism*, 23.

44. Mayhill, *Deed Abstracts*, 90 (G414).

45. Worner, "Church of England (Part IV)," 72, 74–75, 78, 80, 84; Diller and Klein, *History of St. James' Church*, 46–48.

inculcate." Whereas "faction and party strife have been rending the province to pieces," he wrote at the end of the politically turbulent year 1764, his parishioners "behaved themselves as became peaceable and dutiful subjects, never intermeddling in the least." On the whole he believed that "[t]he mildness and Excellency of her Constitution" as well as "her moderation and charity" would eventually gain the Church of England many adherents among Pennsylvania's other religious groups.[46] Sally Bard, a relative of Barton's second wife, Sarah, found him to be a gifted preacher when she heard him on the pulpit in early 1776: "his sermons quite equal Dr. Smiths accompanied with a most agreeable delivery and then flowing from a good heart they must have a good effect upon his hearers."[47]

Barton's letters speak of numerous visits to neighboring Berks County and the regions west of the Susquehanna River, and in 1766 he visited several vacant congregations in New Jersey and Delaware. His circuits not only strained his health but also made him acutely aware of the minority position of the Church of England, whose few adherents were "surrounded by multitudes of Dissenters of every kind."[48] In order to strengthen the position of the Anglican church, Barton supported organizational efforts of the Church of England clergy by participating in a meeting of Anglican ministers from Pennsylvania and neighboring colonies held in Philadelphia in April 1760. In 1767 he had a book of family prayers, which adapted the Church of England's Book of Common Prayer for the use of his congregations, printed at the press of the Seventh Day Baptist Community in Ephrata.[49]

46. Perry, *Historical Collections*, 2:339, 367, 400, 406–7; Worner, "Church of England (Part IV)," 58–59, 66; Wood, *Conestoga Crossroads*, 198. As historian Nancy Rhoden has pointed out, "Anglicans generally defended the role of reason in religion, the importance of free will, and their perception of God as both a rational deity and a model of moral perfection." Ministers of the Church of England "insisted upon the importance of the sacraments to salvation" and "explained spiritual regeneration as a lifelong process and therefore stressed the importance of public worship and regular participation in the church's sacraments. . . . While they generally denounced revivalism's tactics of enthusiasm as indicative of irrationality and weak theology, Anglican ministers adhered strictly to the forms of services articulated in the liturgy and presented the Church of England as a bastion of orderliness" (Rhoden, *Revolutionary Anglicanism*, 11–12).

47. Sara Barton, "The Bartons in Lancaster in 1776," *JLCHS* 52 (1948): 215.

48. Perry, *Historical Collections*, 2:283, 328–29, 339, 343 (quote), 347–48, 358, 387–88, 406, 467; Worner, "Church of England (Part III)," 44, 47–48, 52, and "Church of England (Part IV)," 71.

49. Perry, *Historical Collections*, 2:301, 315, 328; Worner, "Church of England (Part III)," 45, and "Church of England (Part IV)," 67; William Frederic Worner, "Thomas Barton's Family Prayer Book," *PLCHS* 35 (1932): 288–99; Diller and Klein, *History of St. James' Church*, 44. According to an entry in his day book, the Lancaster County attorney and later church warden Jasper Yeates paid 7s. 6d. to William Barton "for 6 Family Prayer Books compiled by his Brother the Rev.d Thos Barton." This entry also proves that the name "William Barton" on the title page was not an error as William F. Worner and others have assumed (Jasper Yeates Collection, 1766–67, MG 205, box 1, folder 31, Lancaster County Historical Society, 69).

As his congregations were too poor to support a household of seven children and two servants, Barton was plagued by financial problems. He felt that he was "obliged to live in a place where every necessity of life must be purchased at a most extravagant rate." While he claimed that he was merely aspiring to "freedom from want—from low and abject dependence," the expenditure of £600 for a town house in 1763 may also have overtaxed his means. In the mid-1760s, therefore, Barton considered going to the Mohawk country as a missionary, to Canada as a chaplain of the British garrison at Montreal, or to Maryland. Only when Governor Thomas Penn offered him a personal gift of £50 and the SPG raised his salary did Barton decide to remain in Lancaster. His connection to the Proprietary Party, which he assiduously cultivated, also helped Barton gain possession of a five-hundred-acre farm on Conestoga Manor in 1768. Interestingly enough, this tract had been inhabited by the Conestoga Indians whom the Paxton Boys had massacred a few years earlier—an action that Barton had vigorously defended in his pamphlet.[50] "[W]ere it not for the Society's bounty and the use of a plantation which the honorable proprietaries of this Province have indulged me with," Barton wrote to the SPG in 1775, "my wants would long before now have obliged me to seek support in some other quarter." There were, he conceded, some "men of property" among his parishioners who were "kind and liberal" to him, but the "great majority" were "persons who are either unwilling or unable to advance anything." Other woes—the prolonged illness of his first wife, Esther, and her death in 1774—proved "almost too many for all the fortitude and resignation I could exercise." But Barton persevered, and his pastorate turned out to be the longest of any clergyman in colonial Lancaster.[51]

During the final years of the colonial period, a select group of prominent English-speaking inhabitants occupied leading positions in the Anglican congregation as wardens and vestrymen. As the following table shows, the congregation valued continuity as lay leaders were usually reelected, and five of these nine men had already served on the vestry prior to 1769. Eight were among the top fifth of the borough's taxpayers. Four were termed "esquires" in the 1773 borough tax list, while one was listed as an attorney and three as artisans in the respectable trades of gunsmith, mason, and coppersmith.

50. Thomas Barton to Richard Peters, February 5, 1767, Peters Papers, vol. 6, p. 47, Historical Society of Pennsylvania; Barton to Peters, June 2, 1768, Peters Papers, vol. 6, p. 58, Historical Society of Pennsylvania; Barton to Peters, August 24, 1768, Peters Papers, vol. 6, p. 62, Historical Society of Pennsylvania; Mayhill, *Deed Abstracts*, 101 (H181); "Notes and Queries," *PMHB* 4 (1880): 119–20; Worner, "Church of England (Part IV)," 59, 63–64, 66–68; Diller and Klein, *History of St. James' Church*, 41–45; Russell, "Thomas Barton," 319, 329; Myers, "Thomas Barton's Authorship," 175–76.

51. Worner, "Church of England (Part IV)," 70, 76–77, 79.

Table 3   Leading laymen of St. James' Anglican Church, 1769–1775

Name	Office and tenure	Profession/rank	Decile on 1773 borough tax list
Atlee, William	W 1769–75	Esquire	2
Bickham, James	V 1769–75	Esquire, shopkeeper	1
Henry, John	V 1769–75	Gunsmith	2
Moore, George	V 1771–75	Mason	1
Ross, George	V 1769–75?	Esquire	1
Sanderson, George	V 1769–75	Coppersmith	1
Shippen, Edward	V 1769–71	Esquire	1
Stone, John	V 1769–75	—	
Yeates, Jasper	W 1769–75	Attorney	2

ABBREVIATIONS: W = warden, V = vestryman

SOURCES: St. James Vestry Minutes, 26, 29–31; Klein and Diller, *History of St. James' Church*, 50–52, 326–27; Egle, *Pennsylvania Archives* 17:454–63.

The group of Anglican leaders included some of the most influential men in Lancaster politics. George Ross sat in the Pennsylvania Assembly from 1768 to 1772 and again from 1773 to 1776. During the latter period he became a delegate to the First Continental Congress. James Bickham was elected to the offices of burgess in 1761 and 1764 and chief burgess in 1762–63. William Atlee, who had come to Lancaster from Philadelphia to study law with Edward Shippen, was admitted to the bar in 1758 and served as the borough's chief burgess from 1770 to 1773.[52] Edward III Shippen (1703–81) himself came from a family established in Pennsylvania since 1694 and had started his career in Philadelphia, where he had become a leading merchant and fur trader by the 1740s and was elected mayor of the city in 1744. He removed to Lancaster in 1752 after his second marriage to the presumed widow Mary Nowland had involved him in a public scandal when her first husband turned out to be alive and residing in Barbados. After his relocation to the backcountry, Shippen continued to cultivate his connections to Governor Hamilton and represented the interests of the Proprietary Party in Lancaster Country as clerk of the Court of Quarter Sessions, registrar of deeds, and prothonotary.[53] Shippen had been an elder of the Presbyterian

52. Ellis and Evans, *History of Lancaster County*, 365–66, 373; Landis, "Juliana Library Company," 240, 243; *Dictionary of American Biography* 8, pt. 2, 177–78; Richard Alan Ryerson, *The Revolution Is Now Begun: The Radical Committees of Philadelphia, 1765–1776* (Philadelphia: University of Pennsylvania Press, 1978), 62, 262–63; Wood, *Conestoga Crossroads*, 176; Robert D. Tunney, "Chart of Historic St. James's Church and Graveyard," *JLCHS* 67 (1963): 128; Henderson, "Ross," 911–12.

53. Charles I. Landis, "Jasper Yeates and His Times," *PMHB* 46 (1922): 199; Randolph S. Klein, *Portrait of an Early American Family: The Shippens of Pennsylvania Across Five Generations* (Philadelphia: University of Pennsylvania Press, 1975), 60–72.

congregation in Philadelphia, and as a committed New Sider he became a founding trustee of the College of New Jersey in 1746. When he moved to Lancaster and did not find a Presbyterian congregation there, he affiliated with the Anglicans. This association continued even after he became involved in the establishment of a Presbyterian congregation, and he was buried in the graveyard of St. James' Church. As one of the wealthiest men in prerevolutionary Lancaster, Shippen owned extensive real estate in Philadelphia and its vicinity, the counties of Bucks and Chester, and west of the Susquehanna, where he founded the town of Shippensburg. His close association with the Proprietary government gave Shippen considerable powers of patronage as well. The prime beneficiaries were men like James Burd, Jasper Yeates, and Peter Grubb, who had married into the Shippen clan.[54]

The case of Jasper Yeates illustrates how quickly a well-connected young man could assume a leading role in the affairs of the St. James congregation, for Yeates was only in his mid-twenties when he became a warden in 1769. The son of a West India merchant, Yeates was born in Philadelphia in 1745 and attended the College of Philadelphia, where he received a B.A. degree in 1761. Four years later, he came to Lancaster to study law under Edward Shippen and was admitted to the bar there at age twenty. He quickly established his legal practice, handling more than two hundred cases before the Lancaster County Court of Common Pleas in 1767. At the end of that year, he married Sarah Burd, a daughter of Colonel James Burd and granddaughter of Edward Shippen. After renting a house from the Moravian shopkeeper Marcus Jung for several years, Yeates purchased his own house in 1775. After a successful start, he went on to a long and distinguished career in the legal profession and in public affairs.[55]

Membership in the vestry conferred prestige on these men but also carried added responsibilities. When a subscription for "the necessary repairs to the belfry and church and for replacing the pulpit cloth" was started in 1775, eight of the twelve men who contributed the initial sum of £41 were members of the vestry. William Atlee was appointed to collect the money, while George Moore and John Henry contracted with the workmen.[56] With their minister Thomas Barton, these men shared a commitment to the Church of England as well as aspirations to

54. Klein, *Portrait of an Early American Family*, 52, 60, 64–72, 85, 92, 116, 143–44, 172; Wood, *Conestoga Crossroads*, 52–53, 115–17, 173, 175–77, 202.

55. Landis, "Jasper Yeates," 199–203.

56. St. James Vestry Minutes, 31, St. James Episcopal Church; Worner, "Church of England (Part IV)," 78–80; Diller and Klein, *History of St. James' Church*, 50.

gentility and respect in colonial society. In 1768, for example, the young attorney Jasper Yeates wrote to the Philadelphia hatter William Jenkins that "[t]he Rev.^d Mr. Barton of this Town has just shewn me a Woman's Hat of your Making, which he lately received, & recommends you to me as an able Workman." Yeates now ordered "a Hat of the same Dimensions in every Particular."[57] While he quickly assumed a leading role in congregational affairs, the young lawyer abhorred religious bigotry and fanaticism. "Our Enjoyments here are much impaired," he wrote in 1770. "*Religion* deformed with a thousand Gloomy Shapes, has made her Appearances amongst us, & the most innocent Recreations are deemed almost sinful & detestable." Yeates was especially put off by those Lancasterians "who consider Mortification a very essential Duty for the Attainment of Happiness in the other Country. We have not had a Dance these ten Months, I don't know when we shall have one."[58] When the Reverend Illing, an Anglican clergyman of German origin who served several congregations in the Susquehanna Valley, ran into an argument with his parishioners in Middletown about the proper use of the liturgy and a delegation came to Lancaster to interview Thomas Barton and the Lutheran pastor Justus Heinrich Christian Helmuth about the matter, Yeates found the dispute "the most trifling one imaginable." The well-read young attorney compared the affair to the "ridiculous Deliberations of the Doctors of the Sorbonne" in Laurence Sterne's novel *Tristram Shandy*.[59]

When Thomas Barton's second wife, Sarah DeNormandie, arrived in Lancaster after a winter journey from New York in January 1776, she was also impressed by the gentility and politeness she encountered. The new Mrs. Barton was greeted with a "most delightful Serenade under the window consisting of two Violins one flute and a hautboy played extreamly well," and her husband "was visited by all the Gentlemen of the place." As Sarah Barton's young travel companion Sally Bard noted, it was "Customary" among the town's social elite to "send cards to all those you would wish to come and have an elegant Collation served up at twelve Clock with wine punch." The estate inventory drawn up after George Ross's death in 1786 likewise included the markers of a genteel lifestyle: mahogany and walnut furniture, several "compleat" sets of china, pictures on the wall, a harpsichord,

57. Jasper Yeates Letterbook, 1767–69, AM 196, Historical Society of Pennsylvania; Jasper Yeates Collection, MG 205, box 1, folder 31, p. 45, Lancaster County Historical Society.

58. Jasper Yeates to Duncan Campbell, January 2, 1771, Jasper Yeates Letterbook, 1769–71, AM 196, pp. 79–80, Historical Society of Pennsylvania.

59. Jasper Yeates to James Burd, February 28, 1774, Shippen Papers, vol. 7, p. 81, Historical Society of Pennsylvania. See also Thomas Barton to James Burd, January 2, 1773, Shippen Papers, vol. 7, p. 63, Historical Society of Pennsylvania.

three coaches, a gold watch, and a "Mulatto Girl named Dinah" to wait on the family. The whole personal estate was valued at more than £3,150.[60]

But while Barton and his leading parishioners might agree on matters of taste and share a refined lifestyle, they differed in their political principles. Unlike his vestry, Barton was a political conservative who supported the imperial policies of the British government and showed no sympathy for colonial resistance. Up to the late 1760s, when politics in Lancaster was still mostly local politics, this difference mattered little. In 1768 Jasper Yeates actually criticized another prominent member of the congregation for mixing religion and politics. When Dr. Robert Boyd, a Presbyterian, sought a public commission, Yeates learned "that Squire George [Ross] has great Objections to his being appointed a Magistrate" and was organizing the opposition against Boyd's candidacy. "To draw in some," Ross suddenly pretended "great Regard to *Christianity*," an issue that was certain to arouse "great Attention in our little Borough." In order "to affect others," Ross allegedly argued that "the Loyalty of the Germans must be in imminent Danger from a Presbyterian & a Man of a republican Turn! Those who know our worthy Member," Yeates concluded, "justly suspect a truer Motive that influences his Conduct, which in short is no other, than that his ungenteel Behaviour towards Dr. Boyd had given him but too just Cause for fear, that he will at least be his adversary in political life."[61]

After the British government had responded to the Boston Tea Party with the Coercive Acts against Boston and Massachusetts, however, imperial politics became a central concern of many Lancasterians, and the conflict between Great Britain and her colonies now prompted the town's Anglican leaders to take sides. Edward Shippen, Jasper Yeates, George Ross, and William Atlee sat on the Committee of Correspondence formed in June 1774, and the next month George Ross presided at a meeting that denounced the Coercive Acts and collected £153 for the relief of Boston's inhabitants. Considered the most influential assemblyman from Lancaster County, the politically moderate Ross embraced the Patriot cause in 1775 and came to support the Continental Congress's decisions to boycott British trade, take up arms against the mother country, and, eventually, declare American independence. He became a member of the Pennsylvania Committee of Safety and was vice president of the convention

---

60. Barton, *Bartons in Lancaster*, 315; "Copy of Inventory of George Ross of Lancaster, Penna.," *PMHB* 31 (1907): 375–76; Wood, *Conestoga Crossroads*, 167.

61. Jasper Yeates to Joseph Shippen, December 20, 1768, Jasper Yeates Collection, 1767–69, MG 205, box 1, folder 1, p. 70, Lancaster County Historical Society.

that drafted the radical new state constitution in 1776.[62] As the colonies moved toward independence after Lexington and Concord, these differences of sentiment would deepen into an unbridgeable gulf between Thomas Barton and his congregation. When Congress recommended that a day of fasting and prayer be observed in July 1775, Barton was among the twelve Anglican ministers in Pennsylvania who assured the Bishop of London that "[m]otives of prudence induced them to observe this day in common with the other denominations," although they deemed their conduct consistent with their "duty as loyal subjects and ministers to the Church of England." The ultimate fate of Barton's ministry, however, depended on the "happy reconciliation" between Great Britain and her colonies, for which he hoped in vain.[63]

PRESBYTERIANS

Although the southern and western parts of Lancaster County were strongholds of Presbyterianism, the denomination evolved only slowly in the town itself. In 1742 the Presbytery of Donegal began to send supply pastors to Lancaster—a practice that continued more or less regularly until 1769. The lack of a resident minister mirrored the numerical weakness of Presbyterianism in the borough as well as the fact that, despite the establishment of indigenous seminaries scuh as William Tennent's Log College and the College of New Jersey, the recruitment and training of ministers did not match the explosive growth of colonial congregations. The fourteen ministers affiliated with the Donegal Presbytery had to supply thirty-eight congregations in 1740 and sixty-five in 1763. The absence of a regular pastor and the loss of practically all local church records before 1800 means that the sources for the history of the congregation are much thinner than for the German Reformed, Lutherans, Moravians, and Anglicans.[64] The

---

62. Diller and Klein, *History of St. James' Church*, 53; Jeffries, "Thomas Barton," 56; Klein, *Portrait of an Early American Family*, 161–62; *Dictionary of American Biography* 8, pt. 2, 177–78; Ryerson, *The Revolution Is Now Begun*, 92–93, 108–11, 122–23, 140, 143, 219, 221–22, 262–63; Henderson, "Ross," 911–12.

63. Worner, "Church of England (Part IV)," 82–83. On the split between loyalist Anglican clergy and patriot laity, see Rhoden, *Revolutionary Anglicanism*, 7. On Anglican clerics' hopes for reconciliation, see ibid., 93–95.

64. Presbyterians in Lancaster, Records of the Presbytery of Donegal, 1742–70, MS D 71, Presbyterian Historical Society, Philadelphia (hereafter Presbyterians in Lancaster, Presbyterian Historical Society); cf. Catherine Courtney a nd John D. Long, "A History of First Presbyterian Church of Lancaster, Pennsylvania," *JLCHS* 90 (1986): 5–6, 8; William F. Early, "Our First 250 Years," in *250 Years of Witness, 1742–1992: First Presbyterian Church, Lancaster, Pennsylvania* (Lancaster, Pa.: History Committee of the

will of the "skin dresser" Robert Patterson, who died in 1748, provides a rare glimpse of a Presbyterian layman in early Lancaster. Patterson willed that if his infant son should die before reaching maturity, his estate was to go to "the Presbytory of Dunnegall in [Lancaster] County to forward, promote and propogate [sic] the Gospell in those parts." Since there was no Presbyterian church in the town, Patterson wished to be buried in the German Reformed churchyard.[65]

In 1760 Donegal Presbytery permitted the Presbyterians in Lancaster and nearby Leacock Township to associate as "conjunct congregations" and apply to the synod for a minister. The congregations' petition was unsuccessful, and when a certain pastor McGraw, who had been preaching in Lancaster for about a year, sought his ordination and a regular call in November 1762, the congregation was divided and the call was apparently never issued. The Presbytery also initiated a collection for the building of a church in Lancaster. The building was begun in 1763 and a lottery held for fund-raising purposes three years later, but the church was not completed until 1770. These pieces of information show that organization of the congregation was a protracted affair. In May 1768 Lancaster and Leacock were granted permission to apply to the Presbytery of New Castle for a pastor, and they eventually secured the services of John D. Woodhull as their first settled minister in 1770. "I suppose," Woodhull later remembered, "there was never a communicant admitted to the Presbyterian Church in Lancaster on examination before I went there. Both congregation and church appear to have been in a rather forming state." Shortly after he began his pastorate, the two congregations were officially placed under the care of the New Castle Presbytery.[66]

Born on Long Island in 1744, Woodhull had entered the College of New Jersey in 1762 and "was swept up in a student revival" there. After graduating in 1766, he received additional training from John Blair at Fagg's Manor, at that time one of the foremost centers of New Side Presbyterianism. Woodhull's association with the New Side was reinforced through his marriage to Sara Spufford,

First Presbyterian Church, 1992), 3, 7–8. For a survey of local church records, see A. Hunter Rineer Jr., *Churches and Cemeteries of Lancaster County, Pennsylvania. A Complete Guide* (Lancaster, Pa.: Publications of the Lancaster County Historical Society, 1993), 199. On the problems of supplying the fast-growing Presbyterian population in the colonies with an adequate number of pastors, see Trinterud, *Forming of an American Tradition*, 129, 137, 199.

65. Lancaster County Will Book A-I-139, Pennsylvania State Archives.

66. Presbyterians in Lancaster, Presbyterian Historical Society; Lancaster County Deed Book N202, Pennsylvania State Archives; Guy S. Klett, ed., *Minutes of the Presbyterian Church in America, 1706–1788* (Philadelphia: Presbyterian Historical Society, 1976), 359, 478; Ellis and Evans, *History of Lancaster County,* 473; Courtney and Long, "History of First Presbyterian Church," 7–8; Wood, *Conestoga Crossroads,* 183–84; Early, "Our First 250 Years," 8, 11.

a stepdaughter of Gilbert Tennent, in 1772. He was known to preach without prepared notes in the tradition of the New Side ministers of the Great Awakening. Woodhull's call to the Lancaster and Leacock congregations also indicates the predominantly rural character of Presbyterianism in Lancaster County: while Leacock promised to pay the pastor £90 annually for two-thirds of his time, Lancaster pledged £40 for the remaining third. Woodhull established his home on a 130-acre farm in Leacock Township known as Harmony Hall, and his later reputation as a "Fighting Parson" in the War for Independence stemmed mostly from the militia troops that he raised in the Leacock area soon after the war began.[67]

By the time Woodhull commenced his ministry, the lay leadership of the congregation also comes into sharper relief. In July 1770 town proprietor James Hamilton deeded a lot on Orange Street "for the use of the Members of the Presbyterian Church in the Borough of Lancaster, in communion with the Church of Scotland" to Edward Shippen, Robert Boyd, William White, Henry Helm, and William Montgomery.[68] The most prominent among these laymen was certainly Edward Shippen, one of the wealthiest and most influential men in colonial Lancaster who was also associated with the Anglican congregation. Of the other Presbyterian leaders, elder Henry Helm accompanied parson Woodhull to Philadelphia on a fund-raising tour for the completion of the church in 1770. Helm was referred to as a shoemaker when he acquired several properties in and near Lancaster in the early 1760s but was listed as a tavernkeeper a decade later. He was assessed among the top 10 percent of Lancaster's taxables in 1759 and among the wealthiest fifth fourteen years later.[69] The innkeeper William White was also listed among the top 20 percent of borough taxpayers in 1759 and owned real estate in town as well as some land in the vicinity, but his fortunes declined after 1770 for his tax assessments dropped sharply.[70] William Montgomery was a farmer and blacksmith in Little Britain Township,

67. Ellis and Evans, *History of Lancaster County,* 473; Courtney and Long, "History of First Presbyterian Church," 9–11; Wood, *Conestoga Crossroads,* 184, 200; Early, "Our First 250 Years," 8–10; William Buchanan Buyers, "The Rev. John D. Woodhull, D.D., 'The Fighting Chaplain,'" *PLCHS* 43 (1939): 131–36; James McLachlan, *Princetonians, 1748–1768: A Biographical Dictionary.* Princetonians 1 (Princeton: Princeton University Press, 1976), 600–602.

68. Lancaster County Deed Book N202, Pennsylvania State Archives; Ellis and Evans, *History of Lancaster County,* 473; Courtney and Long, "History of First Presbyterian Church," 10–13, 63.

69. Mayhill, *Deed Abstracts,* 73 (F214), 93 (H40), 94 (H41), 111 (H349), 190 (M299); Lancaster Borough Tax Assessment List, 1759, Lancaster County Historical Society; Egle, *Pennsylvania Archives,* 458. Cf. Wood, *Conestoga Crossroads,* 63–64.

70. Lancaster Borough Tax Assessment List, 1759, Lancaster County Historical Society; Egle, *Pennsylvania Archives,* 13, 298, 464; Mayhill, *Deed Abstracts,* 72 (F131), 180–81 (M119).

where he owned two hundred acres in 1773.[71] The physician Robert Boyd and the silversmith Charles Hall, who both belonged to wealthiest fifth of Lancaster's taxables in 1773, also ranked among the lay leaders during Woodhull's pastorate.[72] Hall had probably migrated from Philadelphia in the early 1760s. At the time of his death in 1783, he owned a town house, a lot in Musserstown, land in Penns Valley and "at White Deer Hole Creek," and a personal estate valued at £470.[73]

The late organization of the congregation, the slow progress of church-building, the difficulties in obtaining a settled minister, and the continuing association of leading members such as Edward Shippen with other congregations all point to the relative weakness of Presbyterianism in prerevolutionary Lancaster. Only after the War for Independence would this denomination begin to assume a more prominent position in the town's religious landscape and match the organizational efforts of the Lutherans, German Reformed, Anglicans, and Moravians in this confessionally fragmented community.

QUAKERS

Lancaster's Quakers initially belonged to Sadsbury Monthly Meeting, set up in the eastern part of the county in 1737. Members of the Society of Friends constituted only a small minority of the borough's inhabitants but occupied influential positions from its earliest days. Historian Jerome Wood has asserted that Friends "enjoyed local political popularity far out of proportion to their number. . . . In fifteen of the twenty-one years between 1742 and 1763 at least one of the burgesses was a Quaker; in 1761 both burgesses were Friends."[74] Joshua Lowe, who acquired real estate in Hamilton's town in 1735 and owned land near Millersville, was elected county coroner in 1729 and served in that position intermittently until 1740.[75] James Webb (1708–85), who came from a Chester County Quaker family, moved to Lancaster and married Hannah Evans in 1742. He was elected burgess

71. Egle, *Pennsylvania Archives*, 17:70, 370. He had also purchased a house in Lancaster for £900 in 1761 (Mayhill, *Deed Abstracts*, 64 [E156], 76 [F380]). The biographical sketch in Courtney and Long, "History of First Presbyterian Church," 13, is unreliable.
72. Egle, *Pennsylvania Archives*, 17:455, 458.
73. Lancaster County Orphans Court Records, 1772–76, September 3, 1772, p. 50, Pennsylvania State Archives; Lancaster County Will Book D-I-304, Pennsylvania State Archives; Mary N. Robinson, "Charles Hall: A Revolutionary Worthy," *PLCHS* 8 (1904): 177–82; Gerstell, *Silversmiths*, 37–44.
74. Wood, *Conestoga Crossroads*, 31.
75. Heisey, "Borough Fathers," 58, 62.

in 1744 but a few years later moved to the countryside. He owned a large farm in Lampeter Township, and by 1761 he acquired land in Lancaster Township close to the borough.[76]

Peter Worrall also moved to Lancaster from Chester County in the late 1730s. He married Sarah Blunston, the widow of tavernkeeper Samuel Bethel and the daughter and granddaughter of former members of the Pennsylvania Assembly. Worrall ran a tavern in Lancaster and acquired several town properties as well as land on Conestoga Creek. By 1751 he was listed among the top 2 percent of Lancaster's taxpayers. He was appointed one of the first assistant burgesses in 1742 and was elected burgess in 1745. Two years later he became a justice of the peace and was elected to the Pennsylvania Assembly where he served, except for 1750, from 1747 until his resignation in 1756. Worrall had been disowned by the Sadsbury Monthly Meeting after his marriage in 1741 and been engaged in several controversies with other Quakers, but he had rejoined the Friends by midcentury. Following the death of his first wife, Worrall married a wealthy widow from Philadelphia, and this remarriage prompted him to sell several of his properties in and near Lancaster and move to the city on the Delaware in early 1757. Two years later the Worralls returned to Lancaster County and acquired more real estate there, but they finally removed to Burlington County, New Jersey, in 1763 and liquidated their holdings in Lancaster. Until his death in 1786 Worrall remained active in the affairs of the Society of Friends.[77]

Two other prominent Quakers in colonial Lancaster were Isaac Whitelock and Thomas Poultney. The two Friends obviously worked together for some time because in 1754 they advertised in the *Pennsylvania Gazette* a number of properties in and near the town for sale.[78] Isaac Whitelock (1712–84/85) came to Lancaster from Philadelphia, where he sold imported goods from London in his store in the early 1740s. He obtained two lots on Orange Street in 1740, acquired several more around midcentury, and purchased land in the countryside, some of it for speculative purposes. Whitelock ran a brewery and tanyard with Irish indentured servants as well as slaves. As one of Lancaster's wealthiest residents, he was engaged in numerous credit transactions with his English- and German-speaking neighbors,

76. Wright, *Lancaster County Church Records*, 3:14, 25; Ellis and Evans, *History of Lancaster County*, 373; Heisey, "Borough Fathers," 56; Mayhill, *Deed Abstracts*, 27 (C3), 73 (F155, F162), 85 (G264-G268), 106 (H270), 135 (L32), 192 (M329); Wood, *Conestoga Crossroads*, 32.

77. This account relies mainly on Craig W. Horle et al., *Lawmaking and Legislators in Pennsylvania: A Biographical Dictionary*, vol. 2, *1710–1756* (Philadelphia: University of Pennsylvania Press, 1997), 1078–83; cf. also Heisey, "Borough Fathers," 50, 64, 67, 70, 79; and Wood, *Conestoga Crossroads*, 32, 39.

78. *Pennsylvania Gazette*, March 5, 1754.

repeatedly served as burgess from 1752 to 1766, and sat in the assembly. According to the records of the Sadsbury Monthly Meeting, nine children, six of whom died young, were born to him and his wife Mary between 1743 and 1764. Mary seems to have died shortly thereafter, for in 1767 Isaac Whitelock requested a certificate to marry Sarah Raisin, a widow from Maryland. In 1775 Whitelock, his wife, and two unmarried daughters left for Wilmington, Delaware, where his son Charles had already taken up residence.[79] The carpenter Thomas Poultney had also been living in Philadelphia, where he sold ironware and furniture from a shop on King Street, before moving to Lancaster in the mid-1740s. Poultney traveled to Europe during the Seven Years' War but returned in 1762 with a certificate "from Ratcliff Monthly Meeting in Old England." On the eve of the Revolution, he was among the top 5 percent of the borough's taxpayers, but like Worrall and Whitelock he did not remain there. In 1780 he and his family moved to Philadelphia.[80]

By midcentury, this group of wealthy and influential Quakers was anxious to obtain its own place of worship. In 1754 Sadsbury Monthly Meeting reported that "the Friends in and near Lancaster have for some time past . . . kept meetings for worship on First days in Lancaster." The Monthly Meeting now requested the Sadsbury Quarterly Meeting to "appoint some Friends," to visit Lancaster and "consider how far they may be capable to hold and keep meeting for worship with reputation." Several members of the Quarterly Meeting subsequently visited

79. Ellis and Evans, *History of Lancaster County,* 364, 373; Heisey, "Borough Fathers," 60, 75; *Pennsylvania Gazette,* July 9, 1741; December 6, 1745; July 25, 1751; Neible, "Account of Servants (1907)," 462; George W. Neible, "Account of Servants Bound and Assigned Before James Hamilton, Mayor of Philadelphia," *PMHB* 32 (1908): 240; Lancaster Borough Tax Assessment Lists, 1751 and 1759, Lancaster County Historical Society; Wright, *Lancaster County Church Records,* 3:1, 43–44, 47, 49–50; Paul L. Whitely, "A History of Friends in Lancaster County," *PLCHS* 51 (1947): 17; Wood, *Conestoga Crossroads,* 39, 161–62. For his real estate transactions, see Mayhill, *Deed Abstracts,* 39 (D15), 43 (D108), 49 (D250), 52 (D390), 53 (D393), 55 (D441), 87 (G349), 140 (L151). Lancaster County's deed books demonstrate Whitelock's importance in credit networks throughout the 1750s and 1760s; see Mayhill, *Deed Abstracts,* 33 (C211: mortgage of Ludwig Beyerle, 1751), 59 (D511: mortgage of Benjamin Price, 1759), 63 (E102: mortgage of Jacob Backenstos, 1759, and E121: mortgage of William Moore, 1763), 65 (E194: mortgage of Joseph Cookson, 1757), 66 (E223: mortgage of Caleb Sheward, 1758), 67 (E256: mortgage of John Baker to Whitelock and Bernhard Hubele, 1758, and E264: mortgage of John Abraham to Whitelock and Hubele, 1758), 69 (E321: mortgage of Joshua Brown, 1759), 70 (E353: mortgage of Andrew Schwartz, 1759), 71 (F38: mortgage of James Perry, 1760), 73 (F178: mortgage of Adam Foutz, 1760), 93 (H26: mortgage of Samuel Hathorn, 1762), 127 (K124: mortgage of Nathan Brown, 1764), 199 (M462b: mortgage of Caleb Sheward, 1768).

80. Wright, *Lancaster County Church Records,* 3:26, 37, 53; Heisey, "Borough Fathers," 59, 73; Mayhill, *Deed Abstracts,* 70 (F13, F15); Lancaster Borough Tax Assessment Lists, 1751 and 1759, Lancaster County Historical Society; Egle, *Pennsylvania Archives,* 17:461. Six children were born to Poultney and his first wife, Elinor, between 1745 and 1754. After his wife's death in 1754, Poultney married Elizabeth Stockdale (or Stockton) in 1757, and the couple had seven children between 1758 and 1769 (Wright, *Lancaster County Church Records,* 3:6, 16, 33).

the borough, and upon their favorable report the Monthly Meeting authorized the Lancaster Quakers to erect their own meetinghouse in 1755. The leading Friends in town apparently expected this result, for Peter Worrall, Isaac Whitelock, and Thomas Poultney had already obtained two lots on Queen Street from town proprietor James Hamilton in May 1754. Subsequently, funds were collected and contributions solicited for a brick meetinghouse, which may have been completed by 1759. Worrall, Whitelock, and Poultney, who acted as "trustees of the Quaker Society in Lancaster Borough," were also among the largest individual contributors to the new meetinghouse. Isaac Whitelock donated £100, by far the highest sum, while Worrall gave £20 and Poultney £15 in nails. The only other individual who matched their efforts was Caleb Sheward, who contributed £17.[81] Sheward was a brewer and maltster who migrated from Chester County to Lancaster in 1758 and seems to have established his business with a loan from his wealthy fellow Quaker Isaac Whitelock. In 1769 Sheward paid back Whitelock's loan and the family moved to Wilmington, Delaware.[82]

A few other Quakers left traces in local records. Most were retailing or working in the construction trades. Thomas Thornbough, who was variously identified as a mason and a cooper, purchased a house from Peter Worrall in 1749, mortgaged it seven years later, and sold it in 1758. The same year he also made his will, bequeathing £10 to the "Friends of the Meeting of Sufferings of Philad[elphia] . . . to be applied by the said friends in purchas[ing] the lands of the Indians at Opecken."[83] The shopkeeper Caleb Johnson, whose tax payments indicate that he was a man of modest means, married Martha Davis in 1765 and had nine children with her until 1781.[84] The plasterer Caleb Cope purchased a town lot in 1765 and was elected a burgess nine years later. When the British officer John André, who had been captured in Canada in the early months of the Revolutionary War, was held prisoner in Lancaster in 1776, he became a friend of the Cope family and gave his host's sons drawing and painting lessons. Cope also served as a trustee of the Friends' Meeting.[85] Finally, the mason

81. Ellis and Evans, *History of Lancaster County*, 472–73; Coldren and Heisey, "Religious Life," 138–39; Wood, *Conestoga Crossroads*, 183. Whitely, "History of Friends," 6, states that the Lancaster Indulged Meeting was "established in 1753 by Sadsbury Monthly Meeting."

82. Mayhill, *Deed Abstracts*, 66 (E223), 199 (M462b), Wright, *Lancaster County Church Records*, 3:5, 33, 45.

83. Mayhill, *Deed Abstracts*, 58 (D492), 62 (E50), 98 (H118); Lancaster County Will Book B-I-289, Pennsylvania State Archives.

84. Egle, *Pennsylvania Archives*, 17:458; Wright, *Lancaster County Church Records*, 3:7, 16, 41, 44–45.

85. Wright, *Lancaster County Church Records*, 3:4; Mayhill, *Deed Abstracts*, 177 (M38); Ellis and Evans, *History of Lancaster County*, 367, 374; Whitely, "History of Friends," 18; Melvern Evans Jr., "Lancaster Borough: Host to British and Hessian Prisoners of War, 1775–1784," *JLCHS* 89 (1985): 146.

James Webb Jr., son of a prominent Lancaster County Friend, settled in the borough after his marriage to Rebecca Parks in 1757. He was elected county sheriff in 1767 and sat in the Pennsylvania Assembly from 1772 to 1776, where he consistently opposed the movement toward armed resistance and American independence.[86] In addition to their civic offices, several Friends became active in the Lancaster Library Company. Isaac Whitelock was among its first directors in 1759, Thomas Poultney became a director at the time of its incorporation four years later, the two James Webbs were members, and Caleb Sheward served as its secretary in 1765.[87]

More than any other religious group—with the possible exception of the Moravians—the Quakers emphasized the subordination of the individual to the advice and discipline of his co-religionists. Although Lancaster's Friends held their own meetings for worship, the Sadsbury Monthly Meeting remained the forum for monitoring marriages, registering migrations, resolving disputes, and censuring wayward members. In 1750 the Monthly Meeting recorded a complaint against assembly member Peter Worrall "for false speaking." Caleb Sheward complained in 1762 that his fellow Quaker Moses Gilpin "hath been in his debt for a considerable time." Eight years later James Webb brought a complaint against Caleb Johnson for "spreading scandalous reports tending to hurt his character," and Isaac Whitelock charged Joseph Davies for not repaying his debts. Not even the wealthy Whitelock escaped the meeting's censure: in 1762 it found him "guilty of drinking strong drink to excess."[88]

CONCLUSION

While each of the English-speaking religious groups in prerevolutionary Lancaster had its distinct history, several common features stand out. First, they were all relatively small compared to the major German churches in town, and this numerical weakness impeded their organizational efforts. Moreover, the Presbyterians were hampered by the lack of a resident minister and the Quakers by high geographic mobility. Second, each of the three groups had a core of wealthy and prominent members who took the lead in organizing congregations and

86. Mayhill, *Deed Abstracts*, 184 (M190), 196 (M413); Wright, *Lancaster County Church Records*, 3:33; *Pennsylvania Gazette*, October 8, 1767; October 7, 1768; October 12, 1769; Ryerson, *The Revolution Is Now Begun*, 111, 143, 219–20, 262; Wood, *Conestoga Crossroads*, 39.

87. Landis, "Juliana Library Company," 196, 210, 213–16, 241–42, 244.

88. Wright, *Lancaster County Church Records*, 3:29, 37–38, 46.

erecting churches or meetinghouses. Lancaster's English-speaking lawyers and gentlemen gave the Anglican congregation a decidedly genteel character, and these self-conscious lay leaders repeatedly clashed with the clergymen of the Church of England. The town's most influential Quakers, Peter Worrall and Isaac Whitelock, were both subject to censure from the Sadsbury Monthly Meeting, but if it hadn't been for their initiative, there would not have been a Friends' meetinghouse in the borough at all. The same was true of the leading Presbyterian laymen, who took the trouble of building a church although they had to wait for years until an ordained minister took up residence among them. The central role of laypeople in the organization of local churches and in the shaping of the congregational order thus stands out for both English- and German-speaking Protestants.

Third, the approaching Revolutionary War found Lancaster's English-speaking congregations in a particularly vulnerable position. The Anglican pastor Thomas Barton was a political and social conservative who had condemned resistance to the Stamp Act and saw his congregation as a bulwark of order and stability against enthusiasm and fanaticism of every kind. The Presbyterian congregation was still relatively young and unsettled, and the Quakers' principled pacifism, which had already exposed the group to criticism and inner tension during the Seven Years' War, was bound to reemerge as a potent issue in a military conflict with Great Britain. Before we turn to the fate of these congregations during and after the War for Independence, however, we will explore in more detail how the religious diversity of the town affected its inhabitants.

4

RELIGIOUS PLURALISM IN AN
EIGHTEENTH-CENTURY TOWN

PROTESTANT DIVERSITY

In a backcountry town in which several German and English congregations existed side by side, Protestant ministers were highly conscious of religious diversity and competition. The Anglican minister Richard Locke saw the Lancaster region "overrun wth Jesuitism, Moravians and New Lights" in 1748, and these competing groups were gaining "ground very much; as the justices & governing part are all of that disposition." The "Jesuits, New Lights, Quakers, Moravians, Covenanters, Dutch and Irish," Locke wrote on another occasion, "prevail for much here, that an English Clergyman meets with very little Protection & much less charity." Locke's colleague Thomas Barton computed the number of inhabitants of Lancaster County at twenty-four thousand in 1761. Among these, he claimed, "I cannot allow above one in 30 . . . to be actual Members of the Church of England. The rest are Dissenters of I believe every sort in Christendom, divided into sects and parties differing as widely from one another as they differ from us. The Bulk of them however are Calvinists and Mennonists." The Church of England was "surrounded by multitudes of Dissenters of every kind who are all brought up in such narrow principles that they can be no friends to the National Church." While the Anglicans could not claim more than five hundred adherents in Lancaster County, Barton wrote in 1764, the vast majority were "German Lutherans, Calvinists, Mennonists, Moravians, New Born, Dunkars, Presbyterians, Seceders, New Lights, Covenanters, Mountain Men, Brownists, Independents, Papists, Quakers, Jews, &c." His congregation in Lancaster numbered merely thirty families, but "the Presbyterians and such of the Germans as understand English attend also occasionally when they happen to have no service of their own."[1]

While they were wary of their clerical competitors, Lancaster's Protestant pastors also conversed and cooperated on a regular basis. We have already noted that the Anglican and Reformed congregations jointly held a lottery to complete their respective building projects in the early 1760s and that Thomas Barton preached at the consecration of Trinity Lutheran Church in 1766. At times when they did not have the benefit of a minister of their own faith, Lancasterians regularly went to hear another pastor. When no Anglican clergyman was present in the town in June 1749, Heinrich Melchior Mühlenberg preached a sermon for the Anglicans in the Lutheran church. Funerals were also frequent occasions for interdenominational sociability and cooperation. When the Lutheran clergyman Johann Friedrich Handschuh officiated at a funeral on a farm near Lancaster in 1749, for example, people from "all kinds of sects," including several respected Quakers and Mennonites, were present. At a burial in 1767, Heinrich Melchior Mühlenberg met "a Mennonite preacher who was very favorably disposed to hearing and engaging in a Christian conversation concerning practical truths." When Thomas Barton's first wife was buried in June 1774, a "pathetic discourse, well suited to the occasion," was delivered by the Lutheran minister Justus Heinrich Christian Helmuth. In December 1787 the funeral of Matthäus Gottfried Hehl, bishop of the Moravian church, was likewise "attended by many people of various classes and denominations."[2]

The cooperation of Lutheran and German Reformed pastors was certainly facilitated by the pietist inclinations of leading clergymen in both denominations.

1. Owen, "Letters of the Rev. Richard Locke and Rev. George Craig," 467; Perry, *Historical Collections*, 2:252–53, 328–29, 343, 366–67; Worner, "Church of England (Part II)," 88–89; Worner, "Church of England (Part IV)," 61.

2. *Hallesche Nachrichten*, 1:535; Tappert and Doberstein, *Journals of Henry Melchior Muhlenberg*, 2:347; *Pennsylvania Gazette*, June 29, 1774; Worner, "Church of England (Part IV)," 77; Wood, *Conestoga Crossroads*, 187, 202–3; Diller and Klein, *History of St. James' Church*, 49–50; Jeffries, "Thomas Barton," 55; Albert Cavin and August Lerbscher, "Items of Interest from the *Neue Unpartheyische Lancaster Zeitung*," PLCHS 34 (1930): 5–6. On pastors' cooperation across denominational lines, see also Glatfelter, *Pastors and People*, 2:251–52, 264–69; Schwartz, *"A Mixed Multitude,"* 144–50; Splitter, *Pastors, People, Politics*, 34–37.

Heinrich Melchior Mühlenberg, for example, characterized his Reformed colleague Johann Wilhelm Hendel as a man who "loves and seeks to foster the righteousness which is in Christ," and Justus Heinrich Christian Helmuth reported to Halle in 1774 that he and a Reformed colleague were engaged in an initiative for regular pastoral meetings for mutual "edification and brotherly encouragement." When Johann Wilhelm Hendel returned to Lancaster for a second term in 1782, his Lutheran colleague Gotthilf Heinrich Ernst Mühlenberg was delighted, for the Reformed pastor "was learned, communicative, and, best of all, diligent for the cause of Christ," so that Mühlenberg was looking forward to a "period of grace" in Lancaster. When another Reformed pastor, Christian Ludwig Becker, arrived in 1795, Mühlenberg found him open minded and learned and expected him to be a good helpmate.[3]

How did the religious diversity of Lancaster affect Protestant laypeople? Pastors often complained that the bewildering variety of churches and sects confused the laity, and some modern scholars have asserted that colonial Pennsylvanians were "accustomed to ignoring religious differences and relatively indifferent to precisely formulated religious beliefs."[4] On the other hand, the energies that Lancasterians put into the building of congregations and their repeated conflicts with pastors over matters of doctrine suggest that confessional identity did matter to them. The laity's responses to confessional diversity were in fact shaped by a number of factors. In an immigrant society, old-world experiences with and conceptions of other churches and "sects" undoubtedly continued to exert some influence, but these notions of other faiths were reshaped by economic and social interactions in the New World. In the pages that follow, the evidence for interdenominational cooperation, confessionally mixed marriages, and the crossing of congregational boundaries will be examined to arrive at a nuanced portrait of laypeople's attitudes toward religious diversity.

Some laymen and women did adopt a broad, "liberal" attitude toward the rival Christian churches and supported several of them. When Mary Prator, a widow from Earl Township, made her will in 1748 she left bequests to the

---

3. Tappert and Doberstein, *Journals of Henry Melchior Muhlenberg*, 2:465; *Hallesche Nachrichten*, 2:685; Aland and Wellenreuther, *Die Korrespondenz*, 5:488–89, 609; Gotthilf Heinrich Ernst Mühlenberg Personal Diary, vol. 1, entry for March 20, 1795, American Philosophical Society, Philadelphia (hereafter Mühlenberg Diary, American Philosophical Society). On Lutheran-Reformed cooperation in Pennsylvania, which was most conspicuous in the sharing of church buildings, see also Glatfelter, *Pastors and People*, 2:161–70, 272–75; Wolf, *Urban Village*, 221–22; and Nolt, *Foreigners in Their Own Land*, 16, 71.

4. Schwartz, *"A Mixed Multitude,"* 112–15, 120 (quote), 143–44. Cf. also Frantz, "Awakening of Religion," 266–88, esp. 268–69.

Anglican and Catholic congregations in Lancaster and the Lutheran church in Earltown.[5] Other laypeople became religious "seekers" who wandered from one congregation to the next in search of religious fulfilment and spiritual community. The best-documented case can be found in the autobiographical sketch of the gunsmith William Henry, one of Lancaster's most prominent citizens of the Revolutionary period. Born as the son of Irish immigrants in Chester County, Henry was reared as a Presbyterian, the religion of his father. His mother was "a member of the Church of England," but as he pointed out, "there were then no Anglican churches established in Pennsylvania." When he was eleven years old, William Henry was impressed by the preaching of the great revivalist George Whitefield but concluded that it was "too soon" for him to "be converted." After he came to Lancaster and began an apprenticeship with the gunmaker Mathias Roeser around midcentury, he made the acquaintance of "several learned persons" who were religious skeptics. Impressed by the books they gave him to read, Henry "became a decided Deist" himself until he felt a renewed "anxiety for the salvation of my soul." He associated himself with the Anglican congregation for some time, but when he went to an Anglican minister—probably Thomas Barton—and described his troubles to him, the minister dismissed his soul-searching as "mere fancies" and recommended that he "seek gay society, and drink a glass of wine." Henry claimed that he "took great offence at his reply" and resolved "to hold no more communication with this person." On an adventurous business voyage to England in the early 1760s, he made the acquaintance of several Quakers and, after some hesitation, felt "drawn to this denomination." Following his return to Pennsylvania, Henry persuaded his wife, Ann, to join the Society of Friends with him, but she "did not find that edification for which her heart craved" in their meetings, "and all efforts on my part to induce her to join this sect were fruitless." William and Ann Henry eventually met several Moravians and became members of their congregation in 1765, thus reaching the final stage of their spiritual journey.[6]

Henry's account graphically illustrates the range of religious choices available to laypeople who were anxious for salvation, and it highlights the importance of personal encounters in directing a religious "seeker" toward a particular church.

5. Lancaster County Will Book A-I-143, Pennsylvania State Archives.

6. John Ward Willson Loose, "William Henry Memoirs, 1748–1786," *JLCHS* 76 (1972): 60–66; cf. Herbert H. Beck, "William Henry: Patriot, Master Gunsmith, Progenitor of the Steamboat," *Transactions of the Moravian Historical Society* 16, no. 2 (1955): 69–95. Diller and Klein identify Henry as a leading member of St. James' Anglican Church without even mentioning his later Moravian affiliation (*History of St. James' Church*, 66).

The question remains, however, how common such spiritual odysseys were. In fact, the available evidence indicates that they were quite exceptional. As outlined in the first two chapters, a number of Lutherans and several German Reformed joined the Moravians when they formed their own congregation in the 1740s, and several converts to Moravianism experienced complex spiritual journeys. John DeHuff, for example, was originally a member of the Labadist community, a radical pietist group, in the Bohemia district of Maryland. After the death of his father, the sixteen-year-old boy came to Germantown to learn the saddler's trade and associated with local Anabaptists. In Lancaster he became an early leader of the German Reformed congregation but was eventually admitted to the United Brethren in 1748.[7] Leonhard Bender, a leading supporter of pastor Laurentius Nyberg in the Lutheran schism in 1746, was married to a former Mennonite who had been baptized by the Lutheran pastor Stoever in 1737. Conrad Schwartz, another founding member of the Moravian congregation, was of Reformed origin but had associated with the Lutheran church after coming to America in 1740. In 1760 the Moravians expelled him because his frequent fights with his wife were regarded a public nuisance, and he died in wretched poverty five years later.[8] For most of the Lutherans and Reformed who joined the Moravians in the late 1740s, however, association with the United Brethren was a singular, irreversible decision, and during the first seven decades of Lancaster's existence there was no comparable instance of a "mass defection" of laypeople from one particular church to another.

While relations with the Moravians remained tense for at least a generation, many Lutherans had close contacts with German Reformed laypeople, and members of the two groups frequently intermarried. Of the 111 marriages recorded in the Lutheran church book between 1748 and 1751, ten joined Lutheran and Reformed spouses. Not all of these matches were harmonious. In November 1748 the Lutheran Philipp Rudesill did not come to communion "on account of the excuse of an argument with his Ref(ormed) wife," and a few months earlier a Reformed man complained to pastor Handschuh about the disunity and strife in his household after his Lutheran wife had joined the Moravians while their daughter remained in the Lutheran congregation. Nevertheless, Lutheran-Reformed marriages continued to occur frequently. Among the 107 Lutheran Easter communicants in 1749, six were married to Reformed spouses while one

7. John DeHuff obituary in Lancaster Diaries, 1751, Moravian Archives.

8. Smith and Weiser, *Trinity Lutheran Church Records,* 1:8, 407; Lancaster Diaries, 1765, entry for November 8, Moravian Archives.

young woman was the daughter of a Reformed father and a Lutheran mother. Heinrich Melchior Mühlenberg remarked in 1754 that Lutheran and Reformed laypeople were "interwoven" by marriage ties throughout the province.[9]

When 205 people announced their intention to participate in Holy Supper on Easter Sunday 1783, Lutheran minister Gotthilf Heinrich Ernst Mühlenberg counted eighteen people with Reformed spouses among them, and of the roughly fourteen hundred communicants Mühlenberg recorded between 1793 and 1799, more than seventy were married to a Reformed husband or wife.[10] Relations between Reformed lay leaders and the Lutheran congregation were especially close. When a subscription for the new Lutheran church building was set up in 1761, a number of prominent Reformed laymen contributed to it. Wilhelm Bausman and Philipp Leonhard each pledged £10, Johannes Baer £8, and Michael Diffendorfer £5. When the Lutheran congregation introduced pew rents in their new Church of the Holy Trinity in 1766, Reformed leaders Peter Isch, Wilhelm Bausman, Johannes Baer, Michael Diffendorfer, Philipp Graffort, Nicolaus Job, and Valentin Weber—who did not have to pay for the pews in their own church—rented pews there.[11]

To some extent, the close cooperation of Lutherans and Reformed reflected the European heritage of both denominations. Relationships between Lutherans and Reformed in Germany had by no means always been harmonious, but both churches were among the three confessions legally recognized in the Holy Roman Empire under the terms of the Peace of Westphalia (1648), and they shared the tradition of a trained, ordained ministry. In confessionally fragmented territories such as the Electoral Palatinate, Lutherans and Reformed enjoyed comparable civic rights in the eighteenth century, they lived and worked side by side and inter-married with some frequency.[12] In Lancaster, moreover, Lutheran and Reformed lay leaders worked together in institutions such as the borough council, the fire

9. Smith and Weiser, *Trinity Lutheran Church Records*, 1:228–39, 335–39; Handschuh Diarium, entry for June 18, 1748, pp. 20–21, Archiv der Franckeschen Stiftungen; Aland, *Die Korrespondenz*, 2:152. Cf. Hucho, *Weiblich und fremd*, 363–65, 483–89.

10. Smith and Weiser, *Trinity Lutheran Church Records*, 3:254–58, 358–90; cf. Glatfelter, *Pastors and People*, 2:162.

11. Trinity Lutheran Church Documents, vol. 103, pp. 9–10, 15–16, 53–54, Trinity Lutheran Church Archives; Smith and Weiser, *Trinity Lutheran Church Records*, 2:324–25, 344–45, 358–59, 362–63, 366–67, 370–71, 400–401.

12. See Peter Zschunke, *Konfession und Alltag in Oppenheim: Beiträge zur Geschichte von Bevölkerung und Gesellschaft einer gemischtkonfessionellen Kleinstadt in der Frühen Neuzeit* (Wiesbaden: Steiner, 1984); Eva Heller-Karneth, *Drei Konfessionen in einer Stadt: Zur Bedeutung des konfessionellen Faktors im Alzey des Ancien Regime* (Würzburg: Bayerische Blätter für Volkskunde, 1996); Dagmar Freist, "One Body, Two Minds: Mixed Marriage in Early Modern Germany," in *Gender in Early Modern Germany*, ed. Ulinka Rublack (Cambridge: Cambridge University Press, 2002), 275–305.

companies, and the library company, and these experiences may have contributed to a shared sense of public responsibility.

Relationships between "church" and "sect" Germans, on the other hand, required members of both groups to reevaluate their notions and perceptions of each other. According to Stephen L. Longenecker, among the most significant factors contributing to the growth of tolerance in colonial Pennsylvania were "the new socio-economic relationships between German Anabaptists and Lutherans and Reformed." Whereas "European Germans perceived Anabaptists as outcasts, . . . these traditional, hierarchical relationships ended in Pennsylvania, enabling the last to become first."[13] In fact, Anabaptist groups had gained limited toleration and a measure of economic security in southwest German territories such as the Electoral Palatinate and the margravate of Baden-Durlach, where they leased large estates and acquired a reputation as skillful, diligent, and "useful" farmers in the course of the eighteenth century. Nevertheless, they could not become citizens in these territories but were merely tolerated for good behavior. They could not worship in public, had to pay special "protection fees," and in 1744 the Elector Palatine limited the number of Anabaptist families he permitted to settle in his territories to two hundred.[14]

In Pennsylvania, on the other hand, Mennonites had been among the first settlers in the Conestoga Valley, and by the middle of the eighteenth century they owned many prosperous farms in the Lancaster area. As a consequence of their strong economic position, many newly arrived Lutherans worked for Anabaptist farmers as indentured servants. The communicant lists compiled by pastor Handschuh around midcentury identify at least twelve Lutheran men and women as servants of Mennonites, and the communicant Johann Michael Schmiedeknecht was described as a "schoolmaster among the Mennonites." In

13. Longenecker, *Piety and Tolerance*, 25.

14. Jean Vogt, "Wiedertäufer und ländliche Gemeinden im nördlichen Elsaß und in der Pfalz," *Mennonitische Geschichtsblätter* 41 (1984): 3–47; Frank Konersmann, "Duldung, Privilegierung, Assimilation und Säkularisation: Mennonitische Glaubensgemeinschaften in der Pfalz, in Rheinhessen und am nördlichen Oberrhein, 1648–1802," in *Minderheiten, Obrigkeit und Gesellschaft in der Frühen Neuzeit. Integrations- und Abgrenzungsprozesse im süddeutschen Raum*, ed. Mark Häberlein and Martin Zürn (St. Katharinen: Scripta-Mercaturae-Verlag, 2001), 339–75; Mark Häberlein and Michaela Schmölz-Häberlein, "Die Ansiedlung von Täufern am Oberrhein im 18. Jahrhundert: Eine religiöse Minderheit im Spannungsfeld herrschaftlicher Ansprüche und wirtschaftlicher Interessen," in ibid., 377–402; Häberlein and Schmölz-Häberlein, "Eighteenth-Century Anabaptists in the Margravate of Baden and Neighboring Territories," *Mennonite Quarterly Review* 75 (2001): 471–92. In some north German territories Mennonites could even become citizens, albeit with limited political rights. See Michael D. Driedger, *Obedient Heretics: Mennonite Identities in Lutheran Hamburg and Altona During the Confessional Age* (Aldershot: Ashgate, 2002).

June 1748 Handschuh recorded a resolution of the Lutheran church council to inquire about children of Lutheran parents in the service of members of other denominations, and subsequently he made several visits to Anabaptist farmers with Lutheran servants. In September 1748, for example, Handschuh accompanied two elders and a woman from his congregation to a "Mennonite plantation" where the woman's son was in service. The delegation asked the farmer to let the son participate in preparatory classes for Holy Communion, to which the Mennonite agreed "under certain conditions." The next year a widow pleaded with Handschuh to look after her stepson, who had been "sold" to a Mennonite, and in April 1750 he visited the dying servant girl of "separatists." While he supplied Lancaster in 1767, Heinrich Melchior Mühlenberg "was called out of the city early in the morning to a prominent Mennonite's farm in order to visit a sick man, a member of our congregation there."[15] Some Mennonite children also attended the Moravian school in Lancaster. In 1765 the Moravian diarist noted that a former Mennonite named Christian Schenk and his wife, who had been students at the Moravian school many years before, regularly attended the United Brethren's services.[16]

Social and economic contacts between "church" and "sect" people also led to some intermarriage. Pastor Handschuh's communicants Johann Jacob Brehm and Anna Margaretha Mundaffin had Mennonite spouses, and the minister noted that Anna Margaretha had several unbaptized children. In February 1751 Jacob Zinck, a Reformed, and his Mennonite wife had their child baptized by the Lutheran pastor.[17] Handschuh officiated at the marriage of the Mennonite Andreas Muselman and his Reformed wife, Margaretha Helland, in March 1749, and three months later he performed the marriage of a Mennonite man and a Lutheran woman. The following September Handschuh baptized the son of a Mennonite father and an Anglican mother. In January 1750 the Lutheran pastor officiated at Ludwig Huber's marriage to Margaretha Graeff. While Margaretha had been born into a Mennonite family, her parents had joined the Ephrata Dunkers, and Margaretha herself eventually decided to join the Lutheran

15. Smith and Weiser, *Trinity Lutheran Church Records*, 1:333, 337–39, 343, 345–46, 348, 355, 364–65, 369; Handschuh Diarium, entries for June 11 and September 8, 1748, Archiv der Franckeschen Stiftungen; *Hallesche Nachrichten*, 1:531, 541, 547–48; Tappert and Doberstein, *Journals of Henry Melchior Muhlenberg*, 2:354. For the origins of Johann Michael Schmiedeknecht, see Burgert, *Northern Alsace*, 440. On pastors' concern for the spiritual needs of servants, cf. Schwartz, "A Mixed Multitude," 146.

16. Protocoll, entries for May 24, 1755, and April 5, 1761, Moravian Archives; Lancaster Diaries, 1765, "Summarischer Extract," Moravian Archives.

17. Smith and Weiser, *Trinity Lutheran Church Records*, 1:92, 327, 359, 362–63.

church, where she received her first communion in April 1750. Peter Mayer's wife, Dorothea, who was confirmed in the Lutheran church on Palm Sunday 1750, was "a former Dunker, who was baptized three years ago by pastor Brunholtz."[18]

In later years Lutheran pastors continued to marry and bury Mennonites and baptized their children as occasion required. The Mennonite Christian Stehmann was buried by the Lutheran clergyman J. H. C. Helmuth "at his own request" in February 1776. When the aged Cornelius Lahn (or Lane) was buried in January 1780, the Mennonite preacher Martin Boehm delivered the funeral sermon upon the request of the deceased. In his will Lahn bequeathed £10 to the "Elders of the Menonit Meeting" for the the poor "belonging to that Society" and the same sum to the wardens of Trinity Lutheran Church. Four people who took communion in Trinity Lutheran Church between 1793 and 1799 were married to Mennonite spouses.[19]

When Lancaster's Lutheran and German Reformed ministers reported their activities to colleagues in Pennsylvania and Europe, they frequently referred to "sectarians" who desired baptism or wished to join their congregations. Such cases were of high symbolic importance because, from these pastors' viewpoint, they showed that the "true Christian religion" held its ground against the errors of the "sects." Johann Friedrich Handschuh recorded the baptism of a twenty-one-year-old Quaker and a conversation with a former Seventh Day Baptist who had joined the Mennonites and now came to hear the Lutheran pastor's sermons. His Reformed colleague Johann Wilhelm Hendel reported in 1765 that four married women, "who came from the Catholics and from the Men-nonites," had joined his congregation.[20] During a stay in Lancaster in 1767 Heinrich Melchior Mühlenberg learned that Johannes Müller, a "reputable man" who had been baptized by the Mennonites but had later withdrawn from them, had expressed interest to have his three adolescent sons baptized in the Lutheran faith. Müller had even approached Lancaster's departed Lutheran pastor Gerock, "but nothing was done about it." When Mühlenberg visited Müller in his "splendid house," the latter "seemed to be moved and awakened" and affirmed his desire to have his sons baptized, "especially because the young people in this land . . . are led astray by a multitude of alluring examples into unbelief and its depressing consequences." Mühlenberg instructed the three

18. Smith and Weiser, *Trinity Lutheran Church Records*, 1:76, 230–31, 234, 351, 352.

19. Smith and Weiser, *Trinity Lutheran Church Records*, 2:35, 156, 158, 161, 194; 3:53, 74, 115, 135–36, 358–90; Lancaster County Will Book C-I-559, Pennsylvania State Archives.

20. *Hallesche Nachrichten*, 1:536, 546; Hinke, *Minutes of the Coetus*, 236.

youths privately and found them "very much inclined and willing to surrender their hearts to the Redeemer," so that he eventually baptized them in the presence of several elders and deacons.[21]

Mühlenberg's younger colleague Justus Heinrich Christian Helmuth wrote in 1773 that he had publicly baptized two Mennonite women and confirmed them along with a married man who was the son of a separatist. A week before the confirmation ceremony a Mennonite woman who had already received baptism and taken communion with her own people asked to be confirmed by him. Helmuth accepted her for further instruction and was hopeful for her conversion—particularly since the woman's mother had expressed interest in renting a pew in Trinity Lutheran Church. By 1774 Helmuth was regularly preaching to small, confessionally diverse groups of Mennonites, separatists, and others in the countryside. The Mennonites, he claimed, bore such affection for him that several had joined Trinity Lutheran Church and he might easily convert many more. However, he preferred to make "true Christians" of them first. Whereas some leading Mennonites opposed his regular preaching among the Anabaptists, one of their bishops strongly supported him.[22] Gotthilf Heinrich Ernst Mühlenberg informed his father in 1784 that he had recently confirmed fifty-five people, including two former Moravians, one New England-born Presbyterian, and the daughter of a separatist and his Moravian wife. According to Mühlenberg, the young woman was in such a state of spiritual anguish that people thought her mad; she told him about a dream in which the pastor chided her for still being unconfirmed. Mühlenberg took her dream seriously and instructed her, first in private, then together with his other confirmands.[23]

Within Lancaster's English-speaking community, cooperation among Anglicans and Presbyterians is not as well documented as Lutheran-Reformed collaboration on the German side, but it probably was extensive, too. Minister Thomas Barton, who emphasized the doctrinal orthodoxy of the Church of England, did not have a high opinion of Presbyterians, whom he regarded as "a people who are unsteady and much given to change, fond of Novelty, and easily led away by every kind of Doctrine" and therefore "in much disrepute with all the other Sects."[24] The minister's reservations, however, did not prevent a New Side Presbyterian like Edward Shippen from becoming active in the affairs of the Anglican congregation as long

21. Tappert and Doberstein, *Journals of Henry Melchior Muhlenberg*, 2:343–44, 346–48.
22. *Hallesche Nachrichten*, 2:701–2.
23. Aland and Wellenreuther, *Die Korrespondenz*, 5:653.
24. Perry, *Historical Collections*, 2:367–68.

as there was no Presbyterian church in town. Writing in 1825, Edward Burd described his grandfather Edward Shippen as "a very religious and charitable man" who had "family prayers said every morning to which his servants were all summoned," but was also "liberal in his sentiments with respect to the different religious sects." As he thought "that the Episcopal & Presbyterian Religions differed only in non-essentials" and there was no Presbyterian church in town at the time, Shippen "had a pew in the Episcopal Church, but the parson attending two other congregations in rotation in the country & performing divine service in Lancaster only once in three weeks he joined with others in having a Presbyterian meeting built & attended both places of worship alternately."[25] Edward Shippen's own letters show that inner piety was more important to him than confessional doctrine. Thanking James Read for several hymns that Read had transcribed for him, Shippen wrote in 1771: "These holy Songs put me in mind of the Dear Watts, Wesley, Whitefield and other Christian Heroes!"[26]

Interdenominational cooperation across national or "ethnic" lines was still another matter. The German churches in particular held little attraction for the town's English speakers. Only a few members of the English community joined the Lutherans, Reformed, or Moravians. Edward Smout, a prominent justice of the peace who had been a founding member of the Anglican congregation in 1744, attached himself to the Moravians late in his life and left considerable bequests to both religious communities in the will he made in 1751.[27] John Hopson—who was not "of Germanic background," as Jerome H. Wood has claimed, but was born in England in 1720—joined the Moravian church after his marriage to the widow of Matthäus Jung in 1750. He prospered as a shopkeeper and served as an assistant burgess for most of the period from 1762 to 1785. When Hopson made his will in 1804, he left a town lot to "the incorporated society at Bethlehem for the propagation of the gospel among the Heathens" and £50 for the support of the Moravian pastor in Lancaster.[28] Like Hopson, the Irishman Marcus Shee associated with the Moravians after his marriage to a German woman, Anna

25. Edward Burd to William Rawle, December 17, 1825, printed in "Some Biographical Letters," *PMHB* 23 (1899): 202–4 (quotes on 204). See also chapter 3.

26. Edward Shippen to James Read, December 15, 1771, Shippen Papers, vol. 7, p. 57, Historical Society of Pennsylvania.

27. Lancaster County Will Book A-I-196, Pennsylvania State Archives; Coldren and Heisey, "Religious Life," 138. See also chapters 3 and 6.

28. Lancaster County Will Book J-I-100, Pennsylvania State Archives; *Moravian Burial Book*, 28; Wood, *Conestoga Crossroads*, 106, 140, 151, 174. Hopson was assistant burgess in 1762/63, from 1766 to 1775, and from 1778 to 1785.

Christina Kronin, who came from the Palatinate and was reared as a Lutheran. Ten children were born to the couple from 1753 to 1769, and Shee and his wife became members of the congregation in 1759.[29] Margaret Moore, the daughter of a Scottish immigrant, had grown up in Philadelphia and come to Lancaster in 1768 to live with her brother. In February 1769 she married the hatter Matthias Graff, a member of the Moravian congregation. Margaret joined her husband's church and remained in the Moravian fold until her death in 1789. After her husband's death she married the widower John Okely, a native of Bedford in England, in 1780. Okely also became a member of the Moravian congregation. Another English speaker attracted to the Moravian fold was Thomas Edwards, an Irishman from the county of Antrim in Ulster, who married Christoph Reigart's widow, Susanna, in 1785 and died nine years later.[30] As early as 1762 the Moravian pastor Christian Russmeyer had started to offer evening services in English every other week. Although the Moravian diaries noted the attendance of prominent English speakers—the attorney David Stout, a member of the Anglican congregation, was reportedly "much affected" when he attended a session in February 1764—the experiment was a mixed success and was discontinued after a few years. After the Revolution English services were reintroduced and became a permanent feature of congregational life.[31]

The silversmith Charles Hall, a founding member of the Presbyterian congregation, married Maria Salome LeRoy, a daughter of the Swiss watchmaker Abraham LeRoy. This marital alliance brought him into close contact with the German Reformed community, to which he bequeathed £5 in the will he made in 1783. After his death he was buried in the German Reformed churchyard.[32] A sister of Hall's Swiss wife was also married to an English speaker, Wilton Atkinson, whose father and brother were Anglican vestrymen. While the marriage was performed by the Anglican pastor in 1762, their son was baptized in the Reformed church four years later with the pastor's wife, Elisabeth Hendel, acting as sponsor. Relations between Atkinson and his wife's family were less than cordial, however, for when his brother-in-law, Abraham Le Roy, made his

29. Verzeichniß der unter der Brüder Diaconie stehenden Seelen in und um Lancaster, nos. 74–75, Moravian Archives; *Moravian Burial Book*, 17, 19.

30. *Moravian Burial Book*, 17–18, 21–22; Wood, *Conestoga Crossroads*, 213.

31. Kurze Relation, 23, Moravian Archives; Lancaster Diaries, 1763–65, 1784, "Memorabilien," Moravian Archives; Wood, *Conestoga Crossroads*, 194. On Moravians' contacts with English speakers in colonial Pennsylvania, see also Schwartz, *"A Mixed Multitude,"* 130–32, 154–55.

32. Lancaster County Will Book D-I-304, Pennsylvania State Archives; Robinson, "Charles Hall," 177–82; Gerstell, *Silversmiths*, 37–44.

will in 1765 and left the bulk of his estate to his four sisters he ordered that Anna Maria's share should not fall into Atkinson's hands. In fact Atkinson defaulted on his debts only a year later.[33]

While the Moravian and Reformed congregations attracted at least a few English speakers, the Lutheran church remained almost exclusively German. English-speaking men and women were married by the Lutheran pastor or had their children baptized by him in the absence of an Anglican or Presbyterian clergyman, to be sure, but extremely few of them joined the congregation. During his stay in Lancaster in 1768, Heinrich Melchior Mühlenberg baptized Johannes Eichholtz's wife after instructing her in English "because, although she was married to a German, her mother was English." Elizabeth Murray, a communicant at Trinity Lutheran Church in 1780, was identified as "a Welsh person."[34] Among the almost four hundred people who rented pews in Trinity Lutheran church between 1766 and 1782, however, the only clearly identifiable English name is that of Robert Wilson, and he paid for a pew only during the brief period from 1777 to 1779 when the Anglican church was closed on account of minister Thomas Barton's loyalism.[35] The Lutheran congregation's subscription for a new organ in 1771 drew several pledges from Reformed laymen but only one from an English-speaking inhabitant, Caleb Thompson.[36] When the congregation started another subscription for the construction of a steeple in 1785, about a dozen English speakers were among the 394 subscribers, with the largest pledge, amounting to £6, coming from General Edward Hand.[37] Of the more than fourteen hundred people who took communion in Trinity Lutheran Church between 1793 and 1799, only nine were identified as having an English-speaking husband or wife.[38]

Prejudice may have been partly responsible for this low rate of ethnic intermarriage. James Burd Jr., a scion of the influential Shippen-Burd clan, aroused the ire of his relatives when he married a "Low-bred Dutch girl," and a Continental

---

33. Wright, *Lancaster County Church Records*, 2:62 and 3:103; Lancaster County Will Books B-I-148 and B-I-545, Pennsylvania State Archives; Mayhill, *Deed Abstracts*, 66 (E215b), 113 (H375b), 115 (H391); Lancaster County Orphans Court Records, 1772–76, p. 50, September 3, 1772, Pennsylvania State Archives.

34. Tappert and Doberstein, *Journals of Henry Melchior Muhlenberg*, 2:354; Smith and Weiser, *Trinity Lutheran Church Records*, 2:285.

35. Smith and Weiser, *Trinity Lutheran Church Records*, 2:304–465, esp. 438–39.

36. Trinity Lutheran Church Documents, vol. 103, pp. 74–82, Trinity Lutheran Church Archives.

37. Trinity Lutheran Church Documents, vol. 103, pp. 85–99, Trinity Lutheran Church Archives.

38. Smith and Weiser, *Trinity Lutheran Church Records*, 3:358–90: Christine Butin (359), Sus[anna] and Christine Evans (363), Adam Hubley (369), Jens Jansen (371), Martin Kuhns (372), Elis[abeth] McCrackan (377), Maria MacNaughton (379), Regina Philips (380).

Army officer and son of a Presbyterian clergyman who was stationed in Lancaster during the Revolutionary War may have reflected the sentiments of many English speakers when he wrote to his brother in 1781: "I cannot say I will follow your Advice respecting marrying a Dutch Girl, with a good Plantation & a Conestoga Wagon, tho' if I could get the two latter, without the Incumbrance of the former, I should hardly pass them by; but as that is not very likely, I must give over all thoughts of either." Whereas there were "some very genteel English Families" in town, this officer thought, "[t]he inhabitants being generally German, puts sociability out of the Question."[39]

Familiarity with these "very genteel English families" seems to have attracted members of some prominent Lutheran families to the Anglican congregation. Once again, though, the number of cases is small. Adam Simon Kuhn, the eminent German physician, justice of the peace, and Lutheran church elder, had expressed interest in obtaining a pew in St. James' Anglican Church as early as 1757, and Thomas Barton wrote hopefully in 1760 that the "principal Germans" in Lancaster were Lutherans who "might easily be brought to unite with the Church [of England]." They "would gladly embrace every opportunity to teach their children the Religion, Manners and Customs of England" and seemed well disposed toward the Church, but, he added, "the want of an organ of which these people are extremely fond, & in which they place almost half their devotion, has hitherto kept them back." Barton therefore considered purchasing a small instrument with the help of Kuhn.[40] Kuhn may have seen anglicization as a necessary precondition for getting his sons started in their professional careers: three of his sons studied medicine and became physicians. After graduating from the College of Philadelphia and officiating as a deacon in the Lutheran church for two years, Daniel Kuhn was preparing to travel to England in 1771 to seek ordination as an Anglican minister. Recommending him to the Society for the Propagation of the Gospel, Barton wrote that Kuhn "chuses to go into the Church of England where he hopes to be more generally useful as he speaks the English language as well as the Dutch." There was a good prospect of Kuhn becoming "a useful Missionary & of advantage to the Church if he can be well placed where he will have a mixture of English & Germans." Daniel Kuhn,

---

39. Klein, *Portrait of an Early American Family*, 207; Joseph M. Beatty Jr., "Letters of the Four Beatty Brothers of the Continental Army, 1774–1794," *PMHB* 44 (1920): 222.

40. St. James Vestry Minutes, 16, St. James Episcopal Church; Perry, *Historical Collections*, 2:293–95, 315, 408–9; Worner, "Church of England (Part III)," 48–49; "Church of England (Part IV)," 57; Wood, *Conestoga Crossroads*, 195–96; Glatfelter, *Pastors and People*, 2:267–68; Rhoden, *Revolutionary Anglicanism*, 22.

however, eventually received a degree in theology from the University of Uppsala and returned to Pennsylvania as a Lutheran pastor.[41] In contrast to the Huguenots and Dutch Reformed in New York City or the Swedish Lutherans in rural New Jersey, the vast majority of the much more numerous group of German Lutherans in Lancaster withstood the lure of Anglicanism.[42]

Still, several wealthy German Lutherans associated with the Anglican congregation after their marriage. Matthias Slough (Schlauch) married the widow of tavernkeeper George Gibson and continued his business. By the time of the Revolution, his inn, "The White Swan," was a favorite of well-to-do travelers, and Slough extended his activities to wagon transportation and the operation of stage lines. After serving on the borough council (1757–61), as county coroner (1755–68), and county treasurer (1763–69), Slough was elected to the Pennsylvania Assembly in 1773 and was a member of the state assembly from 1780 to 1783. In April 1776 he informed the readers of the *Pennsylvania Gazette* that he "has quit tavern-keeping and devotes all his time now to the dry-goods business and selling wine and rum by the gallon." After the death of his first wife, Margaretha Graff, the wealthy shopkeeper Paul Zantzinger married a daughter of Thomas Barton in 1774. Like Adam Simon Kuhn and Matthias Slough, Zantzinger kept pews in both the Lutheran and Anglican churches and supported building projects in both congregations. Significantly, both Slough and Zantzinger were American-born sons of German immigrants. When Thomas Barton's second wife described Paul Zantzinger as "really an extream genteel polite Man," this certainly implied that he was thoroughly anglicized.[43]

Bernhard Hubele's son Adam, who had grown up in Lancaster, joined the Anglican Christ Church in Philadelphia after his marriage to Jonathan Evans's daughter Mary in 1772. As a successful merchant and auctioneer in the city, Adam Hubley became a political leader during the Revolution and was elected to the vestry of Christ Church in 1784. He was buried in St. Peter's Episcopal churchyard after his death from yellow fever in 1793.[44] When St. James' Anglican congregation

41. Perry, *Historical Collections*, 2:450–51; Worner, "Church of England (Part IV)," 71–72; Heisey, "Borough Fathers," 52–53.

42. Cf. Goodfriend, "Social Dimensions of Congregational Life," 252–78, esp. 262–74; Balmer, *Perfect Babel of Confusion*, 132–40; Fea, "Ethnicity," 45–78, esp. 68–72.

43. Ellis and Evans, *History of Lancaster County,* 396, 401, 489; Ryerson, *The Revolution Is Now Begun*, 111, 143, 262–63; Diller and Klein, *History of St. James' Church*, 83–84; M. Luther Heisey, "A Biography of Paul Zantzinger," *PLCHS* 47 (1943): 113–19; Barton, *Bartons in Lancaster*, 213; Wood, *Conestoga Crossroads*, 174, 213.

44. Lippold, "Hubley Family," esp. 59–61. Cf. Jackson Turner Main, *Political Parties Before the Constitution* (Chapel Hill: University of North Carolina Press, 1973), 433–34; Ryerson, *The Revolution Is Now Begun*, 268–69, 277; Splitter, *Pastors, People, Politics*, 220n4, 236–37, 341.

in Lancaster sought contributors for the church bell it wished to import from London in 1770, Bernhard and Michael Hubele, Adam Reigart, Paul Zantzinger, and Matthias Slough were among the subscribers. The appearance of other German-speaking congregational leaders on the subscription list—Reformed laymen Wilhelm Bausman, Christian Voight, Michael Diffendorfer, and Paul Weitzel, Lutherans Christian Wertz and Georg Mayer, and Moravian Marcus Jung—shows that they deemed it important to cultivate cordial relations with the Anglican church and its local leaders.[45] Considering the rarity of intermarriage, however, Jerome H. Wood has rightly claimed that "Lancaster was still essentially two ethnic communities at the end of the eighteenth century." German- and English-speaking residents regularly did business with each other, they met in taverns and social circles, and they cooperated in civic projects such as the establishment of the Lancaster Library Company. Ethnic intermarriage, however, seldom occurred throughout the eighteenth century. On Sundays and religious holidays, German and English inhabitants generally occupied seats in separate congregations.[46]

These findings are consistent with the results of Laura Becker's study of Reading. Founded in 1752 as the administrative center of newly formed Berks County, about 85 percent of the town's residents were German-speaking on the eve of the American Revolution. Of the residents whose religious affiliation is known, more than half were Lutheran and over 30 percent Reformed in 1773, while Quakers and Anglicans together made up 10 percent of the population, and Catholics—"the only truly ethnically mixed group in town"—constituted 1.7 percent. According to Becker, most inhabitants of colonial Reading married within their own religious group: "Of the 347 different men in Reading in 1767 or 1773, only . . . nineteen are known to have crossed religious lines in marriage, a mere 5.5 %." Intermarriage was not uncommon among Lutherans and Reformed, but seldom occurred between English and German speakers. Friendship, as revealed in the choice of testamentary executors, rarely crossed ethnic lines as well. After the Revolution, Becker finds "only a slight increase of intermarriage" between English and German speakers. "Ethnic differences," she concludes, "created barriers to comfortable interaction among all citizens, and the particular balance of ethnic groups in Reading further complicated affairs. With a small number of British holding most of the prominent economic and political positions while the Germans were completely dominant numerically, no one really 'set a style' in the community."[47]

45. Worner, "Old St. James's Church Bell," 243; Diller and Klein, *History of St. James' Church*, 46.
46. Wood, *Conestoga Crossroads*, 212–15.
47. Becker, "Community Experience," 29–31, 46–48, 81–82, 197, 211, 219, 462.

If marriage across ethnic lines was rare in towns like Lancaster and Reading, so were interdenominational or "ethnic" conflicts. This is all the more remarkable since so many conflicts occurred within Lancaster's congregations. Moreover, when inhabitants of diverse backgrounds did fight with one another, the role of religion or ethnicity remains obscure. In 1752, for example, the prominent Lutheran physician and incumbent chief burgess Adam Simon Kuhn sued Peter Worrall, the Quaker member of the Pennsylvania Assembly, because the latter had allegedly used "Scandalous and contemptuous" language against him in his house, insinuating that a German like Kuhn was unable to understand the responsibilities of a burgess as well as he could. This prompted Kuhn to order Worrall out of his house, but the latter refused. Kuhn then called a constable to escort the legislator out, but Worrall threatened to "raise the Town . . . in a minute" if anyone attempted to lay a hand on him. When the jury declined to indict Worrall, the case was dropped.[48] While this quarrel might superficially be termed an ethnic conflict, we have seen that Adam Simon Kuhn was one of the few German Lutherans who pursued a conscious strategy of anglicization, and he may have found Worrall's remark so insulting precisely because it seemed to deny his aspirations to make himself and his family "English." Moreover, Worrall had been disowned by the Sadsbury Monthly Meeting and Kuhn had been instrumental in driving pastor Handschuh from Lancaster the year before. Both combatants may thus have felt insecure about their religious affiliation. Above all, both were socially and politically ambitious men who were more than likely to have a keen sense of their own reputations, and the sequence of events in this quarrel suggests that reputation—not ethnic prejudice—lay at the heart of the conflict.

CATHOLICS IN A PROTESTANT SOCIETY

The religious diversity of eighteenth-century Lancaster was mainly a diversity of Protestant beliefs. Catholics made up a small minority of colonial Pennsylvania's population, and Lancaster was no exception in this regard. In 1757, when the colony probably numbered about two hundred thousand white inhabitants, the five Jesuit missionaries then active in Pennsylvania counted 1,365 adult members of their faith. Two hundred fifty-one Catholics—two hundred two of German and forty-nine of Irish origin—were reported to live in Lancaster County.[49] Still,

48. Wood, *Conestoga Crossroads*, 29–30; Horle, *Lawmaking and Legislators*, 1081.
49. Samuel Hazard, ed., *Pennsylvania Archives*, 1st series (Philadelphia: J. Severns, 1853), 3:144–45; James Hennesey, *American Catholics: A History of the Roman Catholic Community in the United States*

Catholics were present from the town's beginnings, and they had their own chapel even before the Anglicans or Presbyterians had organized their respective congregations. Several Catholics were wealthy and respected people who lived peacefully among their Protestant neighbors for decades; some were married to Protestants. While the records do provide occasional glimpses of "anti-Papist" sentiments, the overall impression is that the presence of this minority created little tension.

Most early settlers of Lancaster probably were familiar with Catholics before they migrated to Pennsylvania. This was definitely the case for immigrants from southwest Germany, whose area of origin was a patchwork of small Catholic and Protestant territories. Some southwest German villages were jointly administered by Catholic and Protestant princes. In the Palatinate, once a stronghold of the Reformed faith, a Catholic line had succeeded to the elector's throne in 1685, and although the rights of the Reformed majority were guaranteed in the treaty of succession, the new electors actively promoted Catholic settlement. In the religious declaration of 1705, the electors granted liberty of conscience to Catholic, Lutheran, and Reformed subjects, and ecclesiastical properties were divided between the Catholics and the Reformed.[50] In the eighteenth century, members of the three faiths lived side by side in Palatine towns, and while there was friction over the joint use of church properties and public demonstrations of Catholicism such as processions, relations between the different religious groups could be remarkably harmonious.[51] Intermarriage was not unusual: Jacob Eichholtz, who emigrated from the village of Neckarbischofsheim in the Kraichgau in 1737 and became a tavernkeeper in Lancaster, was the son of a Lutheran father and a Catholic mother.[52] In the Lutheran margravate of Baden-Durlach, another

(New York: Oxford University Press, 1981), 50; Jay P. Dolan, *The American Catholic Experience: A History from Colonial Times to the Present* (Garden City, N.Y.: Image Books 1985), 87; Schwartz, *"A Mixed Multitude,"* 241.

50. Meinrad Schaab, "Die Wiederherstellung des Katholizismus in der Kurpfalz im 17. und 18. Jahrhundert," *Zeitschrift für Geschichte des Oberrheins* 114 (1966): 147–205; Alfred Hans, *Die kurpfälzische Religionsdeklaration von 1705. Ihre Entstehung und Bedeutung für das Zusammenleben der drei im Reich tolerierten Konfessionen* (Mainz: Selbstverlag der Gesellschaft für Mittelrheinische Kirchengeschichte, 1973); Anton Schindling, "Andersgläubige Nachbarn. Mehrkonfessionalität und Parität in Territorien und Städten des Reichs," in *1648. Krieg und Frieden in Europa*, vol. 1, *Geschichte, Religion, Recht und Gesellschaft*, ed. Klaus Bußmann and Heinz Schilling (Münster: n.p., 1998), 465–73.

51. Zschunke, *Konfession und Alltag in Oppenheim*; Heller-Karneth, *Drei Konfessionen*. Cf. Ronnie Po-Chia Hsia, "Between State and Community: Religious and Ethnic Minorities in Early Modern Germany," in *Germania Illustrata: Essays on Early Modern Germany Presented to Gerald Strauss*, ed. Andrew C. Fix and Susan C. Karant-Nunn (Kirksville, Mo.: Sixteenth Century Journal Publishers, 1989), 169–80.

52. Burgert, *Kraichgau*, 100.

area of significant German emigration to America, Catholics were granted extensive civic privileges in the new capital of Karlsruhe, where they made up 12 percent of the population in the 1770s, and were allowed to settle in district towns as well.[53] In England, Catholics remained excluded from the Toleration Act of 1689 and therefore had no right to public worship. Still, a number of Catholic peers and gentry had established manorial chapels, which were served by missionary priests and became the focus of Catholic congregations in the countryside. While they remained illegal, neighbors and officials often connived at these ostensibly private, but actually semipublic, forms of Catholic worship.[54] Catholic-Protestant relations in eighteenth-century western and central Europe thus present a contradictory picture of confessional rivalry, complex legal arrangements, and cooperative social relations.

Confessional relations in the American colonies were marked by similar ambivalences. When German immigrants began to arrive in larger numbers in 1727, some Pennsylvanians expressed concern that many of these "Palatines" were actually "Papists," and Governor Gordon claimed in 1728 that it was necessary "to prevent the Importation of Irish Papists & Convicts."[55] Despite these anti-Catholic sentiments, the Jesuits of the Mission of St. Francis Xavier on Bohemia Manor in Cecil County, Maryland, encountered little opposition when they extended their activities to Pennsylvania. In the late 1720s Father Joseph Greaton, a London-born priest who had converted to Catholicism and been assigned to the Maryland mission, began to celebrate Mass in Philadelphia. When a "Romish Chappel" was built under his direction in 1733–34, Governor Gordon claimed that he was "under no small Concern" that some Philadelphians were hearing "Mass openly celebrated by a Popish Priest" in violation of English laws. The Pennsylvania council, however, was uncertain if the English statutes actually applied to the colonial situation, and neither the governor nor the Anglican Society for the Propagation of the Gospel in Foreign Parts actively opposed the celebration of the Catholic Mass. Joseph Greaton also seems to

---

53. Wolfgang Leiser, "Das Karlsruher Stadtrecht, 1715–1752," *Zeitschrift für Geschichte des Oberrheins* 114 (1966): 207–39, esp. 208–11, 222–23, 227; Christina Müller, *Karlsruhe im 18. Jahrhundert. Zur Genese und sozialen Schichtung einer residenzstädtischen Bevölkerung* (Karlsruhe: Badenia-Verlag, 1992), 33–38, 193–94, 196, 222–24, 238, 245.

54. John Bossy, *The English Catholic Community, 1570–1850* (New York: Oxford University Press, 1976); Bossy, "English Catholics After 1688," in *From Persecution to Toleration: The Glorious Revolution and Religion in England*, ed. Ole Peter Grell, Jonathan I. Israel, and Nicholas Tyacke (Oxford: Clarendon Press, 1991), 369–87; Benjamin Kaplan, "Fictions of Privacy: House Chapels and the Spatial Accommodation of Religious Dissent in Early Modern Europe," *American Historical Review* 107, no. 4 (Oct. 2002): 1031–64, esp. 1051–52, 1057–59.

55. Schwartz, *"A Mixed Multitude,"* 89–91.

have visited groups of Catholics in the Conestoga and Conewago settlements around 1730, but between 1734 and 1741 no missionary visits to the Lancaster area are recorded. By the end of the 1730s, the Pennsylvania mission received a boost from the wealthy English convert Sir John James, who entreated the provincials of the Society of Jesus in Europe to send priests and offered generous material assistance. Father Henry Neale, a native of Maryland who had migrated to England, was assigned to assist Greaton in Philadelphia and crossed the Atlantic in 1740. Writing from Philadelphia in April 1741, Neale reported that the "Country Catholics" of Pennsylvania were "very numerous," but since they were mostly "servants, or poor tradesmen," they stood "more in need of charity themselves, than capable of assisting others."[56]

In 1741 two German Jesuits, the Westphalia-born Wilhelm Wappeler from the Lower Rhine province and his colleague Theodor Schneider from the Upper Rhine province of the order, traveled from London to Maryland and then up the Susquehanna to the new town of Lancaster, where they found lodging with the hatter Thomas Doyle. "Our appearance among the German Catholic inhabitants of the city," Wappeler reported to his former superior in Germany, "was as pleasant as it was unexpected. They had always been under the false impression that the entry of German Catholic priests in the land of Pennsylvania was strictly forbidden. They likewise thought that even if it were permitted, no one would decide to minister to such a small group of German settlers amid such danger and inconvenience." The Protestants of Pennsylvania, Wappeler thought, were "divided into more than 50 sects," and "although they never agree in what they teach, are united in one thing—hatred of our holy Catholic religion. Unanimously they persecute not only the missionaries but also the pupils whom they attempt to lead into apostasy."[57]

Despite these apprehensions, Wappeler began to conduct services in a rented house and established "places of assembly" in Yorktown and Conewago west of the Susquehanna, while Schneider settled in present-day Berks County and

56. "Letter of Rev. Henry Neale, Philadelphia, 1741," *American Catholic Historical Researches* 6 (1889): 182–83; Robert Edward Quigley, "Catholic Beginnings in the Delaware Valley," in *The History of the Archdiocese of Philadelphia*, ed. James F. Connelly (Philadelphia: Archdiocese of Philadelphia, 1976), 1–62, esp. 17–19; Edgar A. Musser, "Old St. Mary's of Lancaster, Pa.: The Jesuit Period, 1741–1785," *JLCHS* 71 (1967): 80–91; Hennesey, *American Catholics*, 49, 51; Schwartz, *"A Mixed Multitude,"* 104–5; Joseph C. Linck, "Pennsylvania, Catholic Church in," in *The Encyclopedia of American Catholic History*, ed. Michael Glazier and Thomas J. Shelley (Collegeville, Minn.: Liturgical Press, 1997), 1124–25.

57. Musser, "Old St. Mary's," 91–93; Quigley, "Catholic Beginnings," 19–20; Hennesey, *American Catholics*, 51–52; Linck, "Pennsylvania," 1125.

ministered to Catholic settlers in eastern Pennsylvania and New Jersey. In August 1741 the Catholic mission in Lancaster obtained two lots from town proprietor James Hamilton. Since Wappeler and Schneider, as Catholics, could not be naturalized and therefore could not obtain legal title to property, their English colleague Henry Neale acquired the lots in their stead. A rather inauspicious log chapel was apparently completed on these premises by 1743.[58] The organization of congregations in Lancaster and other backcountry settlements was accompanied by a growing awareness of provincial politicians and Protestant ministers that the Catholic presence was increasing. Proprietor Thomas Penn, who had at one point asked Governor George Thomas to propose legal restrictions on Catholicism to the assembly "by making it very penal for any Priest to exercise his Function in Pennsylvania," told Lancaster's chief burgess Thomas Cookson that he "desire[d] no ground may be granted to any Roman Catholicks," as they held "Tenets destructive of all others."[59] Samuel Blunston, an assembly member for Lancaster County, allegedly "trumpeted about" that "James Hamilton had given a Lot of Ground in the Town of Lancaster to a Roman Catholick Priest to build a Roman Chappel and that he was a great favourer of Jews and Roman Catholicks."[60] Still, there is no evidence that the establishment of the Lancaster mission, or any other Catholic congregation in the Pennsylvania interior, met with serious local opposition.

Wappeler estimated the number of practicing Catholics in the Lancaster-York-Conewago area at about one hundred, and this "little band of Catholics," he wrote in the summer of 1742, was "so scattered throughout the country that it is difficult . . . to gather them for Divine Service and, especially, to instruct them in the faith." In terms strikingly reminiscent of his Protestant ministerial colleagues, the German Jesuit described the laity as a wandering, shepherdless flock who "had strayed from the path of virtue and fallen into wrong ways." As they could not attend Mass and did not have access to Catholic books, "they performed their devotions in the Lutheran or Calvinist prayer house." Since they were deprived of "pure Christian doctrine," Wappeler went on, "[a]n extraordinary lukewarmness and carelessness in attending Divine Service reigned in the Catholic community." The observation of rituals, the celebration of religious festivals, catechetical instruction of the young, and the sacraments were sadly

---

58. Musser, "Old St. Mary's," 95–101; cf. Heisey, "Borough Fathers," 59; Wood, *Conestoga Crossroads*, 13–14. Musser points out that the Lancaster mission was originally known as "St. John Nepomucene," but after a second church was built in 1760, it became known as "St. Mary of the Assumption" (102–3).

59. Schwartz, "*A Mixed Multitude*," 151–52; cf. Musser, "Old St. Mary's," 95–96.

60. Quoted in Wood, *Conestoga Crossroads*, 201.

neglected. Still, Wappeler could report some progress. He had "doubled my little flock of originally 100 people" and established three more "assembly places," which he visited on a monthly circuit. Visits to mission chapels usually began with a celebration of Mass and continued with English gospel readings, catechism lessons, and the performance of baptisms, marriages, and the sacrament of penance as the occasion required. In its outer forms, therefore, Wappeler's labors resembled those of his Protestant colleagues, and like them he peppered his reports to Europe with stories of occasional conversions to the faith and of men, women, and youths who had become "regenerated in Christ."[61]

Wappeler continued his missionary work for seven years before, at the age of thirty-seven, his health began to fail under the strain of constant traveling and he returned to Europe. His mission field was taken over by his former travel companion Theodor Schneider, a native of Hesse who had been educated at the University of Heidelberg. He had already occupied professorships of philosophy at Liège (Belgium) and Heidelberg and the rectorship of the latter university when he asked to be relieved from his duties in order to go to Pennsylvania. After serving the eastern part of the province for several years, Schneider's field of activity comprised all the settled parts of Pennsylvania from 1748 to 1752. He was probably the Catholic priest whom Lutheran minister Johann Friedrich Handschuh met during a ferry crossing of the Susquehanna in April 1749 and whose conversation he described as "modest and sincere."[62] For the next six years, the south German Jesuit Andreas Steinmeyer, who changed his name to Ferdinand Farmer in America, ministered in Lancaster. After Farmer transferred to Philadelphia, where he embarked on a successful ministry of thirty years, Lancaster was visited by Mathias Manners from Conewago for several months until a newly arrived Jesuit from Germany, Jacob (James) Pellentz, took over the post. When Pellentz started his missionary work, anti-Catholic sentiment in Pennsylvania was at its peak on account of attacks on frontier settlements during the first years of the French and Indian War. As early as 1755 a mob had threatened to burn the "Popish" chapel in Philadelphia, and Catholics at Goshenhoppen were suspected of conspiring with hostile Indians. When the log chapel in Lancaster burnt to the ground in December 1760, therefore, it was widely believed to have been at an incendiary's hand. An interdenominational committee made up of chief burgess John Hopson (a Moravian) and assistant burgesses Robert Thompson and

---

61. Musser, "Old St. Mary's," 105–7; Quigley, "Catholic Beginnings," 20–21.

62. Bernhard Duhr, *Geschichte der Jesuiten in den Ländern deutscher Zunge*, vol. 4, pt. 2 (Munich: Manz, 1928), 511; Musser, "Old St. Mary's," 107–12; Quigley, "Catholic Beginnings," 21–22; *Hallesche Nachrichten*, 1:537; Schwartz, *"A Mixed Multitude,"* 152.

Bernhard Hubele subsequently advertised a reward of £20 for the apprehension of the culprit in the *Pennsylvania Gazette*. Meanwhile the congregation, which shared in the fund of four thousand pounds bequeathed by the wealthy English Catholic Sir John James, built a new limestone church in 1761–62 and purchased a third town lot to be used as a churchyard. A fourth lot was donated by a member of the congregation, Catherine Spangler, in 1764. To the Anglican minister Thomas Barton, the fact that a Jesuit priest "had influence enough . . . to get a very elegant chapel of hewn stone erected in this town" seemed quite remarkable. While Barton found the behavior of Lancaster's mostly German Catholic inhabitants "quiet and inoffensive," he added that "they have been often suspected during this war of communicating intelligence to the enemies of our Religion and Country."[63]

In 1768 Jacob Pellentz exchanged mission fields with the priest at Conewago, Jacob Augustin Frambach, who had already supplied Lancaster alternately with Pellentz in 1764–65. Frambach remained for about a year and a half before Lukas Geissler replaced him. The last in the line of German Jesuits who served the town's Catholics, Geissler remained in Lancaster after the suppression of his order by Pope Clement XIV in 1773 and throughout the War for American Independence. In 1775 his congregation purchased an organ from David Tannenberg, the organ-builder who had already worked for the town's Moravian, German Reformed, and Lutheran churches.[64]

According to one scholar, "the reception accorded Roman Catholics" provides clear evidence for the "widespread toleration characteristic" of the colony. "That Catholics lived in Pennsylvania, built churches, and were regularly visited by priests resident in the province was hardly a secret, and was frequently ignored or mentioned without evident animosity."[65] On the whole, the case of Lancaster bears out this verdict. Protestant ministers like Thomas Barton occasionally criticized the Catholic presence, and in some instances pastoral acts caused problems as well. In 1742 Wilhelm Wappeler wrote that he refused to baptize a son of Catholic parents because they had brought along Protestant

63. Thomas O'Brien Hanley, ed., *The John Carroll Papers*, 3 vols. (Notre Dame: University of Notre Dame Press, 1976), 1:406; Musser, "Old St. Mary's," 116–22, 125–26; Coldren and Heisey, "Religious Life," 133; Perry, *Historical Collections*, 2:343; Wood, *Conestoga Crossroads*, 182, 201–2; Hennesey, *American Catholics*, 50, 52. For anti-Catholic sentiments in Pennsylvania during the French and Indian War, see Schwartz, *"A Mixed Multitude,"* 237, 240–42.

64. Musser, "Old St. Mary's," 128–33; Brunner, *"That Ingenious Business,"* 80. On the effect of the papal suppression of the Society of Jesus on its American members, see Dolan, *American Catholic Experience*, 95–96.

65. Schwartz, *"A Mixed Multitude,"* 296.

sponsors, and seven years later pastor Johann Friedrich Handschuh crossed out an entry for a child of Ernst and Maria Eva Micheleis in the Lutheran baptism book. "The mother," Handschuh added in the margin, "wants to have her child baptized by the Catholic priest [vom Catholische Pfaffen], because I would not allow M. Kuntz's Catholic wife to be a sponsor." On the other hand, Handschuh did not refuse private baptism to the son of a Catholic couple or to the son of a Catholic widow in the presence of Anglican sponsors.[66] The following biographical sketches indicate that Catholics integrated easily into Lancaster society and sometimes developed close social relations with Protestants.

Undoubtedly the most prominent Catholic among the early residents was Thomas Doyle, an immigrant from Ireland and a hatter by trade. Doyle, who hosted Wilhelm Wappeler and Theodor Schneider upon their arrival in Lancaster, came to the Conestoga area about 1727 and married Elizabeth Atkinson, the daughter of a fuller, shortly thereafter. Two lots in the new town were assigned to him in May 1730. Doyle owned a hat store in the center of town and acquired considerable real estate. On the borough's earliest tax list, he was assessed for one of the highest property values. In May 1746 an apprentice was assigned to him "for seven years . . . to be taught the trade of a hatter," and a few months later he purchased the labor of a female servant from Ireland. His numerous business dealings brought him into contact with members of various ethnic and religious groups; thus, he sold two hundred acres in Manheim Township to Philipp Quickel, a Lutheran, in 1743. Five years later Jacob Schlauch, then an adherent of the Moravians, purchased a piece of land from him. In 1747 Doyle and the Quaker Isaac Whitelock were among the executors of the will of the Anglican John Foulk and witnessed the writing of the will together with the Anglican minister Richard Locke. The same year the Anglican John Connolly, a native of Ireland, also named Doyle among his executors. A year earlier Doyle bought town properties from the Anglican merchant John Hart and the mason Thomas Thornbough, a Quaker. During the 1750s and 1760s Doyle repeatedly lent money to artisans and farmers.[67] When Doyle, who by

66. Musser, "Old St. Mary's," 106; Handschuh Diarium, entries for February 2 and March 10, 1749, Archiv der Franckeschen Stiftungen; Smith and Weiser, *Trinity Lutheran Church Records*, 1:68, 69.

67. Lancaster Borough Tax Assessment List, 1751, Lancaster County Historical Society; Heisey, "Borough Fathers," 60; Musser, "Old St. Mary's," 92, 94–95; Neible, "Account of Servants (1907)," 366; Neible, "Account of Servants (1908)," 353; Lancaster County Will Books A-I-141 (John Connolly) and I-I-138 (John Foulk), Pennsylvania State Archives; Warrant Register, vol. 16, p. 8, no. 45, Pennsylvania State Archives; Rogers, "Genealogical Gleanings," 134; Mayhill, *Deed Abstracts*, 8 (A161), 14 (B162), 19 (B362, B 364), 20 (B426), 26 (B 612), 30 (C157), 43 (D121), 61 (E12), 67 (E239), 101 (H168), 109 (H319b), 115 (I116–17); Wood, *Conestoga Crossroads*, 75.

then called himself a "yeoman," dictated his will in 1788, he left four houses in Lancaster and three in Philadelphia as well as cash bequests to his wife, three surviving daughters, and several grandchildren. He died as one of the town's oldest residents in 1791. An article in a contemporary newspaper states that he was in the ninety-seventh year of his life and a "large concourse of citizens of all religious denominations attended the funeral" in the Catholic cemetery.[68]

Another prominent Catholic resident was Roger Conner, also a hatter. Conner, who was assessed among the top fifth of Lancaster's taxpayers at midcentury, acquired three town lots in the 1740s, one of them opposite the Catholic chapel. He also owned four houses in Yorktown, which he advertised for sale in 1751, and purchased the labor of indentured servants.[69] In September 1750 Conner and his wife, Elizabeth, brought a son to be baptized by Lutheran pastor Johann Friedrich Handschuh; one of the infant's sponsors, Mary Gibson, was an Anglican. Handschuh also recorded the boy's death less than three weeks after the baptism, and in February 1751 he noted in his diary that a Catholic Englishman—who is identified as Roger Conner in the church record—requested him to come to his house immediately and baptize his weak child. During George Craig's ministry, Conner may have joined the Anglican congregation, for he attended a congregational meeting in August 1751, had a pew erected in St. James' Church two years later, and contributed to a subscription in 1755. The will he made in 1774 does not clarify his religious affiliation. Conner left his whole estate to his wife and three surviving daughters, whom he also named as executors.[70]

German Catholics in the borough were not as well-off as these two men. The wheelwright John Hook (Johann Hoch), identified by a local historian as "one of the original members of St. Mary's congregation," had come to Pennsylvania in 1729 and acquired a lot on which he established his shop. He was succeeded in his trade by his son Michael, who also worked as a clockmaker.[71] In 1762 Michael Hook and the Jesuit priest Jacob Pellentz were named the

68. Lancaster County Will Book F-1-273, Pennsylvania State Archives; Albert Cavin and August Lerbscher, "Items from the *Neue Unpartheyische Lancaster-Zeitung* und *Anzeigs-Nachrichten,*" PLCHS 35 (1931): 35.

69. Lancaster Borough Tax Assessment List, 1751, Lancaster County Historical Society; Mayhill, *Deed Abstracts,* 84 (G233); Heisey, "Borough Fathers," 57, 66, 71, 74; *Pennsylvania Gazette,* August 15, 1751; Eshleman, *Early Lancaster Taxables,* 266, 275; Farley Grubb, *Runaway Servants, Convicts, and Apprentices Advertised in the* Pennsylvania Gazette, *1728–1796* (Baltimore: Genealogical Publishing Co., 1992), 46, 185; Hubley Collection, MG 2, box 3, folder 45, no. 5, Lancaster County Historical Society.

70. Smith and Weiser, *Trinity Lutheran Church Records,* 1:87, 92; *Hallesche Nachrichten,* 2:65; Worner, "Church of England (Part III)," 29, 32, 39; Lancaster County Will Book C-1-134, Pennsylvania State Archives.

71. Heisey, "Borough Fathers," 56; Musser, "Old St. Mary's," 131–32.

executors of the will of the tailor Nicolas Shindleman. Apart from one shilling he left to his "Pretended Son Philip," Shindleman gave Hook £5 "as a reward for attending me during my Illness" and the remainder of his estate to "the Reverend Master Jacob Belance" for "the use and benefit of [the] Roman Catholick Chappel" in the borough.[72]

Alexander Stockslager, who arrived in Philadelphia in 1741, was assessed slightly below the median on the Lancaster Borough tax list in 1751, and eight years later his assessment put him near the median. According to the will he drew up two months before his death in January 1763, he left four houses and lots in Adamstown and Musserstown, two suburbs of Lancaster, to his wife and two stepsons. If both step-sons should die without offspring, his siblings in Germany inherited the property. Should his brother and sisters not come to America to claim the estate, however, Stockslager willed "that the Priest or Minister of the roman Catholick Congrega-tion" in Lancaster was to have "the use, benefit & advantage" of their respective shares.[73] In the years before the Revolution, the cooper Caspar Michenfelder paid the ground rents for the church. His tax payment of four shillings in 1773 puts him in the lower half of the town's taxables; therefore, it must have been a significant loss to him when his apprentice Johannes Marx, a seventeen-year-old German-born cooper, ran away the following year.[74]

Around midcentury, several Catholic-Protestant couples were living in town. In March 1749 Johann Friedrich Handschuh baptized a daughter of Peter Boehm, who regularly went to communion in the Lutheran church, and his Catholic wife, Anna Margaretha, in the presence of a Lutheran man and his Reformed wife. The baptism took place in the parents' home and the child died the next day. Between 1748 and 1766 three baptisms of children of the Catholic Andreas Straube and his Lutheran wife, Anna Catharina, were entered into the Lutheran church register. In October 1749 pastor Handschuh married Joseph Schmidt, a newly arrived Catholic immigrant, and the Lutheran Anna Barbara Kautzmann, another recent arrival. Heinrich Erckenrodt married Susanna Stiessen in the Lutheran church in February 1749 and his wife repeatedly went to com-munion there over the following years. Heinrich remained a devout Catholic,

---

72. Lancaster County Will Book C-I-53, Pennsylvania State Archives; cf. Musser, "Old St. Mary's," 127.

73. Strassburger and Hinke, *Pennsylvania German Pioneers,* 1:310, 312–13; Lancaster Borough Tax Assessment Lists, 1751, 1759, Lancaster County Historical Society; Lancaster County Will Book C-I-50, Pennsylvania State Archives.

74. Musser, "Old St. Mary's," 130–31; Egle, *Pennsylvania Archives,* 460; Grubb, *Runaway Servants,* 106; *Der Wöchentliche Pennsylvanische Staatsbote,* no. 675, December 27, 1774.

however, for in the 1750s the log chapel of the Donegal mission was built on his farm near present-day Elizabethtown. Johann Colman Greiner and his Catholic wife, Ursula, had two children baptized by the Lutheran pastor around mid-century. After Ursula's death, Colman married a Lutheran woman.[75] Christian Hartmann, a Reformed, and his wife, Catharina, a Catholic, brought a daughter into the Lutheran church for baptism in April 1751. Two and a half years later, the baptism of another daughter was recorded in the Reformed church register, while the baptisms of a son in 1755 and a daughter in 1765 were entered into both registers.[76] Catholic-Protestant intermarriage continued on a small scale: from 1783 to 1796, pastor Gotthilf Heinrich Ernst Mühlenberg baptized four children who had a Catholic father or mother. Three of the 285 Lutherans who announced themselves for communion on Pentecost 1785 were married to Catholics, and among the more than fourteen hundred communicants entered into the Lutheran church records from 1793 to 1799, eight had Catholic husbands or wives.[77] Occasionally, Catholics joined the Lutheran church; when he entered Anna Maria Stebin in the communicant register in 1777, pastor Helmuth added that she "came over to us from the Roman church."[78]

Johann Friedrich Handschuh, who officiated at several confessionally mixed marriages, left no doubt that he disapproved of some of these matches. Thus he recorded that "Archiabel Makleas, a Catholic bachelor, and Maria Eva Pfeiffern, of Lutheran parents, have lived together already 1½ years, and were finally married on August 18, 1749, by me in my room in the English language in the

---

75. Boehm: Smith and Weiser, *Trinity Lutheran Church Records*, 1:70, 277, 329, 334, 342, 361, 372; Straube: 1:61, 82, 218; Schmidt: ibid., 1:232, 376; Erckenrodt: ibid., 1:230, 342, 366, 393; Musser, "Old St. Mary's," 117; Greiner: Smith and Weiser, *Trinity Lutheran Church Records*, 1:66, 94, 160, 180, 286, 308, 361, 379. Cf. also Handschuh Diarium, entries for February 16 and February 27, 1749, Archiv der Franckeschen Stiftungen. Several other mixed marriages are recorded: in July 1750 pastor Handschuh baptized the daughter of the Lutheran Andreas Benz and his Catholic wife, Elisabeth, with the Lutheran merchant Michael Gross and his wife acting as sponsors (Smith and Weiser, *Trinity Lutheran Church Records*, 1:85). Anna Maria Hoeltzern, who repeatedly took communion in the Lutheran church in the early 1750s, had a Catholic husband (ibid., 1:353, 367, 376, 390). Catharina Margaretha Seemannin, who went to communion there on Pentecost 1750, was also married to a Catholic (ibid., 1:357). Nicolas Kuntz and his wife, Magdalena, a Catholic, had two children baptized in the Lutheran church in 1748 and 1750. Nicolas Kuntz participated in Lutheran communion on several occasions from 1747 to 1752 (ibid., 1:59, 86, 325, 331, 354, 387). Heinrich Melchior Mühlenberg occasionally noted the presence of Catholic-Lutheran couples in Philadelphia (see Tappert and Doberstein, *Journals of Henry Melchior Muhlenberg*, 1:677; 2:214, 497).

76. Smith and Weiser, *Trinity Lutheran Church Records*, 1:95, 123, 212; Wright, *Lancaster County Church Records*, 2:24, 28, 37.

77. Smith and Weiser, *Trinity Lutheran Church Records*, 3:24, 26, 86, 128, 280–85, 358–90.

78. Smith and Weiser, *Trinity Lutheran Church Records*, 2:271.

presence of two church councilmen." Handschuh obviously tried to keep this marriage as private as possible, and in his diary he wrote that the young woman, "which I had to marry to an Irishman," was born of Lutheran parents, but her religious instruction had been neglected by her stepfather, a Dunker. According to Handschuh, the bride requested him in tears to catechize her and prepare her for communion.[79]

While Handschuh saw this German-Irish match as the result of religious confusion and negligence, some confessionally mixed couples lived together for many years without the least evidence of marital disharmony. A well-documented case is that of the Catholic baker Johannes Utzmann and his Lutheran wife, Albertina. Utzmann, who arrived in Philadelphia in 1738, obtained a warrant for fifty acres of land in Chester County six years later and moved to Lancaster by the late 1740s.[80] There the Lutheran schoolmaster Johann Jacob Loeser and his wife sponsored the baptisms of the Utzmanns' daughter Maria Margaretha by pastor Handschuh in July 1749 and their son Jacob in November 1750. Albertina Utzmann, "whose husband adhere[d] to the Roman Catholic Church," participated in Lutheran communion services at midcentury. In 1749 the Utzmanns employed a recent immigrant, Johanna Maria Paul, as a servant; like her mistress she is listed in the Lutheran communicant lists. From 1766 to 1775 Albertina had rented a pew in the new Lutheran church of the Holy Trinity and regularly went to the Lord's Supper there.[81] As a respected inhabitant, Johannes Utzmann received commissions for Johannes Martin, who was "going to Germany for the autumn fair" in 1752 and was named as executor in the blacksmith Georg Reidenbough's will in 1754.[82] During the 1750s Johannes and Albertina bought and sold several lots in Lancaster and a large piece of land in York County and purchased more than two hundred acres in Manheim Township where Utzmann set up a tavern. To finance their real estate transactions, the couple loaned money from Protestant neighbors like the Lutheran Ludwig Laumann. When he made his will in 1764, Johannes Utzmann named his wife, the schoolmaster Johann Jacob Loeser,

79. Smith and Weiser, *Trinity Lutheran Church Records,* 1:232; *Hallesche Nachrichten,* 1:541.

80. Strassburger and Hinke, *Pennsylvania German Pioneers,* 2:243; Lancaster County Historical Society genealogical notes in file folder "Utzmann, John."

81. Smith and Weiser, *Trinity Lutheran Church Records,* 1:74, 89, 278, 343, 346, 348, 362, 373, and 2:207, 214, 221, 368–69.

82. Edward W. Hocker, *Genealogical Data Relating to the German Settlers of Pennsylvania and Adjacent Territory: From Advertisements of German Newspapers Published in Philadelphia and Germantown: 1743–1800,* 2nd ed. (Baltimore: Genealogical Publishing Co., 1981), 35; Lancaster County Tax Lists, Manheim Township, 1759, Lancaster County Historical Society; Lancaster County Will Book B-I-63, Pennsylvania State Archives.

and Johannes Epple executors of his estate, which included a house in Lancaster and the farm in Manheim Township.[83]

The fact that a confessionally mixed couple like the Catholic Johannes Utzmann and his Lutheran wife, Albertina, integrated themselves seamlessly into local society, built up thriving business relations, and prospered in their worldly affairs while pursuing separate paths to salvation clearly demonstrates that the examples of "religious intolerance" and "bigotry" cited by historian Jerome H. Wood do not convey the full picture of Catholic-Protestant relations in eighteenth-century Lancaster.[84] Expressions of anti-Papist sentiments by prominent Pennsylvanians and the burning of the Catholic chapel at the hands of a presumed arsonist in 1760 should by no means be downplayed, but they should be placed in the context of the regular economic and occasionally cordial social ties that bound members of the small Catholic minority to an overwhelming Protestant society.

JEWS IN A CHRISTIAN SOCIETY

"The presence of Catholics and Jews," Jon Butler has noted, "symbolized not only the growing spiritual heterogeneity of colonial America but the eighteenth century's importance in making it."[85] In Pennsylvania a small number of Jewish merchants and traders established themselves in Philadelphia in the early decades of the century, and Lancaster housed a Jewish community since the 1740s. There were about ten families in the community in 1747, when it obtained a plot of land for use as a burial ground. While most were Ashkenazim, at least three Jewish residents, who had migrated to Lancaster from Georgia and New York, were of Sephardic origin. The household of the wealthy merchant Joseph Simon, an Ashkenazi Jew who had come from England in the early 1740s, was the physical and spiritual center of the small community, which strictly observed the Sabbath laws and other religious ceremonies. Simon "employed a slaughterer of kosher meat, at his own expense, . . . and held services in a room in his home, complete

---

83. Mayhill, *Deed Abstracts*, 48 (D225), 51 (D327), 61 (E24), 62 (E 78, 82); Lancaster County Deed Books Z169, Z17, AA307, AA311, Pennsylvania State Archives; Lancaster County Will Book C-I-99, Pennsylvania State Archives. The estate inventory drawn up after his death listed personal assets of more than £195 (John Utzmann Estate Inventory, 1764, Lancaster County Historical Society).

84. Wood, *Conestoga Crossroads*, 201.

85. Butler, *Becoming America*, 192.

with two Torah scrolls and an ark to house them. Others in the Pennsylvania hinterland, like Myer Josephson of Reading, made their way to Simon's home to observe important holidays." One of the principal merchants of the town, Simon imported hardware, textiles, sugar, coffee, tea, and a variety of other goods from England and the West Indies via Philadelphia, engaged in the fur trade and large-scale land speculation, ventured into the manufacture of liquor, potash, guns, and iron goods, and supplied provisions to frontier troops during the French and Indian War as well as to British and Hessian prisoners of war during the American Revolution. Thus Simon was one of the entrepreneurs who linked the Atlantic commercial world to the colonial backcountry and to the Indian territories in the west. Whereas Simon and a few other Jews lived in Lancaster for extended periods of time, many others made only brief appearances. So central was Simon's importance to Jewish life in Lancaster that the town's Hebrew community faded away with his death in 1804.[86]

While Joseph Simon formed his closest business associations with fellow Jewish traders like David Franks and the Gratz brothers in Philadelphia, relations with some of Lancaster's English-speaking inhabitants were also important. In 1759 he formed a partnership with the gunsmith William Henry that lasted into the Revolutionary War years. Simon and Henry sold hardware from a store in Lancaster, supplied rifles to colonial militia troops in the French and Indian War, and sold arms and military equipment to the Continental Congress and the Pennsylvania Committee of Safety during the War for Independence. They also shipped pig iron, which they had probably obtained from Thomas Smith, iron-master at Martic furnace near Lancaster, to Baltimore, Pittsburgh, and London. Besides, Simon established a business with the Anglican physician Dr. Samuel Boudé in 1757 that manufactured potash and pearl ash on its own premises in Lancaster for about ten years. Further west, Lancaster's preeminent Jewish

86. On the Jewish community and the role of Joseph Simon, see Wood, *Conestoga Crossroads*, 97–104, 197–99, 114–20, 140–41, 148–50, 155, 163, 172, 174, 184; Jacob R. Marcus, *The Colonial American Jew, 1492–1776*, 3 vols. (Detroit: Wayne State University Press, 1970), 1:278, 323, 328–29; 2:568, 587, 595–96, 612, 659, 669–70, 682, 705, 710–11, 725–26, 739–41, 883–84; and 3:976, 981–82, 1007, 1069, 1132–33, 1216, 1264, 1324–25; David Brener, *The Jews of Lancaster, Pennsylvania: A Story with Two Beginnings* (Lancaster, Pa.: Congregation Shaarai Shomayim, 1979), 3–29; Eli Faber, *The Jewish People in America*, vol. 1, *A Time for Planting: The First Migration, 1654–1820* (Baltimore: Johns Hopkins University Press, 1992), 40–41, 86, 90–91 (quote), 95, 109; William Pencak, *Jews and Gentiles in Early America, 1654–1800* (Ann Arbor: University of Michigan Press, 2005), 51, 178, 182–83. Cf. also Sidney M. Fish, *Barnard and Michael Gratz: Their Lives and Times* (Lanham, Md.: University Press of America, 1994), 20, 25, 30–31, 38–40, 43, 45, 49–51, 56–57, 61–63, 71, 84–86, 90–92, 94–98, 100, 113, 116–120, 124, 126–27, 129.

merchant entered into partnerships with the Anglo-Irish fur traders George Croghan and Alexander Lowry.[87] In 1753 the Indian traders John Kennedy and David Lowry mortgaged large tracts of land to Simon, Thomas Harris, and the Philadelphia Jewish merchants Nathan Levy and David Franks. Kennedy was obviously unable to satisfy his creditors, for a year later Simon and Harris bought his land at a sheriff's sale.[88] In 1770 Simon contributed £2 10s. toward the purchase of a bell for St. James' Anglican Church.[89]

English speakers were not likely to have met Jews before their settlement in Lancaster unless they had resided in London, where several thousand Ashkenazi Jews from central Europe were living in the first half of the eighteenth century, or in colonial port cities such as Philadelphia, New York, or Newport.[90] On the other hand, many German-speaking Protestants who crossed the Atlantic in the colonial period had been living in proximity to Jews in their native regions. In the early modern era, Jews gained residence privileges in a number of southwest German territories and established communities—many of them very small—in towns and villages in Franconia, east Swabia, the Palatinate, and the upper Rhine Valley. Jews usually had limited residence privileges and an inferior legal status, and their economic activities and access to communal resources were restricted. Nevertheless, recent research has shown that Jewish traders, pawnbrokers, and moneylenders played important roles in the economy of southwest Germany. Everyday contacts between Jews and Christians were more frequent and more cooperative than has long been assumed.[91] German speakers who came to Pennsylvania were thus likely to be ambivalent about the Jews established there. While they were undoubtedly familiar with traditional stereotypes of Jews

87. Loose, "William Henry Memoirs," 62; Beck, "William Henry," 74–75; Marcus, *Colonial American Jew*, 2:595–96, 669–70, 682, 710–11; 3:1324; Wood, *Conestoga Crossroads*, 148–50; Brener, *Jews of Lancaster*, 8, 12–17; Fish, *Barnard and Michael Gratz*, 136 passim; Faber, *A Time for Planting*, 86; Pencak, *Jews and Gentiles*, 183–85. For Simon's association with Thomas Smith, see also Mayhill, *Deed Abstracts*, 114 (H390).
88. Mayhill, *Deed Abstracts*, 40 (D36, D42), 43 (D118).
89. Worner, "Old St. James's Church Bell," 243.
90. See Todd M. Endelman, *The Jews of Georgian England, 1714–1830: Tradition and Change in a Liberal Society*, rev.ed. (Ann Arbor: University of Michigan Press, 1999); Todd M. Endelman, *The Jews of Britain, 1656 to 2000* (Berkeley and Los Angeles: University of California Press, 2002), 41–77.
91. Recent literature on Jewish-Christian relations in southwest Germany is surveyed in Mark Häberlein and Michaela Schmölz-Häberlein, "Competition and Cooperation: The Ambivalent Relationship Between Jews and Christians in Early Modern Germany and Pennsylvania," *PMHB* 126 (2002): 409–36. Important works include Rolf Kiessling and Sabine Ullmann, eds., *Landjudentum im deutschen Südwesten während der Frühen Neuzeit* (Berlin: Akademie Verlag, 1999); Sabine Ullmann, *Nachbarschaft und Konkurrenz: Juden und Christen in Dörfern der Markgrafschaft Burgau, 1650–1750* (Göttingen: Vandenhoeck and Ruprecht, 1999); and Claudia Ulbrich, *Shulamit und Margarethe: Macht, Geschlecht und Religion in einer ländlichen Gesellschaft des 18. Jahrhunderts* (Vienna: Böhlau, 1999).

as usurers and blasphemers, they also knew about Jews' importance in rural trade and credit networks and the manifold forms of everyday social interaction at markets and fairs and in taverns and private houses.

In Lancaster Joseph Simon's manifold enterprises and business interests often brought him into contact with his German-speaking neighbors. When Elisabeth Mulder and Anna Maria Fischer announced their intention to participate in communion in the Lutheran church in September 1750, pastor Handschuh noted that the two women were living "with the Jew Joseph"; whether they had rented a room in Simon's house or were his servants is not clear. In any case, Fischer was still lodging with Simon in February 1751.[92] In December 1750 Simon witnessed a mortgage of the innkeeper Jacob Eichholtz to the Jewish merchants Nathan Levy and David Franks of Philadelphia, and he bought land in Manheim Township from Jacob Metzger in 1751. In 1754 the innkeeper Andreas Beyerle, a member of the Lutheran congregation, mortgaged a town lot to David Franks and Joseph Simon for £200.[93] Two years later the butcher Michael Fortinet, a member of the German Reformed church, and his wife sold a house to Simon. On the same day in May 1756 the merchant Jacob Friedrich Curteus mortgaged his property on Queen Street to the Jewish trader for the sum of £650. Four years later Simon sold a town lot to Bernhard Brubacher, and in 1767 the tinsmith and pewterer Johann Christoph Heyne paid £600 for a part of Simon's property on King Street.[94]

German-Jewish business contacts apparently intensified during the French and Indian War, which offered enterprising traders new opportunities for profit. Joseph Simon entered into a business partnership with his neighbor, the prosperous tavernkeeper Matthias Slough. In 1763 Slough and Simon organized wagons and teams for the provisioning of troops on the Pennsylvania frontier. Around that time Simon was also indebted to the wealthy Lutheran merchant Michael Gross, while his nephew and associate Levy Andrew Levy had formed a partnership with the Lutheran Michael Hubele for similar purposes as Slough and Simon. By 1764 Simon and his co-religionist Benjamin Nathan also operated a store in Heidelberg Township that "catered especially to the predominantly German population of that

92. Smith and Weiser, *Trinity Lutheran Church Records*, 1:365, 371.

93. Mayhill, *Deed Abstracts*, 28 (C57, C60), 44 (D128). For Eichholtz's and Beyerle's origins, see Burgert, *Kraichgau*, 57–59, 100.

94. Mayhill, *Deed Abstracts*, 63 (E115-E117), 94 (H47); Brener, *Jews of Lancaster*, 8, 12. In the early 1750s Simon's debtor Jacob Friedrich Curteus was engaged in the business of transporting German immigrants from Rotterdam to Philadelphia. His activities can be followed in Wokeck, *Trade in Strangers*, 70–71, 83–84, 103, 105.

region." The partners advertised their goods in German-language newspapers, as did Simon and William Henry. When the Lutherans built their new brick church in the 1760s they bought various items from the Simon and Henry store. Finally, the German blacksmith Johannes Miller produced metal goods for Simon's Indian trade.[95]

While Joseph Simon and Levy Andrew Levy are by far the most visible members of Lancaster's small Jewish community in the records, other Jews came into contact with the town's German speakers as well. Daniel Mendez de Castro's lot on market square bordered on the property of Conrad Schwartz, a German speaker. When Mendez de Castro defaulted on his debts to Nathan Levy and David Franks of Philadelphia in 1750, the sheriff sold his real estate to Peter Spicker, an elder of the German Reformed congregation.[96] The manufacturer Heinrich Wilhelm Stiegel, who operated an iron furnace and a glassworks in northern Lancaster Country, employed the Jewish glass cutter and engraver Lazarus Isaac in 1773. Moreover, Stiegel glassware was "handled in the Lancaster area by Jewish shopkeepers like Myer Josephson, Barnard Jacobs, and Benjamin Nathan."[97] In 1798 Meyer Solomon and Joseph Simon were renting seven houses in Lancaster to English- and German-speaking tenants.[98] And when the Jewish doctor Isaac Cohen, a recent immigrant from the city of Hamburg, appeared in Lancaster in 1797 and announced that he would cure poor patients free of charge, German-speaking inhabitants probably responded to his offer, for Christian patients frequently sought the advice of Jewish physicians in central Europe as well.[99]

The journal of a participant at the Lancaster Indian treaty conference of 1744 provides a rare glimpse of Christian-Jewish sociability beyond the economic realm. "The dancers," noted Witham Marshe, secretary of the Maryland delegation, "consisted of Germans and Scotch-Irish; but there were some Jewesses

95. Marcus, *Colonial American Jew*, 2:596; Wood, *Conestoga Crossroads*, 115, 140–41; Brener, *Jews of Lancaster*, 11–12, 14, 19 (Brener disputes the frequent assertion that Levy was Simon's son-in-law); Fish, *Barnard and Michael Gratz*, 39, 57; Pencak, *Jews and Gentiles*, 183; *Der Wöchentliche Philadelphische Staatsbote*, no. 108, February 6, 1764; Trinity Lutheran Church Documents, vol. 103, and Bills and Receipts, 1761–69, nos. 51, 53, Trinity Lutheran Church Archives.

96. Mayhill, *Deed Abstracts*, 14 (B 79, B 81), 18 (B339); Brener, *Jews of Lancaster*, 4.

97. Heiges, *Henry William Stiegel*, 136; Marcus, *Colonial American Jew*, 1:329–31; 2:537; Brener, *Jews of Lancaster*, 5; *Pensylvanische Berichte*, May 11, 1759.

98. Brener, *Jews of Lancaster*, 9.

99. Marcus, *Colonial American Jew*, 2:546; Brener, *Jews of Lancaster*, 6. For the German background, see Robert Jütte, "Contacts by the Bedside: Jewish Physicians and Their Christian Patients," in *In and Out of the Ghetto: Jewish-Gentile Relations in Late Medieval and Early Modern Germany*, ed. Ronnie Po-Chia Hsia and Hartmut Lehmann (Cambridge: Cambridge University Press, 1995), 137–50.

who had long since come from New York, that made a tolerable appearance, being well dressed and of an agreeable behavior." The ubiquitous Joseph Simon and Levy Andrew Levy would also meet some of their English- and German-speaking Christian neighbors in one of the town's voluntary fire companies and in the Lancaster Library Company.[100] The Anglican clergyman Thomas Barton once recommended Simon to the Indian agent Sir William Johnson as an "eminent trader" who was "a man fair in his dealings and honest from principle." When Barton's second wife arrived in Lancaster in January 1776, the minister "was visited by all the gentlemen of the town of every denomination both Jews and Gentiles."[101]

In his diary Johann Friedrich Handschuh twice noted the presence of Jews. In October 1749 he baptized an Englishman's child in the father's home "in the presence of many English people and five Jewesses, who behaved very decently and outwardly devote, so that I would not have recognized them for Jewesses if I had not been told so afterwards." While Handschuh praised the women's manners, he also betrayed certain preconceived notions about Jews' outward appearance and behavior that did not conform to his experience in this particular case.[102] The second episode reveals the minister's reservations against Jews even more clearly. In July 1750 Handschuh reported the visit of a "former Jewess" who had been living in the Seventh Day Baptist community at Ephrata for nine years with her husband, another convert, and three children. According to Handschuh, the woman and her children had left Ephrata after the husband's death, and she now expressed her desire to join the Lutheran congregation and have two of her children baptized. After some "admonitions," Handschuh asked her to return with her children several days later so that he could get to know her better and examine her more thoroughly. When the "former Jewess" and her children joined him for a meal after a funeral two days later, Handschuh seized the opportunity to "explore her intentions still further and address her conscience."[103] The woman makes another appearance in Handschuh's journal in

100. Brener, *Jews of Lancaster*, 6, 13; Pencak, *Jews and Gentiles*, 181–82. Cf. Landis, "Juliana Library Company," 213–15; Fish, *Barnard and Michael Gratz*, 188, 191.

101. Marcus, *Colonial American Jew*, 2:670; Brener, *Jews of Lancaster*, 9; Faber, *A Time for Planting*, 95; Barton, "Bartons in Lancaster," 214.

102. "[I]m Beisein vieler Engländer und fünf Jüdinnen, welche sich dabei ganz ordentlich und dem Aeußern nach andächtig bewiesen, so daß ich sie wohl vor keine Jüdinnen gehalten hätte, wenn es mir nicht wäre nachhero gesagt worden" (*Hallesche Nachrichten*, 1:542. Cf. Wood, *Conestoga Crossroads*, 188; Pencak, *Jews and Gentiles*, 193).

103. "Damit ich . . . ihre Absichten noch mehr erforschen und an ihr Gewissen reden könnte" (*Hallesche Nachrichten*, 2:60).

February 1751, when she returned to Lancaster after several months of absence and expressed her continuing desire to join the Lutheran church. Her eldest daughter, however, had been "seduced" by her Catholic husband to become Catholic herself, and the pastor, annoyed by the twisted confessional path of the family, noted that "this woman appears to me to have a Jewish heart and earthly intentions, and to be very uncertain." Handschuh offered her instruction for communion after a further probation period of two weeks, but the records of the Lutheran church do not indicate that a "former Jewess" ever joined the congregation.[104]

Handschuh's account of his encounters with this woman reveals a deep ambivalence toward Jewish converts that has also been noted by students of conversions in early modern Germany. While many theologians propagated the millenarian goal of the conversion of the Jews, Christians never really trusted the intentions and motives of converts, who often became alienated from the Jewish community and continued to be marginalized in Christian society.[105] There are occasional glimpses of anti-Jewish sentiment in other records. A German-language newspaper published a critique of the business practices of Joseph Simon and other "Jew landlords" in 1766, and the piece clearly drew on the stereotype of the Jewish usurer. Nevertheless, incidents of open anti-Judaism seem to have been extremely rare in Lancaster or elsewhere in colonial Pennsylvania.[106]

More generally, there is reason to assume that the presence of Jewish storekeepers and traders was a familiar aspect of life for Pennsylvania German farmers and townspeople who had migrated from the small towns and villages of southwest Germany and had to adjust to life in an unfamiliar environment. Indeed, encounters with one of the few Jews in the Pennsylvania countryside would probably have fit German immigrants' prior experience more than contacts with English lawyers and magistrates, Scots-Irish farmers and laborers, African Americans, and Delaware Indians. In the process of migration and resettlement, German speakers had to adapt to a dispersed pattern of settlement, an English legal

104. *Hallesche Nachrichten*, 2:64–65; see also Hucho, *Weiblich und fremd*, 368; Pencak, *Jews and Gentiles*, 193.

105. Manfred Agethen, "Bekehrungsversuche an Juden und Judentaufen in der frühen Neuzeit," *Aschkenas* 1 (1991): 65–94; Elisheva Carlebach, *Divided Souls: Converts from Judaism in Germany, 1500–1750* (New Haven: Yale University Press, 2001). Gotthilf Heinrich Ernst Mühlenberg apparently did not write down his thoughts when he married Joseph Simon's daughter Shinah and her Christian husband, Dr. Nicholas Schuyler, by licence in August 1782; an examination of Mühlenberg's personal diaries from the Lancaster period (American Philosophical Society) has not uncovered any additional information on that case (cf. Smith and Weiser, *Trinity Lutheran Church Records*, 2:203; Brener, *Jews of Lancaster*, 22).

106. William Pencak, "Jews and Anti-Semitism in Colonial Pennsylvania," *PMHB* 126 (2002): 365–408 (see esp. 382–83 on Joseph Simon); Pencak, *Jews and Gentiles*, 191–95.

system, new forms of unfree labor, a pluralist social order, and the requirements of self-government in ecclesiastical and civil affairs.[107] Amid these changes and adjustments, business contacts and neighborly encounters between German-speaking Christians and Jews constituted an element of continuity.

AFRICAN AMERICANS: A PEOPLE WITHOUT A CHURCH

Up to the era of the American Revolution, slavery was an expanding institution in Pennsylvania. The ownership of slaves not only filled the labor needs of wealthy merchants, craftsmen, and farmers but served as an important symbol of rank and status as well.[108] While the proportion of slaves in eighteenth-century Lancaster never exceeded 2 percent of the population, slavery was still an established fact of life. Jerome H. Wood counted twenty-eight slaves in 1764, fifty-four in 1779, and fifty-seven in 1790.[109] Members of all major religious denominations and English- as well as German-speaking inhabitants were among the slave owners. Prominent slaveholders included a number of leading Anglicans—Edward Smout, George Sanderson, Edward Shippen, George Ross, Samuel Boyd, and Jasper Yeates—as well as the Jewish merchants Joseph Simon, Levy Andrew Levy, and Solomon Etting.[110] The "negro woman & boy" listed in the inventory of tanner John Foulk, an Anglican, in 1748 were valued at £50, or almost a quarter of the decedent's personal estate. The estate of Patrick Carrigan, another early Anglican leader, included a black man and woman valued at £50 in 1756; a servant boy and girl were appraised at £15. Innkeeper George Gibson's 1762 inventory itemized "the Negro's Bed cloths."[111]

Neither Quakers nor German speakers were reluctant to acquire slaves in colonial Lancaster. In 1750 Isaac Whitelock advertised that a black slave "with

---

107. These processes have been explored in Roeber, *Palatines*; Fogleman, *Hopeful Journeys*; and the essays in Lehmann, *In Search of Peace and Prosperity*.

108. Greene, *Pursuits*, 131–35; Alan Tully, "Patterns of Slaveholding in Colonial Pennsylvania: Chester and Lancaster Counties, 1729–1758," *Journal of Social History* 6 (1973): 284–305.

109. Wood, *Conestoga Crossroads*, 162. Cf. also Gary B. Nash and Jean R. Soderlund, *Freedom by Degrees: Emancipation in Pennsylvania and Its Aftermath* (New York: Oxford University Press, 1991), 32.

110. Lancaster County Will Book A-I-196, Pennsylvania State Archives; Eshleman, *Early Lancaster Taxables*, 266; *Copy of Inventory*, 376; Wood, *Conestoga Crossroads*, 161–66; Marcus, *Colonial American Jew*, 2:705; Brener, *Jews of Lancaster*, 8–9; Fish, *Barnard and Michael Gratz*, 187–88; United States Bureau of Census, *Heads of Families at the First Census of the United States Taken in Year 1790: Pennsylvania* (Washington, D.C.: Government Printing Office, 1908), 135–38.

111. John Foulk Estate Inventory, 1748; Patrick Carrigan Estate Inventory, 1756; George Gibson Estate Inventory, 1762, Lancaster County Historical Society.

an iron collar around his neck" had run away, and James Webb Jr. was disowned by the Sadsbury Monthly Meeting for buying and selling slaves. In August 1776 Webb requested readmission to the meeting because he had freed his slaves.[112] In 1751 Elizabeth Carpenter, the widow of a Virginia slaveholder, sold several of her deceased husband's slaves to Moravian Georg Graff, Lutherans Andreas Beyerle and Valentin Krug, and Reformed Melchior and Franz Fortinet.[113] The tanner Valentin Krug, one of the wealthiest men in Lancaster at midcentury, mentioned two slaves in the will he dictated in 1757. Krug's son-in-law Caspar Singer, who continued the tannery business, advertised "a handsome young Negro boy" born in America for sale in 1764.[114] The butcher Ulrich Reigart also offered "a likely healthy Negroe boy, about 14 Years of Age" for sale in 1761, emphasizing that he was "fit to wait on a Gentleman."[115]

Matthias Graff, a member of the Moravian congregation, bequeathed his "Negro Boy Jem" and his "Negro Girl Venus" to his wife in 1779. When Wilhelm Bausman, a leader of the German Reformed congregation, dictated his will in 1784, he enumerated the "Negroe Man" Ned, the "Negroe Wench" Diana, her child Nancy, and the six-year-old "Molatoe girl" Jane. The gunsmith Christoph Breitenhart, a member of the Lutheran congregation, bequeathed his "Negroe Wench Esther" to his wife when he dictated his will in 1785. The butcher and tavernkeeper Christoph Reigart disposed of two adult male slaves, an adult female, a girl, and an "old Negroe Wench" in the will he made in 1784.[116] Other prominent German slaveholders in the borough included the tavernkeeper Matthias Slough, who owned five African Americans in 1782, and the shopkeeper Paul Zantzinger, who had three slaves baptized in 1784. As we have seen, Slough and Zantzinger were associated with both the Lutheran and Anglican congregations in town. In nearby Conestoga Township, three German speakers owned a total of thirteen slaves in 1782. In 1790 German speakers Jacob Krug,

112. Mark C. Ebersole, "Abolition Divides the Meeting House: Quakers and Slavery in Early Lancaster County," *JLCHS* 102 (2000): 2–27, esp. 10–11.

113. Mayhill, *Deed Abstracts*, 29 (C128).

114. Lancaster County Will Book B-I-293, Pennsylvania State Archives; *Der Wöchentliche Philadelphische Staatsbote*, no. 136, August 20, 1764. For the Krug-Singer clan, see Clark, "Early Lancaster Notables," 3–9.

115. Wood, *Conestoga Crossroads*, 163.

116. Graff: Lancaster County Will Book D-I-75, Pennsylvania State Archives; Bausman: Lancaster County Will Book E-I-16, Pennsylvania State Archives; Breitenhart: Lancaster County Will Book F-I-126, Pennsylvania State Archives. Cf. Don Yoder, ed., *Pennsylvania German Immigrants, 1709–1786: Lists Consolidated from Yearbooks of the Pennsylvania German Folklore Society* (Baltimore: Genealogical Publishing Co., 1980), 190–91; Reigart: Lancaster County Will Book D-I-404, Pennsylvania State Archives.

Friedrich Anspach, Friedrich Weidele, and Peter Hufnagel were among the borough's slaveholders. These examples clearly reveal that prosperous Germans in eighteenth-century Lancaster were no less hesitant to acquire human property than their English-speaking neighbors. The ownership of slaves was "a testimony, primarily, to the financial and social success of their owners."[117] The passing of a gradual abolition act in Pennsylvania in 1780 met with considerable opposition from Lancaster County residents, including German speakers, and one investigation of voting patterns on antislavery legislation in the state even found that "[t]he German Lutherans and Reformed stood alone as the consistent opponents of abolition." At the turn of the century, however, a number of prominent Lancasterians, including William Montgomery, Josiah Lockhart, Joseph Simon, John Graeff, and Nathaniel Ellmaker, manumitted their slaves, thus contributing to the gradual emergence of a free black population in the town.[118]

Since most of them were unfree and belonged to members of various congregations, blacks in eighteenth-century Lancaster were unable to form their own religious community. Instead, traces of the presence of slaves, free blacks, and "mulattos" can be found in the records of various denominations. The Jesuit Wilhelm Wappeler wrote in 1742 that he had baptized a sick fifteen-year-old black girl in the home of a local physician and hoped to baptize two young Africans, a boy and a girl from Guinea, shortly.[119] The first Anglican minister, Richard Locke, reported to London in October 1746 that he had baptized "8 negros in one Family."[120] When his successor, Thomas Barton, summarized the baptisms he had performed over a twelve-month period in November 1764, he enumerated "115 infants, twelve white adults and two black ones." In 1772 the Anglican schoolmaster Joseph Rathell taught "several Negroes belonging to different families of the church, every Sunday evening, in the school house." He

---

117. Wood, *Conestoga Crossroads*, 163–64; *Heads of Families*, 135–38; Leroy T. Hopkins, "Hollow Memories: African Americans in Conestoga Township," *JLCHS* 101 (2000): 145–64, esp. 148. These findings contrast with those of Laura Becker, who did not find any Germans among the slaveowners of Reading, Pennsylvania, before the Revolution. During the War for Independence, however, several German newcomers brought their slaves with them to Reading (Becker, "Community Experience," 174–76, 445). According to Gary B. Nash, Germans were significantly underrepresented among the slave owners of eighteenth-century Philadelphia (Gary B. Nash, "Slaves and Slaveowners in Colonial Philadelphia," *William and Mary Quarterly* 30 [1973]: 223–56, esp. 254–55).

118. Owen S. Ireland, "Germans Against Abolition: A Minority's View of Slavery in Revolutionary Pennsylvania," *Journal of Interdisciplinary History* 3 (1973): 685–706 (quote on 697); Martha B. Clark, "Lancaster County's Relation to Slavery," *PLCHS* 15 (1911): 43–61, esp. 57–59. For the general course of slave emancipation in Pennsylvania, see Nash and Soderlund, *Freedom by Degrees*; see esp. 108–10 for opposition to slave emancipation in Lancaster County.

119. Musser, "Old St. Mary's," 106.

120. Owen, "Letters of the Rev. Richard Locke and Rev. George Craig," 467–71.

did his best, Rathell claimed, "to instruct them in their catechism of some of the plainest duties of religion and morality, by which I hope these poor creatures will be much benefited."[121]

In 1745 the diarist of the Moravian community in Bethlehem recorded the visit of a "Negro woman from Canastogoe" who "had served among the Mennonites and knows German and can talk quite a good deal about the Christian religion. She knows [the Moravian minister Jacob] Lischy well and also Pastor Nyberg, who has her eight-year-old son with him, and would like to entrust the other, aged ten, to our congregation, but £20 would have to be paid to the Mennonites for this."[122] In 1751 the Moravian minister Georg Neisser privately baptized Sebastian Graff's "negro child" and named it Amalia. Moravian records also document the burials of the unbaptized eleven-year-old slave girl Hannah, who belonged to the shopkeeper Georg Graff, in 1759 and another slave girl of Graff's named Molly in 1764. Hannah, the "negro child" of Jacob Kagey, was interred in 1781. According to Johann Friedrich Handschuh, a black student was among the sixty children who attended the Lutheran parish school in 1750, and a decade later Sebastian Graff asked the Moravian church council for permission to send his black servant girl to the congregational school.[123]

After James Burd's "Negro" Jem had killed a man in Middletown in 1768, the "Dutch Calvinist Minister" was visiting him in prison where he awaited the death sentence. According to Burd's son-in-law Jasper Yeates, the pastor was "endeavouring to prepare the poor unhappy Creature for another State of Existence." The Reformed pastor Carl Ludwig Boehme baptized the child of an English mother who claimed that the father was a "negro" in May 1772. The infant was given to one John Christborn, "who promised to rear it in the Christian religion." John and Sarah Williams, who brought their son Peter to the German Reformed pastor for baptism three months later, were probably black as well.[124] In March 1780, Matthias Slough's slave Cato and George Ross's "negress" Diana were married "according to the required permission on both sides" by the Lutheran pastor Gotthilf Heinrich Ernst Mühlenberg in Maytown. A year later Mühlenberg

121. Worner, "Church of England (Part IV)," 62, 75.

122. Hamilton, Bethlehem Diary, 84.

123. Lancaster Diaries, 1751, entry for November 3/14, Moravian Archives; Moravian Burial Book, 8, 14; Hallesche Nachrichten, 1:545; Protocoll, entries for October 26, 1760, and November 1, 1761, Moravian Archives.

124. Jasper Yeates to Edward Shippen, March 7, 1768; Yeates to James Burd, March 23, 1768, both copied in Jasper Yeates Collection, 1767–69, MG 205, box 1, folder 31, pp. 34–35, 42, Lancaster County Historical Society; Wright, Lancaster County Church Records, 2:75–76. On German clergymen's attitude toward blacks, cf. Glatfelter, Pastors and People, 2:288–90.

married "Mr. Schlauch's Negro, Larry, and Mr. Haverstich's Negress, Nancy" upon their masters' request, and the attorney Jasper Yeates had a coffin made for a black slave named Prime.[125] When Christopher Marshall's slave Dinah died in Lancaster in 1778, on the other hand, her master had difficulties finding people in the community to attend to Dinah's burial since, he believed, "the poor women here" were "rich with imagination." In his diary Marshall noted: "O, what a wretched place is here, full of Religious Professions but not a grain of love or charity, except in words, in the generality of the German inhabitants."[126]

A closer look at the Lutheran and Episcopal church records of the 1780s and 1790s reveals that blacks—both slave and free—occupied marginal positions in Lancaster's Protestant congregations. During the period from 1783 to 1799 sixteen baptisms and five marriages in the Lutheran church involved persons identified as blacks or mulattos. When the adult mulatto Benjamin Wade was baptized in April 1783, no member of the congregation served as his sponsor. Four months afterward a single mother, the maid of one Colonel Butler, brought her daughter to baptism and named the "negro Jacob" as the child's father. Again, no sponsors were entered into the baptism book. Six years later, the black couple Charles Bush and Susanna Casdin had their son William baptized in the presence of Thomas Delvis, another black man, and the slave Esther, who belonged to the widow Breitenhart, received baptism "after appropriate instruction." The mulattos James and Elisabeth Burns had chosen Margaret Williams, a single woman, as godmother of their daughter Margaret. In February 1791 the "free negro" George and Hanna, the black slave of "Mr. Scott," were recorded as the parents and sponsors of the eighteen-month-old child Elisabeth. William, the illegitimate son of the black woman Chinsey Talbert, was baptized in August 1792. The black woman "Johanette," who was "residing with Johan Bausman," brought a child to pastor Mühlenberg for baptism in 1798. There is little evidence that these African Americans felt a deeper attachment to the congregation or were integrated into the Lutheran community. Johannes Kehn, a black, attended communion on Easter 1795, but the pastor recorded that he had "fallen" afterward, and he evidently did not come back. When the forty-two-year-old mulatto woman Hannah Wade died in August 1798, pastor Mühlenberg indicated some familiarity with her by recording that she had borne her long, painful illness as a patient Christian.[127] The sixteen-year-old Johannes (John) Robinson was

125. Smith and Weiser, *Trinity Lutheran Church Records*, 2:190, 196; Landis, "Jasper Yeates," 219.

126. Quoted in Ebersole, "Abolition," 11, and Wood, *Conestoga Crossroads*, 166.

127. Smith and Weiser, *Trinity Lutheran Church Records*, 3:5, 11, 81, 83, 99, 100, 118, 123, 151, 167, 209, 212, 237, 373; 4:34, 232.

baptized in May 1780 and admitted to Holy Communion at the festival of Pentecost. Robinson returned for communion at Easter 1781 and Pentecost 1783, when pastor Mühlenberg identified him as "the negro with the Widow Beckin," and regularly appears in the communicant lists of Trinity Lutheran Church until 1789. Robinson married Rachel Williamson in the Lutheran church in January 1791, and the couple attended communion there on Pentecost 1804. Robinson was the only black who may be termed a regular communicant member of the Lutheran congregation.[128]

A slightly larger number of African Americans appear in the records of St. James' Episcopal Church, which was itself considerably smaller than the Lutheran one. More than twenty baptisms and thirteen marriages of blacks and mulattos were recorded there from 1784 to 1799. Eight baptized blacks were identified as slaves, while one was a servant, one a free black woman, and the remainder were children of free black or mulatto couples. Three of the eight black slaves were baptized as adults, while the others were children of various ages. Flavia, a slave of Paul Zantzinger, was the only black mother who brought two children to baptism during this period, and her son James was the only slave child whose date of birth—January 26, 1786—was precisely recorded. In an unusual instance, on August 31, 1800, eight children of the black couple Isaac and Charlotte Gilmore, aged eighteen months to thirteen years, were baptized. In March 1802 another free black couple, James Corsey and his wife, Ann, brought three children to baptism.[129]

The thirteen marriages recorded at St. James' Episcopal from 1785 to 1796 mostly involved free blacks; only the mulatto Richard, who married the free woman Elizabeth Otley in 1794, was identified as George Ross's servant, and Catherine, who became the wife of Pleasants Tolbet in the same year, was "said to be a slave" of the Jewish merchant Joseph Simon. Moreover, several African American couples showed some attachment to the Episcopal congregation by bringing one or two children to baptism there. After their marriage in September 1791, the free mulattos Benjamin Galloway and Hannah Collins returned with their one-year-old daughter, Betsey, in July 1793 and with their infant daughter, Sarah, in November 1795. Five other children of the couple were baptized in the Lutheran church between 1799 and 1805. The free blacks Charles Carter and Ann Nicholson married in St. James' Episcopal Church in October 1795 and had their one-year-old daughter, Letitia, baptized there in December 1799.

128. Smith and Weiser, *Trinity Lutheran Church Records*, 2:99, 184, 291; 3:232; 4:280.
129. Wright, *Lancaster County Church Records*, 3:76–97.

Finally, the mulatto Jeremiah Marbury (or Maybury) and his wife Mary had a daughter christened by the Lutheran pastor Mühlenberg in February 1793. Mary seems to have died shortly thereafter because Jeremiah and Catherine Boman, another free mulatto woman, were married by the Episcopal pastor in December 1795. Almost a year later, Jeremiah and Catherine received adult baptism in the Episcopal church. Between 1799 and 1803, the couple had three children baptized in Trinity Lutheran Church.[130]

These examples reveal a growing presence of free blacks, at least in the Episcopal congregation, but there can be no doubt that African Americans remained marginal figures in Lancaster's churches throughout the eighteenth century. While the appearance of a black preacher from Maryland who was addressing "sundry people" in an orchard "well for an hour" is recorded as early as 1778, the enslavement of most of the town's blacks prevented them from organizing their religious life according to their own will.[131] In a very real sense, African Americans were a religiously fragmented and poorly integrated group—a people without a church.

CONCLUSION

Pastors who tried to explain the unfamiliar religious situation in Pennsylvania to European correspondents and seek funds from there often referred to the bewildering variety of "sects" and the intense religious competition in Penn's colony, but most of the evidence for the borough of Lancaster indicates that the laity may have been less confused about the range of religious beliefs and choices than the clergy. Lutherans and German Reformed who intermarried and worshipped together merely continued a practice that was well established in confessionally mixed German principalities, and laypeople as well as pastors remained highly conscious of the religious differences separating "church" people from "sect" people. After their break with the Lutherans in 1746, the Moravians attracted several Reformed and a few religious "seekers" like William Henry but remained a fairly small and predominantly German-speaking congregation. Whereas the attractions of the large Lutheran and German Reformed congregations for the town's English-speaking minority remained minimal, the genteel, respectable outlook of the Anglican congregation lured a few prominent first- and

130. Wright, *Lancaster County Church Records*, 3:85, 88–89, 92, 123–27; Smith and Weiser, *Trinity Lutheran Church Records*, 4:36, 55, 81, 88, 114 (Galloway); Smith and Weiser, *Trinity Lutheran Church Records*, 3:123; 4:38, 71, 95 (Maybury).
131. Wood, *Conestoga Crossroads*, 200.

second-generation German speakers. Still, in contrast to the colonial metropolis New York City studied by Randall Balmer and Joyce D. Goodfriend, marriages and conversions rarely cut across ethnic lines.

The presence of small clusters of Roman Catholics and Jews added distinct facets to the religious pluralism of eighteenth-century Lancaster, but on the whole did little to alter its predominantly Protestant character or test the limits of the townspeople's capacity for practical tolerance. To a large extent, the existence of the Jewish community depended on the activism and longevity of its most prominent member, the entrepreneur Joseph Simon. A Roman Catholic presence was maintained by Jesuit missionaries as well as by Irish and German laymen whose relations with their Protestant neighbors appear to have been remarkable free of friction—even at times when anti-Papist sentiment ran high in Pennsylvania politics. Finally, the experience of the town's African Americans sharply contrasts with that of white inhabitants for they were as restricted in their spiritual as in their worldly choices.

5

LANCASTER'S CHURCHES IN THE NEW REPUBLIC

THE REVOLUTIONARY YEARS

Like many communities, Lancaster was affected by the struggle for American independence in numerous ways. Leading inhabitants from all major denominations sat on revolutionary committees, townsmen formed militia units and marched off to battlefields, several hundred captured British and German soldiers were imprisoned in local barracks, inflation and the disruption of trade routes hurt the local economy, and some men prospered from army contracts for military supplies.[1] The war's impact on Lancaster's churches, however, was anything but uniform, and congregational development from 1776 to 1783 depended to a considerable degree on the views and behavior of local clergymen. John D. Woodhull, pastor of the Presbyterian churches at Leacock and Lancaster, represents one end of the political spectrum. Woodhull was an ardent patriot, preached on behalf of the Revolutionary War effort, and accompanied a batalion of Lancaster County militia to the battlefields of Long Island, Germantown, and Monmouth as a field chaplain. Woodhull's military service took him away from Lancaster County during the years 1777 to 1779, and then he did not return to his former parishes but accepted the pastorate at Old Tennent's Church in Freehold, New Jersey.[2]

1. These developments are outlined in detail in Wood, *Conestoga Crossroads.* Cf. also Evans, "Lancaster Borough," 144–51.

2. Courtney and Long, "History of First Presbyterian Church," 11–12; Early, "Our First 250 Years," 10; James McLachlan, *Princetonians,* 1:601–2.

Thomas Barton's political sentiments were diametrically opposed to Woodhull's. The conservative Anglican clergyman had repeatedly denounced colonial resistance to British politics and affirmed his loyal support of existing political and ecclesiastical hierarchies. Moreover, like most Anglican ministers in the northern and middle colonies, Barton depended on the financial contributions of the London-based Society for the Propagation of the Gospel in Foreign Parts for his livelihood. When the Declaration of Independence was proclaimed in July 1776, therefore, he found himself unable to support the new regime and alter the liturgy prescribed in the Anglican Book of Common Prayer. Barton had to close his churches "to avoid the fury of the populace who would not suffer the Liturgy to be used unless the Collects & Prayers for the King & Royal Family were omitted." In a letter to London in November 1776, Barton used whiggish language to express his abhorrence of the American patriots. Although he had "used every prudent step to give no offence even to those who usurped authority & Rule & exercised the severest Tyranny over us, yet my life and property have been threatened upon mere *suspicion* of being unfriendly to what is called the American cause." Anglican ministers "who dared to act upon proper principles" had "suffered greatly" at the hands of the revolutionaries. In short, "the calamities of America, brought on by a few ambitious & designing men here" were "great beyond description." Barred from holding services in the church, Barton went from house to house to give private instruction to his parishioners, visit the sick, baptize and catechize children, and perform other pastoral acts. He thought that his private ministry, which had "somewhat the appearance of the persecution of the Primitive Christians," was having "good Effects" on his parishioners: "it kindled & encreased their Zeal, & united them the closer together." While he had some hope that "the day is near at hand when the Churches will be open & I shall again enter on my *public* duties," St. James' Church remained closed for more than five years.[3]

When he was not visiting his parishioners, Barton explained in a letter to London in late 1778, "prudence & my own safety directed me . . . to confine myself entirely to my own house, which I did for two years." His situation in Lancaster became intolerable, however, when the Commonwealth of Pennsylvania passed legislation prohibiting all people who had not sworn loyalty to the

---

3. Perry, *Historical Collections*, 2:489–91, and 4:130; Worner, "Church of (Part IV)," 84–86, 89; Diller and Klein, *History of St. James' Church*, 55–57; Edgar Legare Pennington, "The Anglican Clergy of Pennsylvania in the American Revolution," *PMHB* 63 (1939): 401–31, esp. 404–11; Jeffries, "Thomas Barton," 58–59; Russell, "Thomas Barton," 313–34, esp. 330–33; Glatfelter, *Pastors and People*, 2:352–53; Rhoden, *Revolutionary Anglicanism*, 104, 110, 112.

new Republican government to leave their county of residence and requiring oaths of allegiance from all adult males. After a petition from Pennsylvania's Anglican missionaries to the state government requesting exemption from these acts had proved fruitless, Barton, "determined never to sacrifice Principle to Interest," decided to request the Supreme Executive Council's permission to move to New York City, the Loyalist stronghold in the mid-Atlantic region. The minister transferred his real estate to his son-in-law Paul Zantzinger and with his second wife, Sarah, took leave from his congregations and his eight minor children in October 1778. He gratefully acknowledged that his congregations in Pequea and Caernarvon, which had with few exceptions "uniformly & steadily retained their attachment to the British Government, & their affection & Loyalty to their Sovereign," had collected his arrears and an additional £50 for him and had removed his children from Lancaster to a house in Caernarvon. Loyalism was apparently much stronger among rural Anglicans than in St. James' congregation. Separated from most of his family and isolated from the people he had served for almost twenty years, Barton was confused about his future course: should he wait for an opportunity to return to his old congregations or "solicit some humble appointment in England"? His "ill state of health" obliged him to spend the summer of 1779 on Staten Island "for the benefit of Bathing & Exercise," but he also "read prayers, preached very often, & baptized several children." Barton's son William, who had recently returned from England, and his son-in-law Paul Zantzinger made repeated attempts to visit the ailing minister in his exile. At the instigation of its member David Rittenhouse, a suspicious Supreme Executive Council finally permitted two meetings in Elizabethtown, New Jersey, in early 1780 but categorically ruled out Barton's return to Pennsylvania. While he was preparing for his departure to England, Thomas Barton succumbed to "a tedious and most painful illness" and died on May 25, 1780.[4]

While the Revolutionary War disrupted congregational life in the English churches, its effects on the German congregations were more subtle. In 1775 Lutheran pastor Justus Heinrich Christian Helmuth gave an account of the siege of Boston and military preparations on the American side that revealed his sympathies for the patriot cause. He found the "enthusiasm that manifests itself

4. Perry, *Historical Collections*, 2:491–93 and 5:129–34; Tappert and Doberstein, *Journals of Henry Melchior Muhlenberg*, 3:160–61; Barton, *Memoirs*, 278–91; Worner, "Church of England (Part IV)," 86–92; Pennington, "Anglican Clergy," 410–11; Diller and Klein, *History of St. James' Church*, 57–61; Milton Rubincam, "A Memoir of the Life of William Barton, A.M. (1754–1817)," *Pennsylvania History* 12 (1945): 179–93; Jeffries, "Thomas Barton," 59–62; Glatfelter, *Pastors and People*, 2:353–54; Rhoden, *Revolutionary Anglicanism*, 97, 120.

under such dark circumstances . . . indescribable" and exaggerated the unity and determination of the colonists: "The people are nearly all raised to the highest pitch of enthusiasm respecting freedom. The whole land from New England to Georgia is all of one mind, to risk body and life in order to assert its freedom. The few who think otherwise, dare not speak otherwise." As a pietistic clergyman, Helmuth was concerned that the colonies thought of their liberty in exclusively secular terms: "Would to God, that men might once assert their spiritual freedom as zealously and unanimously as they here in America rise to the defence of their bodily freedom!" The year before both Helmuth and his Reformed colleague Carl Ludwig Boehme had made a contribution to the relief of the inhabitants of Boston.[5] In a petition to the Supreme Executive Council of Pennsylvania in 1777 Boehme's successor, Johann Albert Conrad Helffenstein, distanced himself from the loyalism of his father-in-law, a Philadelphia butcher, and claimed that "his own Conduct hath always been such, as will convince every impartial observer of his attachment to the Rights and Liberties of America."[6]

In the diaries the Moravian congregation kept during the war years, the writers repeatedly noted that worship services continued undisturbed. There were tense moments in the summer of 1776, when pacifist United Brethren had to shoulder arms and march to the "Flying Camp" in the Jerseys with the Pennsylvania militia, and in October 1777, when fifteen Brethren from Lititz were escorted to Lancaster under armed guard and lodged in the Quaker meetinghouse, which was already full of militiamen. Whatever the reason for their confinement, they were released the same evening and formally discharged the following day.[7] In 1778 the graveyard of Trinity Lutheran Church became the scene of a state funeral when Thomas Wharton, president of the Supreme Executive Council of Pennsylvania, who had died unexpectedly in Lancaster, was buried there. Meanwhile, wartime inflation raised the cost of living for clergymen, and the Lutheran church council decided in 1777 to add £50 to pastor Helmuth's salary and give the schoolmaster and organist a raise "as long as the hard times last." The Reformed church council deemed it necessary to insert a note to posterity in its protocol explaining that the explosion of annual expenses from less than £50 in a normal year to more than £274 in 1777 was due to the extraordinary depreciation of the currency. Since the prices for some goods had risen to twice, three times, or

5. Quoted in Schmauk, "Lutheran Church," 336; cf. Glatfelter, *Pastors and People*, 2:377–78; Heiges, "Evangelical Lutheran Church," 30.

6. Quoted in Glatfelter, *Pastors and People*, 2:380.

7. Lancaster Diaries, 1776–83, "Memorabilien," Moravian Archives.

even ten times their normal levels, the council deemed it a blessing for the congregation that necessary expenses could be met without going into debt.[8]

The Lutheran, Moravian, and Reformed pastors all received passes to visit the German mercenaries held as prisoners of war in Lancaster, and the Reformed pastor Helffenstein preached before them repeatedly. In 1778 Helffenstein married six British and Hessian soldiers, and in 1783 his successor, Johann Wilhelm Hendel, officiated at the marriages of five soldiers captured after the surrender of Cornwallis's army at Yorktown. Several British soldiers were married by the Lutheran pastor from 1781 to 1783, while a number of German prisoners from Brunswick, Hanau, and Waldeck appear in the communicant lists during the same period.[9]

Both the German Reformed and Lutheran congregations had the benefit of regular pastoral services through most of the war. Late in 1775 the German Reformed congregation had called the popular pastor of Germantown, Johann Albert Conrad Helffenstein (1748–90), a native of the Palatinate who had entered the Pennsylvania field in 1772. During his three and a half years in Lancaster, Helffenstein ministered to about 250 families and reported that 137 students attended the two Reformed schools in town. Like many of his predecessors, Helffenstein apparently found Lancaster a difficult place for in 1779 he accepted a call back to Germantown "in the hope of having more fruit there." He was succeeded by another Palatine, Johann Theobald Faber (1739–88), a man who according to one historian felt "[o]bviously more at home in country congregations than in the city." Faber had already declined two earlier calls from Lancaster and left the borough after a pastorate of three years in 1782, to be succeeded by the congregation's "old" pastor Johann Wilhelm Hendel.[10]

In 1779 Trinity Lutheran's pastor Justus Heinrich Christian Helmuth, who according to his older colleague Heinrich Melchior Muhlenberg was working in "harmony and unity" with his congregation in the midst of the war, followed

8. Ellis and Evans, *History of Lancaster County,* 454; Coldren and Heisey, "Religious Life," 130; Heiges, "Evangelical Lutheran Church," 30–31, 33; Records of the First Reformed Church, vol. 10, microfilm no. 88/3, p. 54, Evangelical and Reformed Historical Society; Glatfelter, *Pastors and People,* 2:387; Wood, *Conestoga Crossroads,* 151.

9. Hinke, *Ministers,* 166–67; Coldren and Heisey, "Religious Life," 133; Diller and Klein, *History of St. James' Church,* 57; Evans, "Lancaster Borough," 148–49; Wood, *Conestoga Crossroads,* 195; Glatfelter, *Pastors and People,* 2:381–82; Smith and Weiser, *Trinity Lutheran Church Records,* 2:198, 200, 202, 283, 288, 297, and 3:205, 255, 260, 262, 265.

10. Hinke, *Minutes of the Coetus,* 350, 370, 372, 380, 382; Good, *History (1725–1792),* 551–52, 559–61; Ellis and Evans, *History of Lancaster County,* 454–55; Hinke, *Ministers,* 114, 131–35, 165–68; Glatfelter, *Pastors and People,* 1:39 (quote about Faber), 56. In communities that were closer to the theater of war, by contrast, warfare could have a much more disruptive influence on congregational life (see Wolf, *Urban Village,* 224–25).

a call to Philadelphia. This decision upset many parishioners. When he was preparing to leave, the lay leaders Ludwig Laumann and Michael Hubele visited Mühlenberg and "insisted that Mr. Helmuth must not be called away from their congregation" since it "had been living in peace and harmony with him for the last ten years."[11] After its pleas had proved fruitless, the congregation was temporarily supplied by a neighboring pastor, Christian Emanuel Schultze from Tulpehocken, and by the itinerant Johann Christoph Hartwick until Heinrich Melchior Mühlenberg's son Gotthilf Heinrich Ernst (1753–1815) accepted the vacant position and began his pastorate in March 1780. The call stated that the young pastor had impressed the church council and congregation with his edifying New Year's sermons. The younger Mühlenberg was Trinity's first American-born pastor, but his father had sent the ten-year-old boy to Europe in 1763, where he had been educated with his two older brothers, Johann Peter Gabriel and Friedrich Augustus Conrad in Halle. After his return to America in 1770, Gotthilf Heinrich Ernst was ordained by the Lutheran Ministerium of Pennsylvania and, after several years in New Jersey, became third pastor in Philadelphia in 1774. A committed though not outspoken patriot, he left Philadelphia during the British occupation in 1777 and, after a dispute with senior pastor Johann Christoph Kuntze, resigned in 1779 and went to New Hanover. Although this congregation wished to keep him, he went to Lancaster the next year and spent the remaining thirty-five years of his life there.[12]

While pastors as well as parishioners provided for continuity in the German-speaking churches through the Revolutionary years, tensions lingered beneath the surface. In the midst of the war, a number of Lancaster's elite families, including several leaders of the Anglican, Lutheran, and Moravian congregations, grew tired of austerity and self-sacrifice and formed an "assembly" for dances and other festivities. When pastors Helmuth and Helffenstein were invited to one of their balls in early 1778 they declined, deeming it "quite contrary to the Character

11. Tappert and Doberstein, *Journals of Henry Melchior Muhlenberg*, 3:243; cf. Aland and Wellenreuther, *Die Korrespondenz*, 5:122, 206, 215; Heiges, "Evangelical Lutheran Church," 32.

12. For the congregation's attempts to secure Schultze as its minister, see Aland and Wellenreuther, *Die Korrespondenz*, 5:211, 234, 256, 272. That Mühlenberg wavered for several weeks before accepting the call is evident from ibid., 242–43, 258–59, 262–63, 276, 296, 305–7. Mühlenberg's call is in the Lutheran Archives Center, Mount Airy, Pa. (PM 94 Z3); cf. also Heiges, "Evangelical Lutheran Church," 32–33. For biographical sketches of Mühlenberg, see William B. Sprague, *Annals of the American Pulpit, or Commemorative Notices of Distinguished American Clergymen of Various Denominations*, vol. 9, *Lutheran* (New York: Carter, 1869), 59–66; Paul A. W. Wallace, *The Muhlenbergs of Pennsylvania* (Philadelphia: University of Pennsylvania Press, 1950); Glatfelter, *Pastors and People*, 1:94–95; Charles Boewe, "Muhlenberg, Henry," in *American National Biography*, vol. 16, ed. John A. Garraty and Mark Carnes (New York: Oxford University Press, 1999), 56–57.

of Ministers of Christ to appear at such Places." The clergymen affirmed their conviction "that the most part of the Members of our Congregations are of the same mind with us, and you know that they compose the greatest numbers of the Inhabitants of this Town." The pastors' letter was accompanied by a declaration of "sentiments" penned by Helmuth that cited Christian compassion with the victims of war and compliance with the laws of Congress as reasons for their reprimand. "How strange then is it for men," Helmuth chided, "to play away in this Time of Distress, Whole Hours and Nights in Companys, where they feast perhaps to excess, play and dance. How to account for such Behaviour we hardly Know, for it is certain Heathens would not act worse; and how much more unbecoming it is for such who call themselves Professors of the Religion of our tender and most compassionate Saviour." The reaction of Helmuth's parishioners Matthias Slough, Frederick Kuhn, Paul Zantzinger, and John and Joseph Hubley, who were all members of the "assembly," to this invective is not known, but the pastors seem to have anticipated the sneers of their anglicized members when they apologized about their limited linguistic competence: "The English is not our Mother Tongue, you will find therefore many Faults in consisting with the Idiom of the same; but we know you are too much of a gentleman than to exhaust your Wit about such Trifles."[13]

A petition to the Supreme Executive Council of Pennsylvania for the support of a German weekly newspaper, which dates from the same period and was signed by twenty-four German Lutherans and Reformed, was also headed (and possibly authored) by Helmuth and Helffenstein. As the petitioners reminded the council, many Germans in the state "cannot read English, and some don't understand it." Instead, they were used to German-language papers. As Heinrich Miller's press, which had produced the *Staatsbote* for sixteen years, had been seized and dismantled after the British occupation of Philadelphia and the Saur press had become an overtly Loyalist organ, the petitioners deemed it necessary that a new paper disseminate reliable information on political and military events to the German-speaking public. The State of Pennsylvania subsequently did support a weekly paper, the *Pennsylvanische Zeitungs-Blatt*, which began appearing in February 1778 but expired a few months later.[14] While the two pastors were ostensibly concerned with two very different issues in these instances—social life in Lancaster and the publication of a German weekly—it is notable that they

13. David McNealy Stauffer "The Lancaster Assembly of 1780," *PMHB* 10 (1886): 413–17; cf. Glatfelter, *Pastors and People,* 2:384–85.
14. The petition is printed in Hazard, *Pennsylvania Archives,* 141–42, and is discussed in Glatfelter, *Pastors and People,* 2:384, and Splitter, *Pastors, People, Politics,* 212.

acted as spokesmen for the German-speaking community in both cases and articulated the concerns of a constituency that was conscious of its position as an ethnic group. Helmuth and Helffenstein may have harbored reservations against some of their parishioners' genteel aspirations, but they deemed it essential that the members of their congregations were informed about the momentous events of the American Revolution.

CONGREGATIONAL STABILITY IN THE NEW REPUBLIC

As the preceding chapters have shown, the development of a denominational order in colonial Lancaster had been accompanied by numerous conflicts within the major Protestant congregations. Pastors had been driven away, resigned in frustration, or divided their parishioners. Long pastorates such as those of the Lutheran Johann Siegfried Gerock (1753–1767) and the Anglican Thomas Barton (1759–1776/8) were the exception rather than the rule. After the Revolution, by contrast, stability and continuity became the norm in Lancaster's congregations. The town served as Pennsylvania's state capital from 1799 to 1812 and became a city in 1818, but population growth during the postrevolutionary era, which was a period of comparatively little transatlantic migration, was somewhat slower than colonial population increase. While the number of inhabitants had risen from an estimated fifteen hundred in 1746 to about thirty-three hundred in 1775, 3,772 residents were counted at the time of the first federal census in 1790 and 6,633 people—including 191 foreigners not yet naturalized—were living in the city by 1820. The sixty-six residents with commercial occupations in the latter year indicate that Lancaster continued to play a role in regional trade networks, while the 1,534 inhabitants engaged in manufacture testify to the continuing importance of traditional artisanal trades in a town that had thus far experienced little industrialization.[15]

During the four decades after the Revolutionary War the religious makeup of Lancaster changed only slightly. The major changes were the disappearance of two small religious groups—the Friends' Meeting and the Jewish community—and the emergence of Methodism. Most Quakers left the town in the final decades of the eighteenth century, and "[t]he decreased membership imposed the

---

15. Wood, *Conestoga Crossroads*, 47; United States Bureau of Census, *Heads of Families*, 135–38; United States Census Office, *Fourth Census of the United States, 1820*, vol. 1 (Washington, D.C.: Government Printing Office, 1821).

necessity, on action of Sadsbury Monthly Meeting, of laying down the meeting in 1802. The remaining membership was transferred to Lampeter Preparative Meeting."[16] The Jewish community dwindled away when its members moved to other places or converted to Christianity. Only three Jewish households were left in 1790, and when the last Jewish resident, the eminent merchant Joseph Simon, died in 1804 the community disappeared with him. Jews did not return to Lancaster in significant numbers until the second half of the nineteenth century.[17]

The Methodist movement, which rapidly spread throughout postrevolutionary America, secured a foothold in Lancaster only gradually. The first meetinghouse in the county, known as Boehm's Chapel, was erected at Soudersburg in 1791, but the first appearance of a Methodist preacher in the borough after the Revolutionary War was recorded only in November 1797. William Colbert, who was preaching in Lancaster several times, claimed that Methodism "in this place is in a poor way." In 1803 Henry Boehm is said to have delivered a sermon standing on a butcher's block in the markethouse. Four years later Boehm organized six people into a class in the home of Philip Benedict. In December 1809 the *Lancaster Journal* informed its readers that "the new church built for the Methodist Society in this borough will be opened for divine service" in the presence of three ministers from Philadelphia. The same newspaper announced in July 1810 that the Methodist bishop Francis Asbury was going to preach in the new meetinghouse on August 5, and in August 1811 it announced another visit of Asbury. While the exact size of the congregation is unknown, it probably remained very small before the 1820s.[18] On the whole, Lancaster's denominational order in the early national period still consisted of the six major congregations formed during the colonial period: the Lutheran, German Reformed, Moravian, Anglican (Episcopal), Presbyterian, and Roman Catholic churches.

Lancaster's largest congregation, Trinity Lutheran Church, entered an unprecedented period of stability when Gotthilf Heinrich Ernst Mühlenberg became its minister in 1780. In most respects, the younger Mühlenberg's pastoral record is impressive. In 1784 he baptized 179, confirmed 72, and buried 48 people, while 627 people attended Holy Communion. The number of communicants that Mühlenberg reported at the annual synodical meetings of the Evangelical Lutheran Church fluctuated between six hundred and seven hundred during

---

16. Whitely, *History of Friends*, 6.

17. Brener, *Jews of Lancaster*, 20–25.

18. Ellis and Evans, *History of Lancaster County*, 475; Mary N. Robinson, "Gleanings from an Old Newspaper," *PLCHS* 7 (1902–3): 168; Coldren and Heisey, "Religious Life," 140–42.

the 1780s and 1790s before dropping to between 420 and 550 during the period from 1800 to 1815.[19] Besides his pastoral duties, Mühlenberg devoted considerable time to botanical studies and acquired an international reputation as one of the young republic's foremost students of natural history. He was elected to the American Philosophical Society in 1786 and was a corresponding member of scientific societies in Berlin and Göttingen. In 1787 he became founding president of Franklin College, a "German High School" in Lancaster, and received an honorary doctorate from the College of New Jersey.[20] Like his father, Gotthilf Heinrich Ernst Mühlenberg kept up a regular correspondence with the Francke foundations in Halle and imported books and medicines from there. He also treated patients with medications from Halle and experimented with the production of pharmaceutical substances.[21]

There are many reasons for Mühlenberg's pastoral success. Unlike most colonial pastors, he was not a newcomer to the Pennsylvania field but had spent his early childhood in the province and acquired significant pastoral experience in New Jersey and Philadelphia. At the same time, his education in the Francke foundations connected him to the continental European pietism of his father. The core of his congregation was increasingly made up of second- and third-generation Pennsylvania Germans, a significant portion of whom had acquired wealth and respectability. One aspect of the "Americanization" of the Lutheran congregation was a trend toward feminization. While men and women had taken communion in roughly equal numbers during the peak period of German immigration at midcentury, women outnumbered men at the Lord's Supper in the 1780s. Of the 226 communicants on Pentecost 1784, 141 (62.4 percent) were female, and the following year's 286 Pentecost communicants included 182 women (63.6 percent).[22]

19. *Documentary History of the Lutheran Ministerium*, 263, 270, 277, 285, 292, 299, 305, 310, 317, 325, 335, 345, 354, 369, 376, 392, 402, 413, 429, 439, 450, 463, 480. For accounts of this period in the history of the congregation, see Schmauk, "Lutheran Church," 345–51; Heiges, "Evangelical Lutheran Church," 33–51.

20. See Sprague, *Annals*, 9:60–61; Schmauk, "Lutheran Church," 340–44; Glatfelter, *Pastors and People*, 1:94–95, and 2:422–23, 476–77; and Wallace, *Muhlenbergs*, 178–79, 192–93, 196–97, 266, 270–71, 308–15. On his botanical studies, see Shiu-ying Hu and E. D. Merrill, "Work and Publications of Henry Muhlenberg," *Bartonia* 25 (1949): 1–66; and C. Earle Smith Jr., "Henry Muhlenberg—Botanical Pioneer," *American Philosophical Society Proceedings* 106 (1962): 443–60.

21. Aland and Wellenreuther, *Die Korrespondenz*, 5:543–44, 563–64, 653, 681, 813, 849. See Splitter, *Pastors, People, Politics*, 264–65; Heiges, "Evangelical Lutheran Church," 33–34; and Renate Wilson, *Pious Traders in Medicine: A German Pharmaceutical Network in Eighteenth-Century North America* (University Park: Pennsylvania State University Press, 2001), 152–55, 178–80, 189–202.

22. Smith and Weiser, *Trinity Lutheran Church Records*, 3:271–73, 280–83. On the feminization of American churches, see chapter 2.

Mühlenberg's correspondence and diaries show that he embarked on his ministerial duties with a clear understanding of his own role. "To-day," he wrote in 1781, "I have animated myself anew in increased fidelity—as head of a family in family religion, as pastor, in zealous care for souls, as a theologian, in diligent study, and as a Christian in my calling, that God may be honored, my fellowmen benefitted, that, in one word, I may not live in vain."[23] In a letter to his father in 1785 Mühlenberg outlined his pastoral program. As he explained, he was preaching twice on Sundays. While he chose the topic of the morning sermon freely, either dwelling on remarkable occurrences in his pastorate or on a particularly striking passage in the Bible or some other text, the afternoon sermons specifically addressed Christ's speeches in the Gospels. He pointed out that he attempted to engage his congregation directly and asked his father to comment on this preaching method. On Wednesday afternoons he was holding catechism lessons (*Kinderlehre*), and while there was generally too little time for regular visits to his parishioners' homes, he was visiting sick members without delay, and baptisms in private homes provided him with additional opportunities for *cura pastoralis*. Finally, he deemed it important that parishioners personally announced their intention to take communion and publicly called upon them to visit him. Citing the example of August Hermann Francke, the founder of Halle pietism, he explained that those sermons were most effective in which the exposition of the biblical text was immediately followed by an application to the lives of his listeners.[24] His diaries show that he kept reminding himself of this program. A pastor who intended to be useful, he noted in 1785, should set an example in his own behavior, preach rather more often than necessary, never cancel a sermon without weighty reasons, and devote himself to preparing young people for communion and visiting the sick.[25] While he advocated the introduction of an English class in the Lutheran school and reminded himself to improve his proficiency in English, Mühlenberg conceived of the Lutheran congregation as an essentially German church and continued to preach in German.[26]

23. Quoted in Glatfelter, *Pastors and People,* 1:95.

24. Aland and Wellenreuther, *Die Korrespondenz,* 5:741–45, 764–67. See also the remarks on Mühlenberg's pastoral work in ibid., 324, 337, 397, 447, 484, 489, 596, 608–11, 618, 849. Cf. Heiges, "Evangelical Lutheran Church," 34.

25. Mühlenberg Diary, vol. 1, entry for July 22, 1785, American Philosophical Society. See also entries for July 27 and December 5 and 10, 1788, and November 10, 1792.

26. Ellis and Evans, *History of Lancaster County,* 404; Heiges, "Evangelical Lutheran Church," 35; Glatfelter, *Pastors and People,* 1:95 and 2:480.

The recollections of one of his parishioners confirm that Mühlenberg faithfully carried out this pastoral program. In 1854 Benjamin Keller, who had been a member of Mühlenberg's congregation for nearly eighteen years and went on to become a pastor in his own right, wrote: "He was a profound theologian and original thinker, but his preaching was perspicuous and direct, and came fairly within the range of the common mind. . . . He was uncommonly faithful in his pastoral duties; and even took pains to import from Germany copies of the Scriptures in the German language for distribution among the people. He had a rare gift at imparting religious instruction to the young, by his Catechetical Lectures, preparatory to Confirmation. . . . To these instructions, in connection with the Divine blessing, many beside myself attributed their hopeful conversion to God." Keller, who considered Mühlenberg "a model Pastor," particularly emphasized "another practice to which he always adhered at every Communion season. He appointed two days in the week immediately preceding the Communion for private conversation with those who intended to join in it. This gave him an opportunity at finding out the spiritual state of the communicants, and of counselling, admonishing, encouraging, comforting, as the respective cases might require."[27] A plain, direct preaching style, a strong emphasis on catechizing, visits to parishioners, and private interviews before the Lord's Supper thus were central elements in his pastoral work.[28] Mühlenberg's popularity and the tranquility of his congregation may also be attributed to his willingness to judge his parishioners kindly and not be too stern in rebuking them for their faults.[29] When several members suggested that Mühlenberg conduct private prayer meetings for the "awakened" in 1791, he declined in order to prevent dissension and distance himself from Methodist "enthusiasm."[30]

The German Reformed, who had never retained a minister for more than six years during the colonial era, also entered a period of longer, more stable pastorates. In September 1782 Johann Wilhelm Hendel, who had already served Lancaster during the 1760s and then spent thirteen years at Tulpehocken, accepted a second

---

27. Keller's letter is printed in Sprague, *Annals*, 9:61–62.

28. A typical journal entry reads: "Ohne dringende Noth muß man sich des Klagens über den Zustand der Gemeine enthalten. Ein gehöriger Ehrgeitz einer Gemeine ist gut und ein zur rechten Zeit angebrachtes Lob reicht mehr zum Eifer als offentlicher Tadel, über den solche die draussen sind wohl spotten. Meine Gemeine verdient doch würklich in manchem Betracht Lob" (Mühlenberg Diary, vol. 1, entry for July 8, 1785, American Philosophical Society; see also entries for September 30, 1786, and January 1, 1789).

29. Mühlenberg Diary, vol. 1, entries for July 23, 1791, and October 6, 1791, American Philosophical Society.

30. Hinke, *Minutes of the Coetus*, 386, 391, 401, 408, 414, 423, 430, 440, 447; Good, *History (1725–1792)*, 547

call to the borough and remained there until February 1794. At the meetings of the German Reformed Coetus, Hendel reported that he had 160 to 180 families in his congregation while the number of confirmands fluctuated between twenty-three and forty-nine. According to one early church historian, he regularly held prayer meetings on Thursday evenings. In 1787 Hendel became vice president of the newly founded Franklin College and like his Lutheran colleague Mühlenberg received an honorary doctorate from the College of New Jersey. A leading member of the German Reformed Coetus, which declared its independence from the Synod of Holland in 1792 and constituted itself as the Synod the German Reformed Church of the United States of America, Hendel eventually accepted the prestigious post of German Reformed pastor in Philadelphia, where he died from yellow fever in 1798.[31]

Hendel's successor, Christian Ludwig Becker (1756–1818), also served the congregation for more than a decade. A native of the German principality of Anhalt-Köthen, he had been educated at the University of Halle and served as adjunct pastor in Bremen before his emigration to the United States in 1793. After eighteen months in eastern Pennsylvania, Becker received a call to Lancaster in 1795. Before leaving the borough for a pastorate in Baltimore in 1806, he delivered a farewell sermon in which he thanked his parishioners for the love and trust that they had shown him for the most part. When Becker asked for God's blessing on the people of Lancaster, he specifically included his "beloved ministerial brother," Lutheran pastor Gotthilf Heinrich Ernst Mühlenberg. Becker was succeeded by another pastor from Anhalt-Köthen, Johann Heinrich Hoffmeier, who had migrated to Pennsylvania in 1793 and ministered in Northampton County before coming to Lancaster. Hoffmeier remained for twenty-five years—far longer than any other German Reformed minister to date.[32]

After the Revolutionary War had disrupted congregations and forced many clergymen into exile, the Anglican church reorganized itself as the Protestant Episcopal Church of the United States. The constitution and revised prayer book that the general convention of the church adopted in 1789 "regulated the function of laymen, priests, and bishops in a manner which created a limited

31. Hinke, *Ministers*, 114–16; Glatfelter, *Pastors and People*, 1:58–59.

32. Ellis and Evans, *History of Lancaster County*, 455–56; Cramer, *History*, 61–62, 65–66; James I. Good, *History of the Reformed Church in the U.S. in the Nineteenth Century* (New York: Board of Publication of the Reformed Church in America, 1911), 13–15; Coldren and Heisey, "Religious Life," 133; Christian Ludewig Becker, *Die Lezten Bitten eines Christlichen Predigers an seine Gemeinde, in einer Abschieds-Rede vorgestellet, und seiner ihm theuren Gemeinde zum Andenken hinterlassen* (Lancaster, Pa.: Benjamin Grimler, 1806), 8.

constitutional episcopate divorced from the English monarchy and Parliament."[33] Having weathered a period of upheaval and uncertainty, Episcopalians also rebuilt congregational life at the local level. Like the German Reformed congregation, St. James' Episcopal Church had only three different ministers during the period from the 1783 to 1820. Joseph Hutchins, who held the post from 1783 to 1788, was succeeded by Elisha Rigg, pastor from 1789 to 1796. Rigg, who married a daughter of church warden William Atlee, was interested in education and in 1795 published his plans for a female academy in the *Lancaster Journal*. When he resigned the following year and moved to Maryland, his predecessor, Joseph Hutchins, supplied the parish until the arrival of the thirty-four-year-old Joseph Clarkson in 1799. The son of a prominent Philadelphia physician, Clarkson had graduated from the College of Philadelphia in 1782 and received an M.A. degree from the College of New Jersey three years later. After his ordination by bishop William White in 1787 he ministered in Philadelphia and Wilmington, Delaware, before moving to Lancaster, where he remained until his death in 1830.[34]

In October 1780 Lancaster's Presbyterians joined two rural congregations, Leacock and Middle Octorara, in sending a call for the young licenciate Nathaniel W. Sample (or Semple; 1752–1834) to the Presbytery of New Castle. Sample accepted in August 1781 and served the three congregations until 1821. His forty-year-pastorate exceeded even those of Clarkson among the Episcopalians and Mühlenberg among the Lutherans. Sample had been educated at Robert Smith's academy in Pequea and received an A.B. degree from the College of New Jersey at Princeton in 1776 before returning to Lancaster County for further study under William Foster, pastor of Middle Octorara Church and another Princeton graduate. Licensed to preach by the New Castle Presbytery in 1779, he supplied a congregation in Delaware for half a year before moving back to the Lancaster area for good. Sample's original contract provided for a salary of five hundred bushels of wheat to be paid by the three congregations in proportion to the time the pastor served them. Since Lancaster paid only one hundred bushels while the other two congregations contributed two hundred each, it appears that Sample spent only one-fifth of his time in the borough until 1798, when elder Henry Slaymaker successfully petitioned the New Castle Presbytery for an equal division of the pastor's time among the three congregations. Meanwhile, visiting

---

33. Rhoden, *Revolutionary Anglicanism*, 119.
34. Ellis and Evans, *History of Lancaster County*, 404, 465; Diller and Klein, *History of St. James' Church*, 65–68, 71–75, 79–82.

preachers continued to supplement the resident pastor's services. Sample made his home in Strasburg, a village roughly equidistant from his three parishes, and helped establish a school there in 1790. According to one scholar, Sample "was a popular preacher who tried to entertain his audiences as well as enlighten them. His churches prospered during his long tenure, but the details of his ministry are obscure because he kept no records." After resigning from the pulpit in 1821 Sample started his own academy in Strasburg.[35]

In accordance with its conception as a missionary church, the Moravian church had frequently exchanged ministers in Lancaster during the colonial period, and the turnover of clergymen continued to be higher than in other churches. Six different men ministered to the Moravian congregation from 1785 to 1819. According to a brief historical narrative inserted into the 1820 diary, no Moravian pastor had terminated his life in the town during the first seventy-four years of the congregation's existence; all had left or been called away to other duties.[36] Despite some concern in the 1780s about the migration of members to Maryland, especially to the rising port of Baltimore, which was thought to be the hotbed of a Methodist awakening, the size of the congregation remained stable. Three hundred thirty-four members, including 71 communicants, were counted in 1784, 371 members in 1799, and 368, including 69 communicants, in 1820. In 1784 the Moravians started to hold a public gathering (*öffentliche Versammlung*) in their common hall every other week; according to the diary, these gatherings were attended by numerous non-Moravians. The next year they revived the tradition of *Gemeintage*, which featured a prayer, a reading from the reports of Moravian missions and congregations all over the world, and a brief address. In 1786 they held their first *Gemeinfest* commemorating the founding of the congregation. Brother Klingsohn, who addressed the participants on the occasion, voiced some concern that the "fire" of the founding members had been lost, and there were repeated appeals in subsequent years to attend congregational meetings more regularly. During the late 1790s the diarists bemoaned the spread of unbelief and worldliness and yearned for a spiritual revival. The congregation started a new parochial school in 1810, but attendance did not

35. Richard A. Harrison, *Princetonians, 1776–1783: A Biographical Dictionary.* Princetonians 2 (Princeton: Princeton University Press, 1981), 112–14 (quote on 114); cf. Ellis and Evans, *History of Lancaster County,* 473; Courtney and Long, "History of First Presbyterian Church," 15–16; and Early, "Our First 250 Years," 16–18.

36. Ludwig F. Boehler, 1785–86; John Herbst, 1786–91; Abraham Reinke Jr., 1791–95 and 1803–6; Ludwig Huebener, 1795–1800; Johann Martin Beck, 1800–3 and 1806–10; Constantine Miller, 1810–19 (Lancaster Diaries, 1820, entry for July 23, Moravian Archives; cf. Ellis and Evans, *History of Lancaster County,* 471).

meet the minister's expectations, and in 1817 the members had to be reminded to purchase Bibles and hymn books for family devotions.[37]

The one congregation in postrevolutionary Lancaster that was conspicuous for its instability was St. Mary's Catholic Church. During the ten-year-period from 1785 to 1795 St. Mary's was served by nine different priests from Germany, Belgium, and France. Some of them stayed in the borough for only a few months, and none remained long enough to develop a deeper attachment to the congregation or make a lasting impression on his parishioners' spiritual welfare. In fact, three of these priests—Johann Baptist Causse, Franz Rogatus Fromm, and Wilhelm Elling—were later suspended from the ministry and two of them excommunicated for their wayward behavior and association with schismatic groups. "In view of the extreme needs of Catholics" in the immediate postwar period and "the small number of priests" then residing in the country, America's first vicar-apostolic John Carroll, bishop of Baltimore since 1789, deemed it best "to interpose no obstacle to any pious, learned and prudent priests whose services I could use." According to one scholar, America's first bishop was "forced to accept just about any priest who turned up in the United States."[38] In more than one instance, Carroll found that the priests he placed in Lancaster were not as "pious" and "prudent" as he had hoped.

A letter that bishop Carroll sent to Franz Rogatus Fromm in 1791, for example, contains a veritable barrage of charges against the priest. According to Carroll:

> [T]he Catholics of Lancaster are much dissatisfied with Your Reverence, and have demanded that someone else be sent there as pastor. Since Your Reverence is not sufficiently versed in English either to preach or even to hear confessions, they especially lament the fact that they and their children are unable to further their knowledge of religion; . . . Others complain that you are always harsh and morose when you deal with them, and that religious books, which were recommended by your Predecessors and placed in the hands of the faithful to nourish their piety, are considered by yourself as despicable, and condemned as harmful. They further complain that the catechism which was always used is now disdained; and that you are introducing another or are preparing to do so. They say that you hardly

37. See the "Memorabilien" in Lancaster Diaries, 1784–86, 1788, 1796–99, 1811, 1817, 1820, Moravian Archives.

38. John Carroll to John Causse, August 16, 1785, in Hanley, *Carroll Papers*, 1:193–94 (quote). On Carroll's excommunication of Causse, see ibid., 2:20–22, 31, 56, 92–93; cf. Musser, "Old St. Mary's," 98–119; Dolan, *American Catholic Experience*, 108.

ever celebrated daily Mass during your stay in Lancaster, with the result that there has been a lessening of piety and of devotion towards God and the Blessed Virgin. Finally, . . . they say that, without any reason, you have frequently dealt harshly with a certain widow before the whole congregation.

Since Fromm had not even "been admitted officially to the American clergy," the bishop thought "that it would be better for you to return to a monastery in Germany" since the priest's "labors will bear no fruit for the spreading of the faith here." Although Carroll later added that he did not wish to appoint a replacement if Fromm could "maintain the station at Lancaster in peace and benefit to religion," the priest left the town and went to western Pennsylvania on his own account, where he openly defied the bishop's authority even after Carroll suspended him.[39]

St. Mary's congregation experienced a more tranquil period during the nine-year pastorate of Louis DeBarth, the son of an Alsatian nobleman who had left his native France during the turmoils of the French Revolution. When DeBarth was visiting rural mission churches, several assistants supplied Lancaster in the early 1800s. One of them, the Irishman Michael Egan, was later appointed the first Catholic bishop of Philadelphia. After serving Lancaster from 1795 to 1804, DeBarth transferred to the Conewago church west of the Susquehanna and served as vicar general and administrator of the Diocese of Philadelphia for several years.[40]

When DeBarth departed, congregational harmony vanished with him. The preaching of his successor, Francis Fitzsimons—a recent immigrant from Ireland— aroused the ire of his parishioners almost immediately. According to another Catholic priest, one of Fitzsimons's sermons had caused "an unhappy misunderstanding" and a "division" in the congregation. "It appears evident," the observer continued, "that the utmost necessity compelled him to make money part of his subject, tho' I own, if he had been acquainted with the people of the town, prudence would have suggested some other means." While the "good Catholics" were "unanimous in believing him to be pious and humble and zealous," Fitzsimons was in a hopeless position since "the High Dutch Party headed by John Risdel (who is the richest) is absolutely against him and their prejudices cannot be removed." The Irish priest's inability to speak German highlighted the ethnic

39. Hanley, *Carroll Papers*, 1:493, 502–3, 511–12; 2:75, 90–91, 107, 115–16, 146–54, 241–45.
40. Musser, "Old St. Mary's," 119–129. On Egan, see Arthur J. Ennis, "The New Diocese of Philadelphia," in *The History of the Archdiocese of Philadelphia*, ed. James F. Connelly (Philadelphia: Archdiocese of Philadelphia, 1976), 63–79; Hennesey, *American Catholics*, 90.

and linguistic division within his congregation, and Fitzsimons left Lancaster after only a few months. The experience of his successor, Herman J. Stoecker, was exactly the reverse. His lack of familiarity with English caused his Irish parishioners to petition archbishop John Carroll for an English-speaking priest. "What effect can preaching have," the petitioners complained, "when the hearers cannot comprehend one sentence thereof, which is our case at present." They argued that the appointment of a pastor "that can preach in the English tongue" could not possibly "be the least disadvantage to the German part of the Congregation, as they understand English perfectly well, besides it will give satisfaction to severals [sic], belonging to other Churches, who frequently came to us, when we had English sermons, also several's of the Members of the Legislature during the time of their sitting here, all of which assisted us with money towards repairing the Church." The situation improved during the pastorate of the Austrian Jesuit Johann Wilhelm Beschter (1807–12), who according to archbishop Carroll attended "with incredible zeal three congregations composed of Germans, Americans, and Irish." When Beschter dedicated a new Catholic church in Lebanon, three Lutheran, three Reformed, and one Moravian pastor as well as a number of Protestant laypeople attended the ceremony, thereby giving evidence of their respect for the priest and their generally tolerant attitude toward Catholics. After five years in Lancaster, however, ill health and some "disagreeable arrangements" made by bishop Michael Egan caused Beschter to seek other employment. When he accepted a position at Georgetown College in Washington, D.C., the Irishman Michael J. Byrne became priest of St. Mary's Church but was "afflicted with chronic illness" during his five years in Lancaster. John Joseph Holland, Catholic minister in Lancaster from 1817 to 1823, shared Fitzsimons's handicap that he could not speak German. When German speakers began to defect to the Lutheran and Reformed congregations, the German-speaking priest George Shenfelter (Georg Schönfelder?) was sent to Lancaster as an assistant in 1818. Although he spent a lot of time visiting other congregations, Edgar Musser claims that "the German segment of the congregation considered Father Shenfelter its pastor."[41] The linguistic dualism in St. Mary's Catholic Church thus continued to cast a shadow over the relations between the priests and the congregation. Besides this ethnic cleavage, the conflicts in St. Mary's also testify to a general tendency in American Catholicism during this period—the laity's aspirations for a larger role in congregational affairs. Like many Catholic congregations in the young United

---

41. Musser, "Old St. Mary's," 129–49; Hanley, *Carroll Papers*, 3:187–88. On Beschter and the Lebanon church, cf. Dolan, *American Catholic Experience*, 102.

States, St. Mary's had established a board of trustees to govern congregational affairs by the first decade of the nineteenth century.[42]

The building of church edifices and their adornment with steeples, bells, organs, and galleries had occupied congregations since the colonial period, and these building and decorating activities continued in the early national period. At the end of the Revolutionary War, Trinity Lutheran Church's spacious brick structure still lacked a steeple. In 1785, therefore, the church council decided to undertake construction of a steeple if the funds could be raised to defray the estimated costs of £1,500. Almost four hundred people pledged money for the project, and two members of the congregation, mason Georg Lottmann and carpenter Friedrich Mann, were engaged to do the work, which was overseen by a building committee consisting of Bernhard Hubele, Matthias Slough, Jacob Krug, Valentin Brenneisen, and Melchior Rudesill. Work was begun in the fall of 1785 but had to be interrupted the following year when a height of eighty-six feet had been reached because the costs exceeded the estimates and amounted to £1,100. In 1788 the church council allowed trustee Bernhard Hubele expenses for a journey to Philadelphia to take a look at the steeples there and "consult with intelligent workmen," but it was only in 1791 that council member John Miller was requested to draw up a cost estimate for the completion of the project. Two Philadelphia carpenters, William and Abraham Colliday, signed a contract in December 1791 to resume the work "with such a number of hands as they think necessary in the beginning of next spring and in the course of next summer build and erect the said steeple in a good, durable and workmanlike manner." The price was not fixed but was to be settled between the builders and the church council upon completion, "taking into consideration the time spent thereon and the expense of workmen." Amid ongoing discussions within the church council about the cost of the project, the Collidays and their crew worked on the steeple from April to December 1792 but did not return before August 1794 to finish the job. In early September four carved wooden figures representing the four evangelists were hauled up to their places at the base of the steeple, and at the end of October a large metal ball was placed on top of the spire. The completed steeple had reached a height of 195 feet. In November 1795 William Colliday came to Lancaster to settle accounts. The bill amounted to almost £2,000, and together with the materials the total cost came to £2,370. This sum

42. Musser, "Old St. Mary's," 130. See Jay P. Dolan, "The Search for an American Catholicism, 1780–1820," in *Religious Diversity and American Religious History: Studies in Traditions and Cultures*, ed. Walter H. Conser Jr. and Sumner B. Twiss (Athens: University of Georgia Press, 1997), 26–51, esp. 40–43; and Dolan, *American Catholic Experience*, 110, 114.

burdened the congregation with a heavy debt that could be settled only after an additional subscription and a lottery to raise $3,600 in 1807.[43]

Albeit on a less grand scale than the Lutherans, other congregations also improved their church buildings. The Moravians undertook various repairs at their church and hall in 1788 and purchased a new organ from David Tannenberg in 1799. The dedication of the instrument was attended by the Lititz Trombone Choir and drew a large crowd. The day's collection and a gift of £25 from Catherine Graff helped defray the cost of £260 for the new instrument.[44] The Catholic congregation added a steeple and belfry to its church around 1800.[45] The German Reformed enlarged their graveyard, repaired the parsonage, and spent £232 on the import of two new bells from England in 1784–85. In 1792 the roof of the church was found to need renovation, and it was replaced in 1803. A small organ for the schoolhouse was purchased in 1799, various renovations and improvements inside the church building were undertaken in 1812, and three additional lots of ground were purchased in 1820–21. Finally, the church interior was remodeled in 1822 when the galleries were extended and a new chancel added.[46]

As other congregations were also finding their colonial church edifices too cramped and time-worn, the years around 1820 saw intensive building activities. The Presbyterian church was repaired and a gallery added in the early 1800s, but in 1815 the trustees lamented about its "contracted size and ill construction," and the whole edifice was enlarged and improved in 1820.[47] St. James' Episcopal Church, which had petitioned the state legislature in 1807 for permission to hold a lottery in order to finance necessary repairs, decided in 1818 to raise money through a lottery and subscription. Vestrymen Robert Coleman, Charles

43. Trinity Lutheran Church Documents, vol. 103, pp. 85–102, Trinity Lutheran Church Archives; Mühlenberg Diary, vol. 1, entries for August 4 to October 30, 1794, and November 18, 1795, American Philosophical Society; Ellis and Evans, *History of Lancaster County*, 440–41; John W. Lippold, "Old Trinity Steeple," PLCHS 31 (1927): 127–33; Heiges, "Evangelical Lutheran Church," 34–35, 38–42, 47–48. The archive of Trinity Lutheran Church holds numerous receipts from artisans, workmen, and suppliers of materials from the 1788–96 period.

44. Lancaster Diaries, 1788, "Memorabilien," Moravian Archives; Lancaster Diaries, 1799, entries for January 20–21, Moravian Archives.

45. Musser, "Old St. Mary's," 122.

46. Records of the First Reformed Church, vol. 10, microfilm no. 88/3, pp. 64–67, 70–71, 92, 109, 122, 156, Evangelical and Reformed Historical Society; Ellis and Evans, *History of Lancaster County*, 455–56; Cramer, *History*, 58–60; Coldren and Heisey, "Religious Life," 132.

47. Minutes, Resolutions &c. of the Trustees of the English Presbyterian Church in the Borough of Lancaster, 1804, pp. 27–28, 31, 40, Presbyterian Historical Society, Philadelphia (hereafter Minutes, Resolutions &c., Presbyterian Historical Society); Ellis and Evans, *History of Lancaster County*, 473–74; Courtney and Long, "History of First Presbyterian Church," 16; Early, "Our First 250 Years," 13–14.

Smith, and Adam Reigart formed a committee "to fix upon a proper plan for the new church, to superintend the erection of the same, and to make all contracts" for the necessary materials and workmen. By April 1819 the congregation was "pulling down their present house of worship with the intention of erecting one better adapted to the accommodation of their congregation." The old stone building was replaced by a more spacious brick structure that was consecrated by the bishop of Philadelphia, William White, "in the presence of a large congregation of citizens" on October 15, 1820. When the pews in the new church were assigned two days later, only thirty-six of the fifty-two pews on the main floor and four of the ten pews in the gallery were actually taken up. The vestry saw "no immediate prospect of disposing of them, until the church shall be completely organized, when we shall certainly expect an increase as well of members as of funds." But there was hope for the future: "In cases of this kind, it is not presumptuous to trust to providence for future success and prosperity in our undertaking, with a lively hope of a happy increase of members to our Communion." With the church finished, the vestry also considered "the necessity of having divine service more regularly and frequently performed." Since Joseph Clarkson was preaching only every third Sunday, the congregation proposed to hire William Augustus Mühlenberg, an anglicized descendant of Pennsylvania's most prominent family of Lutheran clergymen, as co-pastor. Mühlenberg was offered a salary of $1,000 if he was willing to preach three Sundays out of four, with Clarkson performing divine service on the fourth Sunday for an annual salary of $200. After some hesitation Mühlenberg accepted, and the first vestry meeting held during his tenure in March 1821 considered plans for building a schoolhouse.[48]

A few weeks before the consecration of St. James' new building, the Moravians had laid the cornerstone of their new brick church. In March 1820 an examination of the old church found it beyond repair, and a majority of the congregation voted for the construction of a new one. In June seven members were chosen to form a building committee, and in July the old edifice was pulled down. The laying of the cornerstone on September 5, 1820, was marked by the presence of pastors from several denominations—Lutheran minister Christian L. F. Endress, Reformed pastor Johann Heinrich Hoffmeier, a visiting Presbyterian clergyman from New York, and independent preacher John Elliott—and festive music performed by the Lititz Trombone Choir. Moravian minister Abraham Reinke addressed a crowd estimated at three thousand to four thousand people, and the

48. St. James Vestry Minutes, 50–56, 60–62 (quotes on 60), St. James Episcopal Church; Ellis and Evans, *History of Lancaster County*, 465; Diller and Klein, *History of St. James' Church*, 88–93; George L. Heiges, "When Lancaster Was Pennsylvania's Capital," *PLCHS* 57 (1953): 107.

laying of the cornerstone was followed by a procession to the Lutheran church where Lancaster's German-speaking Protestant pastors conducted a worship service in an ecumenical spirit. Hoffmeier contributed a "useful" prayer, Moravian pastor Andreas Benade delivered a "powerful" German sermon, and Endress closed with a "short but very suitable" address. On July 8, 1821, Lancaster's Lutheran, Reformed, Episcopal, and Presbyterian ministers, the musicians from Lititz, Moravian dignitaries, and a large crowd of people assembled for the consecration of the new building, thus completing the process of refining the colonial church architecture according to the needs and tastes of Lancasterians in the early national period.[49]

The desire of pastors and laypeople to promote the stability and growth of churches is also evident in other areas of activity. Incorporation now became an important goal of congregational leaders concerned with the security of church property. The Reformed congregation, the only one in the borough that had obtained a charter in the colonial period, had this document confirmed by the Pennsylvania state legislature in 1786, and the Lutheran congregation secured its own charter the following year.[50] In 1804 nine leading Presbyterian laymen obtained a charter from the Pennsylvania Supreme Court as "the trustees of the English Presbyterian church in the borough of Lancaster." The charter provided for the management of church property, the administration of charitable bequests, and the making of rules and ordinances. Trustees were to serve three-year terms, with one-third of the positions to be filled annually by those members who had been enrolled for at least a year, had paid their annual pew rents or made some financial contribution, and were not more than one year in arrears. In subsequent years, the Presbyterian trustees drew up rules for letting the pews, hired supply pastors for the Sundays on which the resident pastor Nathaniel Sample was not in town, and oversaw necessary repairs.[51]

49. Lancaster Diaries, 1820, entries for March 12, June 18, July 23, September 3, and "Memorabilien," Moravian Archives; Lancaster Diaries, 1821, entry for July 8, Moravian Archives; cf. Ellis and Evans, *History of Lancaster County*, 470–71. On church architecture in the early national period, see more generally Richard L. Bushman, *The Refinement of America: Persons, Houses, Cities* (New York: Vintage Books/Random House, 1992), 169–80, 335–48.

50. Records of the First Reformed Church, vol. 10, microfilm no. 88/3, pp. 72–73, Evangelical and Reformed Historical Society; Ellis and Evans, *History of Lancaster County*, 454; Heiges, "Evangelical Lutheran Church," 35–36. For the text of the Lutheran charter, see Smith and Weiser, *Trinity Lutheran Church Records*, 4:1–5. Lancaster's pastor Gotthilf Heinrich Ernst Mühlenberg had discussed the merits of a charter with his father as early as 1780 (see Aland and Wellenreuther, *Die Korrespondenz*, 5:307–9). On the incorporation of Pennsylvania churches after the Revolution, cf. more generally Glatfelter, *Pastors and People*, 2:423.

51. Minutes, Resolutions &c., 1–13 passim, Presbyterian Historical Society.

After the dislocations of the Revolutionary War, the two largest German-speaking congregations revealed a strong concern for renewing church discipline. In 1783 the Lutheran church council resolved to deny burial in the graveyard to suicides, malefactors, wanton sinners, and those who did not contribute toward the support of the minister unless an advance payment was made to the treasury. Illegitimate children could be interred in the graveyard if their parents or grandparents had contributed to the church but had to be buried separately from the other graves and without music or the ringing of bells. During Gotthilf Heinrich Ernst Mühlenberg's pastorate, the council also restored the "ancient custom" of baptizing children in the church and passed regulations regarding the assignment of pews and meetings of the church council. Council members were to appear regularly and punctually, meetings were to be opened and closed with prayer, and all deliberations were to be held in German.[52] In 1815 the church order that Gotthilf Heinrich Ernst Mühlenberg's father had introduced almost half a century before was issued, with minor alterations, in printed form. The printing of the document emphasized that it had stood the test of time and made it easily available to everyone interested.[53]

Like its Lutheran counterpart, the German Reformed church council passed a resolution in 1786 that children should be baptized in the church rather than in private homes. Again following the example of the Lutherans, the Reformed trustees and elders decided in 1787 to exclude those who did not register with the pastor and wanton sinners from rights of membership. Rules for council meetings were agreed upon in 1788 and the following year burial fees were required from those who did not contribute to the support of the pastor and congregation. The regulations governing burials in the churchyard were reaffirmed and proclaimed in church in 1796. Since 1791, moreover, those who were elected to the office of elder were required to have previously served as deacons unless they were living in the countryside or were too old for that office. This ordinance was followed by a 1799 council decision that "no one shall be elected elder who, besides leading a good life, is not of such an age as shall constitute him really venerable enough to be called elder." Two years later the minimum age was fixed at forty-five. In 1805, finally, the Reformed council "established the custom of meeting four times a year as a strictly *spiritual* body, when no other business was to be transacted but such as pertained to 'the establishing and maintaining of Christian order,

---

52. John W. Lippold, "Old Trinity Graveyard," *PLCHS* 32 (1928): 110; Heiges, "Evangelical Lutheran Church," 42; Coldren and Heisey, "Religious Life," 130.

53. *Kirchen-Ordnung für die deutsch Evangelisch Lutherische Gemeine bey der heiligen Dreyeinigkeits Kirche in der Stadt Lancaster, Pennsylvanien, in Nord Amerika* (Lancaster: William Hamilton, 1815).

to the promotion of love to all that is good, and to the advancement of God's honor and glory.'"[54]

In crucial respects, therefore, patterns of congregational life established during the colonial period were continued and reaffirmed during the decades after American independence. Existing churches were enlarged, refined, and eventually replaced, church property was secured through charters of incorporation, and ministers and lay leaders evinced their concern for stability and discipline. The absence of open conflict between pastors and laypeople shows that there was a broad consensus on the need for order and decorum. If the postrevolutionary period was a time of rapid and even revolutionary changes for many American congregations, religious life in Lancaster was little affected by them.

LAY LEADERSHIP IN THE EARLY NATIONAL PERIOD

As the activities in Lancaster's congregations amply demonstrate, ministers of the major Protestant churches shared authority and responsibility with influential lay leaders who raised money for building projects and administered church funds. These leading laymen also attended conferences of ecclesiastical governing bodies on a regular basis. Three delegates from St. James' congregation were present in Philadelphia when the Episcopal church in Pennsylvania constituted itself in May 1785. In 1791 St. James' warden Edward Hand attended a Diocesan meeting in Philadelphia and two years later Henry Bennet traveled there for a state convention of the Episcopal church. On the local level, vestryman John Moore was appointed to meet representatives from other congregations in order to "fix on proper hours for ringing the bell for public worship."[55] Lay delegates from Lancaster attended all meetings of the Evangelical Lutheran Synod from 1793 to 1800 and, after a period of more sporadic attendance, were present at most conferences from 1806 to 1820. Michael Moser, for example, represented Lancaster at Philadelphia in 1795, York in 1796, McAllister in 1800, Lancaster in 1807, and Harrisburg in 1810. Peter Schindel was a delegate at Lebanon in 1808, Hanover in 1809, and Reading in 1813.[56] During the same period trustees and elders of the

54. Records of the First Reformed Church, vol. 10, microfilm no. 88/3, pp. 74, 76–77, 80–81, 91, 104, 113, 118, Evangelical and Reformed Historical Society; Ellis and Evans, *History of Lancaster County,* 455–56.

55. St. James Vestry Minutes, 35–36, 41–42, St. James Episcopal Church; Diller and Klein, *History of St. James' Church,* 65–66, 72–73.

56. *Documentary History of the Lutheran Ministerium,* 261, 269, 276, 283, 298, 304, 309, 324, 332, 366, 376, 387, 398, 411, 448, 486, 499, 511, 526, 548.

German Reformed congregation regularly attended meetings of the Reformed Coetus and Synod.[57]

Before the Revolution the vestry of St. James' Anglican Church had been the socially most exclusive body of lay leaders, and the leadership of St. James' Episcopal Church remained so in the early national period. Five of the eight men on the reconstituted vestry in 1783—William Atlee, James Bickham, George Moore, John Stone, and Jasper Yeates—had already served as vestrymen before 1775, and vestryman Joseph Shippen represented one of the preeminent local families. Over the next seven years, just one new member, the smith Henry Bennet, joined the vestry; his name appears in the records from 1785 to 1804. Twenty new vestrymen were elected from 1791 to 1820. Several came from established Anglican families such as the Shippens, Moores, and Atlees, while a few—George Slough, Adam Reigart, and the hardware merchant George L. Mayer—were anglicized men of German descent. Charles Smith, Richard Gray, William Montgomery, George Slough, James Hopkins, and William Hamilton all served on the vestry for at least a decade, and Jasper Yeates is consistently listed as warden and vestryman from 1783 until his death in 1817.[58] The list of Episcopal vestrymen includes community leaders such as chief burgesses Edward Hand (1789–90) and Adam Reigart (1810–15) and the city's first mayor and recorder after incorporation in 1818, John Passmore and Molton C. Rogers.[59] Moreover, as the following biographical sketches illustrate, the vestry included several men of statewide or even national prominence.

The lawyer William Atlee, father-in-law of the Episcopal clergyman Elisha Rigg, had been chairman of the Lancaster Committee of Safety during the Revolution and was appointed a judge of the second judicial district of Pennsylvania in 1791. He served in that capacity until his death two years later.[60] Edward Hand (1744–1803) had studied medicine at Trinity College in Dublin before he came to Pennsylvania in 1767 as a surgeon's mate in a Royal Irish regiment. After several years in Philadelphia and a tour of duty to Fort Pitt, Hand resigned from military service in 1774 and settled in Lancaster, where he practiced medicine. His

57. Records of the First Reformed Church, vol. 10, microfilm no. 88/3, pp. 86, 89, 96, 99, 107, 111, 115, 118, 119, 122, 124, 126, 130, Evangelical and Reformed Historical Society.

58. Information compiled from St. James Vestry Minutes, 32–55, St. James Episcopal Church; Diller and Klein, *History of St. James' Church*, 326–28. Joseph (III) Shippen opened a dry goods store in Lancaster in 1786, but his business was not successful and he moved to Chester County three years later (cf. Klein, *Portrait of an Early American Family*, 203–4).

59. Ellis and Evans, *History of Lancaster County*, 374–75.

60. Diller and Klein, *History of St. James' Church*, 73; Tunney, "Chart of Historic St. James's Church," 128.

marriage to Catherine Ewing allied him with the town's Anglican elite, and his military career in the Revolutionary War made him a nationally renowned figure. As lieutnant colonel of a rifle batalion, Hand participated in the siege of Boston in 1775, and after taking part in the battles of Long Island, White Plains, Trenton, and Princeton as a colonel of Pennsylvania riflemen, he was promoted to brigadier general in 1777. Hand subsequently served in western Pennsylvania and central New York, was present at the British surrender at Yorktown, and left the Continental Army as a brevet major general in 1783. His military laurels and ties to Pennsylvania's social elite helped him embark on a political career. He was a member of the Continental Congress in 1784–85, served in the Pennsylvania Assembly, was a presidential elector as well as chief burgess in 1789, and attended the state constitutional convention in 1790. As a staunch Federalist, Hand received an appointment as inspector of customs for the third district of Pennsylvania in 1791. His income as a Federalist placeman enabled Hand to lead the life of a country gentleman on Rockford Plantation near Lancaster.[61] Vestryman Stephen Chambers also served as an officer during the Revolutionary War and was a delegate to the state convention that ratified the new federal constitution in 1787, but his career was cut short in 1789 when he was mortally wounded in a duel with the physician Dr. Jacob Rieger.[62]

Since the late 1760s Jasper Yeates had built up an extensive legal practice in the county courts of the Pennsylvania backcountry. During the Revolution he presided over the Lancaster Committee of Correspondence (1775), became captain in a batalion of Pennsylvania Associators (1776), and was a delegate to the state convention that ratified the new federal constitution (1787). A committed Federalist, he was appointed a justice of the Pennsylvania Supreme Court in 1791 and survived an impeachment trial before the Republican-dominated state senate in 1805. Yeates was a close friend of Edward Hand, the husband of his niece, and helped settle Hand's messy financial affairs after the general's death in 1802. When he died in 1817 Yeates left an estate of more than $240,000 that included one of the largest legal and personal libraries of his day as well as valuable investments in stocks and bonds. A conservative investor, Yeates had put most of his money into government loans, bank stock, and shares of turnpike

61. *Dictionary of American Biography* 4:223–24; Paul David Nelson, "Hand, Edward," in *American National Biography*, vol. 9, ed. John A. Garraty and Mark C. Carnes (New York: Oxford University Press, 1999), 976–78; cf. Landis, "Jasper Yeates," 222–25; Diller and Klein, *History of St. James' Church*, 81–82; Wood, *Conestoga Crossroads*, 178; Richard R. Farry, "Edward Hand: His Role in the American Revolution" (Ph.D. diss., Duke University, 1976).

62. Diller and Klein, *History of St. James' Church*, 71–72; Tunney, "Chart of Historic St. James's Church," 133.

companies.[63] Like Yeates, his son-in-law Charles Smith was a lawyer, a vestry-man (1791) and warden (1818) of St. James', and a Federalist politician. He sat in the Pennsylvania legislature from 1806 to 1808 and was a state senator in 1816. In 1820 he became presiding judge of the Lancaster District Court.[64]

After he retired to Lancaster in 1809, the industrialist Robert Coleman (1744–1825) also became active in the affairs of St. James' congregation. Coleman and his son Edward were both elected to the vestry in 1818, and Edward also became the congregation's first registrar. A native of Ulster, Coleman had sailed to Philadelphia in 1764 and had for several years worked as a bookkeeper for a Philadelphia merchant, the prothonotary of Berks County, and the ironmasters Curtis and Peter Grubb at Hopewell Furnace and James Old at Quitapahilla Forge. After marrying Old's daughter Ann in 1773, Coleman established himself as an ironmaster at Elizabeth Furnace in Lancaster County. During the Revolu-tionary War he laid the foundations for his later fortune by producing munitions and other military supplies with the labor of Hessian prisoners of war. In the 1780s he bought shares in several ironworks and forges and subsequently enlarged his holdings into an industrial complex. His wealth and friendship with men like Edward Hand and Robert Morris helped Coleman enter the political arena. He sat in the state legislature in 1783–84, was a delegate to the convention that ratified the federal Constitution in 1787, a member of the Pennsylvania constitutional conven-tion in 1790, and was commissioned associate judge of Lancaster County in 1791. Like Edward Hand and Jasper Yeates a staunch Federalist, Coleman actively supported John Adams's presidential candidacy in 1796 and 1800. After moving to Lancaster in 1809, he became a member of the Select Council, a trustee of Franklin College, and a director of the Bank of Pennsylvania's Lancaster branch.[65]

While Coleman supported the Episcopal church, the German Reformed congregation had occasion to criticize him. In 1811 the Reformed church council voted to bid for a lot adjacent to the churchyard in order to enlarge it and started a subscription. When the councillors learned that Robert Coleman was interested in the lot and might raise the purchase price at auction, a delegation was sent to him with the request that he refrain from bidding. Despite repeated pleas, how-ever, Coleman bought the lot and the council protocol remarked dryly that he

<hr/>

63. Landis, "Jasper Yeates," 203–31; *Dictionary of American Biography* 10, 2:606; Jasper Yeates Estate Inventory, 1817, Lancaster County Historical Society; cf. Diller and Klein, *History of St. James' Church*, 85.
64. Diller and Klein, *History of St. James' Church*, 81.
65. St. James Vestry Minutes, 49–50, St. James Episcopal Church; Frederic S. Klein, "Robert Coleman, Millionaire Ironmaster," *JLCHS* 64 (1960): 17–33; cf. Joseph Livingston Delafield, "Notes on the Life and Work of Robert Coleman," *PMHB* 36 (1912): 226–30.

was obviously more interested in his carriages and horses than in the welfare of a Christian congregation and its dead.[66]

William Hamilton, editor of the *Lancaster Journal* and vestryman of St. James' since 1807, had supported Thomas Jefferson as presidential candidate in 1796, but with so many fellow vestrymen in the opposite camp, it is not surprising that he also became a Federalist. Hamilton sat in the Pennsylvania legislature and was promoted to the rank of colonel in the War of 1812. When the congregation chose William Barton (1754–1817) as a vestryman and Reverend Clarkson picked him as the minister's warden in 1807, finally, this may have been a belated recognition of his father's services to the church. William was the son of the colonial Anglican minister Thomas Barton and had grown up in Lancaster. After four years in England (1775–79) he returned to America and was appointed agent of the Pennsylvania loan office for Lancaster County. In 1797 he moved from Philadelphia to Lancaster, where he assumed the offices of prothonotary (1800), justice of the peace (1808), auditor (1810), and justice (1811) and wrote a biography of his uncle, the inventor David Rittenhouse.[67]

In contrast to the Episcopal church, leadership positions in the German-speaking congregations remained more open to men of middling rank, but as in the colonial period these churches continued to include a number of community leaders. The wealthy Moravian Sebastian Graff Jr. (1744–1791), for example, was a member of the Pennsylvania senate when he died on his estate near Lancaster. According to a local newspaper, a "large concourse of citizens of all denominations, from town and country, attended his funeral" in the Moravian cemetery. Graff, the paper added, "was a useful member of society and served the country in various activities."[68] Henry DeHuff (1738–1799), like Graff a second-generation Moravian, was five times elected chief burgess between 1778 and 1784.[69]

In Trinity Lutheran Church, thirty-seven laymen occupied the positions of trustee, elder, or deacon during the 1780s. Congregational and community leadership were intricately connected and mutually reinforcing: fourteen Lutheran leaders also sat on the borough council between 1777 and 1800, six held county offices during the 1775–90 period, and three—Jacob Krug, Ludwig Laumann, and Matthias Slough—were elected to the Pennsylvania Assembly. Wealthy

66. Records of the First Reformed Church, vol. 10, microfilm no. 88/3, 151 (erroneous double pagination), Evangelical and Reformed Historical Society.

67. Diller and Klein, *History of St. James' Church*, 87–88; Rubincam, "Memoir of the Life of William Barton," 179–93.

68. Albert Cavin and August Lerbscher, "Items from the *Neue Unpartheyische Lancaster Zeitung und Anzeigs Nachrichten*," *JLCHS* 59 (1955): 185; Groff, *Groff Book*, 1:27.

69. Ellis and Evans, *History of Lancaster County*, 374; Clark, "Early Lancaster Notables," 10.

shopkeepers and tavernkeepers who had already been prominent in congregational affairs before the Revolution—Ludwig Laumann, Bernhard and Michael Hubele, Paul Zantzinger, and Matthias Slough—continued to play leading roles. Bernhard Hubele, who had to step down from church office on account of a private scandal in 1769, obviously regained the trust of his fellow parishioners, for he served as trustee in the 1780s. The Lutheran church council, however, remained open to hatters, clockmakers, butchers, bakers, saddlers, shoemakers, and tailors. When the congregation started a subscription for its steeple in 1785, the largest pledges predictably came from wealthy men like Paul Zantzinger, John and Joseph Hubele (Hubley), and the tanners Jacob Krug and Georg Moser, but craftsmen like the butcher Christoph Häger, the saddler Melchior Rudesill, and the joiner Friedrich Mann also pledged sums from £20 to £30.[70]

Whereas Bernhard and Michael Hubele and Ludwig Laumann represented the "old guard" of Lutheran leaders, men like Leonhard Eichholtz and John Hubley stood for a younger, American-born generation. Leonhard Eichholtz (1750–1817) was born in Lancaster as the son of the innkeeper Jacob Eichholtz from Neckarbischofsheim in the Kraichgau. He obtained a tavern licence in 1771 but is identified as a tanner in some sources. His marriage to Catherine, the daughter of Abraham Mayer, was recorded in the Reformed church book in 1772, but the births of all fourteen Eichholtz children—one of whom was the famous painter Jacob Eichholtz—were entered into the Lutheran records. After military service in the War for Independence, Leonhard became active in community affairs as county tax assessor in 1785 and sat on the borough council from 1799 to 1813. In 1778 he had purchased a house and lot from William Montgomery for £3,500 and set up his "Bull" tavern there. Eichholtz bought eight more town properties between 1782 and 1809 and invested in 668 acres of land in present-day Blair County in 1797.[71]

Like Eichholtz, John Hubley (1747–1821) was the scion of a leading German-speaking family. His father, Michael, and his uncle Bernhard had been influential

---

70. Information in this paragraph is based on Trinity Lutheran Church Documents, vol. 103, pp. 148–49, Trinity Lutheran Church Archives; Egle, *Pennsylvania Archives*, 17:753–66; Ellis and Evans, *History of Lancaster County*, 374–75; Splitter, *Pastors, People, Politics*, 219, 236–37, 331–32, 341–42, 345–46, 350, 356, 361. The Lutheran leaders who served as county officers were Michael App (sheriff, 1785–86; coroner, 1788–90), Valentin Brenneisen (assessor, 1770–76), John Hubley (justice of the peace, clerk of the orphans court, recorder of deeds, registrar of wills, and prothonotary, all 1777), Jacob Krug (commissioner of taxes, 1780), Johann Offner (coroner, 1781–88), and Matthias Slough (assistant commissioner of purchases, 1780). In addition, Christian Wertz (commissioner, 1776–79; county sublieutnant, 1777; assistant commissioner of purchases, 1780) had been a member of the vestry before 1775.

71. Ellis and Evans, *History of Lancaster County*, 397; Eichholtz-Rodriguez, *Leonard Eichholtz*, 75–107.

members of the Lutheran church and the community since midcentury. John studied law under Edward Shippen and married Maria Magdalena, a daughter of the wealthy shopkeeper and Lutheran trustee Ludwig Laumann, in 1770. His ties to prominent members of the English and German communities recommended him for positions of leadership, and he was a delegate to the convention that adopted Pennsylvania's first state constitution in 1776, a member of the Pennsylvania General Council of Safety in the same year, and a councillor to the state's Supreme Executive Council in 1777. In addition he was appointed to several county offices. In 1787 he became a delegate to the state convention ratifying the U.S. Constitution, and in later years he served on the committee that oversaw the construction of the Philadelphia and Lancaster Turnpike and a treasurer of Franklin College. "His name," a biographer wrote, "appears on practically every list of subscribers for a philanthropic purpose and public enterprise, while scarce a committee or board seemed complete without it." The inventory compiled after his death in 1821 reveals that Hubley had thoroughly assimilated to prevailing Anglo-American patterns of style and fashion.[72] While public officials, lawyers, physicians, and gentlemen were conspicuous among Lancaster's leading Episcopalians, however, Hubley's career in public office was unusual for the Lutheran lay leaders, who were mostly recruited from the borough's artisanal and commercial ranks.

Like the Lutheran church council, its Reformed counterpart remained open to men of middling rank. Of the thirty-six men elected to offices in the congregation during the years 1780 to 1788, one-quarter had already served in church offices in the early 1770s. Michael Diffendorfer, Caspar Schaffner, and Jacob Frey also sat on the borough council during the 1780s and 1790s. The attorney Peter Hufnagel, elected trustee in 1784 and one of the few professional men among the Reformed leadership, served in the county offices of recorder of deeds and registrar of wills.[73] While trustee Christoph Graffort and elders Jacob Frey, Conrad Haas, and Jacob Schäffer were shopkeepers, most Reformed elders and deacons in the 1780s were artisans. Some worked at the relatively humble trades of shoemaker, weaver, and tailor. A look at the composition of the Reformed church council in the first decade of the nineteenth century reveals that prominent local families such as the Bausmans, Diffendorfers, Fortinets (Fordneys), Freys, and

72. Lippold, "Hubley Family," esp. 62–64. On his estate inventory, see Scott T. Swank, "Proxemic Patterns," in *Arts of the Pennsylvania Germans*, ed. Scott T. Swank et al. (New York: Norton, 1983), 55–56. Cf. Ellis and Evans, *History of Lancaster County,* 363; Ryerson, *The Revolution Is Now Begun,* 242; Splitter, *Pastors, People, Politics,* 236–37, 341–42.

73. Splitter, *Pastors, People, Politics,* 340.

Schaffners continued to be represented among the elders and deacons. John Bausman, for example, was the son of Wilhelm Bausman, an influential church and community leader in the prerevolutionary period. He continued to run his father's tavern until his removal to Maryland about 1814 and occupied the office of burgess in 1803–4 and from 1808 to 1813. Philip Diffendorfer, who likewise followed in his father's footsteps as an innkeeper and Reformed elder, was elected burgess in 1804. Congregation leaders John Messenkop, Jacob Fordney, John Bamberger, and Wilhelm Haverstick were also elected to the borough council.[74]

None of the leading Reformed families epitomized the continuity of leadership as the Schaffners did. Caspar Schaffner II (1737–1826), the son of an early Reformed leader, tread in his father's footsteps when he became town clerk in 1763. He obtained the office of borough treasurer a year later and sat on the Lancaster Committee of Observation in 1774. The second Caspar Schaffner declined his election as burgess in 1777 but did not hesitate to assume the offices of Reformed elder in 1784 and trustee of Franklin College and county commissioner, both in 1787. He eventually served as chief burgess from 1791 to 1795 and was reelected as elder of the Reformed congregation in 1794 and 1800. His roster of influential positions in the community also included a trusteeship of the Farmer's Bank (1810) and the presidency of the Lancaster Trading Company (1814). Caspar Schaffner III (1767–1825) succeeded his father as town clerk in 1788 and was appointed clerk of county commissioners in 1800. He played the organ in the Reformed church but refused the office of deacon in 1795. In the wills they made in 1825, father and son each left $100 to the Reformed congregation.[75] In contrast to the Schaffners, the gold- and silversmith Wilhelm Haverstick (1756–1823) was a newcomer. He had practiced his trade in Philadelphia for a dozen years before coming to Lancaster in the mid-1790s. Apart from gold- and silverware, he retailed a "well chosen assortment of Dry Goods and Groceries, with a variety of China, Glass and Queens Ware." Like many other congregational leaders, Haverstick became active in communal affairs and was elected as assistant burgess (1807–10) and trustee of Franklin College (1813).[76]

The Presbyterian congregation also had several prominent community members among its ranks. John Wilkes Kittera was a state representative from 1791 to

74. Records of the First Reformed Church, vol. 10, microfilm no. 88/3, pp. 57, 58, 62, 64, 68–69, 72, 75, 133 passim, Evangelical and Reformed Historical Society; Ellis and Evans, *History of Lancaster County*, 366, 374, 395, 397, 399, 454; Egle, *Pennsylvania Archives*, 17:753–66.

75. Kieffer, "Three Caspar Schaffners," 181–200.

76. Gerstell, *Silversmiths*, 68–71.

1801. Of the nine trustees who secured the charter of incorporation in 1804 and were consistently reelected until 1809, five—the newspaper publisher William Dickson, Samuel Humes, the storekeeper William Kirkpatrick, the innkeeper Henry Slaymaker, and Henry Pinkerton—also sat on the borough council, while the blacksmith Jeremiah Mosher was county coroner in 1812 and sat in the state legislature from 1815 to 1818. William Kirkpatrick became a director of the Branch Bank of Pennsylvania in 1803 and chairman of an insurance company. Among the eighty-nine people who paid for pews in the first decade of the nineteenth century were Governor Thomas McKean and Timothy Matlack, a leader of Philadelphia radicals during the Revolution who had become state master of the rolls in 1800. Both men were residents of Lancaster while the borough served as Pennsylvania's state capital.[77]

While ministers and leading laymen usually maintained harmonious relations in the postwar years, tensions lingered beneath the surface. Gotthilf Heinrich Ernst Mühlenberg confided many of his concerns to the pages of his personal diary, which provides a unique inside view of relations within a local church council. Like many other eighteenth-century clergymen with a growing family, Mühlenberg was often occupied by financial problems. At the beginning of his pastorate, he noted that his private fortune had melted away during the wartime inflation. Strict parsimony and economy seemed necessary to rescue himself from "utter ruin."[78] In subsequent entries, he repeatedly reminded himself to save.[79] In 1785 he noted that, while his salary had been raised twice since the beginning of his pastorate, the £175 he currently received were barely enough to meet the needs of his family and compared unfavorably to the income of other ministers. Moreover, he was worried that grain contributions from country people and fees for pastoral acts were declining.[80]

If Mühlenberg was anxious about his personal financial situation, the congregation's decision to construct a steeple added to his anxieties. In late 1785 he

77. Minutes, Resolutions &c., 1–7, 14, Presbyterian Historical Society; cf. Ellis and Evans, *History of Lancaster County,* 374, 399, 511; James D. Landis, "Who Was Who in Lancaster 100 Years Ago," *PLCHS* 11 (1907): 394, 398, 403–4; Coldren and Heisey, "Religious Life," 137; Gaspare J. Saladino, "Matlack, Timothy," in *American National Biography*, vol. 14, ed. John A. Garraty and Mark C. Carnes (New York, 1999), 707–8.

78. Mühlenberg Diary, vol. 2, entry for September 19, 1780, American Philosophical Society: "Da mein Vermögen auf die entsetzlichste Art durch die depreciation und den Schluß des Congresses geschmolzen ist, so muß ich durch Sparsamkeit und gute Oeconomie mich von dem gänzlichen Ruin zu retten suchen."

79. See Mühlenberg Diary, vol. 1, entries for July 23 and July 30, 1785; August 12, 1786; and December 28, 1793; and vol. 2, entry for May 20, 1786, American Philosophical Society.

80. Mühlenberg Diary, vol. 1, entry for August 25, 1785, American Philosophical Society. See also entry for November 12, 1786.

was optimistic about the project. In a letter to Halle, he pointed out that his parishioners had subscribed £1,500, and while he expected the whole steeple to cost several thousand, these could easily be raised as long as his congregation, which numbered up to fourteen hundred people, remained united.[81] After he had personally pledged £30, however, he reprimanded himself for promising more than he could really afford and giving people the false impression that he was wealthy.[82] By late 1792 Mühlenberg was convinced that the project had been a mistake—he now considered the steeple too tall and too costly for the congregation.[83]

Mühlenberg's complaints about the inadequacy of his salary and the financial burdens imposed by the building project caused relations between the pastor and the church council to sour. By the summer of 1786 Mühlenberg deemed it a "dangerous symptom" that several council members were considering themselves all too important.[84] A year later he was alarmed that the congregation's income from pew rents was being employed for the steeple project while his own salary was in arrears and his income from fees shrinking. He suspected that the council intended to squeeze him in order to increase its power.[85] By 1788 Mühlenberg was convinced that several members wished to have the pastor "under their feet," for they were not only neglecting the payment of his salary and cutting back on fees but came to church irregularly and appeared vain and saturated. In 1789 he even deemed it necessary to preach against "disturbers of the peace" in the congregation.[86]

Mühlenberg claimed that the principal member of the church council had for a long time shown a bitter enmity and contempt for the pastor. This man, whom Mühlenberg identified as "L." or "L. L." in his diary, allegedly declared in public that one sermon a month was enough for him and the pastor's salary was too high anyway.[87] The old, wealthy, and embittered "L. L." was undoubtedly the

81. Gotthilf Heinrich Ernst Mühlenberg to Sebastian A. Fabricius, November 1, 1785, Mühlenberg Correspondence, 4 C 20: 59, Missionsarchiv, Abteilung Nordamerika, Archiv der Franckeschen Stiftungen, Halle/Saale, Germany (hereafter Mühlenberg Correspondence, Archiv der Franckeschen Stiftungen).

82. Mühlenberg Diary, vol. 2, entries for June 26, 1786, and January 10, 1787, American Philosophical Society.

83. Mühlenberg Diary, vol. 1, entries for December 20, 1792, and November 18, 1795, American Philosophical Society.

84. "Es ist würklich ein gefärlich Symptoma, daß sich jetzt manche so groß fülen" (Mühlenberg Diary, vol. 1, entry for August 21, 1786, American Philosophical Society).

85. Mühlenberg Diary, vol. 1, entry for June 25, 1787, American Philosophical Society.

86. Mühlenberg Diary, vol. 1, entries for February 16, 1788, and unspecified date in May 1791, American Philosophical Society.

87. Mühlenberg Diary, vol. 1, entries for February 16 and April 25, 1788, American Philosophical Society.

shopkeeper and long-time trustee Ludwig Laumann, and while Mühlenberg occasionally complained about other councillors, he considered Laumann to be his chief opponent. In 1791 he noted that Laumann wanted to resign forcibly from his trusteeship, and when he died in 1797, several friends found Mühlenberg's funeral sermon dry and stiff.[88] The cool relationship between the pastor and the trustee is somewhat surprising when we consider that the two men had closely cooperated in the import of books and medicine from Halle in the 1780s.[89] Their conflict may have been caused by the congregation's financial difficulties after the cost of building the steeple had exploded. Another factor was probably the generation gap separating the two men. Laumann had arrived in Philadelphia as an indentured servant seven years before Mühlenberg's birth and became one of the wealthiest men in Lancaster. He may thus have felt more qualified and experienced in the management of congregational affairs than the young pastor who was getting so much recognition as a scientist and college president.

To judge from his diaries, Mühlenberg seems to have experienced the later 1790s as a period of crisis. He still considered his income inadequate and learned that some members of the congregation were criticizing his sermons as too long and unedifying.[90] In 1797 a majority of the church council voted that the schoolmaster, whom the pastor supported, was unsatisfactory and had to leave. When the search for a suitable replacement dragged on for years and threatened to divide the congregation, Mühlenberg in 1800 felt ready to resign.[91] If these problems contributed to the pastor's anxiety, however, they did not lead to open conflict. Mühlenberg did not resign after all but remained pastor of the congregation until his death in 1815. By the early nineteenth century, Trinity Lutheran Church was a large, respectable congregation that worshipped in a stately brick church adorned by an impressive steeple. The regularity with which Mühlenberg performed his pastoral duties also testified to the order and stability

88. Mühlenberg Diary, vol. 1, entries for unspecified date in May 1791 and March 24, 1797, American Philosophical Society.

89. See Gotthilf Heinrich Ernst Mühlenberg to Sebastian A. Fabricius, November 1, 1785, Mühlenberg Correspondence, Archiv der Franckeschen Stiftungen; Tappert and Doberstein, *Journals of Henry Melchior Muhlenberg*, 3:541–43, 601; Aland and Wellenreuther, *Die Korrespondenz*, 5:543–44; Splitter, *Pastors, People, Politics*, 41, 264–65; Wilson, *Pious Traders*, 152–54.

90. Mühlenberg Diary, vol. 1, entries for November 23, 1795; September 14, 1796; October 13, 1796; October 10, 1800; and December 18, 1801, American Philosophical Society.

91. Mühlenberg Diary, vol. 1, entries for August 4 and 9, 1797; February 2, 1798; September 29, 1800; December 30, 1800; and January 12, 1801, American Philosophical Society. The new schoolteacher, John Jacob Strine from Northampton County, was recruited only in 1802 but then served until 1828. He received a yearly salary of £50. See Ellis and Evans, *History of Lancaster County*, 403–4; and Heiges, "Evangelical Lutheran Church," 42–43, 46.

the congregation had achieved. Upon the death of its pastor, the congregation emphatically expressed its attachment to him and its wish for continuity by extending a call to his son Henry Augustus Mühlenberg, then pastor at Reading.[92]

CONCLUSION

The American Revolution affected Lancaster's congregations in different ways. While it caused disruption in the Anglican church on account of the minister's loyalism, the German Protestant congregations had to make subtler adjustments to wartime exigencies, and their moderately patriot pastors repeatedly acted as spokesmen for the town's German-speaking inhabitants. The outstanding features of congregational life in the new republic—a time of momentous religious change on the national level—were order and continuity. There were some changes—the disappearance of the small Jewish and Quaker communities, the growth of Presbyterianism, and the first appearance of Methodism—but their overall effect on the religious landscape of the town was remarkably limited. Most churchgoers continued to worship in the large Lutheran and Reformed congregations, whose lay leadership remained more open and socially inclusive than the Episcopal vestry. Clergymen and lay officers often served for extended periods of time and cooperated in the enlargement and refinement of church edifices, the incorporation of congregations, and the promotion of discipline. With the exception of the ethnically divided Roman Catholics, tensions were submerged in an atmosphere of unprecedented stability.

92. Heiges, "Evangelical Lutheran Church," 52.

6

THE TRANSFORMATION OF CHARITY, 1750–1820

THE BEGINNINGS OF ORGANIZED BENEVOLENCE IN LANCASTER

On February 8, 1815, a number of ministers and laymen assembled in the Lancaster Court House. With the lawyer John Hubley presiding and the Episcopalian minister Joseph Clarkson acting as secretary, the meeting adopted the proposal that the "Lancaster Auxiliary Bible Society" be organized as a branch of the Pennsylvania Bible Society. As a local newspaper put it, the aim of the new association was "to supply the poor of all denominations of Christians in the county with a copy of the Holy Scriptures, without note or comment, in the English or German language, as occasion may require." Following a service in Trinity Lutheran Church at which Gotthilf Heinrich Ernst Mühlenberg preached in German and William Kerr, pastor of Donegal Presbyterian Church, in English, the society held its first business meeting in the afternoon of May 2, 1815. One of the purposes of this meeting was the election of officers. Pastor Mühlenberg was chosen as president, William Kerr and Joseph Clarkson as vice presidents. The merchant Samuel White became recording secretary, the judge and politician Charles Smith, an Episcopalian vestryman, was elected corresponding secretary, and William Kirkpatrick, town clerk and trustee of the Presbyterian congregation, became treasurer. The board of managers included three clergymen—Presbyterian Nathaniel Sample, Moravian Constantine Miller, and Methodist Stephen Boyer—and a number of prominent citizens, many of them vestrymen, trustees, or elders of local congregations. Since pastor Mühlenberg died only three weeks after the meeting, his successor at Trinity Lutheran Church, Christian L. F. Endress, assumed the presidency. By 1818 the society had annual receipts of $445 and expenditures of more than $300 and was distributing large numbers of Bibles in the county. In the 1830s it sent regular annual contributions to the national umbrella organization, the American Bible Society. Each year on the first Tuesday in May the Lancaster Bible Society held its annual meetings featuring English and German addresses from local clergymen, elections of officers, and examinations of accounts.[1]

In July 1816, about a year after the founding of the Bible Society, a group of women assembled in the local Masonic Hall to lay the groundwork for the foundation of a charitable society devoted to the instruction of poor children, and on August 24 the constitution of the Lancaster Sunday School Society was adopted. Only a month later fifty-three women subscribed to the constitution of the Female Benevolent Society, an organization designed "to procure and make up clothing for such as have not the means or ability of providing it for themselves, of visiting the sick and infirm, alleviating their distress, and administering to their wants." While the Female Benevolent Society included women of all ages, the wives and daughters of local ministers, merchants, lawyers, and doctors predominated. The Episcopalian minister Joseph Clarkson's wife and three daughters joined the society, as did four daughters of chief burgess Adam Reigart; Anne and Sarah Franklin, the wife and daughter of a county judge; Mary R. Hopkins, who was married to a state senator; and Sarah Yeates, the wife of Supreme Court Justice Jasper Yeates. No fewer than ten of the fifty-three women belonged to the extensive Hubley clan. While there is no membership list of the Sunday School Society, all but one of its seven directoresses in 1818—Ann Slaymaker, Grace Clarkson, Susan Mosher, Barbara Gundaker, Mary Dickson, Elizabeth Kirkpatrick, and Anne Franklin— were also founding members of the Female Benevolent Society, suggesting that membership of the two organizations was very similar. A contributor to the *Lancaster Journal* who styled himself "A Friend to the Poor" viewed the two organizations as complementary: "Within these few months the ladies have established two charitable societies: one for clothing the poor, the other for educating them, both of which appear to be built upon solid foundations, and which no doubt are the most useful societies ever formed in the borough of Lancaster."[2]

During the first years of their existence, the Sunday School and Female Benevolent Societies benefited from liberal contributions. A report submitted at

---

1. David C. Haverstick, "Lancaster Bible Society, 1815–1915," *PLCHS* 19 (1915): 35–61, esp. 37–46.
2. Landis, *Who Was Who*, 373–421; William Frederic Worner, "The Sunday-School Society," *PLCHS* 33 (1929): 175–88, esp. 178, 180–81. On the varieties of female beneficent activity in the early republic, see

the Female Benevolent Society's first semi-annual meeting in March 1817 acknowledged that generous support had enabled it "to extend a helping hand to the Needy, in instances much more numerous than we originally antici- pated." Within the first six-month period the society had received donations of $322.50 in cash and a number of gifts in kind and had distributed $292.32 in wood, clothing, and groceries to needy women and children over the preceding winter. The society continued to receive cash donations and gifts in kind over the following years and spent almost $420 during the eighteen-month-period from March 1818 to September 1819. Beginning in 1819, however, there were complaints about inadequate funds, and a report issued in 1821 stated that "the Society regrets that its means of relief have been so limited compared with the necessities of the poor." Although the Presbyterian congregation collected $36 for the society and a few wealthy community members like Robert Coleman and John Hubley continued to support it, receipts were shrinking. In January 1823 its funds were reported to be exhausted, and the Female Benevolent Society probably ceased to function shortly afterward.[3]

During the first six months of its existence the Sunday School Society received almost $540 in subscriptions, enabling it to open both a weekly and a Sunday school in 1816. In the weekly school thirty-five children were taught "to read, write and cipher," while the girls were "also taught to sew and knit." After several patrons had moved away or canceled their subscriptions, declining funds forced the society to reduce the number of students to twenty, and the weekly school was discon- tinued after three years. The society then focused its energy on the less expensive Sunday school, where attendance, according to a report published in February 1818, fluctuated between twenty and eighty students. While some Sunday school students were taught to read and write, its "principal object" was a moral one: "to inculcate the principles of piety and virtue; to habituate the infant mind to a proper sense of decorum; to inspire a serious respect for the institutions of reli- gion; to impress upon their minds just sentiments of the Divine Being; and to accustom them to a religious observance of the Sabbath." To promote these goals, students were "required to commit to memory certain portions of Scripture, hymns, prayers, and the catechisms of the several churches to which they belong." In 1819 the society organized separate Sunday schools for girls, boys, and black

---

Hackett, *Rude Hand of Innovation*, 86–87; Lori D. Ginzberg, *Women and the Work of Benevolence: Morality, Politics, and Class in the Nineteenth-Century United States* (New Haven: Yale University Press, 1990), esp. 36–53.

3. William Frederic Worner, "The Female Benevolent Society of Lancaster," *PLCHS* 34 (1930): 11–18.

children and sought to attract new patrons by lowering subscription rates. These efforts received a fatal blow, however, when William Augustus Mühlenberg, the new co-rector of St. James' Episcopal Church, established a parochial Sunday school in May 1821. Other congregations followed suit and the number of students in the society's schools, which had reached more than six hundred at one time, dropped to about one hundred twenty. In August 1821 the fifth annual report defiantly stated: "the Society thinks that the circumstance of *its belonging to no particular sect*, is a very strong argument in favor of continuing the school; particularly as there are several denominations which have not yet established Sunday schools; and there are also many children whose parents belong to no place of worship, and it is believed they would prefer sending them to a school which is not connected with any particular congregation." But the society was fighting a losing battle: annual receipts had declined to less than $170 in 1819–20 and only $52 in 1820–21. The project was probably abandoned soon afterward.[4]

In September 1818 an announcement in the *Lancaster Journal* informed readers that "[a] number of German, and descendants of German, citizens of Lancaster" had formed "an association, headed by the Reverend German clergymen of this city, under the name and title of 'The German Society of Lancaster.'" The society sought to offer advice and help to newly arriving immigrants, ensure "that proper justice be done to German redemptioners," and prevent "impositions which may be attempted by immigrants, by which the charitable disposition of our fellow-citizens may be checked and thwarted, and the honor and welfare of the better immigrants injured." The German Society charged a two-dollar entrance fee and the same sum in yearly contributions and set up a permanent fund from the original subscriptions. At its first quarterly meeting on October 5, 1818, Lutheran minister Christian L. F. Endress was chosen president while his Reformed and Moravian colleagues Johann Heinrich Hoffmeier and Constantine Miller became vice presidents. In an address delivered on New Year's Day 1820, president Endress proclaimed that membership was approaching seventy and that, through the work of the German Society, "our city has been cleared of the swarm of German beggars who once infested it." Moreover, the society had "done some good in ameliorating the condition of some of the serving classes of immigrants, and rendering them better servants to their masters. Upwards of 150 poor and distressed strangers have eaten our bread and received our aid in seeking permanent homes."[5]

4. Worner, "Sunday-School Society," 179–85.

5. William Frederic Worner, "The German Society of Lancaster," PLCHS 35 (1931): 1–8; Hans-Jürgen Grabbe, *Vor der großen Flut: Die europäische Migration in die Vereinigten Staaten von Amerika, 1783–1820* (Stuttgart: Steiner, 2001), 240n179.

The founding of four charitable societies during the brief period from 1815 to 1818 marks the beginning of a new era in Lancaster's history. The rise of organized charity, one of the most striking developments of the early republican period, had finally reached the town. New, voluntary, interdenominational associations were distributing Bibles and religious tracts, offering material aid and religious instruction to poor women and children, and helping recent immigrants. These local societies formed a small part of the thousands of beneficent organizations that sprang up all over the country during those years. Historians have usually interpreted the growth of organized charity as a response to a social and moral crisis and a consequence of the religious ferment of the Second Great Awakening. In the years around 1800 many Americans were deeply worried about the spread of crime, poverty, alcoholism, and other vices, while evangelical reformers were propagating social renewal through individual moral regeneration. Combining these two impetuses, the new charitable societies sought to reform society by offering aid, counsel, and guidance to deserving individuals.[6]

This view of organized charity and moral reform as an outgrowth of the Second Great Awakening has been challenged by Conrad Edick Wright's work on New England, which argues that "in the commercial towns along the Atlantic coast from Portsmouth to Newport the link between organized beneficence and evangelical Christianity was neither as direct nor as complete as scholars have sometimes assumed." Although evangelicals coordinated their reform efforts in the early nineteenth century, the founding of beneficent associations was the outcome of local decisions, and in Wright's view "organized charity was the sum of many smaller initiatives." After the Revolution, New Englanders set up hundreds of mutual benefit associations; humanitarian institutions; and Bible, tract, and missionary societies, many of which predated the evangelical awakenings. Charitable undertakings attracted religious liberals and rationalists along with revivalists, and the membership reflected the heterogeneity of postrevolutionary New England.[7] For Pennsylvania German church people, who made up the majority of Lancaster's population, Steven M. Nolt has demonstrated that "most Lutheran and German Reformed faithful stood apart from the reformist impulse that animated much of American evangelical Protestantism." Ever watchful against outside interference and jealously guarding the autonomy of local communities, Pennsylvania Germans

6. The literature on the topic is vast. I have particularly relied on Ronald G. Walters, *American Reformers, 1815–1860* (New York: Hill and Wang, 1978), 21–37, and Steven Mintz, *Moralists and Modernizers: America's Pre–Civil War Reformers* (Baltimore: Johns Hopkins University Press, 1995), 1–65.

7. Conrad Edick Wright, *The Transformation of Charity in Postrevolutionary New England* (Boston: Northeastern University Press, 1992), esp. 9, 52–54, 92–93.

for the most part rejected "evangelical reformers' desire to shape national values and assume the role of cultural custodian."[8]

In Lancaster the founding of beneficent societies certainly owed less to evangelical revivalism than to the resident ministers and pious laypeople of long-established congregations. The Bible and German societies were organized and headed by local clergymen, elders, and vestrymen, while the Female Benevolent Society was made up of women from elite families and included the wife and daughters of the local Episcopalian rector. On the other hand, the Sunday School Society foundered when individual pastors and congregations withdrew their support. The new charitable societies therefore were not just responses to outside influences but were rooted, in part, in local traditions of beneficence. As pastor Endress explained in his address to the German Society, the history of immigrant aid societies reached back into the eighteenth century. Organized efforts to relieve central European immigrants began with the Philadelphia-based German Society of Pennsylvania in 1764 and continued with the German Societies of Charleston (1766), Baltimore (1783), and New York (1784) before reaching smaller inland towns such as Reading (1802), Harrisburg (1819–20), and Lancaster. Separate aid societies for Irish, Scottish, Welsh, and English settlers were in existence in Philadelphia and New York by the late eighteenth century.[9] The city of Philadelphia in particular had developed a strong tradition of organized beneficence since the 1750s, epitomized in the Pennsylvania Hospital for the Sick Poor, the Bettering House, and local relief societies.[10]

In Lancaster local congregations had long provided material assistance to poor widows and children, operated schools, and looked after recent immigrants and redemptioners. In addition, local congregations had frequently assisted one another in specific projects. Finally, charitable societies that adopted constitutions and bylaws, elected officers, solicited contributions, and administered funds did precisely what local congregations had done for decades. Viewed

8. Nolt, *Foreigners in Their Own Land*, 89–108 (quotes on 90, 93).

9. Worner, "German Society," 4; Erna Risch, "Immigrant Aid Societies Before 1820," *PMHB* 60 (1936): 15–33; Grabbe, *Vor der großen Flut*, 239–40.

10. Carl Bridenbaugh, *Cities in Revolt: Urban Life in America, 1743–1776* (New York: Knopf, 1955), 126–27, 131–32, 321–22; Gary B. Nash, *The Urban Crucible: Social Change, Political Consciousness, and the Origins of the American Revolution* (Cambridge: Harvard University Press, 1979), 254–55, 314, 322, 327–31; A. G. Roeber, "'Troublesome Riches': Protestant and Catholic Stewardship of a Capitalist World, 1698–1815," *Amerikastudien/American Studies* 42, no. 3 (1997): 357–75, esp. 369, 371–72. For a concise overview of charitable societies and charity law in eighteenth-century Pennsylvania, see A. G. Roeber, "The Long Road to *Vidal*: Charity Law and State Formation in Early America," in *The Many Legalities of Early America*, ed. Christopher L. Tomlins and Bruce H. Mann (Chapel Hill: University of North Carolina Press, 2001), 414–41, esp. 427–38.

from this perspective, the formation of charitable societies in the second decade of the nineteenth century was not a new departure but the culmination of older traditions of charity. In order to elucidate these traditions, this chapter explores beneficent activities in Lancaster's congregations and argues that one of the essential roots of organized benevolence lay in long-established practices of congregational charity and interdenominational cooperation.

CHARITABLE BEQUESTS TO CONGREGATIONS

As the previous chapters have shown, laypeople contributed to the building and adornment of churches in many ways. They subscribed money and contributed labor when new church edifices were constructed or old ones repaired; made pledges for the purchase of organs, bells, and burial grounds; donated flagons, chalices, and altar cloths; paid pew rents; and supported pastors, sextons, and schoolmasters. Poor parishioners occasionally received aid from congregational alms funds. Beginning in the late 1740s pious men and women also set aside legacies for local congregations in their wills. As A. G. Roeber has observed, in Pennsylvania and neighboring Maryland "concern for schooling, gifts to the church *ad pias causas*, and acceptance of the idea of obligation toward philanthropy grew very slowly" in the colonial period. Nonetheless, the number and value of charitable bequests in Lancaster did increase throughout the latter half of eighteenth century, enabling several congregations to establish permanent funds in the years after the American Revolution.[11] A detailed examination of these testamentary bequests reveals that they constituted an important local tradition of charity—a tradition that linked the founding generations of Lancaster's churches to their successors in the early national period.

One of the earliest of these testamentary legacies was also one of the most unusual. When Mary Prator, a widow living in Earl Township, dictated her will to the Lutheran pastor Johann Caspar Stoever in 1748 she stipulated £2 of Pennsylvania currency to the Church of England in Lancaster Borough, the same sum to the Lutheran and German Reformed congregations in Earl Township, and £2 to the "popish Church" in Lancaster.[12] While no eighteenth-century Lancasterian is known to have demonstrated a similar irenic spirit, several others did make

11. Roeber, "Troublesome Riches," 373; cf. Glatfelter, *Pastors and People,* 2:182–83.
12. Lancaster County Will Book A-I-143, Pennsylvania State Archives; Coldren and Heisey, "Religious Life," 133; Glatfelter, *Pastors and People,* 2:182, 260.

bequests to more than one congregation. In his final years Edward Smout, a justice of the peace and founding member of St. James' congregation, was attracted to the Moravian faith without renouncing his allegiance to the Anglican church. In the will he made in 1751 Smout gave liberal bequests to both congregations. He ordered a four-hundred-acre tract in York County to be sold and one-half to be applied "towards the repairing and Glazeing the Church of England in the Borough," while the other half was to be used "towards payment of the debts Contracted by the United Brethren for Building the new Stone School House near the Church in the Borough . . . belonging to the said Congregation." If his wife did not give birth to a child within six months after his death, Smout willed one-quarter of his estate for the support of the minister of "the Established Church of England" in Lancaster and one-half for the Christian Indians in Bethlehem.[13] In 1773 the shoemaker Heinrich Baersinger willed £30 to the Lutheran congregation, £5 to the German Reformed church by order of his late daughter Catherine, and £10 to the poor of all denominations, to be distributed by the Orphans Court. Six years later the "yeoman" Cornelius Lane left £10 to the "Elders of the Menonit Meeting" for the poor "belonging to that Society" and the same sum to the trustees of Trinity Lutheran Church for their congregation's poor.[14]

Far more common were bequests to the particular religious group with which the testator identified. As the largest congregation in eighteenth-century Lancaster, Trinity Lutheran Church was the beneficiary of a substantial number of legacies. One of the most significant came from the joiner Ludwig Detteborn in 1752. The childless Detteborn left a town lot, which was later sold for more than £300, and a large Nuremberg Bible to the congregation. Following her late husband's example, Detteborn's widow, Magdalena, also "bequeathed in her will all the money and goods," amounting to £35, "out of praiseworthy religious zeal for the use and benefit of the Lutheran church here" in 1760.[15] Smaller bequests came from Jakob Dannbach, who set aside £2 for the congregation in his 1758 will; Maria Margaretha Herring, who left twenty shillings to the church in 1759;

13. Lancaster County Will Book A-I-196, Pennsylvania State Archives; Rev. George Craig to Richard Peters, January 14, 1754, Lancaster County Manuscripts, vol. 1, 1724–72, p. 93, Historical Society of Pennsylvania; Worner, "Church of England (Part III)," 29.

14. Lancaster County Will Books C-I-27 and C-I-559, Pennsylvania State Archives.

15. Smith and Weiser, *Trinity Lutheran Church Records*, 1:286–87, 306; Trinity Lutheran Church Documents, vol. 103, loose leaf 7, Trinity Lutheran Church Archives. In return, the grateful congregation paid for the widow's mourning gown and for Detteborn's medication (Trinity Lutheran Church Documents, vol. 101, Ledger 1754–82, entries for June 30, 1756, and February 21, 1757, Trinity Lutheran Church Archives).

and Christian Peterson, an unmarried hatter from the duchy of Pfalz-Zweibrücken who gave the congregation £4 in 1760.[16]

The building of the new Lutheran church in the 1760s inspired further bequests. Christoph Wächter, an unmarried forty-three-year-old shoemaker, left £10 before his demise in 1762. The following year the pantsmaker Johannes Böckle "willed whatever remains after the death of his wife" to the church. The congregation's leaders estimated the value of Böckle's house and half lot at about £100 but noted that the bequest yielded little profit because the testator was deeply in debt. The same year Heinrich Baersinger, a "Separatist" of Reformed origin from Berne in Switzerland, requested to be buried in the Lutheran church-yard and bequeathed £30 in return. The widow Sabina Quickel gave £5 in 1765, and the childless butcher Jacob Fissel willed £10 to the elders of Trinity Lutheran Church the following year. When one of the early lay leaders, the baker and tav-ernkeeper Hans Michael Beyerle, made his will in 1766, he left £50 "to the use of our new Holy Trinity Church." The same sum came from the potter Jodocus Dobler in 1767, and Leonhard Lochner bequeathed £25 to the congregation in the same year.[17] In 1771 the wealthy merchant and long-time elder Michael Gross released a debt of £50 that St. Michael's congregation in Philadelphia owed him, gave ten pistoles for the Pennsylvania Hospital, and willed to the elders of Trinity Lutheran Church "a Branch or Lamp or Lustre like to the one as near as can be in the German Lutheran Church in Philad[elphi]a in ffourth Street," which was to be obtained from England on his account. He also donated iron railings for the pulpit and "a Genteel Pulpit Cloath for the same."[18]

In the 1750s the German Reformed congregation also received its first sig-nificant bequests, and a rising number of charitable legacies during the two decades before the Revolution testify to the laypeople's commitment to their church. Heinrich Walter, the treasurer of the subscription for the new church built during Otterbein's pastorate, willed £20 to the congregation in 1754, and the following year the prosperous butcher Franz Fortinet (Francis Fortney) stip-ulated £30 for its use.[19] Philipp Jacob Getz, who had contracted smallpox, wrote

16. Trinity Lutheran Church Documents, vol. 103, loose leaves, 6–8, Trinity Lutheran Church Archives; Lancaster County Will Book B-I-326 (Peterson), and I-I-200 (Herring), Pennsylvania State Archives; Smith and Weiser, *Trinity Lutheran Church Records,* 1:306.

17. Trinity Lutheran Church Documents, vol. 103, loose leaves, 6–8, Trinity Lutheran Church Archives; Lancaster County Will Books B-I-441 (Beyerle), B-I-500 (Dobler), B-I-504 (Fissel), and C-I-27 (Baersinger), Pennsylvania State Archives; Smith and Weiser, *Trinity Lutheran Church Records,* 1:310, 312, 314, 318.

18. Lancaster County Will Book C-I-1, Pennsylvania State Archives.

19. Lancaster County Will Books B-I-92 and B-I-114, Pennsylvania State Archives.

a will in 1757 in which he bequeathed £6 to the "Calvinist Church" in Lancaster "to be applyed towards the purchasing of Organs . . . or paying the Debts of the said Church as the Minister and Congregation shall agree." In 1758 Andreas Bersinger gave his house and half lot on King Street to the congregation. The tanner Friedrich Gervenus, an immigrant from the Palatinate who dictated his will in the same year, bequeathed £12 to the "Presbyteri" for the use of the church. While the formulation is ambiguous, the choice of Reformed leaders Valentin Weber and Christian Buch as executors and the fact that there was no local Presbyterian church at the time suggest that he meant the Reformed congregation. Heinrich Bott, a farmer from Manor Township, donated almost £9 for the benefit of poor members of the congregation between 1765 and 1767. In the mid-1770s, Bott again gave £8 for the poor and £6 for the purchase of new hymn books. Abraham LeRoy, a native of the bishopric of Basle in Switzerland and brother-in-law of the minister Philipp Wilhelm Otterbein, left a legacy of £5 to the congregation in 1765. In 1767 Leonhard Bauser, a native of the Swiss canton of Basle and a farmer in Lancaster Township, gave £5 to the church and £2 for an iron stove in the parsonage. Another Swiss immigrant, Abraham Im Obersteg, specified in his 1767 will that the congregation should receive £10 and his land in Hempfield Township. The former elder Jacob Wilhelm set aside £5 for "the poor and needy of the German Reformed church" in the will he made in 1771. Barbara Mesmer, finally, donated £11 10s. to the church and £11 to the poor of the congregation in 1774.[20] The rising number of bequests and especially the fact that Abraham Im Obersteg's land was alienated from the congregation provided the impetus for the incorporation of the German Reformed Church in 1771. As late as 1812 the Reformed church council made an unsuccessful attempt to recover the Im Obersteg property.[21]

Several wealthy people had joined the Moravians when they broke away from the Lutherans in the mid-1740s and formed their own congregation, and the United Brethren subsequently benefited from their largesse. In the will he made

20. Records of the First Reformed Church, vol. 3, microfilm no. 88/1, pp. 68, 74, 78, 81, 86, and vol. 10, microfilm no. 88/3, pp. 11–12, 49, 55, Evangelical and Reformed Historical Society; Cramer, *History*, 79–80; Lancaster County Deed Book Z452 (Bersinger), Pennsylvania State Archives; Lancaster County Will Books B-I-160 (Getz), B-I-443 (Bauser), B-I-545 (LeRoy), I-I-159 (Gervenus), and J-I-350 (Wilhelm), Pennsylvania State Archives. On Gervenus, see Burgert, *Western Palatinate*, 139. On LeRoy, who was known as Abraham König among German speakers, cf. Gerstell, *Silversmiths*, 79–80. For Abraham Im Obersteg's Swiss origins, see the letter of attorney issued for him in the Canton of Berne in Mayhill, *Deed Abstracts*, 62 (E59).

21. Records of the First Reformed Church, vol. 10, microfilm no. 88/3, pp. 1–7, 153–54, Evangelical and Reformed Historical Society.

in 1777 the shopkeeper Georg Graff made bequests totaling £470 to the Moravians in Bethlehem, Lititz, and Lancaster. These included legacies for the Indian mission, the Widows' and Single Sisters' Houses in Bethlehem, and the single women in Lititz. In 1768 Graff's sister Eva, the widow of Sebastian Graff, had willed £50 each to the Widow's House in Bethlehem and to the congregations in Lititz and Lancaster. The hatter Matthias Graff followed their example in 1779 when he willed £100 for the Indian missions, more than £300 for various institutions and building projects in Bethlehem, £50 each to the Lititz and Lancaster congregations, and sums between £15 and £30 to seven Moravian clergymen, including bishops Nathaniel Seidel and John Ettwein and local pastor Otto Krogstrup.[22] Anton Schneider left £8 for the Brethren's West Indian missions in 1774, and the shoemaker Friedrich Weidele willed £5 to the Lancaster congregation in 1773. A decade later Jacob Kagey, "yeoman," bequeathed £10 to the Reverend Otto Krogstrup or his successor for the benefit of poor Moravians in town.[23]

Lancaster's smaller congregations received fewer bequests but were not without their benefactors. In 1753 the widow Anna Maria Stahl stipulated that £5 were to be paid to "Mr Farmer," the "Roman Minister" in the borough, and Susanna Connolly, also a widow, set aside £3 for repairing the fence around the graveyard of St. James' Anglican Church. Yet another pious widow, Mary Dougherty, bequeathed £5 to the Anglican congregation in 1763 and left the same sum to the Friends' Hospital in Philadelphia. In 1776 the fuller John Davis bequeathed £3 to the Reverend Thomas Barton and £5 to vestryman Jasper Yeates for the use of the church.[24] No Anglican in Lancaster, however, equaled the largesse of Nathan Evans, a member of the Caernarvon congregation who gave £100 "towards finishing the church" and "a glebe of about forty acres . . . for the use of the minister" in the 1760s. Nor did any of them match the generosity of Thomas Morgan, a prosperous farmer in Berks County who set aside enough land and money in his last will to finance the erection of a small stone church.[25]

After the War for Independence laypeople continued to give to their churches. Sixteen testators gave a total of £237 to the German Reformed congregation between 1783 and 1808 (see Table 4). The list of benefactors includes a number of men who had occupied leadership positions on the church council—Wilhelm Busch, Wilhelm Bausman, Michael Diffendorfer, Peter Bier—as well as more

22. *Moravian Burial Book*, 8–9, 12; Lancaster County Will Books A-I-239, C-I-429, and D-I-75, Pennsylvania State Archives.

23. Lancaster County Will Books C-I-259, C-I-395, and D-I-399, Pennsylvania State Archives.

24. Lancaster County Will Books B-I-31, B-I-483, and E-I-36, Pennsylvania State Archives; Worner, "Church of England (Part III)," 34–35.

25. Worner, "Church of England (Part IV)," 59, 65.

Table 4   Gifts and bequests to the German Reformed congregation, 1783–1815

Henry Steib	1783	£15 15s.
Charles Hall	1783	£5
Wilhelm Busch	1786	£50
Wilhelm Bausman	1787	£25
Michael Diffendorfer	1790	£15
Henry Staut	1790	£4
Susanna Roeser	1791	£5
Widow Marburger	1795	£5
Michael Rademacher	1796	£6
Jacob Wilhelm	1797	£20
Heinrich Miller	1800	£5
Heinrich Schweitzer	1800	£10
Peter Bier Sr.	1801	£10
Jacob Ludewig	1805	£25
Philip Diffendorfer	1806	£25
John Stiele	1808	£7 10s.
Andreas Bausman's wife	1813	$50
Andreas Bausman	1814	$300 + shares in Turnpike Company
Widow Herbert (Philadelphia)	1817	$500

SOURCES: Cramer, *History,* 79–81; Records of the First Reformed Church, Lancaster, Pa., vol. 10 (microfilm no. 88⅓), 86; Lancaster County Will Books D-I-304 (Hall), E-I-379 (Bush), G-I-213 (Rademacher), H-I-86 (Bier), K-I-639 (Bausman).

obscure parishioners. In the second decade of the nineteenth century, the Reformed congregation received two particularly large bequests. In 1814 Andreas Bausman, whose wife had already given $50 to the church the year before, bequeathed $300—the interest of which was to be divided among the poor— and shares in the Philadelphia and Lancaster Turnpike Company. The childless Bausman was a wealthy man—he owned several houses in Lancaster, two farms on Little Conestoga Creek, some woodland in Martic Township, and movable goods, mostly stocks and bonds, worth $61,667—and had repeatedly been elected to the position of elder. An even larger legacy came from a widow in Philadelphia three years later.[26]

In 1791 the German Reformed Church council acknowledged that the congregation had repeatedly received gifts and bequests from members who thereby expressed their "gratefulness to God for the blessings he had bestowed on them in their temporal affairs" and their "sincere love for the congregation." Since the congregation had often been obliged to raise money for building projects and

26. Cramer, *History,* 79–81; Lancaster County Will Book K-I-639, Pennsylvania State Archives.

necessary purchases in the past, bequests and donations had always been used to cover expenses. Since all buildings had been completed and debts paid, the council voted unanimously to place all future gifts and legacies in a permanent fund. In the future only the interest was to be spent. The decision was not put into effect immediately—Jacob Wilhelm's bequest was used to paint and repair the church in 1797—but in 1806 the council affirmed that all future bequests should be loaned at interest and Philip Diffendorfer's bequest of £25 should form the basis of a permanent church fund.[27] In 1815 Andreas Bausman's bequest became the subject of further deliberations about the use of charitable legacies. The turnpike company shares, which were originally estimated at $300, were found to be rising in value, and the council voted to cash in on the profits by selling the shares to John Bausman, the testator's nephew and executor, for $400. Meanwhile the interest arising from the cash bequest was to be distributed among poor parishioners as stipulated in Bausman's will. Since the congregation was not facing any necessary expenses in 1817, the widow Herbert's $500 bequest was loaned to congregation member Georg Bamberger at $30 in interest annually. While the interest from this loan was to go toward the support of the poor, $76 in interest accumulated from Bausman's legacy was to be reinvested.[28]

The Lutheran and Moravian congregations also received a number of testamentary legacies after the Revolution. In 1784 the butcher Jacob Yentz willed £50 to Ludwig Laumann for use of the Lutheran church after the death of his wife, and his widow Sophia made a gift of £50 on her own initiative. In 1785 Jacob Stahl gave £25 and Andreas Gattringer £10. In 1788 the congregation received £10 from the estate of the carpenter Heinrich Wagner and £25 from Hans Michael Beyerle's widow, Anna Maria. Adam Derstler, a farmer in Manor Township, willed the substantial sum of £400 to the trustees and elders of Trinity Lutheran Church in 1792. The money was to be put out at interest and the income applied for repair work at the church and the support of the poor. The cordwainer Lorenz Kurtz set aside £30 for the congregation in 1802.[29] John Kraemer of Manor Township willed £5 to John Hopson, trustee of the United Brethren in Lancaster, "to be applied by him or his Successors for the use & Benefit of the said Congregation" in 1785. In 1804 Hopson himself left a town lot to "the incorporated society at

27. Records of the First Reformed Church, vol. 10, microfilm no. 88/3, pp. 87–88, 108, 131, Evangelical and Reformed Historical Society.

28. Records of the First Reformed Church, vol. 10, microfilm no. 88/3, pp. 168–69, 176–77, Evangelical and Reformed Historical Society.

29. Trinity Lutheran Church Documents, vol. 103, loose leaf 8, Trinity Lutheran Church Archives; Lancaster County Will Books E-I-85, E-I-459, F-I-80, F-I-544, and H-I-206, Pennsylvania State Archives.

Bethlehem for the propagation of the gospel among the Heathens" and £50 for the support of the Moravian pastor in Lancaster.[30] The following year a Catholic testator, Mathias Roe, appointed the resident Roman Catholic priest Louis de Barth as his sole executor and named a priest in St. Mary's County, Maryland, as "heir of all the property I leave in this world, to hold it in trust for the use and benefit of the Roman Catholic Priest in Lancaster."[31]

The management of church funds, which became a concern of the German Reformed consistory in the postwar period, was an important theme for the Episcopalian congregation as well. At one of its first meetings after the Revolutionary War, the vestry of St. James' and "several other members of the congregation now present" agreed in 1784 that its real estate—one-half of a gristmill and three tracts of lands in Salisbury Township bequeathed by John Douglass as well as the house and lot in Lancaster bequeathed by Edward Smout more than thirty years before—should be sold. Eight years later the vestry took up the matter again and decided to dispose of Smout's property at a public sale and apply the money "agreeably to the directions of the deed of trust." Trustees Jasper Yeates and Edward Hand accordingly sold it to John Moore, a vestry member, for £140, the purchaser being given ten years' time to pay the price. Since Edward Smout had also willed a lot in Trenton, New Jersey, to the Anglican and Moravian congregations, which "in its present situation" was "in no ways beneficial to the Church or the pastor or minister thereof," the vestry decided to sell its share to the Moravians for £20. When the transaction was completed, the vestry agreed to pastor Elisha Rigg's request "for the said sum to be paid to him to remain in his hands without interest until the vestry of this Church shall think proper and expedient to demand the same . . . for the purpose of supporting a minister." The real estate in Salisbury Township was finally sold for £150 in 1795. Since the sum was insufficient to finance the building of a new parsonage, the interest derived from it was also loaned to the minister without interest. When Juliana Grubb left £150 to the Episcopal congregation in 1804, the vestry decided "that the money . . . be invested in three per cent stock of the United States and the interest thereof be paid to the minister for the time being until further order be taken herein." Warden Jasper Yeates handled the transaction through his relative Edward Burd and a brokerage firm in Philadelphia.[32]

<hr>

30. Lancaster County Will Books E-I-394 and J-I-100, Pennsylvania State Archives; *Moravian Burial Book*, 28.

31. Lancaster County Will Book I-I-394, Pennsylvania State Archives.

32. St. James Vestry Minutes, 35, 37–39, 42–44, 47, St. James Episcopal Church; Jasper Yeates to Edward Burd, July 8, 1799, Jasper Yeates Papers, MG 207, box 2, folder 61, no. 10, Lancaster County

In the early nineteenth century the Presbyterian congregation also received its first large bequests: Juliana Grubb, a half-sister of the ironmaster Peter Grubb who was also a benefactress of the Episcopal church, bequeathed £150 ($400) to it in 1804, Agnes Craig made a legacy of £50 in the will she dictated in 1805, and Josiah Lockhart, who owned several thousand acres of western land and about $60,000 in bank stock, debt certificates, and cash besides a house in Lancaster at the time of his death in 1809, gave the congregation a thousand-acre tract "situate[d] on a branch of Gioga river in the late purchase now Gioga county."[33] In February 1807 treasurer William Kirkpatrick reported to the trustees that he had more than $600 in church funds in his hands and suggested that part of it be invested in stock. The trustees decided to purchase fifty shares of the Lancaster and Susquehanna Insurance Company. In 1809, however, they had to borrow money to pay off an installment on the congregation's shares that became due, and two months later they decided to sell the stock "at a price not less than par" and invest the money "in some other more sure and permanent Fund for the use of said Congregation." The Presbyterian leaders continued to look out for investment opportunities. Four years later they agreed to buy three shares in the Farmers' Bank of Lancaster, but when they found the advance on the stock too high they subscribed for ten shares in the new Union Bank instead. In 1815 the congregation's treasurer reported a balance of $400 in his hands and recommended that the money should be "invested in some productive fund." Several years earlier the trustees had also considered a request from "a certain Mrs. Petre, who formerly belonged to our Church, and who is now old and infirm, and unable to support herself." The old woman proposed to mortgage her moiety of a house and lot in Lancaster to the congregation in return for a weekly allowance. A committee inquired into the matter, and after Mrs. Petre had willed all her property to the church, the trustees decided to pay her $30 and "advance her from time to time, a sum not exceeding seventy five Cents a week." Finally, in December 1809 the trustees decided to apply to the state legislature for permission to sell the land bequeathed by Josiah Lockhart and a lot that the congregation had received from town proprietor James Hamilton.[34]

Historical Society; Diller and Klein, *History of St. James' Church*, 72. For Juliana Grubb's will, see Lancaster County Will Book I-I-172, Pennsylvania State Archives.

33. Lancaster County Will Books I-I-172 (Juliana Grubb), K-I-114 (Josiah Lockhart), and K-I-175 (Agnes Craig), Pennsylvania State Archives. See also Josiah Lockhart Estate Inventory, 1809, Lancaster County Historical Society.

34. Minutes, Resolutions &c., 24, 31, 33, 35–37, 39, 43–44, Presbyterian Historical Society.

To sum up, during the second half of the eighteenth century and the early years of the nineteenth dozens of men and women made charitable bequests to Lancaster's congregations. While individual circumstances and motivations varied, all benefactors demonstrated a strong attachment to one particular or, in some instances, several of the town's churches. Their gifts helped congregations finance purchases and repairs, aid the poor, and eventually set up permanent church funds. The establishment of these funds was an important step, for it demonstrated that the mature church councils of the postrevolutionary era were beginning to conceive of benevolence and congregational development in a long-term perspective. They had passed the phase in which all receipts were used to cover immediate needs and necessary expenses and had reached a stage at which they could set aside money for the future. Two further developments complemented this trend: after the Revolution, Lancaster's congregations regularly supported ecclesiastical and charitable projects in other communities, and they increasingly cooperated across denominational lines in charitable and educational undertakings.

RELIEF AND INTERDENOMINATIONAL COOPERATION

In the colonial period Lancaster's congregations had occasionally supported building projects of their co-religionists in other communities—for example, the Lutherans' contribution to Germantown in 1738. Moreover, members of the Moravian congregation had repeatedly demonstrated their commitment to the United Brethren by collecting money and making bequests for the Indian missions and for institutions in Bethlehem and Lititz. After the War for Independence, however, congregations sent money and aid to other communities much more frequently. The council protocols of the German Reformed congregation allow us to examine these charitable contributions in some detail.

The ministers and elders present at the 1792 meeting of the Reformed Coetus were asked to solicit the support of their congregations for Samuel Helffenstein, eldest son of the deceased Reformed pastor Johann Albert Conrad Helffenstein, since the young man wished to enter the ministry but was unable to finance his studies. The Lancaster church council deemed this a suitable opportunity to "give some proof of the love and esteem, which they held for their former pastor," and agreed to a collection for the purpose. In January 1793 the council voted to give £3 to a frontier congregation in the new state of Kentucky, which had asked for a contribution toward the building of a new church. When the Lancaster

Reformed learned of the sufferings of Philadelphians during the 1793 yellow
fever epidemic, they demonstrated their compassion by sending the money
gathered at the last collection to the Reformed church council in Philadelphia,
accompanied by a "brotherly letter of admonition and consolation." Eventually
more than £55 for the support of poor children of deceased members of the
Reformed congregation were sent to Philadelphia. Four years later the Reformed
collected more than £90 in response to the York congregation's plea for assistance after their church had been destroyed in a fire. In 1797 and 1800 they gave
financial support to the Pequea congregation.[35]

The treasury of the Lutheran congregation was empty for a number of years
since the building of steeple (1785–94) had left it heavily indebted. As late as 1806
the Lutheran church council found itself unable to endorse "a collection . . . for
an institution to train preachers, to send missionaries into distant regions and to
keep preacher's widows . . . because in our present situation it is not advisable."[36]
But the budget constraints of the congregation did not prevent Lutheran leaders
from joining other prominent laymen in a number of charitable and educational
projects. In one of the earliest instances, almost 190 Lancasterians of diverse religious backgrounds pledged sums ranging from several shillings to £10 "for the
relief of the distresses of the poor inhabitants of the town of Boston" in 1774.[37]
In the fall of 1795 an "Association for the Relief of the Poor" collected more than
£106 in the borough's wards and distributed groceries, blankets, and medicine
to needy inhabitants. While the association's treasurer David R. Barton was an
Episcopalian, collectors included prominent Moravian, Lutheran, and German
Reformed laymen.[38] When Philadelphia was struck by another yellow fever
epidemic in 1797, General Edward Hand published an appeal for grain contributions to his fellow citizens in the *Lancaster Journal*, and the paper's editor
asked the "reverend gentlemen of the clergy of every denomination in Lancaster
county . . . to give all the publicity in their power to the foregoing address" and

35. Records of the First Reformed Church, vol. 10, microfilm no. 88/3, pp. 93, 97, 108, 109, 117,
Evangelical and Reformed Historical Society; cf. Cramer, *History*, 78; Lottie M. Bausman, "The Liber-
ality of Lancaster County, 1793–94," *PLCHS* 19 (1915): 315–25, esp. 317; Coldren and Heisey, "Religious
Life," 132.

36. Heiges, "Evangelical Lutheran Church," 47.

37. Henry Frank Eshleman, "Lancaster County Contributors to Relief of Boston, 1774," *PLCHS*
28 (1924): 3–5. According to Conrad E. Wright, contributions for the city "came from nearly one hundred communities across New England and more than thirty towns and counties outside the region,
from Savannah in the south to Montreal and Quebec City in the north" (Wright, *Transformation of
Charity*, 37).

38. William Frederic Worner, "Collections for the Poor in 1795," *PLCHS* 32 (1928): 246–47.

urge the "speedy adoption" of Hand's proposals "to their respective congregations; so that the collections may be made and forwarded in time to answer the benevolent purposes for which they are intended." Paul Zantzinger, a Lutheran merchant with strong ties to the Episcopalian community, oversaw relief efforts in the borough, while Lutherans Michael Moser, Jacob Krug, and Gottlieb Naumann; Reformed Caspar Schaffner Jr. and Philip Messenkop; and Presbyterian Henry Pinkerton acted as collectors. In less than a month more than $720 was collected.[39]

During the severe winter of 1804–5, citizens of several denominations formed committees for soliciting from their fellow inhabitants "such donations in money or otherwise, as their humanity may dispose them to grant, for relieving the sufferings of the poor" and the distribution of relief. A group of young men formed a separate committee to solicit donations among their own age cohort. By the end of April 1805 the distribution committee had handed out almost $530 in cash, groceries, firewood, and other needed items to ninety-one people. Seven of the sixteen committee members had already been affiliated with the 1795 relief association and the 1797 collection for Philadelphia, indicating that Lancaster by the turn of the century had a core of inhabitants who were strongly committed to aid fellow citizens in need. Most of these men—Lutheran Leonhard Eichholtz, Presbyterian Henry Pinkerton, Moravian Matthias Jung, and Reformed John Messenkop and Caspar Schaffner Jr.—were also leaders of their respective congregations.[40] When a fire destroyed several buildings in Lancaster in March 1811, a spontaneously formed committee collected almost $4,000 to help the owners rebuild their houses. Lancasterians also raised money to relieve the victims of disastrous fires that struck Newburyport, Massachusetts, in 1811 and Petersburg, Virginia, in 1814.[41]

While these relief efforts were temporary responses to specific needs and economic crises, interdenominational educational projects required a more sustained commitment. The most important of these cooperative undertakings was the founding of Franklin College, which was incorporated by the Pennsylvania state legislature as a "German College and Charity School" in 1787. As the act of incorporation stated, the college was established for "the preservation

39. William Frederic Worner, "Contributions from Lancaster County for the Distressed Poor of Philadelphia During the Yellow Fever Epidemic of 1797," *PLCHS* 32 (1928): 137–39.

40. William Frederic Worner, "Relief for the Poor in Lancaster," *PLCHS* 32 (1928): 141–43.

41. William Frederic Worner, "Collections in Aid of Sufferers from the Fire in Lancaster in 1811," *PLCHS* 33 (1929): 114–17; William Frederic Worner, "Lancaster's Contribution to Newburyport in the Fire of 1811," *PLCHS* 33 (1929): 117–18; William Frederic Worner, "Contribution to Petersburg (VA) in the Fire of 1815," *PLCHS* 33 (1929): 140.

of the principles of the Christian religion and of our Republican form of government in their purity." According to the prominent physician and political writer
Benjamin Rush, who has been identified as a "prime mover" of the college
along with Lancaster pastors Gotthilf Heinrich Ernst Mühlenberg and Johann
Wilhelm Hendel and their Philadelphia colleagues Justus Heinrich Christian
Helmuth and Caspar Weyberg, Franklin College was "committed chiefly to the
care of the Germans of all sects." But Rush also hoped that it would become a
tool to overcome "the partition wall which has long separated the English and
German inhabitants of the state." The charter required fifteen members of the
board of trustees to be Lutherans and fifteen Reformed, with "the remainder to
be chosen from any other society of Christians." The college president was to be
chosen alternately from the ranks of the Lutherans and the Reformed unless the
trustees should "unamimously agree to elect and appoint two or more persons
in succession of the same religious denomination." Gotthilf Heinrich Ernst
Mühlenberg accordingly became the first president and his Reformed colleague Johann Wilhelm Hendel the first vice president of Franklin College.
The first board of trustees included sixteen clergymen—seven Lutherans, seven
Reformed, one Moravian, and one Catholic—and, besides several prominent
state politicians, a number of leading Lutheran, Reformed, and Episcopal laymen. The cooperative nature of the institution was clearly evident at the opening procession in June 1787, which included the members of the Reformed
Coetus and Lutheran Ministerium as well as the elders and vestrymen of the
Lutheran, Reformed, Moravian, Episcopal, Presbyterian, and Roman Catholic
congregations. Lutheran pastor Mühlenberg delivered a sermon urging the
inhabitants of Lancaster Borough and County, who had already given liberally
to many institutions, to support the new college.[42]

The hopes of clergymen and lay leaders notwithstanding, Franklin College
suffered from a chronic shortage of funds, and in 1818 a committee of the Evangelical Lutheran Synod, which inquired into the situation, found "that this
institution has been so much neglected thus far, and thereby the purpose which
the State, from the beginning, had intended it to serve has been frustrated."
Although the college did not fulfil its founders' aspirations, its establishment

42. Ellis and Evans, *History of Lancaster County*, 414–18; Wood, *Conestoga Crossroads*, 222–24;
Glatfelter, *Pastors and People*, 2:500–508; Nolt, *Foreigners in Their Own Land*, 11–12, 19–20. Cf. also
Heiges, "Evangelical Lutheran Church," 36–37; Diller and Klein, *History of St. James' Church*, 85; Splitter,
Pastors, People, Politics, 280–81. For Mühlenberg's appeal to the citizens of Lancaster, see Gotthilf Hein-
rich Ernst Mühlenberg, *Eine Rede, Gehalten den 6ten Juny 1787, bey der Einweihung von der Deutschen
Hohen Schule oder Franklin Collegium in Lancäster* (Lancaster, Pa.: Albrecht and Lahn, 1788), esp. 14.

demonstrates that clergy and laymen of different faiths were actively working together to promote community projects by the late eighteenth century.[43]

CONCLUSION

Organized benevolence and educational institutions in Lancaster had deep roots in the town's congregations. It was in their churches that local residents became familiar with the principles on which the later voluntary associations and educational institutions operated: the election of officers, the drafting of rules and charters, and the management of funds for charitable purposes. Congregations and religious institutions were the beneficiaries of an increasing number of bequests *ad pias causas*, and church councils contributed to relief efforts and beneficent projects within and beyond the local community. Finally, ministers and lay leaders cooperated across denominational lines to help the poor and promote education. The deep involvement of local religious communities in philanthropic causes highlights, once again, the central importance of the congregation in the town's development and the continuities of congregational life from the colonial to the early national period.

43. *Documentary History of the Lutheran Ministerium,* 517; Glatfelter, *Pastors and People,* 2:509; Nolt, *Foreigners in Their Own Land,* 72.

Conclusion

In a diary entry dated February 17, 1791, Lutheran clergyman Gotthilf Heinrich Ernst Mühlenberg wrote down his impressions of the Methodist movement. Their beginnings had been good, he thought, since they were basically "evangelical Englishmen." He praised their commitment and zeal for conversion but was offended by their emphasis on outward behavior, the raucousness and disorderliness of their meetings, their alleged intolerance, and certain points in their doctrine such as perfectionism, emotionalism, and emphasis on immediate conversion. Methodists, he claimed, were harvesting where they had not sown. In sum, the disciples of Wesley should be met with a mixture of Christian tolerance and watchfulness. Several months later, Mühlenberg expressed his fear that the Wesleyan movement was "degenerating" and criticized its association with Baptists, partisanship, and intolerance of others.[1]

The growth of other denominations continued to occupy the Lutheran minister. In July 1794 he noticed the appearance of a "new sect" that originated in "Otterbein's school" and was rapidly gaining ground west of the Susquehanna. Mühlenberg deemed this group "very dangerous" since it was breathing the "American spirit." Its apostles were coming to Lancaster and holding nightly meetings in private houses. A few years later he noted that more and more people, especially "silent and enthusiastic minds," were finding Emanuel Swedenborg's theological system attractive. By early 1802 "numerous reports" from the west "about a great awakening among the people" were reaching Lancaster. Much good might grow from these revivals, Mühlenberg thought, and some people might be brought to think about their spiritual state. Still, the "disorderliness" of the awakenings and the "rawness of the people" were cause for concern, and their effect on God's realm remained uncertain.[2]

---

1. Mühlenberg Diary, vol. 1, entries for February 17, 1791, and September 7, 1791, American Philosophical Society.

2. Mühlenberg Diary, vol. 1, entries for July 1, 1794; February 14, 1800; January 31, 1802; and December (undated) 1802, American Philosophical Society; translations mine.

By the early 1800s the revivals known as the Second Great Awakening were in full swing, and historians have placed them at the center of narratives about the "democratization of American Christianity."[3] In many accounts of congregational development, the early national period figures as a time of upheaval. Students of New England and New York congregations in particular have noted dramatic changes in the postrevolutionary decades. In their study of Center Church in New Haven, Harry Stout and Catherine Brekus describe "a sudden, remarkable transformation that was more radical and far-reaching than any that had appeared in the earlier life of the . . . congregation and that would not be equaled again until the twentieth century. The War for Independence . . . meant . . . the start of an internal revolution that transformed every institution, including the congregation, according to the new republican orthodoxy of individualism, voluntarism, and the separation of church and state. After 1840, the church recovered from the shocks it had experienced in the Revolution, but only partially. In stark contrast to the colonial era, the most salient fact of life within the Center Church congregation throughout the nineteenth century was change, not stability."[4]

David G. Hackett has portrayed prerevolutionary Albany, New York, as a predominantly Dutch town that retained a communal way of life and relied on extended family networks, social hierarchy, and adherence to the Dutch Reformed church. The hierarchical structure of the community visibly manifested itself in the arrangement of church seats and in the fact that the social and political leaders were often identical with the elders of the Reformed congregation. All this changed during the Revolutionary and early national periods when the effects of war, the massive immigration of New Englanders, and socioeconomic changes associated with the market revolution decisively altered the character of the town. Albany, which was about Lancaster's size in 1790, grew about twice as fast during the following three decades. While the Dutch Reformed church declined in importance, Presbyterianism absorbed the new mercantile, manufacturing, and professional elites. After 1800, workers, petty shopkeepers, and newcomers were increasingly drawn toward Methodism and, eventually, evangelical revivalism. Individualism, religious pluralism, and evangelicalism became hallmarks of Albany society, and American nationalism assumed the character of a "civil ideology that would accommodate unprecedented diversity."[5]

---

3. Nathan O. Hatch, *The Democratization of American Christianity* (New Haven: Yale University Press, 1989).

4. Brekus and Stout, "Center Church," 47–72.

5. Hackett, *Rude Hand of Innovation*, quotes on 20, 155.

For Gotthilf Heinrich Ernst Mühlenberg, the Halle pietist and long-time pastor of the Lutheran congregation in Lancaster, however, the evangelical revivals were distant developments—interesting but also strange and vaguely troubling. While new religious groups and movements seemed to embody the "American spirit," their impact on Lancaster was remarkably slight. As the preceding chapters have demonstrated, the denominational order established during the colonial era remained essentially intact in the early national period. The pluralist religious framework that German- and English-speaking immigrants and their ministers had established since the 1730s survived the Revolution, and the decades after American independence were characterized by long, tranquil pastorates and harmonious relations between pastors and people. Not evangelical revivalism but a plurality of old-world churches that emphasized confessional doctrine, ecclesiastical tradition, a trained ministry, and orderly congregational life continued to dominate religious life. Continental European pietism remained a pervasive influence, but it was a pietism that affected Lutherans, Reformed, and Moravians in distinct ways and was tempered by an overriding concern for stability and order. Also, there was neither a "layman's progress" nor a "triumph of the laity," since laypeople were dominant in the town's congregations from the beginning, and the one group whose position grew more secure over time and whose influence on congregational affairs gradually increased was the clergy.[6] And there was no marked trend toward secularization either since levels of church adherence remained high, laypeople regularly participated in congregational decisions, and building activities as well as a growing number of bequests and donations highlighted the central importance of the congregations in the life of Lancaster's inhabitants.

Religious developments in the borough after the Revolution thus show none of the signs of turmoil, upheaval, and dramatic change that students of New England and New York churches have found. What explains this striking contrast? One part of the answer is that Lancaster's congregations had experienced their period of change and readjustment in the decades just prior to American independence. Most settlers in the new town had been first-generation immigrants from Europe, congregations had been built from scratch, and pastors and people had fought over their respective rights and privileges and the balance of power between them. By the end of the colonial period, all major congregations had a stable core of leaders, had completed major building projects, and had achieved a measure of order and stability. After 1783 Lancaster remained a town

6. These slogans are taken from the titles of Rothermund, *Layman's Progress*, and Westerkamp, *Triumph of the Laity*.

dominated by traders, artisans, and public officials that grew steadily but was not yet affected by the dislocations associated with mass immigration and the industrial revolution. Lancaster's postrevolutionary tranquillity, therefore, was a relatively recent phenomenon that depended to a considerable extent on the continuity of lay leadership.

Furthermore, the religious movements whose dramatic growth redefined American Protestantism in the postrevolutionary period had limited appeal to the German speakers who made up the majority of Lancaster's inhabitants. As Steven M. Nolt has shown, evangelical sects did find some adherents among Pennsylvania Germans, but most of them withstood the lure of evangelicalism. "Lutheran and Reformed resistance to evangelical revivalism," Nolt explains, "relied on a heritage of Continental Pietism, confessional catechesis, and the authority of tradition."[7] Pastors like Johann Wilhelm Hendel, Christian Ludwig Becker, and Gotthilf Heinrich Ernst Mühlenberg made sure that pietism, confessionalism, and respect for tradition remained focal points of German congregational life in postrevolutionary Lancaster.

Laura Becker's study of Reading, another backcountry town mostly settled by German immigrants, shows many parallels. As in Lancaster, the German Reformed and Lutheran congregations were "by far the largest and best organized" in the prerevolutionary period. Like their counterparts in the Conestoga Valley, Reading's Lutherans and Reformed had built stone churches, purchased organs, organized church councils, and held regular alms collections well before the Revolution. Congregational development was impeded, however, by a scarcity of regular ministers and internal divisions. Several Reformed ministers had to leave because of misconduct, and of the seven Lutheran ministers who served the town from 1767 to 1791, most "left as a result of problems with church members." Anglicans had a resident minister and formed a vestry before the Revolution, but they were unable to build their own church before 1800. As in Lancaster, their congregational life was disrupted during the War for Independence because of their minister's loyalism. In addition, tiny groups of Catholics and Quakers had erected a small wooden chapel and a log meetinghouse. The congregational pattern established in the late colonial period essentially survived the Revolution, and with the exception of the Episcopalians, who suffered from declining membership, Reading's churches consolidated in the early national period. The Catholics built a new church and secured a charter of incorporation in 1791. The Quakers reinforced their meetinghouse and added a schoolhouse.

7. Nolt, *Foreigners in Their Own Land,* 47–65 (quote on 57).

The Lutheran and Reformed congregations obtained charters in 1787 and 1790. Moreover, the Lutherans began to collect money for a new church while the Reformed "moved to formalize the meaning of congregational membership." In 1789 their consistory "decided that all members must contribute to the support of the minister and the congregational debt, or else be denied membership and its attendant privileges." In the postwar period "most of Reading's churches continued to strengthen as institutions while their members interacted ever more closely with non-members and contributed to the development of congregations outside the town."[8] In sum, the case of Reading suggests that the progress of Lancaster's churches outlined in this book mirrored developments in other Pennsylvania towns.

It should also be noted that congregational stability in postrevolutionary Lancaster came at a price. The number of communicants in the Lutheran congregation declined after 1800, and tensions lingering beneath the surface of tranquility were only deferred, not resolved. During the pastorate of Gotthilf Heinrich Ernst Mühlenberg's successor, Christian L. F. Endress (1815–27), a controversy over the use of English in church services erupted that tore the congregation apart. Endress preached in English on Sunday evenings since 1815, and four years later the vestry authorized English funeral sermons. When 168 parishioners presented a petition in 1825 for alternate English and German services on Sunday mornings, this proved too much for Lutheran traditionalists. The petitioners argued that they "cannot longer induce our young people, our wives, brothers, sisters, and other relatives and friends to attend our church, because they do not understand the German language sufficiently to derive the benefit which they desire." When the church council approved the change after considerable discussion, a minority of thirty to forty members withdrew and formed a separate German speaking congregation. During the same decade the language issue also divided the Reformed church. While the old pastor Hoffmeier continued to preach in German, several unsuccessful attempts were made to secure the services of a co-pastor who could preach in English and a split of the congregation was narrowly averted. When Hoffmeier resigned in 1831, the congregation decided to hire a pastor who could minister in both languages.[9]

There were other changes in the town's religious landscape. In 1817 the Philadelphia preacher Richard Allen organized a Methodist congregation among African

8. Becker, "Community Experience," 223–33 (quote on 231), 465–69.
9. Heiges, "Evangelical Lutheran Church," 53–54; Ellis and Evans, *History of Lancaster County,* 441, 456. On the language issue in early nineteenth-century German Reformed congregations, see Good, *History (Nineteenth Century),* 7–12; Nolt, *Foreigners in Their Own Land,* 71.

Americans, and four years later the town's black people built the first church and schoolhouse for their own community. A year later the followers of John Elliott, a "reformed" Methodist preacher who had come to Lancaster in 1816, erected a meetinghouse "for use of all denominations." Most of Elliott's adherents eventually joined the movement of John Winebrenner, who began preaching in "Elliott's Chapel" in 1828 and founded the Church of God. In the 1830s adherents of Emanuel Swedenborg formed their own assembly, the Lancaster New Church, and when an itinerant Universalist preacher from New England appeared in town, "a body of Germans rushed into the house as the people were assembling, and shutting the doors threatened vengeance to any who should enter."[10] As these developments show, the stable congregational landscape of the early national period was not to last.

As an ethnically bifurcated and confessionally fragmented community whose major ethnoreligious groups sought to preserve their cultural distinctiveness, Lancaster was evidently not susceptible to religious movements such as evangelical revivalism. Instead, the congregations founded during the colonial period continued to serve the religious needs of the great majority of its inhabitants well into the nineteenth century. In other respects, though, Lancaster appears fairly typical of the experiences of an immigrant clergy and laity who gradually came to terms with religious diversity and congregational self-rule in the American setting. In the early stages of the town's development, ministers' and laypeople's attitudes were strongly shaped by regional traditions. Lutheran pastors from Halle and their Reformed colleagues from Herborn sought to transfer their particular traditions of piety to new-world congregations, while other clergymen and the vast majority of German-speaking parishioners had been reared in the Lutheran and Reformed confessionalism of Protestant territories in southwest Germany and neighboring Switzerland. These diverse religious traditions did not mesh easily, but in the course of time pastors and laypeople jointly formed self-governing German-American Protestant congregations that clearly differed from the Protestant confessionalism prevalent in eighteenth-century German communities. The English-speaking churches likewise accommodated pastors and people from a variety of British, Irish, and American backgrounds, and ministers in the Pennsylvania backcountry had to come to terms with the fact that the shepherds of the English state church tended small flocks amid multitudes of "sectarians" and "dissenters" and lacked the institutional power that the Church

10. Ellis and Evans, *History of Lancaster County,* 478, 480–81; Scott T. Swank, "The Lancaster New Church (Swedenborgian)," *JLCHS* 76 (1972): 69–87; Rineer, *Churches and Cemeteries,* 200, 211; Nolt, *Foreigners in Their Own Land,* 52 (quote on 64).

of England commanded in the mother country. Meanwhile, the small band of Catholics, under the leadership of German-born Jesuits, created the first ethnically mixed congregation in a town that was overwhelmingly Protestant. In the context of Lancaster, "Americanization" of European churches meant the blending of diverse regional traditions, the hammering out of rules and procedures for communal self-government, and the gradual recognition that a thriving congregational life required the benevolence and commitment of its members. It rarely meant the religious enthusiasm promoted by evangelical revivalists that Charles L. Cohen has identified as "Anglo-American Christianity's most distinctive feature."[11] What this study suggests, therefore, is that narratives of American religion may have focused too much on regions of rapid change to the neglect of developments in places that remained outside the evangelical mainstream.

Moreover, many studies have focused on initially homogeneous communities in New England and New York that were fragmented by growing diversity and rapid economic and social change in the eighteenth and early nineteenth centuries.[12] Pennsylvania towns such as Lancaster, Reading, York, and Germantown, however, began their existence as ethnically and religiously diverse immigrant communities in which people of different backgrounds and faiths had to come to terms with one another from the start. These towns experienced rapid change in the middle of the eighteenth century when they were flooded by German and Irish immigrants and were integrated into Philadelphia's geographically and commercially expanding hinterland, but their ethnoreligious communities had stabilized by the end of the eighteenth century. A new period of rapid change did not set in before the rise of immigration and the onset of industrialization after 1830. Therefore they followed a different path to ethnic and religious pluralism than New England communities or Dutch towns in New York. If we look for antecedents of the commercially thriving, ethnically and religiously diverse cities that sprang up in the American Midwest in the nineteenth century, the towns in the Philadelphia hinterland offer a more suitable model than New England communities.[13]

11. Charles L. Cohen, "The Colonization of British North America as an Episode in the History of Christianity," *Church History* 72 (2003): 553–68 (quote on 557).

12. In addition to Hackett, *Rude Hand of Innovation*, see esp. Balmer, *Perfect Babel of Confusion*; Richard L. Bushman, *From Puritan to Yankee: Character and the Social Order in Connecticut, 1690–1765* (Cambridge: Harvard University Press, 1967); John L. Brooke, *The Heart of the Commonwealth: Society and Politics in Worcester County, Massachusetts, 1713–1860* (Cambridge: Cambridge University Press 1989).

13. On ethnoreligious diversity in the nineteenth-century Midwest, see Timothy Smith, "The Ohio Valley: Testing Ground for America's Experiment in Religious Pluralism," *Church History* 60 (1991): 461–79.

Finally, this study shows that religious diversity was not necessarily embraced as an ideal. Rather, Lutheran, Reformed, and Anglican clergymen associated it with competition and potential chaos. Although some wealthy German families gradually anglicized and the Moravians attracted a couple of English speakers, interfaith and especially interethnic marriages and conversions remained relatively infrequent. Still, early Lancasterians practiced pluralism, even if they did not articulate it. Ministers performed pastoral acts for members of various denominations, and people contributed to the projects of other congregations, socialized across ethnic and confessional lines, and engaged in a number of interdenominational projects. Despite the anti-popish and anti-Jewish sentiments voiced by leading Pennsylvanians, the small minorities of Catholics and Jews became part of local business networks, voluntary associations, and social circles. Perhaps the most telling case is that of the Moravians. After they had broken with the Lutherans and formed their own congregation in the late 1740s, relations with the other religious groups in town remained tense for about a generation. To Lutheran, Reformed, and Anglican clergymen, the United Brethren appeared as a dangerous band of proselytizers. In the years between 1780 and 1820, however, Moravians naturally took part in interdenominational educational and philanthropic efforts such as Franklin College, the German Society, and the Bible Society. Lutheran, Reformed, Episcopalian, and Presbyterian pastors and laypeople actively participated in the dedication of the new Moravian church building in 1821. By that time the United Brethren had clearly ceased to be a suspicious "sect" and become a religious community like any other in town. In the final analysis, then, eighteenth-century Lancaster was a laboratory of diversity, a place in which people experienced, negotiated, and adjusted confessional boundaries. The outcome was a remarkably stable denominational order.

Bibliography

MANUSCRIPT SOURCES

American Philosophical Society, Philadelphia, Pa.

Gotthilf Heinrich Ernst Mühlenberg Personal Diary, vols. 1–2

Archiv der Franckeschen Stiftungen, Halle/Saale, Germany

Missionsarchiv, Abteilung Nordamerika
    Johann Friedrich Handschuh Diarium, 1748–53 (4 H 10)
    Johann Friedrich Handschuh Correspondence (4 C 3, 4 D 1)
    Gotthilf Heinrich Ernst Mühlenberg Correspondence (4 C 20)

Evangelical and Reformed Historical Society, Lancaster, Pa.

Records of the First Reformed Church, Lancaster, Pa. (microfilm nos. 88/1–3)

Historical Society of Pennsylvania, Philadelphia

Jasper Yeates Letterbook, 1769–71 (AM 196)
Lancaster County Manuscripts
Penn Papers, Official Correspondence
Peters Papers
Shippen Papers
Society Misc. Collection, Lutheran Church, Lancaster, Pa.

Lancaster County Historical Society, Lancaster, Pa.

Estate Papers, Inventories, and Accounts
    Peter Balspach Estate Papers, 1748
    Patrick Carrigan Estate Inventory, 1756
    John Connolly Administration Account, 1753
    John Foulk Estate Inventory, 1748
    George Gibson Estate Inventory, 1762
    John Henneberger Estate Papers, 1752

William Jevon Estate Inventory, 1767
Jacob Kuntz Estate Papers, 1763
Josiah Lockhart Estate Inventory, 1809
Eberhart Michael Estate Inventory, 1789
Felix Miller Estate Inventory, 1748
Edward Smout Estate Inventory, 1751
David Stout Estate Inventory, 1764
John Utzmann Estate Inventory, 1764
Jasper Yeates Estate Inventory, 1817
Marcus Young Estate Inventory, 1796

Lancaster Borough Tax Assessment Lists, 1751, 1759 (microfilm)

Lancaster County Tax Lists (microfilm)
    Elizabeth Township, 1758
    Leacock Township, 1758
    Manheim Township, 1751, 1756–59
    Manor Township, 1759

Hubley Collection (MG 2)
Jasper Yeates Collection (MG 205)
Jasper Yeates Papers (MG 207)

Landeskirchliches Archiv Stuttgart, Germany

Best. A 26, Bü 373, 1d, nos. 8–10

Lutheran Archives Center, Mount Airy, Pa.

J. H. C. Helmuth Diary, 1772–73 (PH 48 A 1772)
Schaum Correspondence, 1743–55 (PS 313 C)

Moravian Archives, Bethlehem, Pa.

Lancaster Diaries, 1751–1821
Lancaster Elders Conference, 1753–1804
Kurze Relation von den Anfängen der Brüder Gemeine in Lancaster und derselben gnädiger
    Entfaltung biß zum Jahre 1772
Protocoll vom Lancasterischen Gemein-Rath angefangen den 23. August 1754
Verzeichniß der unter der Brüder Diaconie stehenden Seelen in und um Lancaster

Pennsylvania State Archives, Harrisburg, Pa.

Lancaster County Deed Books (microfilm)
Lancaster County Orphans Court Records (microfilm)
Lancaster County Will Books (microfilm)
Pennsylvania Bureau of Land Records, Warrant Register, vol. 16 (microfilm)

Presbyterian Historical Society, Philadelphia

Minutes, Resolutions &c. of the Trustees of the English Presbyterian Church in the Borough of Lancaster, Records of the First Presbyterian Church, Lancaster, Pa., vol. 21, 1804–43 (microfilm)

Presbyterians in Lancaster, Records of the Presbytery of Donegal, 1742–70 (typescript, MS D 71)

St. James Episcopal Church, Lancaster, Pa.

Vestry Minutes of St. James from October 3, 1744, to November 13, 1846 (typescript)

Trinity Lutheran Church Archives, Lancaster, Pa.

Bills and Receipts, 1761–69
Trinity Lutheran Church Documents, vols. 101, 103
Trinity Lutheran Church Documents Acquired at John W. Aungst sale

PRINTED SOURCES

Aland, Kurt, ed. *Die Korrespondenz Heinrich Melchior Mühlenbergs aus der Anfangszeit des deutschen Luthertums in Nordamerika*. 4 vols. Berlin and New York: de Gruyter, 1986–97.

Aland, Kurt, and Hermann Wellenreuther, eds. *Die Korrespondenz Heinrich Melchior Mühlenbergs aus der Anfangszeit des deutschen Luthertums in Nordamerika*. Vol. 5, *1777–1787*. Berlin and New York: de Gruyter, 2002.

Barton, Sara. "The Bartons in Lancaster in 1776." *Journal of the Lancaster County Historical Society* 52 (1948): 213–17.

Barton, William. *Memoirs of the Life of David Rittenhouse*. Philadelphia: Parker, 1813.

Beatty, Joseph M., Jr. "Letters of the Four Beatty Brothers of the Continental Army, 1774–1794." *Pennsylvania Magazine of History and Biography* 44 (1920): 193–263.

Becker, Christian Ludewig. *Die Lezten Bitten eines Christlichen Predigers an seine Gemeinde, in einer Abschieds-Rede vorgestellet, und seiner ihm theuren Gemeinde zum Andenken hinterlassen*. Lancaster, Pa.: Benjamin Grimler, 1806.

Burial Book of the Lancaster Moravian Church, 1744–1821. Lancaster, Pa.: n.p., 1928.

Cavin, Albert, and August Lerbscher. "Items from the *Neue Unpartheyische Lancaster-Zeitung* und *Anzeigs-Nachrichten*." *Journal of the Lancaster County Historical Society* 59 (1955): 184–95.

———. "Items from the *Neue Unpartheyische Lancaster Zeitung* und *Anzeigs-Nachrichten*." *Papers Read Before the Lancaster County Historical Society* 35 (1931): 25–36.

———. "Items of Interest from the *Neue Unpartheyische Lancaster Zeitung*." *Papers Read Before the Lancaster County Historical Society* 34 (1930): 1–10.

"Copy of Inventory of George Ross of Lancaster, Penna." *Pennsylvania Magazine of History and Biography* 31 (1907): 375–76.

Documentary History of the Evangelical Lutheran Ministerium of Pennsylvania and Adjacent States: Proceedings of the Annual Conventions from 1748 to 1821. Philadelphia: Board of Publication of the General Council of the Evangelical Lutheran Church in North America, 1898.

Egle, William H., ed. *Pennsylvania Archives.* 3rd series. Vol. 17. Harrisburg: William Stanley Ray, 1897.

Hamilton, Kenneth G., and Lothar Madeheim, trans. and eds. *The Bethlehem Diary.* Vol. 2, *January 1, 1744–May 31, 1745.* Bethlehem, Pa.: Archives of the Moravian Church, 2001.

Hanley, Thomas O'Brien, ed. *The John Carroll Papers.* 3 vols. Notre Dame: University of Notre Dame Press, 1976.

Hazard, Samuel, ed. *Pennsylvania Archives.* 1st series. Vol. 3. Philadelphia: J. Severns, 1853.

Hinke, William J., ed. "Diary of the Rev. Michael Schlatter, June 1–December 15, 1746." *Journal of the Presbyterian Historical Society* 3 (1905/6): 105–21.

———, ed. *Life and Letters of John Philip Boehm, Founder of the Reformed Church in Pennsylvania, 1683–1749.* Philadelphia: Publication and Sunday School Board of the Reformed Church in the United States, 1916.

———, ed. *Minutes and Letters of the German Reformed Coetus in Pennsylvania, 1747–1792: Together with Three Preliminary Reports of Rev. John Philip Boehm, 1734–1744.* Philadelphia: Reformed Church Publication Board, 1903.

Hocker, Edward W. *Genealogical Data Relating to the German Settlers of Pennsylvania and Adjacent Territory: From Advertisements of German Newspapers Published in Philadelphia and Germantown: 1743–1800.* 2nd ed. Baltimore: Genealogical Publishing Co., 1981.

Kirchen-Ordnung für die deutsch Evangelisch Lutherische Gemeine bey der heiligen Dreyeinigkeits Kirche in der Stadt Lancaster, Pennsylvanien, in Nord Amerika. Lancaster, Pa.: William Hamilton, 1815.

Klett, Guy S., ed. *Minutes of the Presbyterian Church in America: 1706–1788.* Philadelphia: Presbyterian Historical Society, 1976.

"Letter of Rev. Henry Neale, Philadelphia, 1741." *American Catholic Historical Researches* 6 (1889): 182–83.

"Local Items from an Old *Gazette.*" *Papers Read Before the Lancaster County Historical Society* 16 (1912): 116–17.

Mann, W. J., B. M. Schmucker, and W. Germann, eds. *Nachrichten von den vereinigten Deutschen Evangelisch-Lutherischen Gemeinen in Nord-America, absonderlich in Pensylvanien.* 2 vols. Allentown, Pa.: Brobst, Diehl and Co.; Halle: Buchhandlung des Waisenhauses, 1886–95.

Mayhill, R. Thomas, comp. *Lancaster County, Pennsylvania, Deed Abstracts . . . Deed Books A through M (1729 through c1770) with Adjoining Landowners & Witnesses, 5th pr.* Knightstown, Ind.: The Bookmark, 1994.

Mühlenberg, Gotthilf Heinrich Ernst. *Eine Rede, Gehalten den 6ten Juny 1787, bey der Einweihung von der Deutschen Hohen Schule oder Franklin Collegium in Lancäster.* Lancaster, Pa.: Albrecht and Lahn, 1788.

Neible, George W. "Account of Servants Bound and Assigned Before James Hamilton, Mayor of Philadelphia." *Pennsylvania Magazine of History and Biography* 31 (1907): 76–97, 195–206, 355–72, 461–73.

———. "Account of Servants Bound and Assigned Before James Hamilton, Mayor of Philadelphia." *Pennsylvania Magazine of History and Biography* 32 (1908): 88–103, 237–49, 351–70.

"Notes and Queries." *Pennsylvania Magazine of History and Biography* 4 (1880): 119–20.

O'Malley, J. Steven, ed. *Early German-American Evangelicalism: Pietist Sources on Discipleship and Sanctification.* Pietist and Wesleyan Studies 7. Lanham, Md.: Scarecrow, 1995.

Owen, Benjamin F. "Letters of the Rev. Richard Locke and Rev. George Craig, Missionaries in Pennsylvania of the 'Society for Propagating the Gospel in Foreign Parts,' London, 1746–1752." *Pennsylvania Magazine of History and Biography* 24 (1900): 467–78.

Perry, William Stevens, ed. *Historical Collections Relating to the American Colonial Church.* 5 vols. Hartford, 1870. Reprint, New York: AMS Press, 1969.

Record of Indentures of Individuals Bound Out as Apprentices, Servants, Etc. and of German and Other Redemptioners in the Office of the Mayor of the City of Philadelphia, October 3, 1771, to October 5, 1773. Reprint, Baltimore: Genealogical Publishing Co., 1973.

Robinson, Mary N. "Gleanings from an Old Newspaper." *Papers Read Before the Lancaster County Historical Society* 7 (1902–3): 156–73.

Rogers, Sophie Selden. "Genealogical Gleanings from Orphans Court Records of Lancaster County." *Pennsylvania Genealogical Magazine* 24 (1965/66): 15–38, 118–39, 193–223.

Smith, Debra D., and Frederick S. Weiser, eds. and trans. *Trinity Lutheran Church Records, Lancaster, Pennsylvania.* Vol. 1, *1730–1767;* vol. 2, *1767–1782;* vol. 3, *1782–1796;* vol.4, *1797–1810.* Apollo, Pa.: Closson, 1988–2006.

"Some Biographical Letters." *Pennsylvania Magazine of History and Biography* 23 (1899): 202–4.

Sprague, William B. *Annals of the American Pulpit, or Commemorative Notices of Distinguished American Clergymen of Various Denominations.* Vol. 9, *Lutheran.* New York: Carter, 1869.

Stevens, Sylvester K., and Donald H. Kent, eds. *The Papers of Col. Henry Bouquet.* Vol. 2. Harrisburg: Pennsylvania Historical and Museum Commission, 1940.

Strassburger, Ralph B., and William J. Hinke. *Pennsylvania German Pioneers: A Publication of the Original Lists of Arrivals in the Port of Philadelphia from 1727 to 1808.* 3 vols. Philadelphia, 1934. Reprint, Baltimore: Genealogical Publishing Co., 1966.

Tappert, Theodore G., and John W. Doberstein, eds. *The Journals of Henry Melchior Muhlenberg.* 3 vols. Philadelphia: Evangelical Lutheran Ministerium of Pennsylvania and Adjacent States, 1942–57.

Transactions of the Moravian Historical Society 1 (1858–76): 384–87.

United States Bureau of Census. *Heads of Families at the First Census of the United States Taken in Year 1790: Pennsylvania.* Washington, D.C.: Government Printing Office, 1908.

United States Census Office. *Fourth Census of the United States, 1820.* Vol. 1. Washington, D.C.: Government Printing Office, 1821.

Weiser, Frederick S., ed. "Donors to the Lutheran Church in Germantown in 1738." *Der Reggeboge* 19, no. 1 (1985): 8–10.

Wright, F. Edward. *Lancaster County, Pennsylvania Church Records of the Eighteenth Century.* Vol. 2. Westminster, Md.: Family Line Publications, 1994.

Yoder, Don, ed. *Pennsylvania German Immigrants, 1709–1786: Lists Consolidated from Yearbooks of the Pennsylvania German Folklore Society.* Baltimore: Genealogical Publishing Co., 1980.

NEWSPAPERS

Pennsylvania Gazette. Philadelphia: Benjamin Franklin, 1745–71.

Pensylvanische Berichte. Germantown, Pa.: Christoph Saur, 1744–59.

Heinrich Millers Pennsylvanischer Staatsbote. Nos. 696–920. Philadelphia: Heinrich Miller, 1775–79.

Der Wöchentliche Pennsylvanische Staatsbote. Nos. 311–695. Philadelphia: Heinrich Miller, 1768–75.

Der Wöchentliche Philadelphische Staatsbote. Nos. 1–310. Philadelphia: Heinrich Miller, 1762–67.

SECONDARY SOURCES

Agethen, Manfred. "Bekehrungsversuche an Juden und Judentaufen in der frühen Neuzeit." *Aschkenas* 1 (1991): 65–94.

Atwood, Craig D. *Community of the Cross: Moravian Piety in Colonial Bethlehem.* University Park: Pennsylvania State University Press, 2004.

Bach, Jeff. *Voices of the Turtledoves: The Sacred World of Ephrata.* University Park: Pennsylvania State University Press, 2002.

Balmer, Randall. *A Perfect Babel of Confusion: Dutch Religion and English Culture in the Middle Colonies.* New York: Oxford University Press, 1989.

Batchelder, Robert C. "A Lancaster Footnote in American History." *Papers Read Before the Lancaster County Historical Society* 64 (1960): 227–33.

Bausman, Lottie M. "The Liberality of Lancaster County, 1793–94." *Papers Read Before the Lancaster County Historical Society* 19 (1915): 315–25.

Beck, Herbert H. "William Henry: Patriot, Master Gunsmith, Progenitor of the Steamboat." *Transactions of the Moravian Historical Society* 16, no. 2 (1955): 69–95.

Beck, Rainer. "Der Pfarrer und das Dorf. Konformismus und Eigensinn im katholischen Bayern des 17./18. Jahrhunderts." In *Armut, Liebe, Ehre: Studien zur historischen Kulturforschung*, edited by Richard van Dülmen, 107–143. Frankfurt am Main: Fischer Verlag, 1988.

Becker, Laura L. "The American Revolution as a Community Experience: A Case Study of Reading, Pennsylvania." Ph.D. diss., University of Pennsylvania, 1978.

Beiler, Rosalind J. "'Smuggling Goods or Moving Households?' The Legal Status of German-Speaking Immigrants in the First British Empire." In *Menschen zwischen zwei Welten: Auswanderung, Ansiedlung, Akkulturation*, edited by Walter G. Rödel and Helmut Schmahl, 9–23. Trier: Wissenschaftlicher Verlag, 2002.

Bonomi, Patricia U. *Under the Cope of Heaven: Religion, Society, and Politics in Colonial America.* New York: Oxford University Press, 1986.

Bonomi, Patricia U., and Peter R. Eisenstadt. "Church Adherence in the Eighteenth-Century British American Colonies." *William and Mary Quarterly* 39 (1982): 245–87.

Bossy, John. *The English Catholic Community, 1570–1850.* New York: Oxford University Press, 1976.

———. "English Catholics After 1688." In *From Persecution to Toleration: The Glorious Revolution and Religion in England*, edited by Ole Peter Grell, Jonathan I. Israel, and Nicholas Tyacke, 369–87. Oxford: Clarendon Press, 1991.

Brecht, Martin, and Klaus Deppermann, eds. *Geschichte des Pietismus.* Vol. 2, *Der Pietismus im 18. Jahrhundert.* Göttingen: Vandenhoeck and Ruprecht, 1995.

Brekus, Catherine, and Harry S. Stout. "A New England Congregation: Center Church, New Haven, 1638–1989." In *American Congregations.* Vol. 1, *Portraits of Twelve Religious Communities*, edited by James P. Wind and James W. Lewis, 14–102. Chicago: University of Chicago Press, 1994.

Brener, David. *The Jews of Lancaster, Pennsylvania: A Story with Two Beginnings.* Lancaster, Pa.: Congregation Shaarai Shomayim, 1979.

Bridenbaugh, Carl. *Cities in Revolt: Urban Life in America, 1743–1776.* New York: Knopf, 1955.

Brigden, Susan. *New Worlds, Lost Worlds: The Rule of the Tudors, 1485–1603.* London: Penguin, 2000.

Brooke, John L. *The Heart of the Commonwealth: Society and Politics in Worcester County, Massachusetts, 1713–1860.* Cambridge: Cambridge University Press, 1989.

Brunner, Raymond J., *"That Ingenious Business": Pennsylvania German Organ Builders.* Birdsboro, Pa.: Publications of the Pennsylvania German Society, 1990.

Burgert, Annette K. *Eighteenth-Century Emigrants from German-Speaking Lands to North America.* Vol. 1, *The Northern Kraichgau.* Breinigsville, Pa.: Publications of the Pennsylvania German Society, 1983.

———. *Eighteenth-Century Emigrants from German-Speaking Lands to North America.* Vol. 2, *The Western Palatinate.* Birdsboro, Pa.: Publications of the Pennsylvania German Society, 1985.

———. *Eighteenth-Century Emigrants from the Northern Alsace to America.* Camden, Me.: Picton Press, 1992.

Burgert, Annette K., and Frederick S. Weiser. "Seeking a Pastor for Conestoga, ca. 1732." *Der Reggeboge* 24, no. 2 (1990): 62–65.

Burkhardt, Johannes. *Das Reformationsjahrhundert: Deutsche Geschichte zwischen Medienrevolution und Institutionenbildung, 1517–1617.* Stuttgart: Kohlhammer, 2002.

Bushman, Richard L. *From Puritan to Yankee: Character and the Social Order in Connecticut, 1690–1765.* Cambridge: Harvard University Press, 1980.

———. *The Refinement of America: Persons, Houses, Cities.* New York: Vintage Books/Random House, 1992.

Butler, Jon. *Awash in a Sea of Faith: Christianizing the American People.* Cambridge: Harvard University Press, 1990.

———. *Becoming America: The Revolution Before 1776.* Cambridge: Harvard University Press, 2000.

———. "The Future of American Religious History: Prospectus, Agenda, Transatlantic *Problématique.*" *William and Mary Quarterly* 42 (1985): 167–83.

———. *Power, Authority, and the Origins of the American Denominational Order: The English Churches of the Delaware Valley, 1680–1730.* Philadelphia: American Philosophical Society, 1978.

———. "Protestant Pluralism." *Encyclopedia of the North American Colonies.* Vol. 3, edited by Jacob E. Cooke et al., 609–31. New York: Scribner, 1993

———. "The Spiritual Importance of the Eighteenth Century." In *In Search of Peace and Prosperity: New German Settlements in Eighteenth-Century Europe and America,* edited by Hartmut Lehmann et al., 101–14. University Park: Pennsylvania State University Press, 2000.

Buyers, William Buchanan. "The Rev. John D. Woodhull D.D., 'The Fighting Chaplain.'" *Papers Read Before the Lancaster County Historical Society* 43 (1939): 131–36.

Carlebach, Elisheva. *Divided Souls: Converts from Judaism in Germany, 1500–1750.* New Haven: Yale University Press, 2001.

Clark, Martha B. "Lancaster County's Relation to Slavery." *Papers Read Before the Lancaster County Historical Society* 15 (1911): 43–61.

———. "Some Early Lancaster Notables." *Papers Read Before the Lancaster County Historical Society* 8 (1903/4): 3–13.

Coffey, John. *Persecution and Toleration in Tudor and Stuart England, 1558–1689.* Harlow, England: Longman, 2000.

Cohen, Charles L. "The Colonization of British North America as an Episode in the History of Christianity." *Church History* 72 (2003): 553–68.

———. "The Post-Puritan Paradigm of Early American Religious History." *William and Mary Quarterly* 54 (1997): 695–723.

Coldren, Caroline S., and M. Luther Heisey. "Religious Life in Lancaster Borough." *Papers Read Before the Lancaster County Historical Society* 45 (1941): 125–44.

Core, Arthur C. ed. *Philip William Otterbein: Pastor, Ecumenist.* Dayton, Ohio: Board of Publication, Evangelical United Brethren Church, 1968.

Courtney, Catherine, and John D. Long, "A History of First Presbyterian Church of Lancaster, Pennsylvania." *Journal of the Lancaster County Historical Society* 90 (1986): 2–75.

Cramer, W. Stuart. *History of the First Reformed Church Lancaster, Pennsylvania, 1736–1904.* Lancaster, Pa.: n.p., 1904.

Delafield, Joseph Livingston. "Notes on the Life and Work of Robert Coleman." *Pennsylvania Magazine of History and Biography* 36 (1912): 226–30.

Diller, William F., and Harry M. J. Klein. *The History of St. James' Church (Protestant Episcopal), 1744–1944.* Lancaster, Pa.: St. James Church Vestry, 1944.

Dinkin, Robert J. "Seating the Meetinghouse in Early Massachusetts." *New England Quarterly* 43 (1970): 450–64.

Dolan, Jay P. *The American Catholic Experience: A History from Colonial Times to the Present.* Garden City, N.Y.: Image Books, 1985.

———. "The Search for an American Catholicism, 1780–1820." In *Religious Diversity and American Religious History: Studies in Traditions and Cultures,* edited by Walter H. Conser Jr. and Sumner B. Twiss, 26–51. Athens: University of Georgia Press, 1997.

Driedger, Michael D. *Obedient Heretics: Mennonite Identities in Lutheran Hamburg and Altona During the Confessional Age.* Aldershot: Ashgate, 2002.

Dubbs, Joseph Henry. "The Reformed Church in Pennsylvania . . . Prepared at the Request of the Pennsylvania-German Society." Proceedings and Addresses of the Pennsylvania German Society 11. Lancaster, Pa.: n.p., 1902.

Duhr, Bernhard. *Geschichte der Jesuiten in den Ländern deutscher Zunge.* Vol. 4, pt. 2. Munich: Manz, 1928.

Durnbaugh, Donald F. "Pennsylvania's Crazy Quilt of German Religious Groups." *Pennsylvania History* 68 (2001): 8–30.

Early, William F. "Our First 250 Years." In *250 Years of Witness, 1742–1992: First Presbyterian Church, Lancaster, Pennsylvania,* 1–62. Lancaster, Pa.: History Committee of the First Presbyterian Church, 1992.

Ebersole, Mark C. "Abolition Divides the Meeting House: Quakers and Slavery in Early Lancaster County." *Journal of the Lancaster County Historical Society* 102 (2000): 2–27.

Eichholtz-Rodriguez, Janice. "The Lancaster of Leonard Eichholtz, 1750–1817." *Journal of the Lancaster County Historical Society* 79 (1975): 175–207.

Ellis, Franklin, and Samuel Evans. *History of Lancaster County, Pennsylvania, with Biographical Sketches of Many of Its Pioneers and Prominent Men.* Philadelphia: Everts and Peck, 1883.

Endelman, Todd M. *The Jews of Britain, 1656 to 2000*. Berkeley and Los Angeles: University of California Press, 2002.

———. *The Jews of Georgian England, 1714–1830: Tradition and Change in a Liberal Society*. Rev. ed. Ann Arbor: University of Michigan Press, 1999.

Ennis, Arthur J. "The New Diocese of Philadelphia." In *The History of the Archdiocese of Philadelphia*, edited by James F. Connelly, 63–79. Philadelphia: Archdiocese of Philadelphia, 1976.

Eshleman, Henry Frank. "Early Lancaster Taxables—1754." *Journal of the Lancaster County Historical Society* 13 (1909): 263–77.

———. "Lancaster County Contributors to Relief of Boston, 1774." *Papers Read Before the Lancaster County Historical Society* 28 (1924): 3–5.

Evans, Melvern, Jr. "Lancaster Borough: Host to British and Hessian Prisoners of War, 1775–1784." *Journal of the Lancaster County Historical Society* 89 (1985): 144–51.

Faber, Eli. *The Jewish People in America*. Vol. 1, *A Time for Planting: The First Migration, 1654–1820*. Baltimore: Johns Hopkins University Press, 1992.

Farry, Richard R. "Edward Hand: His Role in the American Revolution." Ph.D. diss., Duke University, 1976.

Fea, John. "Ethnicity and Congregational Life in the Eighteenth-Century Delaware Valley: The Swedish Lutherans of New Jersey." *Explorations in Early American Culture* 5 (2001): 45–78.

Fennimore, Donald L. "Metalwork." In *Arts of the Pennsylvania Germans*, edited by Scott T. Swank et al., 211–20. New York: Norton, 1983.

Fish, Sidney M. *Barnard and Michael Gratz: Their Lives and Times*. Lanham, Md.: University Press of America, 1994.

Fogleman, Aaron S. *Hopeful Journeys: German Immigration, Settlement, and Political Culture, 1700–1775*. Philadelphia: University of Pennsylvania Press, 1996.

Frantz, John B. "The Awakening of Religion Among the German Settlers in the Middle Colonies." *William and Mary Quarterly* 33 (1976): 266–88.

Freist, Dagmar. "One Body, Two Minds: Mixed Marriage in Early Modern Germany." In *Gender in Early Modern Germany*, edited by Ulinka Rublack, 275–305. Cambridge: Cambridge University Press, 2002.

Frost, Jerry W. *A Perfect Freedom: Religious Liberty in Pennsylvania*. New York: Cambridge University Press, 1990.

Gerstell, Vivian S. *Silversmiths of Lancaster, Pennsylvania, 1730–1850*. Lancaster, Pa.: Publications of the Lancaster County Historical Society, 1972.

Ginzberg, Lori D. *Women and the Work of Benevolence: Morality, Politics, and Class in the Nineteenth-Century United States*. New Haven: Yale University Press, 1990.

Glatfelter, Charles H. *Pastors and People: German Lutheran and Reformed Churches in the Pennsylvania Field, 1717–1793*. 2 vols. Breinigsville, Pa.: Publications of the Pennsylvania German Society, 1979–81.

Good, James I. *History of the Reformed Church in the United States, 1725–1792*. Reading, Pa.: Daniel Miller, 1899.

———. *History of the Reformed Church in the United States in the Nineteenth Century*. New York: Board of Publication of the Reformed Church in America, 1911.

Goodfriend, Joyce D. "The Social Dimensions of Congregational Life in Colonial New York City." *William and Mary Quarterly* 42 (1985): 252–78.

Grabbe, Hans-Jürgen. *Vor der großen Flut: Die europäische Migration in die Vereinigten Staaten von Amerika, 1783–1820*. Stuttgart: Steiner, 2001.

Greene, Jack P. *Pursuits of Happiness: The Social Development of Early Modern British Colonies and the Formation of American Culture.* Chapel Hill: University of North Carolina Press, 1988.

Groff, Clyde L., Walter B. Groff, and Jane Evans Best. *The Groff Book.* Vol. 1, *A Good Life in a New Land.* Ronks, Pa.: Groff History Associates, 1985.

Grubb, Farley. *Runaway Servants, Convicts, and Apprentices Advertised in the* Pennsylvania Gazette, *1728–1796.* Baltimore: Genealogical Publishing Co., 1992.

Gugerli, David. *Zwischen Pfrund und Predigt. Die protestantische Pfarrfamilie auf der Zürcher Landschaft im ausgehenden 18. Jahrhundert.* Zurich: Chronos-Verlag, 1988.

Häberlein, Mark. "German Migrants to Colonial Pennsylvania: Resources, Opportunities, and Experience." *William and Mary Quarterly* 50 (1993): 555–74.

———. "Transatlantische Beziehungen im 18. Jahrhundert. Die Kontakte südwestdeutscher und Schweizer Einwanderer in Pennsylvania zu ihren Heimatregionen." In *Menschen zwischen zwei Welten: Auswanderung, Ansiedlung, Akkulturation,* edited by Walter G. Rödel und Helmut Schmahl, 45–60. Trier: Wissenschaftlicher Verlag, 2002.

———. "Unfreie Dienstknechte und –mägde im Nordamerika des 18. Jahrhunderts: Migrationserfahrungen, kolonialer Arbeitsmarkt und soziale Mobilität." In *Über die trockene Grenze und über das offene Meer: Binneneuropäische und transatlantische Migrationen im 18. und 19. Jahrhundert,* edited by Mathias Beer and Dittmar Dahlmann, 191–219. Essen: Klartext-Verlag, 2004.

———. *Vom Oberrhein zum Susquehanna: Studien zur badischen Auswanderung nach Pennsylvania im 18. Jahrhundert.* Stuttgart: Kohlhammer, 1993.

Häberlein, Mark, and Michaela Schmölz-Häberlein. "Die Ansiedlung von Täufern am Oberrhein im 18. Jahrhundert: Eine religiöse Minderheit im Spannungsfeld herrschaftlicher Ansprüche und wirtschaftlicher Interessen." In *Minderheiten, Obrigkeit und Gesellschaft in der Frühen Neuzeit. Integrations- und Abgrenzungsprozesse im süddeutschen Raum,* edited by Mark Häberlein and Martin Zürn, 377–402. St. Katharinen: Scripta-Mercaturae-Verlag, 2001.

———. "Competition and Cooperation: The Ambivalent Relationship Between Jews and Christians in Early Modern Germany and Pennsylvania." *Pennsylvania Magazine of History and Biography* 126 (2002): 409–36.

———. "Eighteenth-Century Anabaptists in the Margravate of Baden and Neighboring Territories." *Mennonite Quarterly Review* 75 (2001): 471–92.

Hackett, David G. *The Rude Hand of Innovation: Religion and Social Order in Albany, New York, 1652–1836.* New York: Oxford University Press, 1991.

Hans, Alfred. *Die kurpfälzische Religionsdeklaration von 1705: Ihre Entstehung und Bedeutung für das Zusammenleben der drei im Reich tolerierten Konfessionen.* Mainz: Selbstverlag der Gesellschaft für Mittelrheinische Kirchengeschichte, 1973.

Harbaugh, Henry W. *The Life of Michael Schlatter: With a Full Account of His Travels and Labors Among the Germans in Pennsylvania, New Jersey, Maryland and Virginia.* Philadelphia: Lindsay, 1857.

Harbold, Peter M. "Schools and Education in the Borough of Lancaster." *Papers Read Before the Lancaster County Historical Society* 46 (1942): 1–44.

Hark, J. Max. "The Beginnings of the Moravian Church in Lancaster, Pennsylvania." *Transactions of the Moravian Historical Society* 11 (1931): 179–86.

Harrison, Richard A. *Princetonians, 1776–1783: A Biographical Dictionary.* Princetonians 2. Princeton: Princeton University Press, 1981.

Hatch, Nathan O. *The Democratization of American Christianity*. New Haven: Yale University Press, 1989.

Haverstick, David C. "Lancaster Bible Society, 1815–1915." *Papers Read Before the Lancaster County Historical Society* 19 (1915): 35–61.

Heal, Felicity. *Reformation in Britain and Ireland*. New York: Oxford University Press, 2003.

Heiges, George L. "The Evangelical Lutheran Church of the Holy Trinity, Lancaster, Pennsylvania. Part One, 1730–1861." *Journal of the Lancaster County Historical Society* 83 (1979): 2–7.

———. *Henry William Stiegel and His Associates: A Story of Early American Industry*. 2nd ed. Manheim, Pa.: The Arbee Foundation, 1976.

———. "When Lancaster Was Pennsylvania's Capital." *Journal of the Lancaster County Historical Society* 57 (1953): 81–108.

Heisey, M. Luther. "A Biography of Paul Zantzinger." *Papers Read Before the Lancaster County Historical Society* 47 (1943): 113–19.

———. "The Borough Fathers." *Papers Read Before the Lancaster County Historical Society* 46 (1942): 45–82.

Heller-Karneth, Eva. *Drei Konfessionen in einer Stadt: Zur Bedeutung des konfessionellen Faktors im Alzey des Ancien Regime*. Würzburg: Bayerische Blätter für Volkskunde, 1996.

Henderson, Roger C. "Matters of Life and Death: A Demographic Analysis of Eighteenth-Century Lancaster Reformed Church Records." *Journal of the Lancaster County Historical Society* 91 (1987/88): 43–77.

Hennesey, James. *American Catholics: A History of the Roman Catholic Community in the United States*. New York: Oxford University Press, 1981.

Hinke, William J. *Ministers of the German Reformed Congregations in Pennsylvania and Other Colonies in the Eighteenth Century*. Lancaster, Pa.: Historical Commission of the Evangelical and Reformed Church, 1951.

Holifield, E. Brooks. "Toward a History of American Congregations." In *American Congregations*. Vol. 2, *New Perspectives in the Study of Congregations*, edited by James P. Wind and James W. Lewis, 23–53. Chicago: University of Chicago Press, 1994.

Hopkins, Leroy T. "Hollow Memories: African Americans in Conestoga Township." *Journal of the Lancaster County Historical Society* 101 (2000): 145–66.

Horle, Craig W., et al. *Lawmaking and Legislators in Pennsylvania: A Biographical Dictionary*. Vol. 2, *1710–1756*. Philadelphia: University of Pennsylvania Press, 1997.

Hu, Shiu-ying, and E. D. Merrill. "Work and Publications of Henry Muhlenberg." *Bartonia* 25 (1949): 1–66.

Hucho, Christine. *Weiblich und fremd: Deutschsprachige Einwandererinnen im Pennsylvania des 18. Jahrhunderts*. Frankfurt am Main: Lang, 2005.

Ireland, Owen S. "Germans Against Abolition: A Minority's View of Slavery in Revolutionary Pennsylvania." *Journal of Interdisciplinary History* 3 (1973): 685–706.

Jacobsen, Douglas C. *An Unprov'd Experiment: Religious Pluralism in Colonial New Jersey*. Chicago Studies in the History of American Religion 9. Brooklyn, N.Y.: Carlson, 1991.

Jeffries, Theodore W. "Thomas Barton (1730–1780): Victim of the Revolution." *Journal of the Lancaster County Historical Society* 81 (1977): 39–64.

de Jonge, Eric. "Johann Christoph Heyne: Pewterer, Minister, Teacher." *Winterthur Portfolio* 4 (1968): 168–84.

Jütte, Robert "Contacts by the Bedside: Jewish Physicians and Their Christian Patients." In *In and Out of the Ghetto: Jewish-Gentile Relations in Late Medieval and Early Modern Germany*, edited by Ronnie Po-Chia Hsia and Hartmut Lehmann, 137–50. Cambridge: Cambridge University Press, 1995.

Kaplan, Benjamin. "Fictions of Privacy: House Chapels and the Spatial Accommodation of Religious Dissent in Early Modern Europe." *American Historical Review* 107, no. 4 (Oct. 2002): 1031–65.

Kieffer, Elizabeth Clarke. "Three Caspar Schaffners." *Papers Read Before the Lancaster County Historical Society* 42 (1938): 181–200.

Kiessling, Rolf, and Sabine Ullmann, eds. *Landjudentum im deutschen Südwesten während der Frühen Neuzeit*. Berlin: Akademie Verlag, 1999.

Klein, Frederic S. "Robert Coleman, Millionaire Ironmaster." *Journal of the Lancaster County Historical Society* 64 (1960): 17–33.

Klein, Randolph S. *Portrait of an Early American Family: The Shippens of Pennsylvania Across Five Generations*. Philadelphia: University of Pennsylvania Press, 1975.

Konersmann, Frank. "Duldung, Privilegierung, Assimilation und Säkularisation: Mennonitische Glaubensgemeinschaften in der Pfalz, in Rheinhessen und am nördlichen Oberrhein, 1648–1802." In *Minderheiten, Obrigkeit und Gesellschaft in der Frühen Neuzeit. Integrations- und Abgrenzungsprozesse im süddeutschen Raum*, edited by Mark Häberlein and Martin Zürn, 339–75. St. Katharinen: Scripta-Mercaturae-Verlag, 2001.

Lambert, Frank. *Inventing the "Great Awakening."* Princeton: Princeton University Press, 2000.

Landis, Charles I. "Jasper Yeates and His Times." *Pennsylvania Magazine of History and Biography* 46 (1922): 199–231.

———. "The Juliana Library Company in Lancaster." *Papers Read Before the Lancaster County Historical Society* 33 (1929): 221–45.

Landis, James D. "Who Was Who in Lancaster 100 Years Ago." *Papers Read Before the Lancaster County Historical Society* 11 (1907): 363–421.

Landsman, Ned C. *Scotland and Its First American Colony, 1683–1765*. Princeton: Princeton University Press, 1985.

Langford, Paul. *A Polite and Commercial People: England, 1727–1783*. Oxford: Clarendon Press, 1989.

Lehmann, Hartmut et al., eds. *In Search of Peace and Prosperity: New German Settlements in Eighteenth-Century Europe and America*. University Park: Pennsylvania State University Press, 2000.

Leiser, Wolfgang. "Das Karlsruher Stadtrecht, 1715–1752." *Zeitschrift für Geschichte des Oberrheins* 114 (1966): 207–39.

Lemon, James T. *The Best Poor Man's Country: A Geographic Study of Early Southeastern Pennsylvania*. Baltimore: Johns Hopkins University Press, 1972.

———. "Urbanization and the Development of Eighteenth-Century Southeastern Pennsylvania and Adjacent Delaware." *William and Mary Quarterly* 24 (1967): 501–42.

Lippold, John W. "The Distinguished Hubley Family of Lancaster." *Papers Read Before the Lancaster County Historical Society* 40 (1936): 53–72.

———. "Old Trinity Graveyard." *Papers Read Before the Lancaster County Historical Society* 32 (1928): 109–17.

———. "Old Trinity Steeple." *Papers Read Before the Lancaster County Historical Society* 31 (1927): 116–33.

Lodge, Martin. "The Crisis of the Churches in the Middle Colonies." *Pennsylvania Magazine of History and Biography* 95 (1971): 196–221.

Longenecker, Stephen L. *Piety and Tolerance: Pennsylvania German Religion, 1700–1850.* Pietist and Wesleyan Studies 6. Metuchen, N.J.: Scarecrow, 1994.

Loose, John Ward Willson. "William Henry Memoirs, 1748–1786." *Journal of the Lancaster County Historical Society* 76 (1972): 58–68.

MacMaster, Richard K. *Land, Piety, Peoplehood: The Establishment of Mennonite Communities in America, 1683–1790.* Scottdale, Pa.: Herald Press, 1985.

Main, Jackson Turner. *Political Parties Before the Constitution.* Chapel Hill: University of North Carolina Press, 1973.

Marcus, Jacob R. *The Colonial American Jew, 1492–1776.* 3 vols. Detroit: Wayne State University Press, 1970.

Martin, C. H. "Life of Andrew Byerly." *Papers Read Before the Lancaster County Historical Society* 33 (1929): 3–8.

McKnight, Evajean Fortney. *The Fortineux—Fortinet Family (Fortney, Fortna, Fordney, Furtney) in America.* Salem, W.Va.: Walsworth, 1989.

McLachlan, James. *Princetonians, 1748–1768: A Biographical Dictionary.* Princetonians 1. Princeton: Princeton University Press, 1976.

Mintz, Steven. *Moralists and Modernizers: America's Pre–Civil War Reformers.* Baltimore: Johns Hopkins University Press, 1995.

Müller, Christina. *Karlsruhe im 18. Jahrhundert: Zur Genese und sozialen Schichtung einer residenzstädtischen Bevölkerung.* Karlsruhe: Badenia-Verlag, 1992.

Müller, Thomas J. *Kirche zwischen zwei Welten: Die Obrigkeitsproblematik bei Heinrich Melchior Mühlenberg und die Kirchengründung der deutschen Lutheraner in Pennsylvania.* Stuttgart: Steiner, 1994.

Musser, Edgar A. "Old St. Mary's of Lancaster, Pa.: The Jesuit Period, 1741–1785." *Journal of the Lancaster County Historical Society* 71 (1967): 69–136.

Myers, James P., Jr. "The Rev. Thomas Barton's Authorship of *The Conduct of the Paxton Men, Impartially Represented* (1764)." *Pennsylvania History* 61 (1994): 155–84.

———. "The Rev. Thomas Barton's Conflict with Colonel John Armstrong, c. 1758." *Cumberland County History* 10 (1993): 3–14.

———. "Thomas Barton's *Unanimity and Public Spirit* (1755): Controversy and Plagiarism on the Pennsylvania Frontier." *Pennsylvania Magazine of History and Biography* 119 (1995): 225–48.

Nash, Gary B. "Slaves and Slaveowners in Colonial Philadelphia." *William and Mary Quarterly* 30 (1973): 223–56.

———. *The Urban Crucible: Social Change, Political Consciousness, and the Origins of the American Revolution.* Cambridge: Harvard University Press, 1979.

Nash, Gary B., and Jean R. Soderlund. *Freedom by Degrees: Emancipation in Pennsylvania and Its Aftermath.* New York: Oxford University Press, 1991.

Nolt, Steven M. *Foreigners in Their Own Land: Pennsylvania Germans in the Early Republic.* University Park: Pennsylvania State University Press, 2002.

Norton, Mary Beth. "The Evolution of White Women's Experience in Early America." *American Historical Review* 89 (1984): 593–619.

O'Gorman, Frank. *The Long Eighteenth Century: British Political and Social History, 1688–1832.* London: Arnold, 1997.

O'Malley, J. Steven. *Pilgrimage of Faith: The Legacy of the Otterbeins.* Metuchen, N.J.: Scarecrow, 1973.

Pencak, William. "Jews and Anti-Semitism in Colonial Pennsylvania." *Pennsylvania Magazine of History and Biography* 126 (2002): 365–408.

————. *Jews and Gentiles in Early America, 1654–1800*. Ann Arbor: University of Michigan Press, 2005.

Pennington, Edgar Legare. "The Anglican Clergy of Pennsylvania in the American Revolution." *Pennsylvania Magazine of History and Biography* 63 (1939): 401–31.

Peters, Jan. "Der Platz in der Kirche. Über soziales Rangdenken im Spätfeudalismus." *Jahrbuch für Volkskunde und Kulturgeschichte* 28 (1985): 77–196.

Plakans, Andrejs. *Kinship in the Past: An Anthropology of European Family Life, 1500–1900*. Oxford: Blackwell, 1984.

Po-Chia Hsia, Ronnie. "Between State and Community: Religious and Ethnic Minorities in Early Modern Germany." In *Germania Illustrata: Essays on Early Modern Germany Presented to Gerald Strauss*, edited by Andrew C. Fix and Susan C. Karant-Nunn, 169–80. Kirksville, Mo.: Sixteenth Century Journal Publishing, 1989.

————. *Social Discipline and the Reformation: Central Europe, 1550–1750*. London: Routledge, 1989.

Pointer, Richard W. *Protestant Pluralism and the New York Experience: A Study of Eighteenth-Century Religious Diversity*. Bloomington: Indiana University Press, 1988.

Pritzker-Ehrlich, Marthi. "*Michael Schlatter von St. Gallen*: Eine biographische Untersuchung zur schweizerischen Amerika-Auswanderung im 18. Jahrhundert." Ph.D. diss., University of Zurich, 1981.

Quigley, Robert Edward. "Catholic Beginnings in the Delaware Valley." In *The History of the Archdiocese of Philadelphia*, edited by James F. Connelly, 1–62. Philadelphia: Archdiocese of Philadelphia, 1976.

Rechcigl, Miloslav, Jr. "The Demuth Genealogy Revisited: A Moravian Brethren Family from Czechoslovakia." *Journal of the Lancaster County Historical Society* 92 (1989/90): 55–67.

Rhoden, Nancy L. *Revolutionary Anglicanism: The Colonial Church of England Clergy During the American Revolution*. New York: New York University Press, 1999.

Rineer, A. Hunter, Jr. *Churches and Cemeteries of Lancaster County, Pennsylvania. A Complete Guide*. Lancaster, Pa.: Publications of the Lancaster County Historical Society, 1993.

Risch, Erna. "Immigrant Aid Societies Before 1820." *Pennsylvania Magazine of History and Biography* 60 (1936): 15–33.

Robinson, Mary N. "Charles Hall: A Revolutionary Worthy." *Papers Read Before the Lancaster County Historical Society* 8 (1903–4): 177–82.

Roeber, A. G. "The Long Road to *Vidal*: Charity Law and State Formation in Early America." In *The Many Legalities of Early America*, edited by Christopher L. Tomlins and Bruce H. Mann. Chapel Hill: University of North Carolina Press, 2001: 414–41.

————. *Palatines, Liberty, and Property: German Lutherans in Colonial British America*. Baltimore: Johns Hopkins University Press, 1993.

————. "Der Pietismus in Nordamerika im 18. Jahrhundert." In *Geschichte des Pietismus*. Vol. 2, *Der Pietismus im 18. Jahrhundert*, edited by Martin Brecht and Klaus Deppermann, 666–99. Göttingen: Vandenhoeck and Ruprecht, 1995.

————. "The Problem of the Eighteenth Century in Transatlantic Religious History." In *In Search of Peace and Prosperity: New German Settlements in Eighteenth-Century Europe and America*, edited by Hartmut Lehmann et al., 115–38. University Park: Pennsylvania State University Press, 2000.

————. "'Troublesome Riches': Protestant and Catholic Stewardship of a Capitalist World, 1698–1815." *Amerikastudien/American Studies* 42, no. 3 (1997): 357–75.

Rothermund, Dietmar. *The Layman's Progress: Religious and Political Experience in Pennsylvania, 1740–1770*. Philadelphia: University of Pennsylvania Press, 1961.

Rubincam, Milton. "A Memoir of the Life of William Barton, A.M. (1754–1817)." *Pennsylvania History* 12 (1945): 179–93.

Russell, Marvin F. "Thomas Barton and Pennsylvania's Colonial Frontier." *Pennsylvania History* 46 (1979): 313–34.

Ryerson, Richard Alan. *The Revolution Is Now Begun: The Radical Committees of Philadelphia, 1765–1776.* Philadelphia: University of Pennsylvania Press, 1978.

Schaab, Meinrad. "Die Wiederherstellung des Katholizismus in der Kurpfalz im 17. und 18. Jahrhundert." *Zeitschrift für Geschichte des Oberrheins* 114 (1966): 147–205.

Schilling, Heinz, ed. *Die reformierte Konfessionalisierung in Deutschland: Das Problem der "Zweiten Reformation": Wissenschaftliches Symposion des Vereins für Reformationsgeschichte 1985.* Gütersloh, Germany: Mohn, 1986.

Schindling, Anton. "Andersgläubige Nachbarn: Mehrkonfessionalität und Parität in Territorien und Städten des Reichs." In *1648: Krieg und Frieden in Europa.* Vol. 1, *Geschichte, Religion, Recht und Gesellschaft*, edited by Klaus Bußmann and Heinz Schilling, 465–73. Münster: n.p., 1998.

Schmauk, Theodore Emanuel. "The Lutheran Church in Pennsylvania, 1638–1800 . . . Prepared at the Request of the Pennsylvania German Society." Proceedings and Addresses of the Pennsylvania German Society 11. Lancaster, Pa.: n.p., 1902.

Schmidt, Leigh Eric. *Holy Fairs: Scottish Communions and American Revivals in the Early Modern Period.* Princeton: Princeton University Press, 1989.

Schwartz, Sally. *"A Mixed Multitude": The Struggle for Toleration in Colonial Pennsylvania.* New York: New York University Press, 1987.

Shiels, Richard D. "The Feminization of American Congregationalism, 1730–1835." *American Quarterly* 33 (1981): 46–62.

Smaby, Beverly P. *The Transformation of Moravian Bethlehem: From Communal Mission to Family Economy.* Philadelphia: University of Pennsylvania Press, 1988.

Smith, C. Earle, Jr. "Henry Muhlenberg—Botanical Pioneer." *American Philosophical Society Proceedings* 106 (1962): 443–60.

Smith, Timothy. "The Ohio Valley: Testing Ground for America's Experiment in Religious Pluralism." *Church History* 60 (1991): 461–79.

Splitter, Wolfgang. *Pastors, People, Politics: German Lutherans in Pennsylvania, 1740–1790.* Trier: Wissenschaftlicher Verlag, 1998.

Stauffer, David McNealy. "The Lancaster Assembly of 1780." *Pennsylvania Magazine of History and Biography* 10 (1886): 413–17.

Steckel, William Reed. "Pietist in Colonial Pennsylvania: Christopher Sauer, Printer, 1738–1758." Ph.D. diss., Stanford University, 1949.

Stoeffler, F. Ernest, ed. *Continental Pietism and Early American Christianity.* Grand Rapids, Mich.: Eerdmans, 1976.

Swank, Scott T. "The Lancaster New Church (Swedenborgian)." *Journal of the Lancaster County Historical Society* 76 (1972): 69–87.

———. "Proxemic Patterns." In *Arts of the Pennsylvania Germans*, edited by Scott T. Swank et al., 35–60. New York: Norton, 1983.

Tanis, James. "Reformed Pietism in Colonial America." In *Continental Pietism and Early American Christianity*, edited by F. Ernest Stoeffler, 34–73. Grand Rapids, Mich.: Eerdmans, 1976.

Tracy, James D. *Europe's Reformations, 1450–1650.* Lanham, Md.: Rowman and Littlefield, 1999.

Trinterud, Leonard J. *The Forming of an American Tradition: A Re-examination of Colonial Presbyterianism.* Philadelphia: Westminster, 1949.

Tully, Alan. "Patterns of Slaveholding in Colonial Pennsylvania: Chester and Lancaster Counties, 1729–1758." *Journal of Social History* 6 (1973): 284–305.

Tunney, Robert D. "Chart of Historic St. James's Church and Graveyard." *Journal of the Lancaster County Historical Society* 67 (1963): 128.

Ulbrich, Claudia. *Shulamit und Margarethe: Macht, Geschlecht und Religion in einer ländlichen Gesellschaft des 18. Jahrhunderts.* Vienna: Böhlau, 1999.

Ullmann, Sabine. *Nachbarschaft und Konkurrenz. Juden und Christen in Dörfern der Markgrafschaft Burgau, 1650–1750.* Göttingen: Vandenhoeck und Ruprecht, 1999.

Vogt, Jean. "Wiedertäufer und ländliche Gemeinden im nördlichen Elsaß und in der Pfalz." *Mennonitische Geschichtsblätter* 41 (1984): 3–47.

Wallace, Paul A. W. *The Muhlenbergs of Pennsylvania.* Philadelphia: University of Pennsylvania Press, 1950.

Walters, Ronald G. *American Reformers, 1815–1860.* New York: Hill and Wang, 1978.

Weiser, Frederick S. "The Origin of Organized Lutheranism in Lancaster County, Pennsylvania." *Journal of the Lancaster County Historical Society* 107 (Winter 2005): 110–33.

Westerkamp, Marilyn J. *Triumph of the Laity: Scots-Irish Piety and the Great Awakening, 1625–1760.* New York: Oxford University Press, 1988.

———. *Women and Religion in Early America, 1600–1850: The Puritan and Evangelical Traditions.* London: Routledge, 1999.

Whitely, Paul L. "A History of Friends in Lancaster County." *Papers Read Before the Lancaster County Historical Society* 51 (1947): 1–33.

Wilson, Renate. *Pious Traders in Medicine: A German Pharmaceutical Network in Eighteenth-Century North America.* University Park: Pennsylvania State University Press, 2001.

Wokeck, Marianne S. *Trade in Strangers: The Beginnings of Mass Migration to North America.* University Park: Pennsylvania State University Press, 1999.

Wolf, Stephanie Grauman. *Urban Village: Population, Community, and Family Structure in Germantown, Pennsylvania, 1683–1800.* Princeton: University Press, 1976.

Wood, Jerome H., Jr. *Conestoga Crossroads: Lancaster, Pennsylvania, 1730–1790.* Harrisburg: Pennsylvania Historical and Museum Commission, 1979.

Wood, Stacy B. C., Jr. "A John Eberman Legacy: Eight Lancaster, Pennsylvania, Clockmakers." *Journal of the Lancaster County Historical Society* 91 (1987/88): 90–128.

———. "Rudy Stoner, 1728–1769: Early Lancaster, Pennsylvania, Clockmaker." *Journal of the Lancaster County Historical Society* 80 (1976): 112–27.

Woolverton, John Frederick. *Colonial Anglicanism in North America.* Detroit: Wayne State University Press, 1984.

Worner, William Frederic. "The Church of England in Lancaster County (Part II)." *Papers Read Before the Lancaster County Historical Society* 40 (1936): 79–92.

———. "The Church of England in Lancaster County (Pt. III)." *Papers Read Before the Lancaster County Historical Society* 41 (1937): 25–54.

———. "The Church of England in Lancaster County (Pt. IV)." *Papers Read Before the Lancaster County Historical Society* 41 (1937): 57–92.

———. "Collections for the Poor in 1795." *Papers Read Before the Lancaster County Historical Society* 32 (1928): 246–47.

———. "Collections in Aid of Sufferers from the Fire in Lancaster in 1811." *Papers Read Before the Lancaster County Historical Society* 33 (1929): 114–17.

———. "Contributions from Lancaster County for the Distressed Poor of Philadelphia During the Yellow Fever Epidemic of 1797." *Papers Read Before the Lancaster County Historical Society* 32 (1928): 137–39.

————. "Contribution to Petersburg (VA) in the Fire of 1815." *Papers Read Before the Lancaster County Historical Society* 33 (1929): 140.

————. "The Female Benevolent Society of Lancaster." *Papers Read Before the Lancaster County Historical Society* 34 (1930): 11–18.

————. "The German Society of Lancaster." *Papers Read Before the Lancaster County Historical Society* 35 (1931): 1–8.

————. "Lancaster's Contribution to Newburyport in the Fire of 1811." *Papers Read Before the Lancaster County Historical Society* 33 (1929): 117–18.

————. "Old St. James's Church Bell." *Papers Read Before the Lancaster County Historical Society* 35 (1931): 239–46.

————. "Relief for the Poor in Lancaster." *Papers Read Before the Lancaster County Historical Society* 32 (1928): 141–43.

————. "The Sunday-School Society." *Papers Read Before the Lancaster County Historical Society* 33 (1929): 175–88.

————. "Thomas Barton's Family Prayer Book." *Papers Read Before the Lancaster County Historical Society* 35 (1932): 288–99.

Wright, Conrad Edick. *The Transformation of Charity in Postrevolutionary New England.* Boston: Northeastern University Press, 1992.

Zschunke, Peter. *Konfession und Alltag in Oppenheim: Beiträge zur Geschichte von Bevölkerung und Gesellschaft einer gemischtkonfessionellen Kleinstadt in der Frühen Neuzeit.* Wiesbaden: Steiner, 1984.

Index